T0315009

EMPIRES OF VICE

HISTORIES OF ECONOMIC LIFE

Jeremy Adelman, Sunil Amrith,
and Emma Rothschild, Series Editors

Empires of Vice

THE RISE OF OPIUM PROHIBITION
ACROSS SOUTHEAST ASIA

DIANA S. KIM

PRINCETON UNIVERSITY PRESS

PRINCETON & OXFORD

Published by Princeton University Press
41 William Street, Princeton, New Jersey 08540
6 Oxford Street, Woodstock, Oxfordshire OX20 1TR

press.princeton.edu

Library of Congress Cataloging-in-Publication Data

Names: Kim, Diana S., 1982– author.
Title: Empires of vice : the rise of opium prohibition across Southeast
    Asia / Diana S. Kim.
Description: Princeton, New Jersey : Princeton University Press, [2020] |
    Series: Histories of economic life | Includes bibliographical references and index.
Identifiers: LCCN 2019029698 (print) | LCCN 2019029699 (ebook) |
    ISBN 9780691172408 (hardback) | ISBN 9780691199702 (paperback) |
    ISBN 9780691199696 (ebook)
Subjects: LCSH: Opium trade—Southeast Asia—History. | Opium trade—Political
    aspects—Southeast Asia. | Opium trade—Malaysia—Malaya—History. |
    Opium trade—Indochina—History. | Opium trade—Burma—History. | France—
    Colonies—Asia—Administration. | Great Britain—Colonies—Asia—Administration.
Classification: LCC HV5840.S643 K57 2020 (print) | LCC HV5840.S643 (ebook) |
    DDC 364.1/77095909034—dc23
LC record available at https://lccn.loc.gov/2019029698
LC ebook record available at https://lccn.loc.gov/2019029699

British Library Cataloging-in-Publication Data is available

Editorial: Eric Crahan and Thalia Leaf
Production Editorial: Mark Bellis
Jacket Design: Leslie Flis
Production: Merli Guerra
Publicity: Alyssa Sanford and Kate Farquhar-Thomson
Copyeditor: Theresa Kornak

Jacket Credits: poppy from the Missouri Botanical Garden, St. Louis;
ledger courtesy of Archives nationales d'outre mer, France, INDO/NF/88/880

This book has been composed in Arno

Printed on acid-free paper. ∞

Printed in the United States of America

10 9 8 7 6 5 4 3 2 1

Dedicated to my parents and Julia

CONTENTS

FIGURES

TABLES

ACKNOWLEDGMENTS

WRITING THIS BOOK has been a much longer, harder, yet always more reward-ing process than I had originally envisioned. I am first and foremost grateful for the support of my dissertation advisors, Bernard Harcourt, Dan Slater, and Andrew Abbott. Through their exemplary scholarship and warm encourage-ment, each has durably shaped the way I see and puzzle about the political world. I am also grateful to the wonderful colleagues, teachers, and friends whom I met at the University at Chicago, including Kathy Anderson, Mark Bradley, Michael Dango, Sofia Fenner, Joe Fischel, Minnie Go, Bob Gooding-Williams, Daragh Grant, Chris Haid, Gary Herrigel, Eric Hundsman, Iza Hussin, Juan Fernando Ibarra del Cueto, Sarah Johnson, Samip Mallick, J. J. McFadden, Claire McKinney, Jeremy Menchik, Sankar Muthu, Jim Nye, Jonathan Obert, Willow Osgood, Josh Pacewicz, Jong-hee Park, Jennifer Pitts, Jon Rogowski, Bill Sewell, Erica Simmons, Nick Smith, Matthias Staisch, Paul Staniland, Tekeisha Yelton-Hunter, and Lisa Wedeen. My particular gratitude goes to Matthias for always being there for me, with every imaginable form of caffeine, alcohol, wit, and patience.

Over the past years, I have been very fortunate in finding welcoming inter-disciplinary homes among historians, economists, and political scientists. As a postdoctoral prize fellow with the Center for History and Economics at Har-vard University, I had the pleasure of meeting and sharing ideas with Sunil Amrith, Abhijit Bannerjee, Allan Brandt, Ian Brown, Claire Edington, Cathe-rine Evans, David Doupé, Allegra Giovine, Ben Golub, Johannes Haushofer, Kalyani Ramnath, Emma Rothschild, James Rush, Paul Sager, Padraic Scanlan, Amartya Sen, Brandon Terry, Alicia Turner, and Kirsty Walker. Since joining the faculty at Georgetown University and living in Washington D.C., I have also benefited from discussions with and the friendship of Peter Andreas, Celeste Arrington, Carol Benedict, John Buchanan, Marc Busch, Victor Cha, Katha-rine Donato, Mike Green, Kristen Looney, Kimberly Morgan, Kate McNamara, Marko Klasnja, Abe Newman, Irfan Nooruddin, Charles King, Christine Kim,

Melissa Lee, Zachariah Mampilly, John McNeill, James Milward, Puja Rudra, Nita Rudra, Diya Rudra Sundaram, Jordan Sand, Joseph Sassoon, Joel Simmons, Ravi and Kitcha Sundaram, Yuhki Tajima, Dennis Quinn, Jim Vreeland, and Erik Voeten. The formative ideas for this book are also inextricably linked to a co-taught seminar with Kirsty Walker, my brilliant friend and partner in crime for all matters relating to the history of vice in colonial Southeast Asia, as well as the insights of thoughtful students including Nathaniel Bernstein, Daye Lee Cho, Max Paterson, Catherine Killough, David Showalter, Wonik Son, Hannah Rosenfeld, Kim Mai Tran, and Bohesa Won.

I would like to express appreciation to several organizations for their support in developing this book: the Southeast Asia Research Group (SEAREG), a remarkable collective of political scientists committed to marrying positive social science with deep area studies, especially feedback from Allen Hicken, Amy Liu, Eddy Malesky, Quynh Nguyen, Alexandre Pelletier, Tom Pepinsky, Sarah Shair-Rosenfeld, Jessica Soedirgo, Dan Slater, Risa Toha, and Meredith Weiss. I also acknowledge financial support from the American Philosophical Society, Council of American Overseas Research Centers, the Nicholson Center for British Studies at the University of Chicago, the Mortara Center for International Studies and the Carnegie Foundation's Bridging the Gap grant, as well as the staff at the following institutions for their assistance and expertise: the British Library, the Center for Khmer Studies, Center for Research Libraries, National Archives of Cambodia, Myanmar, Vietnam, and the United Kingdom as well as France's National Archives for Overseas Territories. It has been a pleasure working with Princeton University Press with the steadfast support of the editors for the Histories of Economic Life Series, Jeremy Adelman, Sunil Amrith, and Emma Rothschild. I am also grateful for the acumen and patience of my editors Eric Crahan and Thalia Leaf, as well as Amanda Peery for her help during earlier stages of the manuscript's development, to Mark Bellis for bringing it to production, and to Theresa Kornak for copyediting. I have also benefited immensely from the constructive criticism and suggestions of three anonymous reviewers.

The pleasure in writing this book has come from people who have been with me constantly. I am happy to acknowledge the friendship of Yoonsun Hur and Mia Jeong, as well as Jean Lachapelle, who has been both my most astute critic and caring audience. My younger sister and best friend, Julia Sue Kim, is an unfailing source of energy and laughter. Without her, I would not have been able to complete this book. My greatest debts are to my parents, Mi Sun Kim and

Sun Chang Kim. I am the daughter of two scientists, who love history and politics. They were my first teachers and remain my warmest mentors today. And there are few aspects of my professional and personal life that are not inspired by the creativity, passion, and discipline they have demonstrated throughout their own careers. With much love, this book is dedicated to them.

NOTE ON TERMS USED

THROUGHOUT THE BOOK, I use the generic terms *opium* and *consumption* when actually referring to a much wider range of the drug's forms and sumptuary practices. *Chandu* is a sweeping term for opium processed for the purpose of smoking. *Madak* is a mixed form of smokable opium, prepared by first dissolving raw opium in water, straining it through cloth, and boiling it down to a syrup, and mixing it with charred leaves of acacia, betel, or guava. *Dross* is the residue left in an opium pipe after it is smoked. *Kunbon* refers to betel leaves fried and smoked in opium. Opium consumption encompasses a diverse range of modes of ingestion that include smoking, eating or chewing, and swallowing.[1]

For most of the time period I examine, neither the word "Southeast Asia" nor its reference to what we understand today as a bounded regional unit existed.[2] I have nonetheless chosen to use the ahistorical term because it is the clearest way to convey the geographical scope this book covers to different audiences that include non-specialists of this part of the world. For similar reasons, I use terms like "Vietnamese" and "the Hmong in Laos" even though a polity called "Vietnam" or "Laos" did not yet exist. My decision to reproduce labels that may have uncomfortably pejorative connotations such as "native," "indigenous," as well as "the Burman," "Annamite," or "Chinaman" reflects an aim of conveying British and French administrative language during the nineteenth and twentieth centuries, and I hope to avoid any hint of condoning the colonial logics that produced these terms. Unless noted, all translations are my own.

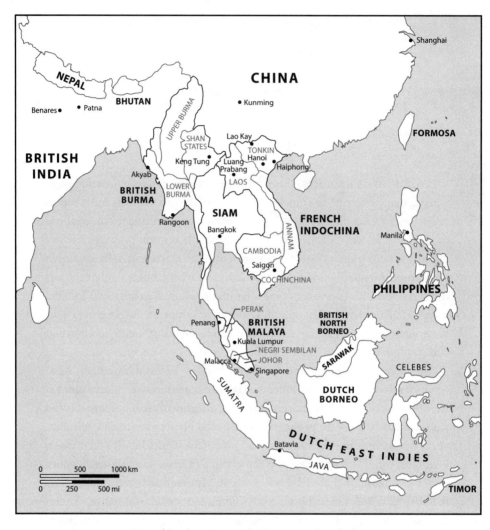

FIGURE 0.1. Map of Southeast Asia under European colonial rule, 1870s–1940s.

Part I

1

Introduction

UNTIL THE LATE NINETEENTH CENTURY, European powers defended opium as integral to managing an empire. "Opium was one of those things," declared one imperial politician in 1875, "which enabled us to serve God and Mammon at the same time."[1] Colonial states in Southeast Asia taxed opium consumption as a vice, at once collecting revenue and claiming just reasons for doing so. During peak years, the British and French collected more than 50 percent of colonial taxes from opium sales to local inhabitants, while other European rulers across the region reported smaller yet still significant shares sustaining the public coffers.[2] It was possible, an administrator stationed in Burma wrote, that this drug could "raise for the public benefit, the greatest amount of revenue with the smallest possible consumption."[3]

Into the first half of the twentieth century, however, the same powers were disavowing opium as a proper source of revenue and reconfiguring rationales that had once aligned the fiscal might and moral right of imperial rule. Before Parliament, John Morley referred to the British Empire's anti-opium resolve as "that civilizing mission of the regeneration of the East," while the French senator Édouard Néron wrote approvingly that "[o]ur commitment to ending the consumption of opium in Indochina has been made unambiguously clear" at an international conference in Geneva organized to combat dangerous drugs.[4] By the 1940s, all major beneficiaries of colonial opium were restricting once permissible habits of opium consumption, closing down opium shops and punishing violators of these new interdictions.

The prohibition of opium altered the foundations of colonial government and justifications for European rule across Southeast Asia. It involved reconfiguring old fiscal arrangements and fashioning new claims to authority, as opium went from being a significant source of public revenue to an official danger that states condemned. This remarkable transformation is the subject of this book.

Specifically, *Empires of Vice* puzzles over this historical process in two respects. First, prohibiting opium entailed abandoning a key source of revenue for colonial states. Thus, it sits uneasily against influential theories that view modern states as guided by efforts to maximize revenue.[5] Second, a shared turn against opium unfolded unevenly across Southeast Asia under European rule. There were diverse experiences, with the timing and tenor of opium-related reforms differing not only between empires but also among colonies of the same empire. Such variations complicate conventional understandings of colonial opium policies as following metropolitan regimes that medicalized drug control or as a response to religious actors and transnational activists who altered the moral conscience of the world.[6]

How did colonial states come to prohibit opium in such different ways? This book addresses the question, focusing on the British and French Empires—two powers that relied especially heavily on opium revenue collected from vice taxes—and tracing how they restricted opium sales and consumption in Burma, Malaya, and Indochina from the 1890s to 1940s. I argue that local administrators stationed in each colony are key to understanding when and how such reforms were possible. Prohibition involved unraveling a state's deep-seated opium entanglements, a process enabled by a loss of confidence deep within the bureaucracy about the drug's contributions to colonial government. Local administrators played a pivotal role in constructing official problems, which internally eroded the legitimacy of opium's commercial life for European colonial states across Southeast Asia.

Local administrators were minor agents of imperial rule, far removed from greater intellectual debates of their times and seldom directly involved in the high decision-making of empires. Yet, these actors exercised surprisingly strong powers, as they produced official knowledge about opium in overseas colonies that provided evidentiary bases for major legal administrative reforms. They were poor theorists but rich empiricists of colonial reality. By way of doing what lowly administrators do on a day-to-day basis—implementing policies and keeping records—they developed commonplace philosophies about opium consumption as a colonial vice and forceful opinions about profits gained from the ills of others, while generating copious records that described and explained what challenges, what dangers, what wickedness seemed to mar local order. Seemingly radical reversals to Empire's approach to opium in each colony were the sum of accumulated tensions arising from longstanding efforts to manage opium markets. Anti-opium reforms occurred at different times for different reasons, depending on the ways in which local administrators defined opium problems and affirmed them as politically actionable causes. But commonly, prohibiting opium was made possible through the work of anxious overseas bureaucracies.

The power of a state is felt intimately when it declares new interdictions. In the case of Southeast Asia, opium had long been a part of both the public and private lives of people. When nineteenth-century colonial rule began, opium was sold openly in the busy ports of Singapore under British rule and French Saigon to sailors and dockhands, in tin mines of Malaya where Chinese and Indian migrant workers toiled, as well as at opium shops in bustling bazaars throughout the region. The ones in Rangoon "are like gin shops in London with conspicuous signboards and often attractive in appearance particularly at night," described one British official living in Burma in the 1880s.[7] A French doctor named Angélo Hesnard remembered the Saigon opium manufacturing factory where "busy Chinese, half naked, covered in sweat, labored in a vast hall . . . filled with the infamous odor of 'boiled chocolate.'"[8] As a sumptuary practice, consuming opium touched the lives of both the rich and the poor, the pious and the profane, as a habit associated with the highest of pleasures and the lowest of pains. For those who smoked, ate, or otherwise ingested it, opium was a drug "at once bountiful and all devouring, merciful and destructive, sustaining and vengeful," in the words of the novelist Amitav Ghosh.[9]

This everyday world changed under prohibition. Vendors faced restrictions on who they could sell opium to, at what price, and at what times of the day, while some saw their businesses taken over altogether by the same authorities who had issued sales licenses. In turn, people changed how they acquired and consumed a good that disappeared from respectable markets, from well-off merchants in Saigon to impoverished rickshaw pullers in Singapore who smoked opium excessively in pursuit of brief reprieves from the physical hardship, disease, and profound loneliness that came with working as a migrant away from home.[10] Some individuals were summoned before authorities to register as opium addicts and avow the state's way of defining their experiences. Others did not and became labeled as illicit, illegal, and indeed criminal actors. By demonstrating how this shift was made possible through the nitty-gritty work of local administrators, this book tells a larger story about how states transform themselves.

The Underbelly of Bureaucracies

The bureaucracy holds a privileged place for understanding modern states. It enforces laws, oversees taxation, provides public services, and allocates resources to people. Such administrative activities can introduce and naturalize fundamental categories through which individuals understand their place in groups, society, and a nation, while inculcating a sense of the inevitable presence or self-evident utility of the state. Bureaucracies have and continue to assume a powerful role organizing the exercise of physical and symbolic forms of state power.

While many scholars now agree that the state is not a monolithic entity with a unified purpose, we have been slower to acknowledge the bureaucracy in a similar way.[11] In the shadow of Max Weber's ideal type of the professional bureaucracy— an organization ordered by hierarchy, routinized tasks and rules, internal meritocracy, and the triumph of rational-legal authority—many conceive of administrative activity as first and foremost a rule-bound process of executing top-down directives.[12] Public choice theorists also favor a minimalist view of bureaucracies comprising principal–agent relationships, hampered by frictions that arise from misaligned interests between implementing administrators and the ministers, regulators, and technocrats who formulate policies.[13] Both perspectives posit a general logic to bureaucracies as pursuing goals set by upper echelons of the organization, seeking to efficiently implement policies formed from above.

This conventional wisdom tends to pathologize the discretion of low-level officials. From a high vantage point at the center, low-ranking administrators who act by their own volition are sources of bureaucratic inefficiency. From a Weberian perspective, these actors defy the rules of an organization and thwart its ability to realize goals. Everyday administrators who implement policies imperfectly and produce imprecise paperwork, vague records, as well as gaps between professed objectives and achieved results are suspect agents who exploit their principal's relative lack of information and difficulty monitoring in order to implement alternative polices or pursue private ends. Discretionary power within bureaucracies often has a negative connotation, from misleading superiors and shirking responsibilities to rent-seeking behaviors and outright corruption[14]: The desk officer who sidesteps procedure. The tax collector who reports ambiguous numbers. The financial officer who misreports funds and blurs entries in the budget. The wayward official who alters, contradicts, or even challenges given directives. Typically, all are familiar as willful figures who distort the rational workings of a bureaucracy.

But when we actually look within a bureaucracy, these administrators are no longer so familiar. This book argues that the discretion they exercise represents commonsense acts in the contexts in which they work, as solutions to problems with perceived urgency. They acquire felt imperatives to act, which vary widely depending on the history and inherited precedents for their particular realm of administrative activity. More than mere disobedience or corruption, the ways that low-ranking administrators behave differently from the bidding of superiors reflect their own reasons for easing tensions, making accommodations, and exercising authority on a day-to-day level of work.[15] Thus, to understand discretionary power within bureaucracies, it is necessary to understand what problems fueled the everyday work of minor officials. From the perspective of these insiders, the bureaucracy was not a coherent organization but a messy structure defined by multiple logics of operation, shifting objectives, as well as contradictory reasons for action. Political scientists have long stressed that bureaucracies are mired in politics, arising from external ties to elected politicians and legislators, business interests, professional communities, intellectuals, and activists, as well as through interactions with everyday citizens. I tell the lesser known story of micropolitics *within* bureaucracies. This requires exploring the concrete and granular workings of administrative governance, focusing on what actors deep within the underbelly of a bureaucracy actually did and wrote.

Contributions

This book's approach to bureaucracies and opium in colonial Southeast Asia offers several interpretive and theoretical contributions. First, for scholarship in political science and sociology on the modern state, it places the everyday bureaucracy and power of ideas at the center of how we think about states and their claims to govern. A growing literature on symbolic dimensions of state capacity recognizes the ways that seemingly banal administrative categories, labels, classifications, and regulatory rubrics can profoundly order and organize socioeconomic life.[16] When explaining how bureaucrats develop and implement such administrative schemes, most studies focus on external interactions with political actors and social forces. But less sustained attention has been paid to the interpretive work that actors *within* bureaucracies do: how they choose and puzzle over objects of regulation, how they define the meaning of their own work, and how they develop narratives about the necessity and viability of official action. This inner world of bureaucratic activity is important for understanding how states govern concretely and claim authority to rule.

For comparative historical studies of colonialism and state building, this book's focus on opium illuminates an often overlooked realm of fiscal capacity and authority for European colonial states: the vices of subject populations. Taxing colonial vices enabled rulers to exercise social control, collect revenue, and assert moral claims to govern. It simultaneously gave institutional expression to imperial logics of domination based on difference, while instantiating Empire's ambivalence about the terms on which to articulate reasons for differentiating among and dominating presumed others. Yet, few studies have treated colonial vice taxes as a central subject of inquiry or been curious about how exactly this system operated.[17] *Empires of Vice* does both. It situates the regulation of vice at the heart of European colonial state building, focusing on policies and arguments for regulating opium consumption as a peculiar vice among non-European subjects through excise taxation.

Finally, for histories of opium and empire, this book gives reason to be more puzzled about how opium prohibition happened across Southeast Asia under European rule since the late nineteenth century. The anti-opium turn of empires has been best understood from global perspectives that center on the political economy of China and India, transnational forces behind international norm changes, as well as the role of the United States and League of Nations. Seen as a region, however, Southeast Asia merits special consideration, not least due to the distinctive regulatory conundrums that taxing opium consumption posed for colonial states. Using a diverse range of administrative sources, I give access to the inner lives of bureaucracies on colonial ground and elucidate the variety of administrative challenges that different colonial states faced by identifying the authors of official facts about opium problems invoked in major anti-opium reforms, the architects behind administrative categories, the creators of revenue numbers and government statistics on crime and diseases relating to opium, as well as the narrators of public transcripts of the state with their descriptive, causal, and normative assessments of colonial reality. In doing so, this book aspires to tell a history that compares, in the words of Frederick Cooper, without "sweeping the particular under the global."[18] It also underscores the imperfect and incomplete nature of this process of change, in ways that demonstrate how Southeast Asia today bears the lasting legacies of colonial opium prohibition.

Symbolic State Power and Everyday Bureaucracies

States are powerful, with a capacity "to name, to identify, to categorize, to state what is what and who is who."[19] They can impose categorical distinctions on society by officially defining, declaring, and sometimes naturalizing the basic terms on which people understand the world they live in. While the modern state is most famously the wielder of physical coercion par excellence, it is also an entity that exercises a more subtle yet equally forceful presence by generating formal categories, shared vocabularies, and frameworks of reference that guide human interactions. If a claim to monopolize the legitimate use of violence distinguishes the state from other entities capable of coercing, disciplining, and ordering society, then the state is also distinct in its claim to centralize control over symbolic realms of social and economic activity, constituting as "given" what people experience as meaningful.[20]

In recent decades, studies acknowledging the importance of symbolic state capacity for understanding historical dynamics of state formation and contemporary governance have gained much currency. They provide valuable correctives to canonical theories of the modern state focusing predominantly on the military, police, and bureaucracy in establishing and defending territorial jurisdictions, waging war, and extracting revenue, by shifting attention to the many other composite institutions of the state and its additional pedagogical, corrective, and ideological roles.[21] In this revisionist vein, studies on symbolic power generally give sustained attention to cultural and ideational dimensions of state capacity; recognize the importance of legitimate authority for exercising power; challenge blunt separations of material versus immaterial, hard versus soft forms of influence; and stress the ways by which coercive and extractive acts occur alongside, or indeed require, nonmaterial capacities that shape an individual's ideas, beliefs, values, as well as his or her social, linguistic, and practical relationships with others.[22]

The pervasive presence of bureaucracies in people's lives has proven a fruitful vantage point for understanding how administrative capacities emerge and evolve to reconfigure social hierarchies, construct the taken-for-granted, and mask the intrusive presence of the state. The census; registries for birth, marriage, death, disease, and criminal behavior; cadastral maps; tax lists; land surveys; and passports mark but a few of the many sites where seemingly mundane bureaucratic arrangements "can become powerful instruments of state rule, as they help constitute what they appear merely to represent."[23] For instance, the census classifies, quantifies, and serializes people in ways that at once enabled the rise of imagined political communities, grammars of resistance against it, as well as the remaking of ethnic and racial identities and struggles for political recognition.[24] Even the most microlevel administrative practices such as creating surnames and standardizing units of measurement can render society "legible"—generating knowledge about local practices into standardized forms—in ways that facilitate efficient fiscal extraction and social control.[25] In the international realm, everyday patterns of action that perform competency can shape war, diplomatic cooperation, and conflict, as well as the efficacy of international organizations through reiterative interactions that "embody, act out, and possibly reify background knowledge and discourse in and on the material world."[26] Banal, yet clearly existing forms of political authority may prevail through administrative practices that produce official statistics, conduct surveys, and employ technologies to map, label, and narrate supranational entities as a social fact.[27]

This book advances the current literature by taking the lens of everyday practices further inside the bureaucracy. Many studies on symbolic power have focused on state–society interactions: between bureaucrats and citizens, elites and nonelites, technocrats and laypersons, official and unofficial actors, those who govern and those who are governed.[28] This reflects a predominant approach to studying the power of administrative categories in light of what people recognize as legitimate, of how society regards the state. But if we pause to ask where a state's vocabularies, narratives, and professed ways of knowing come from, then the existing literature tells a partial story. There is a prior step of fashioning labels, attaching referents in the empirical world, transforming words into official names, and entering them into the formal lexicon of the bureaucracy. State actors enact public transcripts that are produced through very prosaic acts of paperwork, recordkeeping, sorting, and scripting that tame unwieldy and abundant information into seemingly coherent narratives. Low-level bureaucrats also express their own convictions about what is or should be treated as real about objects of administration. Such convictions are formed cumulatively, by way of dwelling on regulatory precedents, internal archives, and shared commonsense about the possibilities and limits of administrative action. Put simply, in addition to looking outwardly, everyday bureaucrats look inwardly and backwards at their own pasts and construct official realities that they themselves find persuasive.

The inner workings of bureaucracies are messy, murky, and often hidden from sight. Understanding them requires a critical stance that steps back from established ways of asking how states wield symbolic state power through administrative categories. Who does the actual work of producing official knowledge and what does the process look like? What fidelity do bureaucrats have to the languages they use and when do the state's own agents recognize formally sanctioned ways of categorizing and classifying the world as legitimate, appropriate, or absurd? Why do some constellations of ideas, interests, and sentiments shared among administrators become official narratives while others do not; and through what mechanisms does a bureaucratic realm of imagination guide state action? I address these prior questions that concern how administrative actors come to act, speak before, and interact with society in the ways that they do.

A sustained focus on administrative narratives about rule and revenue laden with symbolic power runs counter to how social scientists typically study policies relating to economic, fiscal, and financial matters. The words that official actors use are often treated as either secondary to hard material interests or as smokescreens for unspoken alternative goals. There is also a tendency to discount what bureaucrats say, assuming that efforts to explain, record, or hide their activities are guided by insidious intents such as misleading superiors, pleasing external audiences, or performing otherwise absent competency.

This book pushes against such preconceptions. I insist on the importance of language for bureaucratic activity and approach the self-regarding ways that administrators articulate reasons for action (or lack thereof) as interpretive acts. Even the lowliest of officials can justify their decisions, without necessarily seeking to perform competency before, or conceal corruption from, superiors, but because it is an everyday practice that makes sense in their narrow worlds. They can fashion and weld together labels and idioms, conceptual frameworks, presuppositions and biases, standards of necessity, causal and descriptive explanations, as well as worldviews that may appear odd and even hypocritical to outsiders but still make sense internally. An absurd quality may color a repetitive and almost comically self-referential process that nonetheless has a method to its madness, "conjur[ing] up . . . visions that are at once accepted and understood by the whole of a social group."[29] The narratives that administrators use may enact and express ideas to accord with these visions. And desires to find meaning in actions taken in their official role may give these agents of the state reason to actually believe in the categories they construct.

This prior layer of interpretation within bureaucracies has political consequences. It sets the boundaries of a state's officially acceptable speech by generating guidelines for what information and truth claims can be made publicly and what must remain unspoken. It defines formally actionable causes by establishing criteria for the necessity and feasibility of state action among those most intimately involved in actual administrative work. It decides (or negates) reasons for policy change and produces narratives that explain why certain initiatives succeed (or fail). It invents political facts by abstracting information and generalizing knowledge that bureaucrats produce. It induces state actors to believe in, defend, or at least justify their own ideas publicly and behave accordingly. It constructs realities that become taken for granted as obvious objects of state action.

In sum, this book approaches bureaucracies from the inside out. It takes seriously the importance of language and knowledge in administrative work and locates what political scientists might call endogenous sources of policy change in struggles *within* the bureaucracy. Even the most minor officials and their seemingly petty ideas can have major influence over how states wield symbolic power, by constructing official realities. Throughout this book, I refer to the surprising strength of weak actors to capture this link between micro- and macrolevel dynamics of change and trace the processes through which everyday bureaucratic practices and ideas have real, observable political consequences.

Taxing Colonial Vices

The vices of others formed a hidden pillar on which colonial states were built. Empires were obsessed with deviant sexualities, illicit addictions, and perverse moralities, developing regulatory regimes that collected revenue and policed unfamiliar societies, while also defining what constituted abnormal behavior among subject populations. An interdisciplinary literature on colonial history recognizes the regulation of vice as simultaneously manifesting logics of colonial domination, while also serving purposes of social control and managing boundaries.[30] State interventions that presupposed the difference of colonized subjects involved in prostitution, gambling, drinking, and use of narcotics—to name just a few of the most studied vices—are understood as both constitutive of the fundamental nature of colonialism and instrumental to its maintenance. Many scholars have focused on the paternalistic regard of European rulers toward non-European subjects, while some have also explored how people blurring distinctions of race, class, and gender commanded the attention, anxiety, annoyance, but also sympathy of colonial states.[31]

The ambivalence of official actors has become a key thematic guiding students of colonial vice who historicize the regulatory role of the state. An earlier generation of scholars influenced by subaltern studies and critical

Marxism as well as social and cultural historians focused more on the colonized and their agency, seeking to move beyond reductionist views of victimhood attached to people at the ostensible margins of colonial society.[32] More recent studies have reconsidered the colonizer, dissatisfied with blunt characterizations of the colonial state as a monolithic entity with primary goals of exploitation. According to one especially influential line of reasoning indebted to the works of Michel Foucault, even if colonial impositions clearly worked to the detriment of people's welfare, economy, identity, and dignity, we risk drawing overly straight lines between the state's intentionality and consequences in ways that run roughshod over processes of implementation, reversals, as well as unobserved state–society interactions that profoundly shaped not only lived experiences of the past but also later outcomes.[33] Now, serious references to the state's gaze or colonial mind acknowledge its fractured and context-dependent nature, as well as the polyvalence of discourses that may coexist and comply with numerous political agendas at once.

Existing scholarship as such, is attentive to the many and conflicting imperatives that shaped the regulation of colonial vice. Historians of empire studying gender and sexuality have produced an especially vibrant research agenda showing how policies dealing with prostitution and trafficking in women and children not only reflected but also impacted evolving concerns about race and class difference, public health and hygiene, as well as labor productivity and security that pulled state authorities in conflicting directions: to both protect and punish presumed inferiors, to both acknowledge and disavow sources of disrupted social order, to both police and condone illicit intimacies.[34] The colonial state, as Philippa Levine demonstrates lucidly, "frequently found itself in the curious and ambiguous position of upholding the moral and political authority of the modern Western judicial mode but simultaneously seeking to reassure the foreign population subject to that mode that it would not unduly interfere with either their laws or customs."[35] Studies of colonial crime and deviance also establish the ways that European authorities regarded gambling, drinking, and drug use among native populations as both troubling but understandable, worrisome but necessary.[36] These works enrich our understanding of how regulatory regimes for colonial vice wrought profound changes over peoples' lives without being confined to asking whether authorities succeed or failed to actualize their intended changes. They enable us to acknowledge but not halt at the normative implications to questioning why states behaved in the ways they did and who bears responsibility for the improvement (or worsening) of people's welfare and developmental outcomes under colonial rule. This growing literature thus opens opportunities to become newly curious about the nature of colonial governance and its effects.

This book's focus on the bureaucracy pursues one such line of inquiry. Given the ambivalence of administrative actors toward colonial vice regulation, how did they settle on specific policies? If European officials perceived of prostitution, drunkenness, excessive drug use, and gambling among the colonized as problematic yet inevitable, then what explains the emergence of certain regulatory approaches? I argue that the nuts-and-bolts aspects of administrative work can generate a slow-moving process through which official problems that the state deems worth solving are constructed, translating general ambivalence into specific policy.

It often starts small. Minor disruptions to routine abound at the level of everyday administration. From so many occasions where little things can go wrong, modest officials gain recurrent reasons to reflect on the causes and significance of such disruptions. Introspection occurs frequently, as biased and always partial assessments of what obstacles, what challenges frustrate the work of lowly bureaucrats. Routines continue. Disruptions repeat. And as these actors continue to ponder imperfectly, so accumulates anxiety within the bureaucracy. Documentation of felt sources of worry are archived, giving paper reality to perceived problems alongside names and labels, causal narratives, as well as numbers and ways of calculating that affirm already presumed reasons for concern. A process of escalation ensues, fueled by the regularity of routine administrative work. Bureaucrats at once reaffirm problems of their own making and struggle to solve them. They may gain remarkable discretionary power over defining what constitutes an actionable cause for the state by authoring official facts, assessing the necessity and viability of policy changes, and producing the language through which the state explains publicly the purpose of its actions (or reasons for a lack thereof).

Southeast Asia's experience with regulating opium consumption as a colonial vice illustrates this process, which I call the bureaucratic construction of official problems, with particular clarity. European rulers gained a substantial fiscal base from indirect taxes collected from non-European subjects who consumed opium. Yet, local administrators held deeply ambivalent positions about the legitimacy of revenue collected from what was deemed a peculiarly Asian vice and debated the proper nature of state involvement. Opium consumption in Southeast Asia under European rule thus represents a colonial vice with high fiscal stakes for which the meaning of regulation was especially contested. It took a near half-century-long process of bureaucratic problem solving for opium consumption to become a taken-for-granted object of state control and prohibition.

More generally, a study of the bureaucratic making of colonial vice regulation invites scholars of modern state formation to consider how states arrogate authority to themselves by constructing official problems, dangers, and threats to society that make top down interventions seem obviously necessary.[37] Chares Tilly once famously likened states to criminal organizations. The activities of a classic Weberian state, he observed, bears striking resemblances to a protection racket, a scheme to produce both a danger and at a price, the shield against it. "If protection rackets represent organized crime at its smoothest," Tilly reasoned, "then war-risking and state-making . . . qualify as our largest examples of organized crime."[38] This analogy has durably shaped how social scientists think about the state. Many ask how states provide protection in the comforting sense of the word—how do rulers ensure the security of society; with whom do they bargain, what sorts of contracts do they establish, and by what mechanisms do effective and credible shelters endure?

However, Tilly reminds us, the word protection also sounds an ominous tone. The distinctive brand of protection common to the state and disreputable practitioners of organized crime also involves producing shields from threats that may be real or imaginary, threats that states themselves "simulate, stimulate, or even fabricate."[39] This darker sort of statecraft has received less sustained attention. Remedying this asymmetry, this book explains how states come to define official problems, construct dangers, and reify them through everyday bureaucratic work.

Opium Prohibition across Southeast Asia and Colonial State Building

For nineteenth- and twentieth-century histories of opium and empire, what distinguishes this study is the greater weight given to asking *how* anti-opium reforms occurred in European colonies in Southeast Asia rather than explaining *why*. The many causes behind the rise of global prohibition regimes against opium have been established by prominent studies about the religious origins of transnational activists who morally condemned opium, galvanized a change in international norms, and mobilized policy changes in metropolitan and international arenas.[40] We also know a great deal about the geopolitical tensions and ideological forces that weighed upon the British and French to ban opium smoking in their colonies during this period, especially in light of the United

States' entry into Asia as an imperial power and its efforts to assert global leadership through a moralizing antinarcotic position.[41]

Few, however, have been curious about the process through which the sinews of overseas rule built on opium were dismantled and how official narratives justifying this practice were reversed. Seminal histories have sidestepped this aspect as obvious, following either one of two lines of reasoning: that collecting and justifying opium revenue became untenable for European imperial powers in a world with new anti-opium norms, and colonial states transitioned to alternative fiscal bases while realigning official discourses to echo the lofty dictates of an international community and peer empires.[42] Or, as those dealing more squarely with opium in Southeast Asia more often suggest, colonial states never really changed their practices but better hid them from external scrutiny, and bureaucratic language about gradual opium suppression served as smokescreens.[43] Especially trenchant versions of this second perspective draw attention to institutions called opium monopolies (also called *régies*) that centralized control over opium markets, replacing tax farming systems that had delegated the management of opium sales and distribution to private entrepreneurs with direct management by state officials and their appointed agents. The base fact that states effectively continued to oversee opium sales to local populations and collected revenue has been taken as evidence that the monopolies were profit-seeking entities, hardly serious about restricting the drug's commercial life and popular opium consumption in the colonies. Many have discounted the bureaucracy's justifications, regarding the opium monopolies as primarily profit-maximizing institutions, centralizing systems for efficient revenue extraction.[44]

However, the archival records of the opium monopolies for multiple British and French colonial states that I have consulted cannot be read solely through the lens of avarice. They also contain traces of anxiety, frustration, remorse, pride, boredom, as well as conflicting expressions of irrational confidence and profound skepticism about the integrity of the monopolies. "The history of the East is strewn with the wrecks of control schemes, of one kind or another, as regards opium," acknowledged one administrator in 1936, even as he pondered ways to design yet another such scheme.[45] Expressions of overt acceptance of colonized people injured by opium consumption are preserved in the official record alongside equally conspicuous concerns with the welfare of vulnerable others. Evidence of keen alertness among local administrators based in the colonies regarding Empire's damaged reputation and lost prestige couples with blatant exasperation with, diffidence toward, and indeed disregard for what politicians, activists, and others outside the bureaucracy thought about opium policies on the ground. In other words, it is difficult to see just untrammeled pursuits of profit, desires for social control, or the conceit of civilizing missions within the opium monopolies. All were present.

I would like to explore rather than presume rationales for administrative action. Therefore, I give more weight to the words of official actors than is conventional and interpret the emergence of the opium monopolies as the rise of opium prohibition, which was what involved administrators called it at the time. When doing so, the monopolies begin to make more sense as vexed institutions mired in problem-solving rather than simply profit-seeking entities.[46] Grappling with the ideas that state actors expressed, both publicly and privately, reveals practices of governance that were not necessarily hidden but less visible from the outside, including mechanisms for "officializing" facts about opium's significance for colonial society (Chapter 4), calculating opium revenue and converting it into a source of investment wealth (Chapter 5), as well as simultaneously reporting and disguising degrees of fiscal dependency (Chapter 6). The foundations of Southeast Asia's colonial states were tightly entangled with opium in ways that belie any notion that their dismantling was ever an easy or obvious task.

An untold story of prohibition through the opium monopolies thus emerges, as the continuation of colonial state building rooted in administrative struggles dating back to initial moments of territorial conquest. European rulers began to levy taxes on opium based on preconceptions about its consumption as a vice among local inhabitants of non-European territories, but with inchoate understandings about what exactly defined its evil, harm, and injury. If modern states "puzzle before they power" and must formulate conceptions about societies they govern in order to develop policies, then most colonial states in Southeast Asia did the opposite. They powered before puzzling, by collecting revenue and intervening in people's lives first, and clarifying reasons for doing so afterwards.[47] This reverse ordering durably shaped the work of subsequent administrators in the colonies. From early overreach came backward looking practices for managing opium markets, oriented toward solving problems arising from haphazardly formed, imperfect policies of the past. By way of doing their regular work, administrators came to conceive of certain challenges as more formidable than others, as threats to the stability and integrity of governance and eventually, as major challenges warranting forceful solutions. Over time, these actors came to lose confidence in the viability of the opium-based foundations of colonial states that they were tasked with managing, enabling anti-opium reforms.

I stress the inadvertent ways that low-level officials transformed the colonial state from within, using terms like haphazardness, unintended outcomes, and perverse consequences to describe how regulatory changes eluded the control of any single actor, yet were constantly propelled through the actions and ideas of individuals. But to be clear, I do not mean to suggest that administrators had given intentions that were thwarted or straightforward visions of ideal outcomes to be achieved that failed. Rather, these were captured actors within a flawed bureaucratic apparatus who were engaged in routinized work that had escalatory effects. Major anti-opium reforms were possible when those most intimately involved in everyday administration persuaded themselves of the reality of constructed opium problems and deemed them politically actionable causes.

This book thus tells a colonial history of opium prohibition that focuses squarely on the administrative state's perceptions and regulatory practices. It excavates a more tenuous and fragile side to the opium monopolies than what existing histories have recognized. Opium in Southeast Asia is best known as a drug that often had detrimental effects on the health and livelihoods of colonial populations, a good associated with Chinese migrant workers, tax farmers, and business families, a commodity integral to colonial political economies of labor and trade, as well as a form of contraband.[48] Usually, the state represents a constant, an entity that injured people, tax farmers and entrepreneurs bribed, opium consumers reproached, and smugglers evaded in diverse ways.[49] By contrast, this book reveals a more dynamic side to the colonial state, focusing on the inner anxieties that riddled its everyday bureaucracy.

Colonial Legacies

Today, the region of Southeast Asia hosts an especially dense cluster of countries that sanction capital punishment for drug trafficking and certain forms of consumption. Currently, only around thirty countries in the world retain the death penalty for nonviolent drug offenses, but one-third of them are concentrated in this region.[50] Such draconian drug laws are matched by aggressive policing strategies or "drug wars" that employ both extrajudicial and state-sponsored forms of violence. The world's second largest illegal poppy cultivation area is also located in this region, anchored in the highlands of Burma and sprawling across borders into northern Laos and Thailand.[51] Alongside concerns related to "social ills" stemming from opiate addiction and urban disorder, drug-fueled conflict and corruption, real and rumored, animate popular and political discourse. This book demonstrates how Southeast Asia's vexed opium-entangled political and economic landscape today is a product of its colonial experience with opium prohibition. A more general imprint left by colonial opium prohibition has been the recurrence of sharply delineated conceptions of illicit and dangerous aspects of commercial activity, which once found strong expressions in paternalistic rationales for external rule and are emerging during the twenty-first century as leitmotivs for state interventions and coercive controls over people's lives. By attuning scholars and policymakers to these themes, *Empires of Vice* invites the reader to pause and reflect on the assumptions and anxieties lying beneath our ongoing conversations about the harms of drug addiction, trafficking, and criminal undergrounds. How do we understand these seemingly obvious problems? What shapes our sensibilities of the need for policy action? What renders the criminality of vice visible, but masks the corresponding roles of the state and law, with their claims to moral authority? How did we get to where we are today and what has been lost sight of along the way? This book makes the case that the only way to fully understand these questions is to address them through historical inquiry, by illuminating the colonial legacies that have profoundly shaped contemporary Southeast Asia's illicit economies and punitive states.

Organization of Chapters

Chronologically, this book spans eight decades of British and French rule in Southeast Asia, beginning in the 1870s and ending in the 1940s after World War II. Chapter 2 presents the guiding concepts, theoretical claims, and analytical frameworks that guide the book. How did colonial states come to ban opium consumption, a once permissible vice that they had taxed and justified collecting revenue from? The change was the product of longstanding tensions within the colonial bureaucracies. The everyday work of managing opium markets involved makeshift solutions to small problems that accumulated over time and escalated into large perceived challenges to the legitimacy of colonial governance. Local administrators played a key role in this process by constructing social, fiscal, and financial problems relating to opium, through their everyday work. Chapter 2 lays out this argument in detail, while clarifying definitions of colonial vice, prohibition, and the state that the book uses throughout.

Chapter 3 surveys the opium monopolies of Southeast Asia from the 1890s to the 1940s, laying out differences in regulatory reforms for restricting opium sales and popular consumption. For readers unfamiliar with the nineteenth- and twentieth-century history of opium in Asia, this chapter provides background on key events and developments that inform existing scholarship on colonial opium prohibition: the decline of the India–China trade, the US annexation of the Philippines, and imperial entry into Southeast Asia, as well as the emergence of medicalized drug control regimes in Britain, France, and internationally under the League of Nations. The chapter also aims to persuade those already familiar with this history to be more puzzled about the colonial institution of an opium monopoly. Looking across multiple empires, I show how differently European powers implemented policies restricting opium that not only differ on a colony-by-colony basis in ways that challenge conventional understandings of opium monopolies as arrangements for maximizing revenue collection, but also do not map neatly onto major metropolitan and international developments. In this regard, Chapter 3 argues that prohibition unfolded unevenly across Southeast Asia as local administrators constructed official problems in ways that were responsive to but not necessarily reacting to external pressures; thus, there is reason to pay more attention to what was happening locally in the colonies.

Part II examines the opium monopolies of British Burma, Malaya, and French Indochina in detail. I focus on periods in the lifespans of each monopoly that are especially illustrative of the bureaucratic construction of official problems and proceed chronologically, with each chapter beginning in the decade where previous chapter ended: Burma from the 1870s to 1890s (Chapter 4), Malaya from the 1890s to 1920s (Chapter 5), and Indochina from the 1920s to 1940s (Chapter 6). Together, these cases are layered temporally to cover a long period of eight decades, with the aim of conveying detailed microlevel narratives about individual administrators while situating their ideas and actions in macrolevel political economic developments.

Chapter 4 begins with Burma in the 1870s. It traces a twenty-year process through which the British colonial state came to define a crisis of "moral wreckage" caused by opium and introduced an opium monopoly, while enacting an unprecedented ban on Burmese opium consumption in 1894. Chapter 5 turns to Malaya, another site of British rule, where the monopoly was introduced more than a decade later in 1910, without expressed concerns about indigenous opium consumption or sumptuary restrictions. It shows instead how the British colonial state was highly reliant on opium revenue; and the monopoly emerged as local administrators were reversing longstanding acceptance of such dependency as a natural condition of colonial government. Over the course of several decades, taxing opium sales became conceived of as an untenable practice and challenge to fiscal order, culminating in the introduction of an opium revenue reserve fund in 1925 to enable the substitution of opium taxes. Chapter 6 looks to Indochina in the 1920s, when the French colonial state was reporting comparably high shares of revenue from opium taxes to British Malaya. This chapter identifies a very different set of concerns animating local administrators who misreported official revenue numbers while struggling to manage an opium monopoly that ran itself into bankruptcy. I trace a process through which a minor accounting measure in 1925, originally designed to allow emergency liquidity for purchasing foreign opium, became an entrenched mechanism for artificially balancing the budget, which slowly accumulated into a crisis of overdrawn accounts and unpaid debts that threatened the financial viability of colonial government.

Part III addresses the contemporary and theoretical implications to understanding Southeast Asia's experience with colonial opium prohibition. Chapter 7 traces the lasting legacies of the opium monopolies, linking the infrastructures they established for restricting opium's commercial life to the region's post–World War II illicit opium economies and harshly punitive laws against drug trafficking. It also utilizes a set of historical photographs to dwell on what alternative visions of state power and perspectives on vulnerability are rendered visible by better understanding the colonial history of opium prohibition. Chapter 8 concludes by reflecting on the analytical and normative significance to this book's approach toward colonial bureaucracies and inner anxieties of the administrative state.

Method and Sources

This book provides a comparative method for explaining a complex process of historical change, which prioritizes identifying hitherto neglected similarities and differences across multiple sites. Colonial opium prohibition represents an event with a "lumpy" temporality that unfolded at uneven paces across multiple locations.[52] For the context of Southeast Asia, where received wisdom about colonial state behavior regarding opium regulation as driven by moral concerns with imperial reputation and revenue is especially strong, the anti-opium reforms that transpired during the late nineteenth and early twentieth centuries seem obvious enough that spatial and temporal variations within this process are often overlooked. A paucity of inter-empire and cross-colony histories of opium has further limited opportunities to compare and contrast the regulatory activities of European powers across the region.

I present three case studies of British Burma, Malaya, and French Indochina as layered comparisons: each builds on the previous one to clarify how differently local administrators worked in contexts in which one might expect more similarities in administrative responses to opium-related problems as colonies of the same national empire (Burma and Malaya) and with high fiscal dependency on opium revenue (Malaya and Indochina).

It is worth being clear upfront about what these case studies do and do not do. Each case privileges contexts that mattered for administrators who played pivotal roles in constructing opium problems, for instance, figures like Donald MacKenzie Smeaton in British Burma, who inscribed the official label of "moral wreckage" in government records; Arthur Meek Pountney, who designed the opium revenue replacement reserve fund for the Straits Settlements; and Joseph Ginestou, who oversaw the near bankruptcy of Indochina's opium monopoly. Empires were multiscalar concatenations of evolving legal administrative frameworks, "located in wider global fields of conflict and competition . . . reach[ing] across, through, and down to more localized settings of power relations." [53] In turn, administrators situated in the colonies felt such reach with varying degrees of intensity and shifting importance. What constitutes pertinent extra-bureaucratic influence—from the dictates of international conventions and metropolitan scrutiny to the input of professional experts, knowledge communities, and the media—thus differs for each case. Some events famously associated with opium in Asia remain in the background (such as the end of the India–China opium trade and World War I), while other events figure more prominently (including border tensions with China and World War II). In other words, these three case studies do not offer general histories of opium regulation by colony, but present dense contexts salient for understanding state actors consequential for pivotal anti-opium reforms.

Layered comparisons are well suited for explaining differences in policy-making and implementation for connected sites that defy standard comparative case study methods in the social sciences, which require presuming independence across cases to test causal arguments. [54] I draw inspiration from innovative approaches like Iza Hussin's use of networked cases (which examines the making and remaking of colonial law in light of dense interchanges in ideas, strategies, and modalities of translation and extrapolation that connected India, Malaya, and Egypt under British rule) and works by sociologists who extend the metaphors of ecologies and fields in reference to arenas of contestation that extend beyond nation-state boundaries. [55] The additional value to layering cases lies with elucidating contrasts and interrogating what politics and struggles are uniquely bound to a given site despite its clear connection to other sites.

Burma, Malaya, and Indochina were embedded in a densely interconnected world of ideas and interests vested in opium's commercial life. Until the end of World War II, the illegality of this realm had yet to be defined clearly as empires and states, colonial and independent, debated the terms on which international law might collectively restrict opium traded between countries and limit the drug's legitimate use to medical purposes. Asia represented the core of this global political economy of opium. In 1922, conservative estimates placed the world's annual opium production at 8,000 tons, of which more than half was grown in the southern provinces of China; around 2,000 tons in eastern India; and 1,100 in Turkey and Persia combined. Poppy cultivation itself was not limited to Asia; the flower that yielded a precious milky latex sap also bloomed in Greece, France, parts of today's Slovenia and Serbia, as well as Latin America. But the networks, capital, and knowledge necessary for commercializing its produce as a trade commodity had flourished earlier in Asia. British India served as the main hub for supplying opium to the world, dominating exports until 1935.

On the receiving end, small amounts of legal opium entered metropolitan Western Europe, usually Turkish and Iranian opium that had high morphine contents profitable for pharmaceutical industries.[56] The vast remainder of the world's opium, mostly from China and India, was destined for territories in Asia under the purview of what the World Peace Foundation once called the "opium smoking powers": Britain, France, Japan, the Netherlands, and Portugal.[57] Their colonies in Southeast Asia imported opium that was sold to local inhabitants for popular consumption.

Figure 1.1 shows these territories on a 1929 map produced by a League of Nations commission. The bold lines trace the itinerary of this commission, which was tasked with ascertaining the peculiarities of opium colonies in Europe's Far East (which I discuss in detail in Chapter 2). This map illustrates how observers during the early twentieth century placed these countries, which encompass what are today regarded as three subregions of South, Southeast Asia, and East Asia, within a common framework relating to opium.

Burma, Malaya, and Indochina illustrate the context-specific administrative tensions that opium taxation and vice regulation posed with particular clarity, as the British and French operated opium monopolies across multiple colonies. Whereas the opium monopolies for the Dutch East Indies and Portuguese Macao were limited to one colony, the sprawling reach of British and French

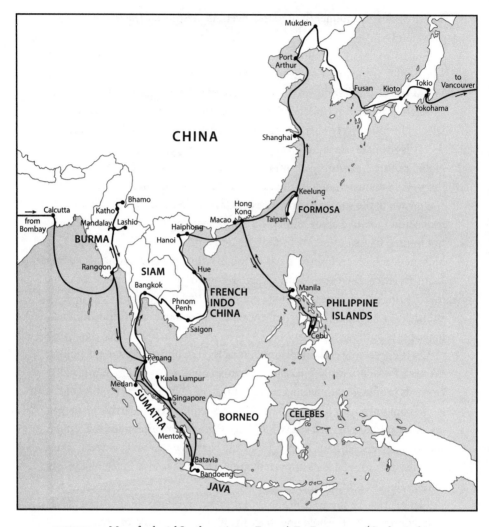

FIGURE 1.1. Map of colonial Southeast Asia in Europe's Far East, c. 1929. (Credit: Archives nationales d'outre mer, France, INDO/GGI/43095.)

empires rendered opium administration a messier affair, raising difficult questions about regulatory precedents, their transferability, as well as whether colonies under the same imperial power were comparable at all.[58] The British established separate opium monopolies for India, Burma, Hong Kong, Malaya, as well as Brunei, Sarawak, and North Borneo. Burma was administered as a part of India until 1935, but its monopoly operated differently without involvement in production and trade, unlike the India monopoly, which famously oversaw poppy cultivation, opium manufacture, as well as exports. The Malaya opium monopoly was in fact two monopolies: one for the Straits Settlements of Singapore, Penang, and Malacca, which comprised a Crown Colony under direct British rule and another for the indirectly ruled Federated and Unfederated Malay States; and it operated closely alongside three monopolies for Brunei, Sarawak, and North Borneo in the British-claimed parts of the Malay Archipelago. The French established opium monopolies for Indochina; in China for the leased territory of Kwang-Chou-wan; in India for the settlements of Chandernagor, Pondicherry, Yanaon, Karikal, and Mahé; as well as for the French protectorate of Oceania in the Polynesian Islands of the South Pacific. The Indochina opium monopoly was the largest, combining five older subregional monopolies for the colony of Cochinchina and protectorates of Tonkin and Annam, Cambodia, and Laos.

The colonial states of empires with multiple opium monopolies had distinctive experiences. Although local administrators actively learned from each other and shared information, these actors were also engaged in an intricate politics of comparison.[59] "Comparisons in the hands of colonial officialdom were also conceptual assessments and grounded interventions," Ann Stoler reminds us, and "[c]olonial agents disagreed over what constituted comparable contexts, often sharply aware that these choices had potent political effects."[60] Such choices were especially loaded for local administrators of the British and French Empires. As much as they could stress similarities and make analogies between different sites to argue for converging opium policies, these actors could also contrast their jurisdiction's imperatives to others under the same imperial power and declare unique local circumstances. The notion of an empire's general approach to opium was a fiction fashioned on high diplomatic stages. There was a reality of incoherence and accommodation to locally defined exigencies that underwrote the rise of opium prohibition across Southeast Asia. This process was common to the region, but unfolded in especially complicated ways for the British and French territories.

To trace this process, I consulted records collected over the course of twenty-two months of archival research in multiple repositories in Britain, Cambodia, France, Myanmar, Vietnam, and the United States. Administrative records concerning the opium monopolies and prohibition that involved officials produced represent the most proximate sources for reconstructing the insider's perspective of a colonial state. They are also the more tedious archives of the state, preserved in serialized records, internal correspondence, minutes of meetings, policy memos and drafts, as well as papers compiled for commission inquiries. These documents span a wide spectrum of granularity, moving from town and village-level assessments to district-level and colony-wide monthly and annual reports, across departments and offices overseeing customs and excise, taxation, finance, jails and prisons, crime and policing, as well as medical hygiene and medical services. When available, I also consulted the private papers, family correspondences, and diaries of local administrators, as well as commentary in the press concerning their activities.

I treat the writings of these actors as containing theories, opinions, and interpretations about social and economic realities of overseas colonies, following approaches by Jon Wilson and Karuna Mantena, who have examined imperial administrators in their capacities as less remembered political thinkers of empire.[61] A few of the local officials I examine were also well-known figures of their day who left behind texts containing glimpses into their petty philosophies. More often however, my protagonists were uncelebrated figures, politically inconsequential, whose names appear in passing as authors of government reports, some altogether anonymous. Yet, in some instances, the rich administrative records have made it possible to chase these individuals in the archives and trace a genealogy of ideas and ways of reasoning.[62]

Abundance is not always a blessing. It may amplify the myriad biases, misrepresentations, willful and inadvertent distortions, as well as troubling acts of violence and enduring forms of misrecognition that occur through the production and preservation of bureaucratic paperwork.[63] This aspect of government records gives reason not to abandon, but to be more vigilant when studying the colonial state that pursued this particular form of documentary life.[64] I have found the administrative paperwork perplexing, especially in its often messy, onerous, and redundant forms. The pedantic tones of annual excise reports, for instance, are sometimes interrupted by odd labels, categories, and commentaries that break the placid façade of routinized paperwork. Records show that even the most seemingly blatant pursuits of domination and efficiency-driven administration had different textures. Depending on the level of administration, certain illegal and corrupt bureaucratic practices are surprisingly visible in the archives, left in plain sight. To understand why and to what effect requires looking closely at what those producing the records said they were doing and asking why they claimed to use the language, categories, and forms that they did.

To be clear, it would be a mistake to see these administrative narratives as coherent wholes. Rather I view them as amalgamating profoundly human attempts to describe and judge the lives of others, which contain and condense the biases, mistakes, and hubris of actors who wrote them. As inner narratives of the state, they are thus valuable for a study of the administrative construction of official dangers. The records also yield many moments when authorities acknowledge non-European subordinate officials, informants, and friends of different genders and races who shaped their worldviews. I have incorporated these voices when they appear, such as in the field notes of subdistrict officers who questioned village elders about known opium addicts with the help of indigenous informants, in responses to unhappy Chambers of Commerce in Rangoon, Singapore, and Saigon and Haïphong, during "native" witness testimonies solicited by official commissions, as well as in official photographs that rendered certain types of social actors hypervisible as addicts and criminals. Of course, there was much more to the lives of opium consumers beyond how they appeared in official records, which this study attempts to convey by inquiring into why—for what reasons and upon what summons—their words were coopted in the state's archives. However, with regards to the lived experiences of the larger universe of people who do not appear in the records, I defer to others who do proper justice to their everyday politics in the history of colonial Southeast Asia.[65]

In sum, this book reconstructs the small worlds of officials stationed overseas, and when possible, embeds their ideas and expressed interests within broader intellectual and political economic contexts of their day. As historical contexts in which local administrators saw and spoke of their surroundings, the three colonies I examine capture vividly a regulatory world in flux where individuals held complex positions, combining concrete tasks of managing opium market with abstract reflections on the place of morality in colonial government, the boundaries between commerce and society, as well as just reasons for assumed differences about lived experiences in Europe's Far East.

These are narrow worlds: partial and inward looking, taking shape from what a small group of privileged British and French administrators wrote about what they did, said, and claimed to believe. Those writing were also mostly men, almost all white. The disproportionate attention I give to European administrators bears neither an apologist intent nor defense of the opium monopolies that they managed. It is more informed by a discomfort with the arrogant confidence of those who rule over others, and at the same time, a fascination with how even "the meanest of men has his theory" and must envision his own just reasons for action.[66]

2

A Shared Turn: Opium and the Rise of Prohibition

BEGINNING IN THE LATE NINETEENTH CENTURY, European empires established institutions across Southeast Asia called opium monopolies or *régies*, which centralized state control over opium markets within a colony. According to involved administrators at the time, these arrangements were efforts to prohibit opium consumption and protect colonial societies. A monopoly's professed goal was to gradually suppress a problematic drug, possibly achieving its eventual abolition. Most contemporary observers as well as later scholars have held this claim in deep skepticism, regarding the monopolies as quintessential expressions of colonial exploitation. It was "[a] complete, systematic arrangement, by which the foreign government profited at the expense of the subject peoples under its rule," according to the decorated journalist and American nurse Ellen Lamotte, who traveled to the region in 1916.[1] In Indochina, explained a French doctor living in the colony in 1925, "collective narcomania, coupled with this odious colonial policy" deprived the French nation of moral prestige.[2] "In no other region of the world did so many governments promote mass drug abuse with such unanimity of means and moral certitude," notes Alfred McCoy in his seminal 1972 monograph, *The Politics of Heroin in Southeast Asia.*[3] When writing about opium and empire, it is conventional to view the colonial monopolies in light of the revenue collected from and injury occasioned by opium consumption.

This chapter has three interrelated objectives. First, it sheds new light on the rise and development of the opium monopolies across Southeast Asia as a puzzling process of colonial state transformation. Existing studies have not been particularly curious about the half century-long era during which these

institutions operated, in part because most regard the state's language of prohibition and promises for gradual suppression as the alibi of the powerful,
apologist rhetoric or a form of imperial humanitarian aimed at protecting
commercial interests.[4] However, from the 1890s to 1940s, the opium monopolies also oversaw a vast range of regulatory reforms that slowly restricted the
commercial life of opium. This entailed a great shift to the economic bases of
government revenues and official justifications for colonial rule. Opium prohibition represents an often overlooked process of incremental change that
becomes visible only when we explore the nitty-gritty ways that an opium
monopoly actually worked and take seriously the rationales for its day-to-day
operations that involved officials told themselves and others.

Second, this chapter explains how such a transformation on part of colonial
states was possible. For this was hardly an obvious or easy task. When European rulers began territorial conquest across the region earlier in the nineteenth century, most levied indirect taxes on the popular consumption of
opium, raised revenue, and justified this practice in various ways. An especially
prevalent set of arguments centered on the regulation of colonial vice, which
posited the smoking of opium as a sumptuary act peculiar to inhabitants of the
Far East territories.[5] Yet, opium consumption was a tolerated vice among
many and not obviously destined to become an object of state control. Moreover, by the turn of the twentieth century, opium revenue and official narratives citing necessary profits, moral policing, as well as a colonizer's obligation
to protect the vulnerable from harm served as established fiscal and discursive
bedrocks for colonial states. Conflicting narratives could simultaneously rec-
ommend and warn against the involvement of the state in opium-related economic and social activities. Given such entanglements and ambivalence, how
were colonial states across Southeast Asia able to turn against opium, reconfiguring what was once a defensible source of revenue into an officially denounced danger?

The answer, I argue, lies with the everyday work and ideas of local administrators stationed in the colonies. Officials on site constructed administrative
problems that delegitimized the colonial state's reliance on opium from within.
Anti-opium reforms were enabled by an erosion of confidence deep within the
bureaucracy, a product of long accumulated tensions rooted in how European
rulers had first established arrangements for taxing opium consumption as a
colonial vice among non-European subjects, reversing a conventional sequence
of state building of puzzling before powering.[6] This chapter lays out this

argument in detail, emphasizing the surprising strength of seemingly weak actors who played a pivotal role in shaping the anti-opium turn of colonial states.

It is important to note that European administrators stationed in Southeast Asia constructed colonial opium problems within a transnational context of evolving political economic considerations and ideas concerned with opium during the late nineteenth and early twentieth centuries, and that overseas bureaucracies were embedded in more complex governance structures of empires with global reach.[7] This chapter focuses squarely on the inner life of a colonial state, because it is necessary to first grapple with the micropolitics of bureaucracies—namely, what struggles, anxieties, interests, ideas, and imaginations animated the everyday work of administrators on ground—and what made the monopolies operate in the ways that they did, before explaining how they fit in broader contexts. I will turn outward in the next chapter, situating the opium monopolies in Southeast Asia amid major global and imperial developments.

Finally, this chapter clarifies the significance of this argument for scholarship on state building and colonialism, by explaining the discretionary power of local administrators and identifying the bureaucratic construction of official problems as a mechanism for exercising symbolic state power.[8] The act of officially defining problems that justifies state involvement takes place in the underbelly of bureaucracies, where the habitual work and ideas of everyday administrators can generate taken-for-granted categories and classification that orient how states see society. And while it is tempting to assume that states that wield such symbolic power are strong because they can invent reasons to govern, this is only half of the story. Constructing official problems, I contend, serves as a double-edged sword for the purposes of legitimating governance. While it may help justify the state's presence and top-down interferences into society, the act of officially defining problems also binds the state to solving them in ways that not only self-impose obligations of accountability but also risk undermining the state's own authority when it fails to demonstrably remedy acknowledged problems. I elaborate on this duality of symbolic state power and highlight its irony in colonial contexts, where even when subject populations and metropolitan authorities could not hold colonial states accountable, bureaucracies struggled to explain their actions to themselves in ways that provided internal constraints.

The Rise of Opium Prohibition
across Southeast Asia

Prohibition was the name that European administrators stationed in Southeast Asia gave to reforms establishing the state as the sole locus of control over opium-related commercial activities within the colonies from the 1890s to 1940s. These monopoly arrangements generally had three components: (1) laws declaring the state as the only legitimate importer and manufacturer of opium; (2) licensing systems for sellers of opium, who were placed under supervision of government officials with police powers; and (3) policies restricting who could buy opium from these shops. All alternative forms of trade, sales, and consumption were deemed illegal and illegitimate.

The era of the opium monopolies was called the era of prohibition. Looking back, the ways that state-supervised opium markets prevailed does not look much like what we usually recognize as prohibition in terms of the constitutional ban on alcohol sales in the United States during the early twentieth century or laws criminalizing gambling in old Regime France, sodomy in Victorian Britain, and consuming "hard drugs" like cocaine or methamphetamines today.[9] Looking back, the European approach to opium consumption in Asia under colonial rule was one of tight state regulation over a legalized drug, which culminated only in the full abolition of opium markets and criminalization of drugs after independence. However, when looking forward from the past, extraordinary restrictions were being imposed on opium consumption, a colonial vice that was controversial but not yet seen as the self-evident danger requiring state control through punishment that it would become.

Permissive Days: When Opium Made
Empires and Colonial States

It was not obvious that European powers in Southeast Asia would ban opium consumption. As a trade commodity, opium had long been integral to imperial expansion. Early modern mercantile companies bearing the flags of British, Dutch, French, and Portuguese sovereigns competed to monopolize routes that shipped opium grown in India, Persia, and Turkey to the world.[10] Until the seventeenth century, Portuguese merchants and the Dutch East India Company had dominated these trade routes. During the 1660s, the British East India Company supplanted its Dutch rival and in 1797 established a trade monopoly over opium produced in India. Exporting opium to China opened avenues for

European economic influence over sovereign rulers in Asia and wars of conquest. Most famously, the British used opium to address trade deficits with China and recover losses of silver bullion arising from the popularity of China's tea, silk, and porcelain among British consumers without corresponding demand among the Chinese for European goods. By transporting cotton and opium from India to China, the British reversed the flow of silver and pressed China to release restrictions on foreign trade more generally. Two "opium wars" were waged (1838–1842 and 1856–1860) as the British, later joined by the French, militarily defeated China and compelled it to open many ports to non-Chinese merchants and legalize opium, which had been hitherto banned by the Qing emperor.[11]

Through the opium trade, European mercantile companies also gained territorial footholds into Southeast Asia. The British and Dutch East India Companies shipped Indian opium to the Malay Archipelago and Java. Writing in 1727 about Malaka, one observer remarked "[t]he Company sends a great deal of Cloth and Ophium [sic] there, and brings gold-dust in Return," and by the 1760s, Batavia alone was receiving around 100 tons of opium.[12] British merchants who had established private firms in India that shipped opium to China—known as country traders—transited through the Straits of Malacca and traded opium in major ports on the way. Across Southeast Asia, most sovereigns banned opium imports and use: King Rama III of Siam expressly outlawed opium trade in his 1826 treaty with Britain, while in 1820, the Dai Viet Emperor Minh Mang suppressed opium consumption vigorously.[13] However, by the mid-nineteenth century, "either through outright invasion, diplomatic pressure, or the corruption of their own subjects and officers, all were forced to accept the European presence and with them, opium."[14] During the 1860s, the King of Burma yielded to British demands to allow Indian opium to pass through his country to reach China, while upon the conquest of Saigon, the French began to collect duties on opium entering Cochinchina.[15]

Opium also played a pivotal role in building colonial states and the emergence of capitalism throughout Southeast Asia. Across the region, as European rulers asserted territorial claims to governance, they collected revenue from opium consumed by local inhabitants through opium tax farms. Tax farms were monopoly concessions by which the state subcontracted the collection of indirect taxes to private entrepreneurs for a set period of time, and these individuals paid regular fees and kept the margin of profit generated within a given territory.[16] The selection of opium tax farmers occurred either through auctions (in which the entrepreneurs made competitive bids for a contract to exercise exclusive control over importing, manufacturing, and selling opium) or through appointment by the colonial administration. The fees that a selected opium tax farmer paid could be fixed before his contract began or renegotiated in the process of operating the tax farm; and some colonial administrations required tax farmers to pay security deposits upfront and reduced the regular payments, while others collected the fees as shares of usually biannual or yearly profits. These were indirect taxes levied on opium consumption, usually categorized as a type of excise revenue or directly labeled as opium revenue in colonial budgets. The opium tax farmer, in effect, claimed rights to temporary monopolies over the entire supply chain after imported opium entered a colony until it reached the consumer: from warehouse to factory and boiling plants, to distribution depots, retail shops, smoking dens, as well as households where individuals had their own opium pipes. Tax farmers also actively policed contraband and protected their assets with private security forces and informants.[17]

In many European colonies, most opium tax farmers were domiciled Chinese with strong social and business ties who commanded key sectors of colonial economies.[18] In Dutch Java, auctions for the opium farm were called "the battle of the kings" as they involved the wealthiest of Hokkien merchants who partnered with coethnic investors to maximize collective capital (known as *kongsi*) and commanded their own security forces (called *mata-mata*).[19] Similar arrangements prevailed in the British Straits Settlements and Burma where Chinese opium tax farmers employed members of local triad organizations as private police forces. For instance, during the 1870s in Burma, the Rangoon opium farm was held by a Chinese secret society from Macao called the Ghehin sect, which the British considered "the most influential and steadiest members of the community."[20] There were also non-Chinese entrepreneurs who ran opium tax farms, as was the case of Cochinchina during the 1860s, when two French businessmen acquired contracts as well as in Burma during the early 1890s when a Burmese man served as opium tax farmer for Thayetmyo.[21]

Prominent sites for opium tax farming included labor-intensive tin and gold mines and plantations for gambier, pepper, coffee, and rubber.[22] Throughout the region, migrant laborers (called *coolies*) from southern China represented the most visible group of opium consumers. The largest shares of domiciled and migrant Chinese resided in the British Straits Settlements representing more than 50 percent of the total enumerated population, followed by the Dutch East Indies and French Indochina (around 2 percent), and British Burma (less than 1 percent).[23] Opium smoking was generally regarded a predominantly Chinese sumptuary practice, favored among the working class.[24] In 1848 Singapore, for instance, a British surgeon estimated that around 85 percent of Chinese

laborers smoked opium and "amongst the principal are carpenters, box makers, blacksmiths, barbers, hunters, coolies, boatmen, and gambier planters
including gardeners."[25] Migrant workers from India also consumed opium.
The Indians working at the Rangoon rice mills "take opium regularly every
day, and the practice is . . . almost universal, it being exceptional to find a man
who does not take it," recalled a mill manager named C. Findley who had resided
in Burma during the 1880s."[26] Indigenous populations represented a smaller
but still significant consumer base for opium. Working in the silver mines of
Namtu, "Burmese foresters and elephant men all ate opium to keep away the
fever," as did laborers from Laos in the teak forests of Siam and Javanese workers on the tobacco estates of Sumatra.[27]

Opium tax farms contributed to the development of private enterprise in
Southeast Asia. Carl Trocki has shown comprehensively how the Chinese-run
tax farms operated as vehicles of capital accumulation that privileged coethnic
entrepreneurs and brokers, while creating docile labor forces, large and usually
reliable cash flows, as well as opportunities for low-risk long-term investments in
ways that allowed Chinese investors to expand and diversify their operations.[28]
Opium tax farms also often doubled as banks that enabled savings and contributed to the flourishing of urban consumer economies, which laid the groundwork
for a distinctively Chinese form of transregional capitalism, based on powerful
"syndicates constitut[ing] a large, segmented network of interconnected *kongsi*
stretching from Burma to Shanghai and extending as far south as Australia."[29]
Within Southeast Asia's colonies as well, opium had many economic lives. According to James Rush's influential study of opium in Java, the tax farms bolstered
the patronage structures of Chinese-Javanese *peranakan* elites, while serving
as village credit institutions and overseeing retail trades that linked peasants
to rice-buying traders. In this Dutch colony, argues Rush, "[i]t was no wonder
that the rice trade, partial monetization of the rural economy, and the full-scale
development of the opium [tax] farm system occurred hand in hand."[30]

In tandem, European colonial states were able to extract revenue without
directly building infrastructures for tax collection and policing. The opium tax
farms provided the colonial state's first customs agents, police forces, and bureaucratic structures, which not only helped build political authority through
"the fact that they [Chinese tax farmers] themselves recognized the sovereignty
and legitimacy of the new colonial order," but also "solved a crucial problem
of colonial finance in that they were a supplement to colonial revenue."[31]

During the tax farming era, opium sales to local consumers became one of
the largest local tax sources for most European colonial states in Southeast Asia.

Around 60 percent of the local revenue of the British Straits Settlements (1819–1910) came from indirect taxes on opium collected through the farm contracts, more than 50 percent for French Cochinchina (1861–1899), and 35 percent for the Dutch in Java (1886–1895).[32] British Burma had a relatively lower level of fiscal dependency on opium revenue at around 10 percent (1826–1894) (see Appendix Figure A.6). For all, this source of local tax revenue was tightly entwined with the operations of colonial government. Opium revenue helped pay for the electricity that lighted Singapore's Horsburgh Lighthouse, maintaining the docks of this active port as well as financing the upkeep of the British Empire's naval base that defended it.[33] In the Philippines, wrote the Spanish civil servant and political Rafael Comenge in 1894, opium revenue made it possible to sustain a colonial justice system, "from the justice of the peace up to the Registrars of Property and Notaries."[34] "If Indochina has developed infrastructure, improved agriculture, and transformed its once putrid swamps into paddy fields, it owes this in part to the opium tax," acknowledged local administrators in the French colony.[35] In addition to directly financing public works and administrative salaries, opium revenue indirectly contributed to economic growth under the purview of colonial states.[36]

From the beginning, opium was a much debated source of colonial revenue but not necessarily destined to become an object of prohibition. Its consumption, from the perspective of early European administrators, was initially one among many vices that subjects, migrants, workers, and others residing in Southeast Asian colonies were seemingly injured by. Opium consumption was problematic but not uniquely so, opined James G. Scott, a Scotsman and prolific nineteenth-century journalist who also served the British colonial administration in Burma. "There are, of course, cases of excess," he acknowledged, "but the opium victim is never the hideous spectacle of the man sodden with alcohol or the repulsive bestiality that the man becomes who takes food to excess."[37] The vice of drunkenness in particular, agreed Charles Saunders, who worked in the Straits Settlements, was more disruptive to society as "drunkards and sots injure other people, [but] opium smoking only affects the smoker and his family."[38] Those who consumed opium excessively were seen as a limited part of the colonial population. For instance, "among the Dutch, it was a vice associated only with the weaker 'half-bloods,' and the "bad ones' who disappeared into the kampungs and the slums."[39] If anything, the vice of gambling was seen as more laden with potential to diffuse to the general public: the British in Burma viewed the lottery played by the Chinese with trepidation as "[i]t is the most insidiously seductive game, and I," explained one administrator, "have known and heard of whole families of unsuspecting simple Burmans who have been fed by the false hope of retrieving their losses, and after a few months, irretrievably ruined." He bemoaned how "even children share in the frenzy."[40] At least, according to an administrator in Indochina, opium consuming was hardly a "disastrous vice" as "the addict does not transmit his vice to his sons."[41] The French colonial state publicly displayed its own label—the letters "R.O." for *Régie de l'opium* or opium monopoly—on both the uniforms of administrators and on flags fixed to state-owned opium shops.[42]

Then how did consuming opium, a colonial vice among many, become an object of state control? What did this shift look like, and how was it possible, given the entanglements of opium with the social and fiscal order of colonial states? The following section addresses these questions in two steps. First, it explains the ambiguity of colonial vice for European rulers and the tensions that taxing and regulating opium consumption as a colonial vice among inhabitants of Southeast Asia posed. Second, it argues that local administrators came to construct this particular colonial vice as an object of state control, in the process of struggling to address small challenges and developed imperfect solutions. Their everyday work and ways of puzzling retrospectively not only gave bureaucratic reality to perceived problems at hand but also begot newly visible ones against the backdrop of clarified official knowledge. The accumulation of administrative anxieties escalated into an erosion of confidence within the colonial state. In other words, the rise of opium prohibition involved a sort of double selection process: the first in which, out of many tolerated colonial vices, habitual opium consumption became regarded as an especially dangerous problem, and the second in which, among the many possible ways to solve such problems, the colonial state (rather than religious authorities or market forces) emerged as the seemingly proper locus of control.

Defining Colonial Vice

Vice referred variously to prostitution, homosexuality, gambling, as well as the excessive consumption of stimulants such as alcohol, tobacco, and drugs. Grouped together, these were human acts that did not inflict physical damage on others, but risked offending another's sensibilities of good or proper behavior.[43] For European officials in non-European colonies, the vices of local inhabitants were a sweeping label for seemingly perverse expressions of sexuality, illicit addictions, compulsive behaviors, and dangerous desires. They connoted immoral and degrading aspects of an individual's life that had

complaints about hawking and contraband. While opium administrators were formally members of departments of excise and finance, because opium markets were so embedded in colonial societies, these officials also weighed in on matters of prison administration (when criminals were opium smokers), public health (when opium smokers were ill), labor and immigration (when ability of migrant opium smokers to work was at stake), as well as border policing (when opium smokers, suppliers, and their paraphernalia moved in and out of a colony). In doing so, they were interpreting, explaining, and writing about opium's significance to colonial political economy and local societies.

Against the backdrop of a growing internal archive, local administrators encountered problems relating to opium. Many were at first minor and technical, stemming from borrowed regulatory templates ill-fit for local circumstances or policies that failed in the face of new expediencies. For instance, British excise officials found India's templates for counting opium users among Hindus and Muslims inadequate for Burma with its Buddhist majority, while in Indochina, French administrators in Cochinchina struggled to find bidders for its opium tax farm. Small adjustments were made—the British added the label of "Burman" to enumerating templates based on religion; the French shortened the length of the tax farm's contract. Short-term solutions, in turn, created larger problems. The British found that large numbers of indigenous inhabitants of Burma could still not be categorized as Burman; the French were confronted with tax farmers who found loopholes in new policies and underreported profits; unforeseen shortages in opium stocks encouraged smuggling; fixed prices for retail sales further aggravated contraband. Administrators obsessed over such issues; readjusted policies; and, at the margins of each reform, encountered more problems.

Small problems accumulated, as these officials continued to implement policies and keep records. A thickening administrative archive enabled retrospective answers to questions that had been sidestepped initially, including what defined opium consumption as a colonial vice and why the state taxed it the way it did. Local administrators "discovered" reasons for intervention from their own records, reinterpreting prior moments of expediency as situations of necessity, recounting precedents of policies as guided by clear imperatives that had not existed at the time. By way of clarifying why existing regulatory regimes worked the ways they did and generating supporting evidence, local administrators came to more clearly discern irregularities in market dynamics and disrupted social orders, which obtained a documented reality. When tax farms underperformed periodically, it became evidence of troubling inefficiencies and the suspicious nature of Chinese business practices. With the imposed label of Burmese opium consumers came an enumerable population of indigenous opium smokers and estimates of its worrisome growth under British rule. Thus within the bureaucracy, challenges to colonial governance arising from opium-related problems became increasingly believable among those most immediately involved in everyday administration.

In effect, these actors were affirming the reality of problems of their own making with regard to opium consumption. And this particular vice became subject to state control when local administrators persuaded themselves of verifiable threats warranting official action. For instance, the British endorsed an official vision of a crisis of colonial society from "morally wrecked" Burmese due to a small but spreading habit of opium smoking, and banned the popular opium consumption in 1894 (Chapter 4). The French adjusted retail prices for opium and expanded control over poppy cultivation in parts of Indochina, on deeming a dependency on imported opium as a fundamental source of instability to the colony's finances (Chapter 6). Such were the sorts of dangers that administrators came to construct relating to opium consumption.

With hindsight, these seem like obvious fallacies to building a state on opium. For instance, enlisting Chinese proto-capitalists to run opium tax farms fostered a powerful economic elite that could challenge the European authorities.[62] Where opium revenue was a large share of local tax revenue, it follows that colonial states might become slow to diversify their fiscal bases and became vulnerable to economic downturns, famines, and other crises that affected the pockets of subjects, residents, and workers of the colony who bought the drug. Smuggling would, of course, also occur. Precisely as Eric Tagliacozzo's compelling works have shown for the British and Dutch, colonial states policing contraband—drugs, people, guns, counterfeit goods traveling in and around the Malay world and East Indies—necessarily faced backlash.[63] Moreover, throughout the period when European powers were taxing opium consumption, the social meaning of this sumptuary practice was a controversial topic, and into the first half of the twentieth century, the Far East opium smoking colonies were subject to much external scrutiny from metropolitan governments, their electorates, and the media.

These challenges, however, emerged *in the process* of governing a colony, not as foreseeable obstacles for administrators who either began with a blank slate upon which to build states or with clear visions of what sort of order they wanted to achieve. They struggled with such issues as they arose, constrained by precedents, initially from borrowed and makeshift policies and subsequently the product of their own actions. Crises of upset social order, fiscal dependency, and financial instability, as well as curtailed prestige, were not sufficient in and of themselves to provoke administrative reforms, but required a recognition within the bureaucracy as an actionable cause. This entailed winnowing down multiple formulations of problems and possible solutions into a master narrative about exceptional challenges to colonial governance that required the state's involvement.

In sum, European colonial states struggled to reform an especially unwieldy administrative hand, which had initially begun collecting revenue from opium for reasons of expediency, justified vaguely in reference to vice regulation, which subsequently spiraled beyond its control. This process was riddled with myriad tensions that local administrators tasked with managing the colony at once addressed and amplified, including ill-fitting labels for opium-consuming people that became categories for officially problematic populations, borrowed templates for indirectly taxing opium that had perverse consequences, as well as ad hoc justifications for regulating immoral and harmful activities. Once instituted, these arrangements were difficult to alter, and states acquired conservative biases against political action, whether banning opium or collecting revenue, given how they were initially built up and fiscally sustained by realms entwined with vice regulation. These opium-based foundations were a source of anxiety for those tasked with their management. Prohibition was what involved administrators called the many adjustments, initiatives, and policies aimed at solving accumulated challenges arising from taxing opium as a colonial vice. The everyday work and ideas of these middling actors were influential in shaping the process of opium prohibition across Southeast Asia.

Administrators and Their Discretionary Powers

British and French administrators based in overseas colonies exercised considerable discretionary power over opium affairs. These actors were the purveyors of archives that imperial bureaucrats, politicians, and legislators in London, Calcutta, Paris, and later diplomats to Geneva relied on for information about opium consumption in the colonies and assessments for the viability of anti-opium legal administrative reforms. They also presided over fiscal and financial arrangements that some metropolitan authorities paid attention to but struggled to make sense of, while others sought plausible deniability over.

Initially, the loftier minds of Empire were not particularly curious about opium in Southeast Asia. Europe's gaze focused more India's opium production and export trade to China, and opium tax farming represented a minor theme in the great political and intellectual debates about opium's significance in Europe's involvement in Far East territories (see Chapter 3).[64] In this context, local administrators went about relatively unencumbered in their mundane work of revising, adjusting, abandoning, and reintroducing pricing schemes and zoning arrangements for opium sales, licenses for retail venues, fees on individual consumers, and penalties against rule violators. They explained and recorded what they believed to be true about the colonial world around them, and developed shared practices for collecting and counting revenue from opium. Some arrangements were deliberately misleading for outside observers, while others were developed not necessarily to hide but to pave over what administrators themselves deemed unseemly.

During the second half of the nineteenth century, however, these administrators found newly receptive audiences for situated ways of knowing. For one, it was a time of expansion to what David Ludden calls "orientalist empiricism," an epistemological approach to making sense of colonized others, which took authority from an Enlightenment rubric of objective science that posited an observable reality, verifiable and independent of any subjective colonizing will.[65] "Freed from politics," Ludden writes, this empiricism was expressed in authoritative facts that were "conventionalized and then fixed as a factual basis for inference in theory," which solidified in official minds as commonsense.[66] For the British Empire, social theories that embraced "facts" about the fixity of village communities in India and tradition accorded special status to methods of ethnographic inquiry, and by elevating "direct observation as a methodological imperative," "provided an enormous fillip to . . . a genre of official anthropology by civil servants."[67] Learned communities in late nineteenth century France were also turning away from the earlier aggressions of physical anthropology that posited anatomical difference and biologically essential others, toward what was called the colonial sciences that favored field research on site, interviews, comparative statistics, and ethnographic modes of inquiry as ways of producing official knowledge about non-European people.[68] In this context, what local administrators professed to know about local colonial opium markets and societies became valued as privileged forms of expertise based on direct observation and proximate experiences.

A new "problem space" for European empires and their opium entanglements was emerging, i.e., an "ensemble of questions and answers around which a horizon of identifiable stakes hangs," in which metropolitan authorities sought more information about opium in the colonies.[69] There was greater curiosity about the nature of opium consumption within Southeast Asia. From afar, both critics of and stakeholders in imperial rule held divided opinions about the immorality, harm, and injury of opium, based on diffuse sensibilities about its consumption as a peculiar vice among non-Europeans but with tenuous evidentiary bases. Who was buying opium in Saigon-Chôlon, where more than 70 percent of Indochina's opium was being sold? How many Chinese migrants in Singapore smoked opium? How did their experiences compare to that of their countrymen in China? Were the Burmese injured by their opium habits and how did any ill effects differ from those experienced by Indians? What explained the absence of opium consumption among Malays and the unusual resilience of certain groups in Indochina who did smoke the drug? Answers to these questions, literal and demandingly granular, were sought from local administrators.

Into the first half of the twentieth century, imperial decision-makers in Britain and France continued to yield a privileged autonomy to local administrators stationed overseas in Southeast Asia. Empires developed a spate of multilateral agreements that enshrined a humanitarian norm that committed a self-avowed civilizing power to restrict the legitimate use of opium to medical and scientific realms and end the world's opium problems (Chapter 3). In this context, the existence of opium monopolies and their regulatory regimes, especially as they related to raising revenue from taxing opium consumption, was like the proverbial elephant in a room that all were aware of but loathe to acknowledge. For those removed from the day-to-day reality of colonial governance, the persistence of opium revenue and the slow pace of regulatory reforms that almost imperceptibly restricted the commercial life of the drug were embarrassments. And for high diplomats addressing peer imperialists, the fait accompli of colonial opium administration could serve as a reason why the total abolition of opium was impractical; for ranking bureaucrats held accountable to worried politicians, the reality on colonial ground could be cited as a reason for imperfect change. Thus, the regulatory realm of opium in the Far East persisted as an opaque one over which local administrators wielded a near monopoly over.

Stylized differences between British and French approaches to colonialism tend to invite a separation of opposing doctrines of indirect rule versus assimilation, as well as differing bureaucratic capacities, processes for the selection and education of colonial civil servants, work cultures, as well as organizational structures of imperial bureaucracies. In terms of size, the French administration in Indochina was larger than its British counterparts for Burma and Malaya, and among the managerial core, the former brought in more individuals from a lower middle-class background and outside of Paris, while the latter had higher middle-class Oxford and Cambridge graduates.[70] The French in Indochina were also quicker to create salaried positions for "natives," and those sent from the metropole received less formal training in local languages and technical aspects of administration. High-ranking French officers served for shorter periods than their British counterparts, who received pre–post training in native law, local administration, tropical hygiene, accounting, and surveying.[71] Also, in a very general sense, the British gave less formal autonomy to the colonies in Southeast Asia over the financial management of opium revenue compared with the French, and the political influence of religious antiopium movements was strong in Britain's Parliament without parallel in France's Senate and National Assembly.[72]

However, at an everyday level of administrative work, such distinctions between British and French Empires were not always so stark. Situated bureaucrats had biases, sentiments, and ideas that were shaped by but hardly the direct product of different organizational hierarchies and ideologies of rule. As Julian Go's comparative study of the British and American empires has shown persuasively, "[c]olonial policies were not shaped by national character, value, or styles but by the very spaces and scenes they aimed to manipulate and manage."[73] For policies regulating opium consumption in Southeast Asia as well, the situated experiences, interpretations, and power struggles of local administrators were deeply formative. Distinctions between the British and French blur even more for the middling officials involved in the opium monopolies. Whether Briton or Frenchman, the day-to-day work that absorbed local administrators similarly ranged from the basest of practical politics—how such funds would be used, how much would it cost to close down opium markets, who should pay for lost tax revenue, and how to actually enforce a ban with limited resources—to higher ideas about what legitimated the collection of opium revenue and the proper role of rule and regulation over the vices of others—what justified taxation in a non-European dependency, who was a fiscal subject among assumed nonequals, as well as what obligations of protection a colonial state should assert over those deemed especially vulnerable among already inferior people.

Local administrators pursued answers to these questions in a relatively insulated fashion, with strong biases against external input from nongovernment actors. Those intimately involved in operating the opium monopolies also acquired a peculiar impatience against the expertise of others asserted on moral and scientific grounds deemed divorced from their administrative reality. This echo chamber–like quality to the regulation of opium consumption as a vice tax distinguishes it from other colonial policy domains, which were powerfully shaped through interactions with indigenous elites, colonized subjects, and professional experts.[74] With regard to opium consumption, local administrators were acutely aware of, but increasingly dismissive toward, groups outside of the bureaucratic apparatus, including missionaries (who collected and dispersed information about opium-related injuries based on their own observations in the colonies), medical professionals (who were better informed about and adapted advances in scientific knowledge about opium consumption in the tropics), social activists (including intellectuals, community leaders who conveyed the opinions of opium-consuming people in the colonies), journalists (who compared and wrote about what they saw as foreign about opium in the Far East), as well as other nonofficial actors.

The Strength of Weak Actors

A rich and growing body of scholarship on colonial administrators reveals and instates these actors as major forces behind colonialism and Empire. Earlier studies tended to focus narrowly on imperial administrators as rulers in conquered societies, especially works written by former members of colonial overseas civil services.[75] This post–World War II generation of scholars found something special about this particular group of bureaucrats, their behavior, and a general esprit de corps—Philip Woodruff called them "picked men, picked from picked men," an elite within an elite—and sought to explain the sources of this distinctiveness.[76] On the British, G. M. Trevelyan noted the diminished salience of class differentiation among graduates of the Indian Civil Service and overseas colonial bureaucrats more generally.[77] Students of the French overseas administrators noted the strong imprint of their humanistic training at the Colonial School.[78] Subsequent inquiries surveyed factors such as procedures of selection and recruitment, family background, educational systems, and socialization opportunities to understand what shaped the special disposition of individuals for imperial service, their cohesiveness as a group, and this group's guiding beliefs and ideals. Anthony Kirk-Greene's rich monograph *Britain's Imperial Administrators, 1858–1966* reflects on the concepts that have since informed debates on "the fashioning and nature of a ruling elite" in colonial settings, which include

> Bottomore's cohesiveness of an administrative elite, Goldthorpe's image of a service class, and Mason's influential label of Platonic guardians trained to rule according to their own understanding of the Good and the Beautiful; from Potter's norms and values of the gentlemanly mode, Wilkinson's easy exercise of gentlemanly power and Raven's postulate that rule and administrative were the special provinces of the gentleman; and even from Ranger's deflationary formulation of neo-tradition which, invaluable overseas Service commodity that it was, required regular renewing in order to sustain its hold and continuity.[79]

If earlier studies focused on the formation of administrative elites, subsequent work centered on what consequences this particular breed of elite bureaucrats had for overseas rule. For some, the European administrator in non-European settings represents Empire's "man on the spot," a faithful agent building structures of exploitation and domination on the ground. For instance, British district commissioners in 1920s Africa prevailed as "chiefs in their own country—men who considered it their birthright to rule, and who did so by habit."[80] The well-trained and carefully groomed imperial administrator served to fortify the capacity of colonial states to make laws work, implement extractive and discriminatory legal policies, efficiently transform metropolitan directives into change overseas, as well as effectively repress local dissent.[81]

For others, imperial administrators represent a chink in the armor of overseas imperialism. Principal–agent problems plagued the large-scale apparatuses driving European expansion.[82] "Expansion by means of extending and multiplying agency relationships was a two-edged sword," Julia Adams points out, as "while it promised gains in the principal's efficacy and reach, it also created problems of monitoring agent's activities and enforcing compliance through sanctions."[83] Physical distance and inadequate communication and transportation technologies limited the sorts of real sanctions that imperial administrators faced. They worked within a procedurally streamlined institutional environment, one relatively free of the usual political, economic, and social pressures constraining policymaking in the metropolis. Also, the incentives of overseas administrators did not necessarily align with those of their metropolitan counterparts, especially when the former identified less as members of a public bureaucracy and more with private interests. For the Dutch and Spanish in Southeast Asia, James Scott explains that the "[c]olonial office until the

20th century was regarded more often than not as an investment in an exclusive franchise that was expected to yield a good return to the political entrepreneur who acquired it."[84] George Orwell's literary portrayal of the *pukka sahib*, the men who haunted the Pegu Club in British Burma, vividly typifies the corrupt, inept, and insecure imperial administrator who had a negative impact on colonial rule through his rent-seeking behavior and his unbridled ability to broker, manipulate, and even interrupt local–metropolitan ties by pushing policies in ways that undermined the symbolic masculine authority of the colonial state.[85]

Greater nuance given to the role and impact of overseas administrators serves as a salutary advance for studies of colonialism and Empire across disciplinary boundaries of political science, sociology, and history. Karuna Mantena's important work on Henry Maine during his tenure in British India as a legal member of the Viceroy's council demonstrates how the writings and ideas of this scholar-administrator served as a critical conduit between social theories of his time and practices of British imperial rule.[86] Maine's conception of native societies in crisis and evolutionary view of European modernity—as a trajectory of progress from ancient and primitive village communities to representative government—contributed to the late nineteenth century British Empire's ideological shift toward indirect rule as well as to the development of land reform strategies in India that would purportedly rehabilitate native customs and institutions and protect fragile communities. Similarly, Keally McBride's study of James Stephen in his capacity in the Colonial Office elucidates the discretionary power of an imperial administrator who, as undersecretary for the colonies and legal counsel, profoundly shaped the rule of law for nineteenth- century British colonies.[87] McBride underscores how the ways that Stephen and his family vigorously defended bureaucratic principles of legal proceduralism also entailed overseeing the law's transformation into an instrument of social control and propaganda. Imperial administrators were also imaginative actors, who competed among themselves to acquire and enact ethnographic acumen, as Steinmetz's magisterial analysis of the formation and implementation of native policy across German colonies shows.[88] He demonstrates how discourses and representations about an essentialized Other were inflected heavily by metropolitan intraelite class conflicts that were displaced onto the colonies and expressed through competition for reciprocal recognition of "ethnographic capital, of the acuity of their perception and judgment with respect to exotic cultures and indigenous subjectivities."[89] Steinmetz illuminates with particular clarity the psychic registers on which colonial administrators across Southwest Africa, Qingdao, and Samoa cultivated forbidden fantasies, cross-identifying with a specific *imagos* of the colonized. These situated actors "engaged in both symbolic projects and narcissistic, imaginary ones," with real effects.[90]

The well-recognized figures who exercised significant formal and informal influence over colonial policy, law, and ideologies while stationed outside of metropolitan Europe are often those who served as colonial governors, senior bureaucrats, legal counsels, and district or provincial commissioners. These imperial administrators represent the higher minds of Empire's overseas bureaucracy, with direct say in judicial and legislative decisions, as well as abilities to issue minor ordinances, directives, and emergency orders that had legal effects.[91] They made declarative statements and utilized official languages and categories that at once drew on and reproduced a complex politics of knowledge production that included the invention of colonial facts, gaps between governance in practice and its articulations and aspirations, as well as misrepresentations of reality, both willful and unintended, anchored in dispositions ranging from alarm, fear, and suspicion to ignorance and sympathy.[92]

There is an additional, often overlooked layer of activity undergirding high bureaucratic expressions of official knowledge. The act of writing official statements and drafting policy texts, the task of collecting village- and district-level reports and producing summary findings that consolidated an abundance of messy observations into a neat narrative, the many different ways to calculate and record revenue returns, the selection of descriptive terms for labels, categories, and classification schemes. These nitty-gritty aspects of everyday administration entailed a bewildering array of choices, which gave opportunity for even the pettiest of officials to insert his ideas, opinions, reflections, and biases into the basic terms on which colonial knowledge took formal expression.

Such work was repetitive, often uneventful, and likely tedious. Yet, curtailed forms of creativity emerged from routinized work, a brand of specialized expertise based on situated experiences and a serialized archive of self-elicited problems and solutions, which supplied an evidentiary basis on which policy changes could occur, shaping their direction, as well as the tenor of reforms. Under certain conditions, their grounded ways of knowing were summoned by higher powers as a testimonial form for legal and administrative decisions in the colony; sometimes their ideas traveled to metropolitan and international arenas for decision-making. Seemingly weak administrators could wield surprising strength as such, generating a remarkable capacity on the part of the colonial state to officially define society's dangers and self-legitimate its presence.

A Shallow Sort of Symbolic State Power

For the opium-entangled colonial states of Southeast Asia, local administrators represent the diffident wielders of symbolic state power, an ability "to name, to identify, to categorize, to state what is what and who is who" makes a state powerful.[93] They were incidental state-builders who described, explained, and reported on local circumstances in ways that claimed privileged authenticity based on direct observation. The act of formally asserting "what is what and who is so" did not necessarily create identities to which subjects adhered, nor did it create new ways of thinking about the world that people took for granted as inevitable. Rather, it was powerful in a shallower sense of providing authorities with internal evidence and a shared vocabulary to mobilize resources to rule over others. Put simply, constructing official problems enabled colonial states to self-authorize their presence. There was a tragic ease to how forcefully European rulers could claim to govern on behalf of the colonized. Protection over putatively vulnerable others served as a key idiom of colonial rule; and there was perhaps no better place to "simulate, stimulate, or even fabricate" dangers from which to protect society than the murky realms where colonial vices prevailed.[94]

However, such ways of exercising symbolic power also rendered colonial states precarious. They did not allow for an unbridled exercise of power over society because a state that defined official problems was in turn compelled to solve them. If protecting vulnerable subjects was invoked as a reason for more policing, completely eradicating the threats from which people were protected also did away with justifications for such powers. At the same time, an inability to deliver on promises for protection risked enervating paternalistic claims to govern. Administrators entrapped themselves, constrained by a self-imposed horizon for problem-solving that simultaneously could but should not be reached. States were at once inexorably strong because they could renew claims to a raison d'être for protecting endangered societies, yet always fragile because they must constantly acknowledge an upset social and moral order to establish such claims. In this sense, colonial vice represented an attractive piece of grist for making the fundamental bricks of state-building that could easily turn into dust in the hands of those who touched them.[95]

There was something peculiar about how the bureaucratic construction of official problems worked in a colonial context. Usually, an impetus for states to introduce, adjust, or abolish regulatory regimes emerges from society, from moral entrepreneurs or people "with strong notions about appropriate or desirable behavior in their community," who are often motivated by empathy, altruism, and ideational commitments, as well as intermediate groups between citizens and the state who aspire to change widely shared existing values.[96] But the colonial world was always less just, with a fundamental asymmetry of power that limited the accountability of state authorities to those they professed to protect, while restricting the latter's collective expressions of grievance. Officials intimately involved in opium administration heard and worried about, but did not necessarily heed the voices of people consuming opium who might object to paying higher prices for their regular fix. Even as intellectuals and the media expressed loud complaints and made impassioned pleas to the authorities to address urban disorder, the corrupt morals of youth and society, as well as crises of poor hygiene and public health, their voices fell short of persuading anxious agents of the colonial state to change what they were already used to doing. In the British and French colonies of Burma, Malaya, and Indochina that we will soon explore, worries about popular legitimacy and societal agitation were seldom sufficient to persuade local administrators to change entrenched practices for managing opium sales, distribution, and collecting revenue. And only infrequently could their bureaucratic superiors in Calcutta, London, or Paris effectively dictate reforms, given the vast realm of knowledge and minute practices for actually regulating opium under the purview of administrators on the ground, to which the rest of the empire was beholden.

Yet, local administrators could neither govern as they pleased nor alter arrangements relating to opium's commercial life at whim. For by way of continuing to tax the drug's consumption as a colonial vice, they inherited and affirmed problems to solve, and became bound by their own words and anxieties. Rarely could the underclasses of a colonial society hold the colonial state accountable for whether the revenue it collected was reasonable, how such money would be used, and what obligations were assumed toward the vulnerable people the state avowed to protect. But in an ironic twist, local administrators posed and answered these questions themselves, constraining the colonial state from within.

Conclusion

In 1901, a French military commander stationed in Indochina named Fernand Bernard dwelled on the colony's bewildering array of indirect taxes, which civilian administrators levied on "the ferries, the markets, the gamblers, the pawnshops, and opium, alcohol, and salt." [97] The entire fiscal landscape, he argued "was adapted not to the real state of the country, but to the ignorance of those who administered it."[98] It was "a strange method" that was nonetheless practiced with some pride on the ground, wrote Bernard in a book on the problems that France's colonial empire faced entitled *Indochina: Errors and Dangers*.

This chapter's argument suggests that there was more than ignorance and pride underlying the seemingly strange ways that colonial administrators in Southeast Asia approached opium. The regulatory approaches that local officials followed had a problem-solving logic, with a backward-looking orientation, rooted in early moments of colonial conquest when opium consumption was taxed as a colonial vice, despite tenuous conceptions of what defined a vice among colonized subject. Subsequent administrators at once built upon and reconfigured these makeshift arrangements, which further embedded tensions arising from retrospective attempts to clarify objects of taxation and reasons for regulation. Through repetition, small tensions found in bureaucratic procedure and paperwork escalated slowly into larger problems that preoccupied local administrators. And their everyday work would continue stubbornly, even amid eventful changes in global opium trade patterns and emergence of international regimes for drug control. In the next chapter, I situate these administrators in these broader contexts of the late nineteenth and early twentieth centuries to show how Southeast Asia fits uneasily within major political and economic developments that existing scholarship associates with the region's experience with anti-opium reforms.

3

The Different Lives of Southeast Asia's Opium Monopolies

BETWEEN THE 1890s and 1940s, opium monopolies oversaw regulatory reforms that incrementally restricted the commercial life of opium across Southeast Asia under the aegis of centralized state authority. These reforms were varied, often mutually contradictory, and ranged from minor acts of relabeling existing arrangements for opium sales and altering official categories for opium consumers to more major amendments to empire-wide laws that sanctioned forceful policing and redefined what constituted legal and legitimate opium-related activities in Europe's overseas colonies.

This chapter situates the opium monopolies of Southeast Asia and the diverse regulatory reforms they oversaw in the broader global and imperial context of the nineteenth and twentieth centuries. The previous chapter explored the inner lives of opium-entangled colonial states, explaining how local administrators constructed official opium problems in ways that contributed to the reversal of longstanding practices of taxing opium consumption as a colonial vice. We now look outward, at the busy and shifting world of commerce and ideas in which these actors were located.

This chapter is organized as follows. The first section presents an overarching view of opium monopolies across Southeast Asia and colony-by-colony differences, using a rich cross-national survey of regulatory approaches conducted by the League of Nations in 1929. Focusing on the British- and French-ruled territories, this section identifies a striking misalignment between how colonial bureaucracies defined and gathered evidence about opium problems in their jurisdictions and what they reported to external audiences, by cross-referencing the League of Nation's final report and interview transcripts with the internal records and private correspondence of administrators who spoke to the League's delegates. The gap is due, I contend, not to insidious intents on the part of state actors to deceive or mislead, but rather to a necessary disjuncture between what local administrators knew and others from afar wanted to know. I also suggest that this gap captures tensions between what is made visible about an opium monopoly when approaching its operations from the inside out and what is overlooked when looking at it from the outside in.

The second section further develops this critical perspective, by reviewing existing histories of opium and empire as well as literature on the colonial politics of opium in Southeast Asia. There are three key developments that are usually credited with Empire's anti-opium turn around the early twentieth century: the decline of the India–China opium trade; the emergence of religiously inspired transnational moral crusades and metropolitan legislative reforms for drug control; and the internationalization of drug control under the League of Nations. Against this backdrop, I draw attention to several aspects of colonial state-opium market relationships in Southeast Asia that unsettle prevailing wisdom, and clarify how the timing and tenor of regulatory reforms were influenced by, but did not necessarily follow, the dictates of the surrounding global economy and imperial world of ideas.

Specifically, unlike China and India, which had domestic production economies for opium aimed at export, Southeast Asia relied almost predominantly on imported opium to supply domestic consumers. Such within-region market demand mixed the tastes of foreign migrants and diaspora communities with indigenous inhabitants of the colonies. In addition, when European administrators initially began to collect indirect taxes from opium, they had enlisted, coopted, and cooperated with existing entrepreneurs who commanded social and economic networks for selling opium and policing contraband, many of whom came from immigrant Chinese families or business collectives indebted to Chinese capital. As a result, for Southeast Asia, any colonial state's attempt to alter its regulatory approach to opium raised a set of complicated governance concerns that included the tenuous stability of a heavily import-dependent sector of the colonial economy; the ambiguous rights and obligations of foreign entrepreneurs before an equally foreign state; as well as the desires of and tensions among an ethnically, racially, and socioeconomically diverse opium-consuming population. Recall that Chapter 2 argued that seemingly weak local administrators wielded strong discretionary power over evidentiary bases that animated regulatory changes. Here, I build on this argument to make a case for approaching these actors as inhabiting a small world of precedent-bound ideas and habitual work upon which macrostructural trends certainly weighed heavily, but did not determine how it operated.

The third section underscores the value of paying more sustained attention to distinguishing characteristics of opium regulation in Southeast Asia under European colonial rule. It presents an overarching picture of the region's opium import trends, reported levels of opium revenue collection and a timeline of legal administrative reforms from the 1870s to 1940s, which illustrate overlooked cross-colony variations in the timing and tenor of anti-opium reforms that sit uneasily against prevailing narratives about opium prohibition. Every colony had its own complicated history of opium-indebted state building, which was rooted in precedents of vice taxation over opium consumption that in turn bequeathed administrative problems, real and imagined, along with different imperatives for solving them. These inherited tensions animated varying problem-solving dynamics within local bureaucracies, which were always incremental but had a common cumulative effect of banning opium markets and restricting popular consumption over time. This section emphasizes the value of viewing colonial states through the lens of the micropolitics of bureaucracies, and lays out an approach for doing so, which attends to the peculiar creativity of routine work, ideas and administrative language.

A Bird's Eye View

In 1929, the League of Nations conducted an unprecedented study of opium in Asia. European empires had avowed to address problems of opium consumption in their Far East colonies. The League appointed three men as impartial observers—esteemed diplomats of Sweden, Belgium, and Czechoslovakia—to ascertain local circumstances, focusing on the extent of opium smoking and ongoing government efforts to control it. Over the course of six months, these observers traveled to thirty-four cities in territories under British, French, Dutch, Portuguese, American, and Japanese rule, as well as independent Siam—beginning in Rangoon on September 24, 1929 and ending in Tokyo on April 11, 1930. It was called the Ekstrand Commission, after the Swedish envoy Eric Einar Ekstrand, who chaired the inquiry.

The Ekstrand Commission found it "desirable to conduct the enquiry on similar lines in all the territories to be visited, so as to ensure . . . a complete view

of the whole problem in general and in each territory, based on material collected under a uniform scheme."[1] Thus, a common questionnaire was precir-
culated to local administrators in Burma, the Straits Settlements, Federated
Malay States, Java and Sumatra, Siam, Indochina, Hong Kong, the Philippines,
Formosa, Japanese and French leased territories in China, as well as Chosen
Korea.[2] The three men interviewed 606 individuals over the course of six
months, posing a similar set of questions to officials of opium monopolies and
departments of customs, finance, sanitation, labor, education, and police, as well
as nonofficials including judges, lawyers, doctors, leaders of church and missionary organizations, heads of Chinese and indigenous communities, bank-
ers, employers of labor, and nineteen opium smokers.[3]

The Ekstrand Commission's approach elucidates a tension between what
international observers, who needed to standardize information in order to
compare across multiple sites, learned about colonial opium monopolies, and
what local administrators provided as evidence from their respective jurisdictions. In this regard, the commission was part success, part failure. At one
level, it successfully compared the extent of opium consumption and related
policies, providing a sweeping picture of differences and similarities across
opium monopolies in Europe's Far East. In fourteen territories, there were
opium monopolies that centralized control over imports and manufacturing,
while managing state-owned retail shops that restricted opium sales to a small
number of people with legitimate needs. All, according to the Commission's
final report, were attempting to control harmful forms of opium smoking with
the aim of gradually prohibiting the drug's consumption completely, but there
were differences in local circumstances and specific approaches.[4] The final
report produced standardized maps that rendered such distinctions comparable for Burma, Indochina, and the Dutch East Indies (see Appendix
Figures A.1, A.2, and A.3). It also discerned that generally across the Far East,
opium was consumed mainly by foreigners, especially Chinese migrants, but
the number of indigenous people using opium was increasing. "In proportion
to the total racial population, the Chinese are everywhere more addicted to
opium-smoking than other Asiatic races," and "[c]ontact with Chinese immigrants has . . . usually been the cause of the indigenous population acquiring
the opium-smoking habit," learned the Commission.[5] In order to understand
the extent of opium consumption for both foreign Chinese people and "among
the Burmese, the Malays, the Javanese and other indigenous races in the Netherland Indies, the Siamese, various races and tribes inhabiting the Union of

Indochina and the Philippine Islands," it was necessary to first ascertain the number of opium smokers.[6]

Thus, Ekstrand asked Émile Chauvin, the French Assistant Director for Customs and Excise for Cochinchina: "Do you have an idea of the total number of smokers? How many are Chinese? Which Chinese tribes smoke the most? Do the Europeans smoke as well?"[7] Chauvin was one among more than 200 local administrators who answered such questions and prepared reports on opium consumption in their jurisdictions for the Ekstrand Commission. Based on this information, the League's representatives compared the extent of opium smoking across the Far East territories: the British Straits Settlements (7.3 percent) and Dutch East Indies (4.1 percent) had the largest shares of opium consumers among the general population, while French Indochina and British Burma had the smallest, less than 1 percent of the total population (see Table 3.1, column 1. See Appendix Table A.2 for more details).

The opium monopolies also operated retail shops but had different arrangements for actually distributing and selling to consumers. For one, observed the Commission, the numbers of shops varied, with upwards of 2,000 in Indochina to fewer than 200 across Burma, two territories of roughly the same size, both with relatively small opium-consuming populations. Some monopolies directly appointed state employees to run these shops, while others licensed private individuals, which entailed different ways of compensation: in the Dutch East Indies, employees were paid fixed salaries; vendors in French Indochina paid license fees and were allowed to set retail prices to recover these costs. Relatedly, there were many different pricing arrangements for opium retail sales: a uniform price was set for the entirety of the Malay Peninsula, whereas the monopoly in Indochina divided the colony into four zones with different retail prices in each (see Table 3.1, column 2).

Again, the Ekstrand Commission asked local administrators for information: Did the monopoly limit the number of retail shops? How much opium was sold? Did they restrict access to women and minors? Did people smoke on the shop's premises or did the monopoly operate smoking dens and divans? Were these venues licensed or government run? How much did a license cost? How much did opium cost? In general, government-run shops were mostly in British and Dutch colonies while the French and Japanese opted for licensed vendors. The Dutch East Indies set the highest retail prices for opium, nearly twice those in British Malaya, and more than three times those in British Burma and French Indochina. To facilitate comparison, the commission converted the many different units for retail sale, types of opium, and currencies used across the fourteen territories into a common Swiss franc per tahil, which amounted to roughly thirty-eight grams (see Table 3.1, 3).

In doing so, the Ekstrand Commission further compared how much opium revenue the Far East monopolies collected and their levels of fiscal dependency. Opium revenue came from license fees, retail sales, and other channels that differed on a territory-by-territory basis. Again, the Commission relied on rich descriptive statistics about revenue that local administrators provided and converted local currencies into Swiss francs to take different exchange rates into account. As a percentage of net opium revenue to total revenue for 1929, reported fiscal dependency was highest, at around 20 percent, for the British-ruled small territories in the Malay Archipelago and Portuguese Macao. Burma was unusual among the British colonies, deriving a relatively small share of opium revenue (3 percent), comparable to with Japanese Formosa (3 percent), and the Dutch East Indies (6 percent) (see Table 3.1, column 5).

At another level however, the Ekstrand Commission failed its mandate to ascertain local conditions relating to opium consumption and government policies in the Far East. In a most obvious sense, it posed questions ill-suited for collecting information from respondents. Emile Chauvin, the French administrator in Cochinchina, found the Commission's request for numbers on opium smoking in Indochina difficult to meet. "Mr. President," Chauvin addressed Ekstrand, "we calculate the number of opium smokers in major cities, smaller urban sites, and in the villages, as we try to reduce the number of licensed vendors as much as possible and to avoid the habit of opium consumption from spreading."[8] But Chauvin did not know the precise number of opium smokers. He was aware that neighboring territories were registering opium consumers and able to provide headcounts, but his administration was different. Chauvin informed Ekstrand that in Cochinchina:

[W]here the population is composed of indigenous Annamites and Cambodians, some Malays and Chinese; and the Chinese are among the most significant opium consumers. We calculate that 3 out of 1,000 indigenous people, 9 out of 1,000 male adults living in Cochinchina are opium smokers. The most important group is the Chinese ... and in 1928, the monopoly sold [approximately] 32,000 kgs of opium to the Chinese. Assuming that each Chinese consumes 15 grams, their per capita consumption rate is 0.007 grams. [This is] around 70–80 smokers out of every 100 Chinese.

TABLE 3.1. Ekstrand Commission of Enquiry's Comparison of Opium Monopolies c. 1929

Colonial Power	Territory	1 Estimated number of smokers (share of total pop.)	2 Retail distribution method (number of shops)	3 Sales prices per tahil in Swiss francs	4 Percentage of net opium revenue to total revenue (1920)	5 Percentage of net opium revenue to total revenue (1929)
British	Burma	100,000 (0.8%)	Government shop managed by licensed vendors (121)	14	2	3
	Straits Settlements	73,000 (7.3%)	Government shop (65)	37	46	15
	Federated Malay States	53,000 (3.5%)	Government shop (113)	37	14	12
	Unfederated Malay States	50,000 (5%)	Government shop (106)	37	20–29	17–23
	Brunei	500 (2%)	Government shop (8)	29	17	20
	Sarawak	5,000 (0.8%)	Government shop (1)	23	18	14
	British North Borneo	5,100 (2%)	Government shop and estate managers (53)	29	29	19
	Hong Kong	120,000 (12%)	Licensed shop (70)	24	28	9
Dutch	Netherland Indies	216,000 (4.1%)	Government shop (1,065)	62	13	6
	Siam	110,000 (1%)	Government and licensed smoking shop (856)	32	23	16
French	Indochina	115,000 (0.6%)	Licensed shop (2,277)	16	14	5
	Kwang-Chow-Wan	22,000 (11%)	Licensed shop (70)	5	14	5
Portuguese	Macao	87,000 (54%)	Licensed shop (43)	4	45	22
Japanese	Formosa	55,000 (1.4%)	Licensed shop (447)	10	3	3
	Kwantung Leased Territory	96,000 (11%)	Licensed shop(104)	7	24	6

Source: League of Nations 1930. On estimated number of smokers, see vol. 1, p. 21, column 10; for total population count, see p. 154; on retail distribution methods, see p. 149, column 4; for number of shops, see vol. 2, pp. 11, 58–59, 97, 125, 142, 156, 173–174, 196, 250–252, 301, 329–330, 349, 390, 416, 445; on retail sales prices, see vol. 1, p. 42; on percentage of net opium revenue to total revenue, see vol. 1, pp. 48–51.

"So, what is the total number of smokers?" Ekstrand asked.

"It's difficult to know. I have numbers for the total population and a percentage. [And] not all Chinese smoke [opium]," responded Chauvin.

"Perhaps you might have an idea [or] an opinion," countered Ekstrand.

"Maybe 150,000 or 160,000," guessed Chauvin.

But, the French administrator continued to caution the Swedish diplomat: "I cannot provide exact numbers, and the ones I have given you are not certain. For such numbers, one must visit all homes, all dwellings, family by family."[9] Ekstrand and his colleagues were in Indochina for only two days. So they calculated approximately 115,000 opium smokers based on an annual per capita consumption rate of 1 kg, which were estimates that accorded neither with Chauvin's nor the Government of Indochina's officially provided numbers.[10] In its final report, the Commission reported the number of opium smokers in French Indochina as unknown, while noting in the margins that although local administrators had admitted that there were about 54,000 opium smokers in the colony, the Commission estimated much higher numbers, around 115,000 smokers.[11]

The misaligned conversation between Chauvin and Ekstrand reflects a deeper tension between what the League of Nations wanted to know and a local colonial administrator's ways of knowing. There was little indication of a grand conspiracy to hide the machinations of the opium monopoly or of systematic efforts to mislead external observers. Rather, the two men talked past each other because the League's questions were not the relevant ones for those managing the monopolies. Coming from afar, unable to "visit all homes, all dwellings, family by family," the Ekstrand Commission could not but fail to discern deeper differences underlying the varying numbers of individuals consuming opium, opium shops, sales regimes, and shares of opium revenue that administrators were recording.

Layered Comparisons: British Burma, Malaya, and French Indochina

Who should an opium monopoly count as a legitimate consumer? In Burma, the act of tallying such individuals was not a straightforward task. It had started in the 1890s as a way to affirm a category of people meriting special attention from the colonial state. There had been longstanding worries among local administrators about opium consumption as linked to the "moral wreckage" of the Burmese people, associated with rising trends of petty crime and ruined families that affected at least 11 percent of the indigenous population (Chapter 4). In 1894, the British introduced the monopoly amid expressed concerns that opium-induced moral wreckage was spreading. Burmese opium consumption was banned in general, but at the same time some Burmese were exempt from this interdiction, who were officially registered as habitual opium consumers and permitted to buy opium in small amounts from the state's retail shops. During its first year of operations, the opium monopoly counted approximately 15,000 such individuals and labeled them as legitimate opium consumers. Every year after, administrators continued to register people under this label, which morphed beyond its original referent (a small subset of Burmese subjects uniquely harmed by their opium habits) to encompass all inhabitants of the territory, including Chinese and Indian migrants, for more reasons than to restrict their sumptuary practices. By the 1920s, counting opium smokers in British Burma was an act of defining whose social behavior was problematic and why.

For the Straits Settlements and Federated Malay States, the British introduced an opium monopoly in 1909, and it was not until nearly two decades later that indigenous opium consumers were counted and registered. A Malay's smoking of opium did not preoccupy local administrators in the same way that those in Burma expressed anxieties about vulnerable Burmese subjects. To be clear, it was not that Malays did not consume opium: opium smoking was also considered a colonial vice for inhabitants of the Malay Peninsula, and non-official reports on the alarming problems caused by indigenous consumption abound. "The most famous of Malayan words in English, best known in the phrase *to run amok*," referred to a homicidal frenzy among indigenous people that medical experts and ethnologists associated with opium smoking.[12] For a Malay, "[t]o run amock [*sic*] is to get drunk with opium . . . to sally forth from the house, kill the person or persons supposed to have injured the Amock, and any other person that attempts to impede his passage," wrote the famed British explorer James Cook in his *Voyages*.[13] Indeed, such tropes were common, and to some extent, every territory had some variant of an official argument citing opium's unique dangers to its indigenous subjects. However, these social problems did not escalate into reasons for policy action in Malaya as they did in Burma.

Rather, a different set of questions weighed upon local administrators in this British colony. Indirect taxes levied on opium consumption had long constituted a key source of revenue for the strategically and economically important Straits Settlements, and Singapore paid annual fees to London for the naval defense of this Crown Colony. Initially, a high level of dependency on opium revenue to sustain the Straits Settlements was accepted as a pragmatic reality, but over time became regarded by local administrators as a precarious state of affairs, with worrisome repercussions for other parts of the Malay Peninsula. Attempts to find ways to reduce reliance on opium revenue culminated in the creation of an opium revenue reserve fund in 1925, which set aside 30 million Straits dollars taken from the Straits Settlement's currency surplus and added yearly transfers of 10 percent of the Straits Settlement's total revenue (Chapter 5). By the late 1920s, when the Ekstrand Commission was visiting Singapore and Kuala Lumpur, a large sum had accumulated and the questions that absorbed local administrators were along the lines of: to whom did the money in this reserve fund belong and how should it be used?

The contemporaneous experience of Indochina provides an instructive contrast to British Malaya. Since its inception, the French colony had also relied heavily on indirect taxes collected from opium sales, and the state-run monopoly similarly normalized the opium consumption of foreign populations with muted official concerns about opium smoked by indigenous subjects. However, a high fiscal dependency on opium revenue did not worry those in French Indochina in the same ways as in British Malaya, and into the 1920s neither pursuits for an opium revenue reserve fund nor comparable measures to substitute this fiscal base preoccupied local administrators.

Instead, local administrators in French Indochina worried about precarious finances that challenged the stability of colonial governance. During the early days of the opium monopoly's operations, officials had used an accounting practice that allowed temporary liquidity to purchase foreign opium through advance purchases. Over time, this became an entrenched mechanism for artificially balancing the monopoly's budget by declaring fictitious sales (Chapter 6). By the 1920s, recurrent struggles to procure and pay for opium culminated in the near bankruptcy of the monopoly. Around the time when Emile Chauvin was providing Erik Ekstrand with information about the extent of opium smoking that the League of Nations was curious about, he and other administrators were more concerned with questions about how the monopoly could pay off its debts; how to secure opium that it did not have sufficient funds to pay for; as well as how to minimize the scrutiny of metropolitan auditors regarding an embarrassing situation. The French opium monopoly in Indochina as such had a vexed inner life. It was not unique in this regard. Each monopoly established in Southeast Asia under European colonial rule had its own set of anxieties embedded in its day-to-day operations, a layer of administrative activity that was busy, messy, and stubbornly tied to precedents, with many differences over which the Ekstrand Commission could not but run roughshod over.

Conventional Neglect

The oversights of the Ekstrand Commission have parallels in existing scholarship that has neglected the varieties of opium monopolies across Southeast Asia. First, histories of opium prohibition and empire have focused predominantly on the end of the opium trade between India under British rule and China and emergence of international drug control regimes, with less attention to how multiple imperial powers continued to manage opium markets within overseas colonies until the 1940s. Second, studies of opium in Southeast Asia tend to assume the revenue-maximizing intentions of colonial states and regard the opium monopolies as obvious arrangements for centralizing control and modernizing bureaucratic administration. Consequently, scholars have not been very curious about why the monopolies operated in the ways they did and are often dismissive of officially expressed objectives to prohibit opium as mere alibis of the powerful.

Histories of Opium and Empire

In 1907, the British Empire and China signed an agreement to reduce India's opium exports and China's domestic poppy production within ten years. In 1909, Europe's great powers convened in Shanghai to discuss opium problems in the Far East territories. These two events represent crucial turning points in the history of opium and empire, toward the end of the opium trade between India and China, and the birth of multilateral frameworks for drug control with global jurisdiction. The 1909 Shanghai conference focused centrally on Chinese opium, while the 1912 Hague Opium Convention brought more countries into a cooperative framework that avowed to domestically restrict opium production, manufacture, and distribution in Asia. The end of World War I helped formalize this multilateral resolve, as ratification of the 1912 Convention was made a condition of the 1919 peace treaties of Versailles. The consolidation of an international system for controlling drugs took place under the auspices of the League of Nations' (1920–1946) Opium Advisory Committee and gatherings in Geneva (1925), which sought to improve transnational control and in Bang-kok (1931) that led to the 1936 Geneva Convention for the Suppression of the Illicit Traffic in Dangerous Drugs, the first international instrument to make certain drug offenses international crimes.

The centrality of the great India-China opium trade's end and rise of global drug control regimes for how we understand the history of opium prohibition in Asia today has its own history. Indian opium long held a privileged place in the global imperial economy.[14] For nearly 150 years between 1789 and 1935, the British in India exported a total of 5.6 million chests of opium (approximately 970,000 tons).[15] During peak decades of the nineteenth century, opium was "one of the most valuable commodities moving in international trade" and the object of two trade wars pitting Britain and later France against the Qing court of China. On the eve of the First Opium War (1839–1842), the British East India Company was exporting approximately 36,000 chests of opium annually, of which nearly 90 percent went to China. By the end of the Second Opium War (1856–1860), which opened China's ports to foreign trade, India's opium exports to this country had doubled in volume.

Dismayed observers at the time compared the opium trade to the trans-Atlantic slave trade in terms of its immorality and toll on human lives. Opium sent from India was responsible for 20 million opium smokers in China, of whom at least 1 million died annually as a result, "a more appalling mortality than ever was the case in the Slave Trade," in 1857 declared Lord Shaftesbury, the prominent British statesman who would later become the president of the Society for the Suppression of the Opium Trade (SSOT), a Quaker-led anti-opium reform movement with strong political ties.[16] With the supply of British Indian opium to Chinese subjects, "loom[s] between the East and West, a problem that, in its magnitude and potentials for strife, will outstrip the magnitude and forces of that long-since and happily settled slavery question," noted the American physician and later U.S. Opium Commissioner Hamilton Wright.[17] When the Second Opium War ended in 1860, with China's defeat and the birth of unequal treaty systems limiting her sovereignty, the India-China opium trade preoccupied the loftiest of thinkers who disagreed about its political-economic significance. Karl Marx condemned it as an illegitimate commerce that could contribute to a crisis in world markets, "by raising the dreams of an inexhaustible market and by fostering false speculation."[18] Others, such as John Bowring, redeemed the opium trade as part of a laudable trend of free trade opening access to "an empire [Qing China] amounting to 414 million men, that is to say, a third of the human race, that gave Europe an immense market and could provide diverse products."[19] The flow of opium between India and China as such represented a deeply divisive yet firmly embedded feature of the imperial world.

Thus, when this opium trade finally came to an official end in 1907, so radical a change did it seem that many contemporary observers wrote of it as making sense only as somewhat accidental. The great powers were "suddenly passionate about this fashionable question," noted Paul Gide, a French scholar who described how "we are witnessing a strange spectacle of the West repelling with terror the same poison that it had once forced on the East."[20] John Kennaway, a British Member of Parliament who presided over the Church Missionary Society, found it compelling that "as if it were by an electric flash, England and China have awakened almost simultaneously to the disgrace and danger of the continuation of the opium trade."[21] On both sides of the channel, religious commentators were especially prolific and pleased to explain the suddenness of successful negotiations with China as the product of divinely guided moral consciences. Their writings diffused widely, through both English and French language periodicals including the *Friend of China* issued by the SSOT and the *Bulletin du Comité de l'Asie française*, which was published by a committee in France's Chamber of Deputies. There was also much cross-fertilization of ideas and opinions, with Protestants in France paying attention to the British, translating speeches by the SSOT president outlining the state of anti-opium reforms.[22]

Initial English-language scholarship focused on the India–China opium trade's demise, echoing the sense of chance that pious writers of the first half of the twentieth century had expressed. For instance, David Owen (1934) examined how "the chain of events which led to the suppression of the trade from India was started almost fortuitously."[23] In *The Genesis of International Narcotics Control*, Peter Lowes located the origins of the 1909 Shanghai gathering in "how quite fortuitously three entirely separate events" came together in 1906— "the House of Commons resolution of May 30, 1906; the letter from Bishop Brent of the Philippines to President Roosevelt of July 24, 1906; and the Imperial Edict in Peking of September 20, 1906."[24]

Scholars have since explored each of these events closely for Britain, the United States, and China. For Britain's apparent change of heart against the opium trade, many acknowledge the powerful role of the SSOT, which lobbied Parliament and raised public awareness in Britain about opium in the Far East.[25] Kathleen Lodwick's work has stressed the informational role that Protestant missionaries in China played in educating the British public about the moral

and medical problems caused by opium through missionary journals, conferences, and public talks as well as surveys of medical opinion on opium consumption in China.[26] Social and medical historians have also identified an underlying shift in popular attitudes within Britain against opiate use that enabled such
political changes domestically. Following Virginia Berridge's influential 1981
study of the medical construction of problems of opium use among urban working classes, many have explored the role of jurisdictional struggles within the
medical profession, the rise of new addiction science, as well as the press and
moral panics in establishing Britain's domestic regulation for narcotic control
more generally.[27]

Looking at the US side, historians and political scientists have also paid
close attention to the missionary impulses behind American efforts to assert
moral leadership in international arenas and diplomatic negotiations leading
to drug control agreements under the purview of the League of Nations.
"American missionaries in the Far East . . . played the greatest part in inducing
the United States to take the lead in the movement against the traffic," wrote
Arnold Taylor in 1969, stressing the humanitarian concerns of religious leaders with strong political ties such as Charles Brent—an influential Episcopal
bishop in the Philippines who became the American chief delegate to the
1909 and 1912 international opium gatherings—who urged President Roosevelt to take an active stance against the opium trade in his 1906 letter.[28] Bishop
Brent's persuasiveness has been further situated in the Progressive era political
climate sympathetic to anti-opium reforms, as well as prior public anxieties
about drug addiction among the white middle class and social constructions of deviance associated with opium-consuming Chinese immigrants on the
West Coast.[29]

Finally, counterbalancing Anglo-American narratives, scholars of China have
identified factors that conditioned the Qing Court's diplomatic resolve in 1906
to cooperate with Britain and to suppress opium production, ranging from the
growth of interior political economies for poppy cultivation that financed provincial warlords, reformist zeal following the Boxer Rebellion (1900) and its
disastrous aftermath, and concerns with foreign interference. Moreover, public
worries about dangers of spreading opium consumption dovetailed with campaigns for general social reform and nationalism. Thus, China in 1906 becomes
less surprising in light of ongoing efforts to secure social order, and ongoing ebbs
and flows of campaigns to suppress opium use among the Chinese and restrict
domestic production and smuggling.[30]

Building on rich understandings of the rise of anti-opium movements and political reforms, scholars placed such national developments more squarely in imperial contexts. In 2000, Timothy Brook and Bob Wakabayashi wrote of how "in the last few years, the scholarly community has started to see opium as a more complex phenomenon with a multi-stranded history."[31] Regarding China for instance, R. Bin Wong situates the anti-opium edict of 1906 in a context of imperial state building with eighteenth-century origins in campaigns to promote agrarian social order, espouse Confucianist values, and mobilize elite support that helped discipline populations.[32] David Bello's work shows clearly how the Qing opium prohibition policies must be understood in light of the empire's earlier eighteenth-century territorial expansion, focusing on Western China and ways in which the court struggled with limited administrative control.[33] He demonstrates how the central government's approach to opium was shaped in interaction with the localities, especially opium traffickers from Central Asia into the northwest province of Xinjiang as well as poppy producing areas in the southwestern provinces of Yunnan, Guizhou, and Sichuan, with tensions arising from attempts to manage ethnolinguistic diversity along this interior frontier. Cultural histories of opium consumption have emphasized the extent to which opium smoking was already a part of Chinese everyday life under the Qing empire, tracing how its valence shifted since the early nineteenth century from "a hobby among both the high and the low in officialdom," a practice of the leisure class, to despised habits of the urban lower-class, to a vehicle of ruin for the general population by the early twentieth century.[34]

A turn to empire is also clear in global histories of the US role in international anti-opium crusades. Anne Foster has drawn attention to how the annexation of the Philippines gave rise to a nascent empire's struggles to fashion an imperial identity in contradistinction to European powers in Asia. She shows how US colonial officials in the Philippines embraced a strong rhetoric that equated an anti-opium agenda with a civilizing mission that morally elevated the United States over existing British, Dutch, and French administrations that raised revenue from opium consumption.[35] A forceful stance against opium consumption therefore answered a question of "what American colonialism would look like—how it would demonstrate the superiority of American institutions."[36] Daniel Wertz argues that opium's central role in fashioning US imperialism in the Philippines had international repercussions in terms of giving new momentum to Bishop Brent and American missionaries to launch a lagging anti-opium movement into a global cause for moral action.[37]

Likewise, now Britain's anti-opium turn relating to India requires appreciating the evolution of poppy cultivation and growth of an export-oriented opium industry in Bengal as a complex political task for imperial state builders. Historians of South Asia attentive to the place of opium in agrarian societies and trade economies stress how closely entwined the colony's opium political economy was with metropolitan Britain.[38] John Richards' work has demonstrated the positive impact of state-sponsored poppy cultivation for peasant growers, along with the benefits of the opium trade to the general Indian economy.[39] He situates these developments in imperial contexts, first by showing both how opium profits tied to silver bullion imports from China enabled India to pay the costs of wars of conquest as well as remit private British savings and transfer investment profits to stakeholders of the East India Company during the early nineteenth century. Second, Richards clarifies the disconnect between economic reality in India and the propaganda of later nineteenth century British moral reformers who, despite critiques of complicity between opium and empire, exercised their own form of cultural imperialism as they "ignored Indian sensitivities by denying any cultural and social value to the use of opium."[40] Amar Farooqui's works show how the western India's poppy cultivation and vibrant coastal opium trade centered in Bombay and Portuguese Daman, which he identifies as a source of capital accumulation for early Indian bourgeoisie operating under colonial constraints.[41]

A key contribution of existing scholarship on opium and empire lies in identifying the wide spectrum of actors outside of conventional seats of power who galvanized anti-opium causes and transnational moral crusades. There were busy networks of activists and global coalitions comprising alert medical experts, lobbyists and their political agents, as well as drug diplomats and Christian missionaries. Recent histories of narcotics have placed particular emphasis on situating this cast of characters in context, shedding light on their inconsistent ideas and varied interests in ways that clarify the contingency of metropolitan–colonial connections.[42] This is a welcome development, not least because it encourages attention to countries that were deeply entwined with Britain, China, and the United States, yet seldom studied together, including France, Japan, and parts of the Middle East and North Africa.

Histories of the French empire's experience with opium have advanced separately from English-language literature focusing on the Anglo-American and Chinese powers. France fought alongside Britain during the Second Opium War; the eventual end of the opium trade between India and China was also a subject of active conversation among the French. In December 1860, following the signing of the Treaty of Tientsin (which concluded the Second Opium War), the Paris Society of Political Economy invited John Bowring to speak about the opium trade at the Society's regular meeting, and Bowring's debate with the esteemed political economist, Joseph Garnier, was published in the Paris Society's *Journal des économistes*.[43] Armand Lucy, a French military officer who had served in China during the war, wrote in 1861 about the hypocrisies of the British.[44] "Our brave allies are greedy and build their power on a criminal opium trade," Lucy noted.[45] He opined that the only way to counterbalance Britain's wrongs and bring "[t]he strongest, the most decisive, the most French result of our glorious campaign" was to restore the Catholic faith and moral superiority through the work of missionaries.[46] The French popular imaginary was also filled with opinions and complaints about the India–China trade, in ways that mirrored British commentaries, as Figures 3.1 and 3.2 illustrate.[47]

Contemporary French writers addressing the end of the India–China trade focused on the British intent behind the 1906 House of Commons decision, echoing Lucy's disparagement of British conduct in China and extending similar criticism of Britain's "two faces" in India: "one that invoked the great financial resources that India brought through opium; the other . . . [invoking] moral preoccupations."[48] Like the Anglophone commentators, the French paid most attention to the United States, especially when explaining the emergence of international drug control regimes and activities of the League of Nations. In 1925, one author noted the number of publications on his topic of interest, counting upwards of 3,000 texts in the bibliographies of American writers.[49] By contrast, less was written about France's own involvement in the India–China trade and its role in the international politics of opium prohibition. More recent studies remedy this tendency by addressing the participation of French diplomats in the US-led multilateral conversations preceding the 1909 Shanghai conference and the endurance of opium concessions in French settlements within British India until the mid-twentieth century.[50]

Over the past two decades, a greater attentiveness to France's empire has been evident in studies of opium prohibition and narcotic control, moving away from a general tendency to treat the metropole and the colonies separately with regard to drugs. On the one hand, national histories have focused on the medical profession and criminalization of drug addiction, stressing the harshly punitive nature of laws that emerged during the early twentieth

FIGURE 3.1. French popular depiction of Second Opium War, c. 1859. The French caricaturist Honoré-Victorin Daumier's cartoon shows a French soldier pouring opium down the throat of a Chinese official. It was published in the illustrated weekly magazine *Le Charivari* in 1859 as part of a series called "In China" that ran from December 1858 to April 1860.

FIGURE 3.2. British popular depiction of Second Opium War, c. 1858. This cartoon is an illustration for an article entitled "Piety, Pounds, Shillings, and Pence" from the British magazine *Punch* from October 1858, which shows a British man forcing a treaty down a Chinese official's throat.

century.[51] Valuable works by Jean-Jacques Yvorel and Emmanuelle Retaillaud-Bajac have added nuance by demonstrating an overseas component to the emergence of France's key antidrug legislation of 1916, based on security concerns, with French naval officers serving in Indochina acquiring opium smoking habits and negative associations between drugs and migrants from Asia and the Middle East.[52]

On the other hand, French colonial histories of opium have been deeply indebted to the seminal work of Chantal Descours-Gatin, who demonstrated how Indochina's opium tax farming system and opium monopoly financed local governance while posing reputational and political challenges for French colonial rule.[53] Subsequent scholars have explained the eventual anti-opium reforms in Indochina in reference to the imperial context in which French colonial authorities worried about prestige and reputation. Most notably, Philippe Le Failler has situated the colony's anti-opium reforms in Indochina within the international anti-opium movements of the early twentieth century and world economic crisis of the 1930s, while recent work by Ami-Jacques Rapin underscores the tensions between local administrators and metropolitan officials that erupted in these contexts.[54] An invaluable study by Yann Bisiou has shown how the French Empire's opium monopoly extended beyond Indochina to drug monopolies across Oceania and settlements in India, Tunisia, and Morocco.[55]

A focus on transnational contexts has also provided opportunity to recognize the significance of Japan and its empire for the global politics of opium prohibition. Mid-nineteenth-century Japan embraced a strong anti-opium stance, drawing lessons from the negative example of China's "victimiz[ation] . . . by means of opium, Christianity, and aggressive warfare" with Western powers.[56] In addition to enacting diplomatic treaty provisions banning opium imports, Meiji-era laws against drug use were punitive, as Wakabayashi demonstrates, grounded in stigma against resident Chinese that spurred fears of spreading opium addiction and crime within Japan. Recent studies show how policies for regulating opium in Taiwan, Korea, and Manchuria into the first half of the twentieth century reflected Japan's aspirations to signal its modernity to Western powers and assert membership in an international community of civilizing powers.[57] Miriam Kingsberg makes a forceful case that the moral value of abstinence from narcotics lay at the core of Japan's nationhood and imperial identity. She shows how diverse actors came to define and police such norms, including Japanese scientists and researchers keenly attuned to foreign medical developments, journalists and intellectuals with pan-Asian sensibilities, as well as well-traveled merchants and businessmen.[58]

Finally, while poppy cultivation in British India and its eastbound opium trade to Asia has dominated the existing literature, Turkey and Iran also had longstanding domestic economies for producing and exporting opium that reached East and Southeast Asia. Histories of narcotics in the Middle East and North Africa clarify sites under the Ottoman Empire as well as interwar Mandate territories that influenced international anti-opium agendas. For instance, Philip Robins argues that Turkey, initially a "rejectionist power" against multilateral drug control efforts in the 1900s, came to play a key role in defining what constituted the national self-interest of a drug-producing country after World War I, under the antinarcotic treaty regimes of the League of Nations.[59] Liat Kozma demonstrates the ways by which the concerns of Egyptian elites with cannabis shaped British colonial attitudes during the 1924 Geneva Opium Conference, which instituted an international ban on cannabis trades.[60] Drawing attention to the nineteenth-century emergence and evolution of illicit opium production in Anatolia and trafficking through Istanbul on the Mediterranean coast, Ryan Gingeras traces ties of collusion over the transit of drugs between Asia and Europe that interwove Turkish state officials, Western traders, as well as both local and transnational criminal actors.[61] Cyrus Schayegh's study of interwar narcotic trafficking across the Middle East reveals the sprawling network of smugglers across the region matched by the French police forces for mandate territories, providing a rare lens into inconsistent approaches to drug control across far-flung corners of the twentieth-century French Empire.[62]

There are clear upshots to gaining a fuller understanding of the forces behind the decline of the India–China opium trade and emergence of international drug control regimes. Explanations for the origins of global prohibition have become more nuanced, with a keener sense about the power struggles and tenuous nature of consensus building, which replace earlier senses of surprise with a seemingly fortuitous confluence of events or foreordained moral imperatives. Yet, there are also risks to privileging transnational connections in an age of empires. By blurring metropolitan and periphery distinctions, regulatory changes in different sites are too readily seen as always and already knitted into global changes, and thus distinctive experiences discounted. There is a tendency to presume rather than demonstrate how exactly different colonies fit into global economic, ideational, and regulatory changes, overlooking the extent to which local administrators were inside of, but not necessarily reacting to, a shifting world of imperial interests and laws. The experience of Southeast Asia under European rule is instructive in this regard, because of several region-specific aspects to its experience with opium regulation and colonial state building.

The Regional Peculiarities of Southeast Asia

First, opium prohibition across Southeast Asia was a temporal process that unfolded alongside but not in tandem with the end of the India–China opium trade. The many European powers dividing the region continued to import opium from India well *after* the 1907 Anglo-Chinese Opium Agreement was signed and the British colony officially exported its last chest of opium to China in 1913. Figure 3.4 shows how while India's opium trade dramatically shrank in volume after 1913, it continued to supply Southeast Asia: the British Straits

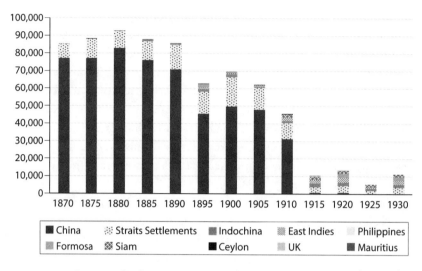

FIGURE 3.3. Quantity of Indian opium exports to key destinations, 1870–1930 (in chests).

Settlements became the largest recipient of Indian opium, followed by French Indochina and the Dutch East Indies, with smaller quantities imported by Siam and Japanese Formosa.[63] The end of the India–China trade as such did not herald the end of India's exports to these territories. It was not until 1926 that the Government of India announced all opium exports for commercial purposes would be reduced annually and halt completely by 1935[64] (see Appendix Figure A.1 for detailed statistics on India's opium export quantities post-1913).

The opium-consuming colonies of Southeast Asia under European rule not only continued to import opium from British India, but also diversified their foreign sources, as international accords were still setting terms on which to define opium's legitimate use as limited to medical purposes. Figure 3.5 shows the post-1913 total volume of opium imports for the region's five largest importers—the Straits Settlements, Indochina, the East Indies, Siam, and Japanese Formosa—which officially reported opium from Persia, China, and Turkey, in addition to India. It demonstrates that Southeast Asia's declining opium imports began two decades after the great India–China opium trade ended.[65]

Second, both indigenous and migrant populations residing in Southeast Asia consumed opium. For the British and French alike, the opium habits of people living in colonized territories raised more complex governance concerns compared with those associated with opium consumed in China among people

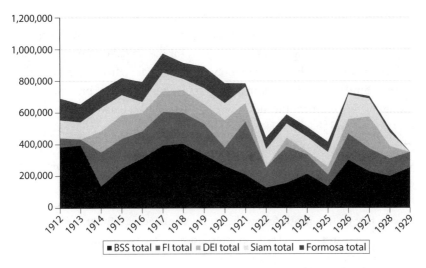

FIGURE 3.4. Quantity of imported opium from India, Persia, and China to key destinations in Southeast Asia, 1912–1930 (in kg).

ruled by their own sovereign. One concerned the Chinese diaspora in Southeast Asia. The region experienced a mass influx of immigrants from China between the 1840s and 1940s: during this century, around 20 million Chinese emigrated overseas, 90 percent of whom went to Southeast Asia.[66] The migration boom of the mid-nineteenth century onward comprised largely wage laborers from Southern China, who found work in tin mining industries and commercial agriculture for gambier, tapioca, and pepper, largely in the hands of coethnic entrepreneurs. European authorities bluntly associated all Chinese laborers with opium consumption, and the moral fervor of anti-opium reforms was constantly weighed against the potential impact of restricting opium upon labor productivity in key sectors of colonial economies and anticipated reactions of different members of the wealthy and often politically influential Chinese diaspora.

At the same time, opium consumption across Southeast Asia was not limited to the Chinese but was also a sumptuary practice among migrants from India; indigenous Burmese in Burma; Malays in Malaya; the Vietnamese, Cambodians, and Laotian in Indochina, as well as people who have been sweepingly referred to as the "natives," "tribal groups," and ethnic and racial minorities of Shan, Kachin, and Miao (Hmong) descent residing in the northern inland areas of Burma and Indochina. Given preconceptions of opium consumption as a predominantly Chinese habit, British and French observers and administrators made sense of the extent to which it prevailed among the non-Chinese under rubrics of tradition (for those who cultivated poppy appeared to have longstanding rituals for ingesting opium and using it for medicinal purposes), religion (which became a catch-all term for nonsecular behaviors that perplexed the European mind), as well as colonial progress (in terms of the consequences of economic development that occasioned greater contact between the enterprising Chinese and "backward" indigenous people). In other words, the diversity of colonial societies of Southeast Asia in which composite groups were associated in different ways with opium consumption rendered its regulation an especially complex affair.

Third, the colonial opium policies of Southeast Asia emerged and evolved in ways that neither neatly follow the timing of major metropolitan reforms nor anti-opium mandates set forth on international arenas. During the first half of the twentieth century, both Britain and France introduced metropolitan laws restricting opium as a dangerous drug that had limited applications for overseas colonies. France in 1908 passed an Opium Decree (that promulgated an existing 1845 law restricting opium as a poisonous substance) that strictly controlled commerce and the use of opiates, and later introduced laws in 1916 to prohibit the trade and nonmedical use of opium.[67] For Britain, Section 40B of the 1916 Defense of the Realm Act (DORA) made the nonmedical possession and sales of narcotics including opiates a criminal offense, laying the ground for more comprehensive legislative controls under the 1920 Dangerous Drugs Act.[68] However, these landmark legislations did not extend to Southeast Asia in ways that weighed directly upon colonial regulation. For instance, in the case of France's 1908 decree, metropolitan authorities allowed for a dual approach to restricting opium in some colonies: the version promulgated for Indochina omitted opium smoking, which was the common form of consumption in the colony, and tacitly allowed the state-run monopoly to remain.[69] Similarly, a diminished version of the 1916 anti-opium law was applied to Indochina, as the Minister of Colonies recognized that "The strict and immediate application of the new law would bring in the balance of this budget [of Indochina] a disturbance which must be taken into account."[70]

Such regulatory gaps between metropole and colony on opium issues make sense in light of what Howard Padwa calls the antinarcotic nationalism that shaped punitive drug laws in Britain and France oriented around citizens, not colonized subjects.[71] During the decades preceding World War I, each country came to view imminent threats to its national communities occasioned by drugs and Padwa argues: "in France, worries about social cohesion and loyalty colored discourses about opiates, while in Britain, [worries were] expressed through concern about the economic impact of open availability and consumption."[72] Wartime exigencies intensified already existing anxieties about opiate addiction and contraband that partly stemmed from contact with Far East territories. In France, military officials worried about the spread of opium smoking brought over by servicemen stationed in Indochina and its negative impact on military discipline and health.[73] In Britain, alarm grew over increasing Chinese immigration in port districts of London and Liverpool, already perceived as a threat to British shipping industries. During World War I, both countries adopted harsher restrictions against drugs as matters of protecting France "from a potential agent of national decay and betrayal, thus preserving the solidarity of a republican nation" and Britain, to prevent disruptions to the supply of drugs to soldiers that were more generally linked to concern with Chinese traders smuggling opiates abroad.[74] As a result, the antinarcotic laws that emerged during the early twentieth century were national rather than imperial in scope. In turn, metropolitan Europe and its drug laws and politics represented a removed backdrop against which colonies of Southeast Asia managed opium-related issues.[75]

Gaps also abound between colonial opium-related reforms and international obligations professed on the part of imperial diplomats and politicians. The 1912 Hague Convention was the first multilateral agreement that formalized obligations on the part of major European powers, including Britain and France, to introduce domestic legislations that would "gradually and effectively . . . suppress the manufacture and trade in prepared opium [i.e., opium suitable for consumption other than medical]."[76] The Hague Convention's aspirations were interrupted by World War I, but became widely ratified postwar. In British Burma, however, restrictive measures relating to opium consumption were already set in place in 1894, well before 1912 whereas in Indochina, the French took "the particular circumstances of our overseas possessions" into account to promulgate a much less restrictive version of the Hague Convention, limited to curtailing international trade.[77] The next major anti-opium international convention emerged from two conferences held in Geneva in 1924 and 1925, which focused on improving transnational controls on drug imports. Historians have shown how the diplomatic preparations and disputes leading up to the Geneva conferences and ensuing opium conventions had direct bearings on colonial opium policies.[78] This was especially true for British Malaya, and introducing registration for opium consumers in the

Straits Settlements was a result of the 1925 Geneva Convention's recommendations. However, the French in Indochina explicitly refused this measure, indicating the limits of international pressures in fully understanding regulatory changes in the colonies. In these regards, the colonial Southeast Asia's opium-related reforms fit awkwardly within key developments for restricting non-medical opium on international stages.

Within each colony, there were many microreforms to local "opium regimes"—following Brook and Wakabayashi's definition of "a system in which an authority declares its right to control certain practices and develops policies and mechanisms to exercise that right within its presumed domain."[79] In the cases of Burma, Malaya, and Indochina, each opium monopoly's approach to sales, distribution, and consumption changed often and subtly, at the discretion of local administrators who revised, retracted, and reintroduced measures for their presumed domains, which could be as narrow as a district, a village, or, as we will see in Chapter 4 on Burma, a single prison. As a result, every opium monopoly had a spate of regulatory shifts that were sensitive to what local administrators perceived as proximate to their day-to-day work more than metropolitan and international dictates from afar (see Appendix Figure A.2 for a detailed timeline).

Histories of Colonial Southeast Asia and Opium

Within existing histories of colonial Southeast Asia, that the opium monopolies enabled imperial powers to pursue profit is a story often told, but not well explained. Better known are the negative consequences of opium consumption for subjects and residents of each colony. For British Malaya, James Warren's study of male Chinese rickshaw pullers in Singapore conveys poignantly how opium addiction aggravated debt, unemployment, and "a sense of hopelessness, shame, and [desire to] escape from pain" among this migrant community that contributed to high rates of suicide.[80] Using inquest records, Warren finds an abnormally large number of suicides taking place between 1918 and 1939, especially during periods of economic downturn, and demonstrates the tragic vulnerability of rickshaw pullers who smoked opium or injected morphia, "always in desperate need of more money to pay for rent and sufficient food for their family on top of the expenses of their habit."[81] In French Indochina as well, disease, despair, and death accompanied opium consumption patterns that spread under colonial rule. L'Écho annamite reported opium-related suicides or attempted suicides nearly every year of its circulation from 1922 to 1940. In

1925 in Saigon-Chôlon, for instance, at least five men and women sought to take their lives by overdosing on opium to ease the pain of "heartache," "accusations of thievery," "nostalgia for home," and "jealousy," suggesting the easy accessibility of the drug to the urban poor.[82] In colonial prisons as well, as Peter Zinoman has shown, prevailing habits of opium consumption among Vietnamese inmates rendered them vulnerable to the predation of guards, who organized rackets that allowed smuggled opium into the prisons in exchange for a share of the drug or "routinely trad[ing] gay sex for opium or cash."[83]

Historians have also demonstrated the promises and pitfalls to opium consumption among workers on pepper and gambier plantations, as well as tin mines, namely, sites of large-scale organized labor for industries that provided the lifeblood of empires. Chinese coolies migrating temporarily to the Malay Peninsula, Borneo, and Sumatra under Dutch rule became dependent on opium supplied by their employers.[84] "Laborers ultimately found themselves deeply in debt to the capitalists, and frequently addicted to opium as well," writes Carl Trocki, who portrays vividly the reasons for which these individuals would turn to opium.[85]

> In most cases they [Chinese coolies] had few opportunities for relief or entertainment. They lived in all-male communities where even prostitutes were scarce. They worked long hours in very difficult conditions: clearing the rainforest; digging out the hills; keeping their crops clear of weeds and pests; constructing and maintaining mining equipment and often standing in bone-chilling water up to their knees shoveling the ore through the sluices. Opium killed their pain and eased their loneliness. It was also their only form of medicine . . . a sovereign painkiller . . . [and] it stopped up bowels loosened by dysentery and relieved the fevers of malaria and other tropical microbes.[86]

Migrants were not alone in their unhappy experiences with opium sold under the purview of colonial states. Indigenous opium smokers in Indochina sought "Western" medical care as a last resort and yet, according to estimates by Philippe Le Failler, 1 to 6 percent of the deaths in the colony's hospitals during the late 1930s were due to opium addiction.[87] In addition, "[o]piomania was taken as a Vietnamese ethnic if not racial predilection," associated with pederasty and syphilis in ways that rudely stigmatized Vietnamese men and women as promiscuous and agents of infection.[88] In Burma, injuries to the health and dignity of people included the Burmese as well as the Shan, Karen, and Kachin.

Robert Maule and Alfred McCoy have shown how poppy cultivation expanded under British rule, and the lasting legacies of this shift in agricultural practices include post-independence patterns of polarization of wealth distribution within Karen communities, territorial disputes, and drug-related violence involving Shan groups seeking to finance secessionist struggles.[89] Recent works by Christian Culas and Ami-Jacques Rapin also note the ways by which French approaches to selling opium encouraged market-oriented poppy cultivation among the Hmong residing in Laos and Siam, which endures today.[90]

The socially marginalized were not the only ones affected by opium consumption. Opium reconfigured the lives of wealthy entrepreneurs and elites involved in colonial economies and societies as well. In the Dutch East Indies, for instance, Lea Williams stressed the financial destruction and terror felt among the Chinese in the 1890s who held tax farms for opium as well as licenses for running gambling houses, ferry boats, slaughterhouses, and also monopolies on collecting edible bird's nests, as these economic elites faced colonial authorities who were about to destroy the "rights of countless Chinese dealers in goods and services."[91] In the Straits Settlements, influential Chinese intellectuals approached anti-opium reforms as a political issue that struck at the heart of their overseas national identity, and mobilized collectively during the early twentieth century with aspirations to "foster the rebirth of 'civilized' Chinese in order to restore their faith and pride which had been undermined by the addiction to opium."[92] In Indochina, Phung Nhu Cuong, a member of the Grand Federal Council for Vietnamese elites, encouraged the wartime Vichy regime to ban opium consumption, framing it as a matter of "humanitarian work proper to the National Revolution that contributes to the bodies and morals of the Indochinese race."[93] More famously, Ho Chi Minh criticized the French who "to weaken our race . . . forced us to use opium and alcohol," as he declared Vietnam's Declaration of Independence in 1945.[94]

While colonial histories of opium recognize diverse social and economic experiences with regards to opium consumption, the state retains a curiously rigid presence. Conventional wisdom has moved beyond simplistic portrayals of "wily Europeans peddling harmful products to simple dupes across the rest of the world whose governments were powerless to protect them," and as James Mills and Patricia Barton make clear in an important collection of essays on modern imperialism and intoxication, there is something "unsatisfactory and indeed . . . echoes of Orientalist fantasies and the civilizing mission" in narratives that demonize European empires as conscious and willing agents of addiction in non-Western societies.[95] Most acknowledge that colonial states had many agendas, not just a single one, when regulating this psychotropic substance, with its overlapping lives as a global commodity, means of labor management, medicinal good, local currency, as well as an infamous object of moralizing criticism. Yet, there is also a stubbornly fixed assumption that colonial states in Southeast Asia ultimately sought to maximize revenue from indirect taxes on opium consumption.

Specifically, many presume that the guiding logic of opium monopolies was one of pursuing improved efficiency over fiscal extraction; and administrative agents of a colonial state were primarily concerned with opium revenue while superficially addressing criticism about the immorality of profiting from the drug's consumption. Ashely Wright's study of British Burma notes how regulating opium consumption followed "a pattern of concern for profits masquerading as social responsibility" that echoed mercantilist approaches of the British East India Company toward the opium trade.[96] In other British colonies, opium monopolies have been described as projects for running an "empire on the cheap" or a type of "prolonged rearguard action" to preserve vested interests in taxing opium to maximize revenue.[97] Similarly for French Indochina, the opium monopoly is best known in light of its role in financing the creation of the colony.[98]

The ways in which existing scholarship tends to presume profit and revenue-centered state motives echo the criticism of former observers of the opium monopolies as quintessential expressions of colonial predation. From the vantage point of social actors, opium sales in British Burma, for instance, were always but "a chain prepared, pre-arranged, and supervised by the Government itself in its every link, from the licensed poppy field in Bengal to the licensed poisoner in Arakan," and this "unbroken chain . . . connected the ruin of Burmese lads with the filling of the [British] Indian treasury."[99] The administrators of Indochina "sing the glories of a double-headed alcohol-opium, monster and . . . for reasons of a purely fiscal nature, the double poison is offered to, sometimes forced upon, the natives," reported one French doctor, condemning a "collective narcomania . . . coupled with an odious colonial policy, which causes the Nation to lose most of its moral prestige."[100] The renowned Vietnamese journalist Tam Lang saw the greed of French colonial rule literally etched upon the face of the monopoly's opium shops in Hanoi that bore signs with the tricolor flag, while his contemporary Vu Trong Phung vividly portrayed illicit economies for drug use entwined with prostitution that sustained the insidious fiscal interests of the colonial government.[101]

Metropolitan authorities also posited revenue hunger on the part of those tasked with managing the colonies on the ground, suspecting maladministration and graft. The French politician Marius Moutet wrote a scathing criticism in 1916 of the Indochina opium monopoly as "a scandal by its mere existence," opining that "the fiscal zeal of our Indochinese administration all too easily forgets that a good administration must aim, if not to reform the mores [of colonized subjects], to at least not itself become an agent of corruption and demoralization."[102] The British administrators of the Straits Settlements, complained V. Fox-Strangways from the Colonial Office, appeared to have designed a revenue reserve fund for opium in 1925 for rent-seeking purposes: "It actually seems to have been their intention to build up a fund so large, that the interest upon them would equal the opium revenue which is to be lost and the Governments would then live like rentiers upon their savings."[103]

Local administrators were certainly revenue conscious but not single-mindedly so. The stakes to complicating the motives of these actors become clear, first, when reflecting on the timing of introduction for opium monopolies. In British Burma and Malaya, decades before centralizing control over opium sales and distribution, officials were already keenly aware of the inadequacies of opium tax farming from a revenue perspective. Yet, this did not necessarily translate into reasons to centralize control. Accommodation, rather than reform, was the more common reaction to many situations in which tax farmers failed to deliver promised returns. In 1883 Singapore, for instance, the Chinese opium tax farmer Chiu Sin Yong was on the verge of defaulting on his payments to the British, in part because his business was undermined by smugglers from a competing Chinese syndicate conspiring to destroy their rival.[104] Instead of taking over, the authorities reduced Chiu's license fees and helped the tax farmer confront his competitors by passing a law restricting opium exports. "It is not a revenue question" stated the Governor of the colony explicitly as he explained the legislative change. Anticipated losses in opium revenue and misreported sales from tax farmers were common.[105] Yet, such knowledge only occasionally became reasons for reforms to better monitor these agents of the colonial state.

Similarly, in French Indochina, local administrators long tolerated graft, rumored and real, as par for the course of colonial government in Asia. For instance, local administrators reacted with quiet irritation to revelations of the misconduct of two French merchants running the Cochinchina opium tax farm in the 1860s, who had concealed their opium sales by keeping separate accounts.[106] Yet rather than overhaul a flawed arrangement for monitoring private interests, officials opted to replace the old entrepreneurs with new Chinese merchants. Only in 1881 did the French begin to directly oversee opium imports and distribution in Cochinchina, taking direct control over the tax farms. And it was not until 1899 that a general opium monopoly for the entirety of Indochina replaced all opium tax farms. In short, there were many reasons to abolish a decentralized system of control over revenue collection; and it is difficult to draw a straight line between administrative desires to make opium tax collection more efficient and the timing when an opium monopoly was introduced.

Second, the opium monopolies endured well into the 1940s, even after they stopped being profitable for colonial states. For Indochina, Philippe Le Failler has shown how the high expenditures of running the French opium monopoly left the administration with little net profit by the 1930s. The lasting shock of the Great Depression had pushed the French to incur significant debts in order to maintain their Saigon opium factory and thousands of retail shops, and financing their antismuggling police forces.[107] For the British opium monopoly in the Straits Settlements, Harumi Goto-Shibata demonstrates how the 1930s ushered in a period of sharply reduced revenue returns from opium sales, not least because the economic downturn made it difficult for opium consumers to afford the officially sold product.[108]

If colonial states were driven primarily to maximize profits from opium sales, we might expect these downturns to lead to significant reorganizations of the opium monopolies, most likely toward the direction of downsizing or even abolishing such arrangements altogether. Yet, despite high expenditures and shrinking real revenue gains, monopolies continued to operate.[109] The internal records of each monopoly that I have consulted are also consistent with the claim that opium monopolies outlived their profitability to colonial states. Figure 3.6 traces the share of net opium revenue from taxes collected locally.[110] It plots general trends in fiscal dependency that each opium monopoly reported officially (see Appendix Figure A.3 for region-wide trends including the Dutch East Indies, Hong Kong, and Siam).

For all colonial states, reliance on opium revenue declined during the decades following an opium monopoly's introduction. In Burma, after 1894, there was brief increase in reported revenue (1903–1905), but after 1906, fiscal dependency on opium revenue steadily declined from 10 percent to around 5 percent by the late 1910s, around 3 percent by the late 1920s, and less than 1 percent by the 1930s. For the Dutch East Indies, fiscal dependency on opium revenue declined from 12 percent in the 1910s to less than 6 percent in the 1920s to less

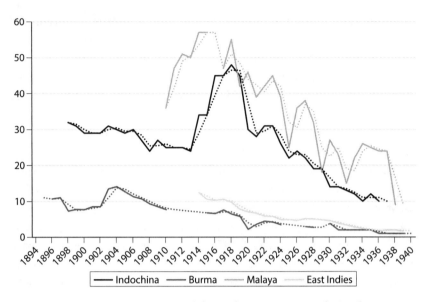

FIGURE 3.5. Comparing reported shares of net opium revenue for Southeast
Asia, 1890s–1930s (%).

than 2 percent by the late 1930s. In short, these opium monopolies appear to
have continued under the official sanction of states for decades, as they were
becoming increasingly unprofitable. Therefore, it is unsatisfying to regard these
stubbornly persistent arrangements as oriented solely toward revenue
extraction.

In British Malaya and French Indochina, a secular downward trend is also
manifest, although a few caveats apply. In Malaya, immediately following the
opium monopoly's introduction, reported fiscal dependency rose from
36 percent in 1909 to a peak of 57 percent in 1915, but decreased afterwards to
less than 30 percent by the late 1920s. Indochina's opium monopoly reported
decreasing shares of net opium revenue from upwards of 30 percent in 1899 to
less than 20 percent by the late 1920s. The spike during World War I (1914–1918)
is due to a change in how the French calculated opium revenue during the war
by temporarily including opium sales from the leased territory of Kwang-chou-
wan in China. Post–World War I, the French separated opium revenue from
Kwang-chou-wan from the general budget for Indochina. Overall, however,
these opium monopolies experienced a general decline in each colony's fiscal
dependency on opium revenue into the 1920s.

It is difficult to read the records of opium monopolies and envision a colonial state obsessed with maximizing opium revenue, or indeed find evidence

of local administrators cagily hiding profits. For there was so much more going on. For instance, in 1924 Malaya, as we will see in Chapter 5, the colonial Treasurer Arthur Meek Pountney was busily designing the opium revenue reserve fund, pondering ways to reduce this tax base, with expressed optimism that "schooling ourselves to a reduced revenue will react in schooling us to a reduced expenditure."[111] After all, he opined, "[w]e do not want to leave to posterity an annual bill which it cannot meet without a very great reduction of efficiency or a drastic reduction in the maintenance and upkeep of the systems and institutions of Government."[112] In the same year in Indochina, Marie-Alphonse Kircher, the head of the French opium monopoly, was beginning to overdraw funds, launching a spiral of debt into the 1930s that would lead to false reports of the colony's opium revenue numbers, while leaving local administrators with no profits to pocket.

Finally, there is reason to rethink the opium monopolies beyond blunt functions of revenue collection because of the many and conflicting rationales of their institutional purpose that involved actors articulated. Some considered the opium monopoly as an institution of atonement for the past wrongs of earlier colonial administrations who had introduced a new and dangerous habit to natives such as "the Burmese and Arakanese [who] could not resist indulging to excess whenever opium was placed before them."[113] Simultaneously, it was a self-righteous institution respectful of existing uses of opium as a traditional medicine, an analgesic in Buddhist rituals for tattooing, a frowned upon but acceptable social habit among locals that "I would not say a curse [but] it is recognized as a vice, with drinking, womanizing, and gambling," one administrator in Singapore explained.[114] An opium monopoly was also an inconsistent institution that registered individuals to both enable and restrict opium consumption. It gave rations to those deemed addicted, sold to mine owners and plantation managers employing manual laborers who smoked the drug, while also limiting physical access to opium retail shops and raising prices in ways that rendered opium smoking a prohibitively expensive habit. It was a contradictory institution that at once expressed concerns with labor capacity of Chinese opium smokers, pity for the "social status and hygienic conditions . . . at such a low level that these workers seek at all costs a distraction that makes them forget, however temporarily, the miseries of life," while also comfortably asserting that the Chinese race was impervious to the usual harms of opium to Asians.[115] Among the Chinese in Saigon-Chôlon, explained the city's mayor in 1908, "we seldom encounter those individuals suffering from the physiological decay so often heard about."[116] Therefore, an opium monopoly also operated as a pragmatic institution supplying opium to those who consumed in moderation, while striving to prevent harms from excessive smoking or by especially vulnerable people. It also operated as an aspirational institution, as a means to an end for the total eradication of opium. Citing a civilizing power's obligation to care for its subjects, other administrators reasoned as follows: given the scope of existing drug users in the colony and smugglers, an incremental approach was necessary—to reduce consumption, care for addicts, and build capacity to police contraband—which was best assumed through centralized control.

All of these arguments were expressed by local administrators in colonies throughout the half-century during which opium monopolies prevailed across Southeast Asia. Some arguments were true, others false; some wishful, others deceitful. To distinguish among them, it is necessary to begin by suspending skepticism that such expressed opinions were disguising a more insidious scheme by a colonial state to profit from the vices of the colonized. As an alternative point of departure, let us take seriously what involved officials at the time said. The British in late nineteenth century Burma declared the era of the opium monopolies as beginning a "general prohibition against the use of opium."[117] Let us start by doing the same.

Conclusion

The global and imperial contexts in which the colonial opium monopolies of Southeast Asia emerged and endured were complex. This chapter has focused on three major developments of the late nineteenth and early twentieth centuries: the end of the India–China opium trade, the internationalization of drug control under the League of Nations, and metropolitan anti-opium crusades and legislation. I have argued that these developments weighed upon but did not necessarily determine when and how shifts in colonial opium policies restricting opium's commercial life occurred. I have also stressed the peculiarities of Southeast Asia as a region since the nineteenth century, in light of general dependency on opium imports from India, the profitability of taxing opium consumption as a colonial vice, and an influx of Chinese migrant laborers associated with opium smoking. In doing so, this chapter has aimed to clarify the risks of overlooking variations in regulatory approaches that followed logics of problem solving that differ on a colony-by-colony basis, rooted in precedents of state building. It underscores the extent to which a small and busy world of local opium administration was embedded within but not always reacting to the external pressures of religiously inspired moral crusaders with political clout, imperial diplomats concerned with the empire's reputation, as well as social actors protesting government-organized opium sales.

Part II moves into these small worlds, focusing squarely on the micropolitics of bureaucratic realms overseeing opium matters in Burma, Malaya, and Indochina. For each colony, the three chapters will peer into the day-to-day of local administrators, tracing what they did, said, and wrote, and demonstrating the significance of the problems they constructed, affirmed, and officialized.

Part II

4

"Morally Wrecked" in British Burma, 1870s–1890s

IN 1894, the British colonial state in Burma introduced an opium monopoly and declared an official ban on popular opium consumption. Previously permissible habits of smoking and eating opium were deemed illegal, and opium markets for selling opium were placed under state control. The British placed particular emphasis on restricting Burman subjects from accessing opium freely. This interdiction was among the first of its kind instituted by a European power governing territorially in Southeast Asia, and marked the beginning of a long and uneasy era of opium prohibition.

British Burma's late nineteenth century experience as such has been often underappreciated, in part because many have been profoundly skeptical of the expressed intentions of official actors to ban opium consumption while establishing a state-run monopoly. It is conventional to view the British as only reluctantly adopting anti-opium reforms to placate the international community, especially under pressure from the United States. Often, the impetus behind the British Empire's eventual turn to prohibition is located in the American Empire's moral crusade against opium, especially after conquering the Philippines and abolishing the former Spanish colony's opium tax farm in 1898, while consolidating a forceful anti-opium stance by 1908.[1] The United States, as a late-comer imperial power, aspired to define its identity as a civilizing power in contradistinction to the older opium-complicit European empires, especially the British.[2] Prevailing scholarship also establishes how European rulers, in addition to worries about international reputation and lost prestige, had reason to restrict opium markets based on anti-Chinese sentiments: authorities saw opportunities to displace wealthy Chinese capitalists who controlled opium tax farms, and coopt their economic bases of power while also perceiving threats from poorer migrant Chinese workers whose seemingly unruly behaviors were associated with opium smoking habits.[3]

However, despite a relatively small number of Chinese inhabitants with weaker economic clout compared to other colonies, British Burma banned opium consumption before the US colonized the Philippines. What explains Burma's early move against opium? This chapter situates the emergence of the 1894 ban in a context of longstanding struggles within the colonial bureaucracy to articulate and quell perceived problems for governance that associated opium consumption with crime and disorder. It demonstrates a wealth of already existing arguments favoring anti-opium reforms and moralizing narratives that local administrators in Burma had developed since the 1870s, and traces two decades of subsequent endeavors to address the drug's perceived injury to local populations, which came to include but did not necessarily originate in reference to the colony's Chinese inhabitants.

This chapter argues that the ideas and everyday work of on-site officials guided British Burma's reforms by constructing an official problem of "moral wreckage" that posited opium consumption as causing the ruin of 11 percent of the indigenous Burmese population. This specific narrative and number had a distinctive genealogy within the bureaucracy, which I trace, using a diverse range of records that capture the multilevel nature of paperwork that administrators generated across the colony's jail and prisons, as well as departments for excise, customs, public health, and finance relating to opium. To explore the antecedent and underlying layers of information collection and interpretation behind official statements and public testimonies, I consulted sources that include the personal diaries of excise officers, early and revised drafts for district records and annual reports, confidential memos prepared for official inquiries, and related internal correspondence. The granular process of administrative knowledge production that this chapter unveils both enriches and unsettles existing analyses of well-known documents that expressed the colonial state's official position, including Chief Commissioner Charles Aitchison's 1880 memorandum on opium consumption in Burma and the Royal Opium Commission's 1895 report, by tracking the original authors of authoritative categories, assumptions, and statistics used at the time.[4]

Examining British Burma and its 1894 ban on opium consumption in light of the bureaucratic construction of official problems of "moral wreckage" is important for understanding the rise of opium prohibition across Southeast Asia more generally. Burma's anti-opium reforms represented an exception to the British Indian Empire's general approach to regulating opium during the late

nineteenth century, which eschewed intervening directly regarding the sumptuary practices of subject populations. The ban on Burman consumption was
introduced despite worries in high seats of power in Calcutta and London about
indigenous discontent and resistance, as well as anticipated losses in revenue.[5]
Seemingly minor low-level administrators in Burma wielded surprisingly strong
discretionary powers by providing arguments and evidence that persuaded senior bureaucratic officials and political actors of the unique urgency of local
circumstances. This chapter shows how these actors haphazardly produced a
particular strand of colonial knowledge that claimed privileged authenticity
based on direct observation and physical proximity that guided the introduction of the 1894 Burma Amendment to the 1878 All India Opium Act and the
creation of opium consumer registries—two institutions that gave first and formal expression to the British Empire's turn against opium in Southeast Asia.

The "Morally Wrecked"

In April 1892, the Financial Commissioner of Burma, Donald Mackenzie Smeaton, wrote with great concern about "an injury of great magnitude . . . being
done to the people of Burma by opium."[6] "[T]he evil effect of opium on mind
and body are much more marked in Burmans than in other races," according
to Smeaton, who described how "when a Burman lad comes back to his home
after he has been known to have contracted the [opium] habit, he is looked upon
as a man who comes back really to thieve."[7] Known as a *beinsa*, the opium-
addicted thief was hardly a violent individual, but an oddly petty criminal. As
Smeaton would later explain, a *beinsa* specialized in stealing "from his own
father's or mother's or mother-in-law's house, reaping crops from other
people's paddy fields . . . robbing from stacks and taking clothes and food."[8] His
infractions were so minor that they "would hardly come within the cognizance
of a criminal court at all," but the prevalence of *beinsas* nonetheless indicated
a grave crisis in the colony, according to Smeaton.[9]

Other administrators agreed. *Beinsa* crimes were a large problem in 1890s
Burma, "likely to lead to a great demoralization of the people" worried Major
Butler, the Deputy Commissioner for Henzada.[10] A "general slackness, both
physical and moral," could be seen among Burmans for whom "in too many
instances one has only to scratch the opium-eater or smoker to come on the
criminal," observed Major Peile, the Inspector General of Police.[11] And once
convicted, "the Burman resembles a mummy, always apathetic and down-
hearted, besides being quite disorderly in his habits," noted the superintendent

of the Sandoway jail.[12] There was a typical "downward course" that many officials recognized in which "[w]ith the love of ease that is characteristic of the race, the listlessness induced by the drug is intensified, and in the process of time honest labor is given up, nourishment is irregularly taken, the appetite for proper food abates, while that for the drug is stimulated."[13] The opium-consuming Burman thus "becomes a social outcast and is obliged to consort with those who are themselves addicted to the vice."[14] This figure, in Smeaton's words, was "morally wrecked."[15]

Supporting statistical evidence that moral wreckage was a general phenomenon across the colony, coupled with a conviction that Burma was incomparable to other parts of the Indian Empire, led the British to introduce a state-run opium monopoly and ban popular opium consumption at a time when other imperial powers were not. On January 1, 1894, the Chief Commissioner's office announced that Burmans in Lower Burma were no longer allowed to purchase opium or smoke the drug, unless they chose to register with the state as a habitual opium consumer. A few months earlier in 1893, the Excise Department had finished registering 7,513 such individuals deemed likely to suffer "real hardship" from a sudden ban on opium and issued certificates that would permit them to purchase small amounts.[16] Otherwise, the new year of 1894 ushered in a new world of sumptuary restrictions. Going forward, the colony's twenty-odd opium shops would cater only to the addicts, the Indians and the Chinese, while the everyday Burman found in violation of the ban faced up to three months of imprisonment and fines.[17] Two interrelated hypotheses underwrote this anti-opium reform: first, that opium consumption caused social crimes of a moral nature; second and relatedly, that this inimical opium effect was unique to a Burman in Burma.

Burma Unlike India

These arguments and the 1894 ban were significant because of Burma's place as a province of British India at the time. Over the course of three wars—the First, Second, and Third Anglo-Burmese wars of 1824–1826, 1852–1853, and 1885—the British had incrementally conquered territories of the Kingdom of Burma and placed them within a common regulatory framework with India with regards to opium. Under the East India Company's rule until 1857, the sale and distribution of opium in Burma were under the jurisdiction of the Bengal Board of Revenue.[18] After 1857, the Government of India used four laws that combined to centralize state control over the trade, production, and excise of opium—the

1856 Bengal Abkaree Act (XXI), the 1857 and 1878 Opium Acts (XIII of 1857 and I of 1878), and the 1878 Sea Customs Act.[19] All were formally extended to British Burma.[20]

Within this framework, it was unusual but not impossible for British authorities India to grant exemptions for Burma, based on what the former deemed persuasive and urgent reasons to create special amendments. For instance, in 1857, the Government of India reversed the British East India Company's (EIC) longstanding approach to opium tax farming (which auctioned a limited number of licenses to private entrepreneurs permitting them to hold submonopolies over local sales and distribution) and introduced what was called the "free market" system (which granted a much larger numbers of opium supply licenses and allowed more open competition among licensed private vendors).[21] Initially, this free market system was extended to Burma under the Bengal Abkaree Act, but five years later in 1862, Burma was permitted to switch back to opium tax farming following a successful petition to the Government of India made by the Chief Commissioner of Burma citing widespread smuggling problems unique to his jurisdiction.[22] Exceptions citing Burma's unique circumstances were also granted in 1871 (to abolish opium farming); in 1874 (to adjust the scope of licensed vendors from district to retail shop); in 1887 (to allow the reselling of seized contraband opium); and in 1888 (to permit poppy cultivation in northern frontier areas).

Until 1894, however, the British authorities in India refused to allow those in Burma to directly intervene in matters relating to the opium consuming habits of subject populations. While the Government of India had sanctioned some indirect measures aimed at controlling excessive use through raised sales prices and reduced numbers of opium shops, it stopped short of authorizing what was deemed an overly intrusive state interference into colonial society.[23]

There are several aspects of Burma's political economy and society during the nineteenth century that at once shaped its status as a special province within British India and provided the context in which local administrators would come to persuade the Government of India to finally authorize a ban on popular opium consumption. Since the 1850s, the expansion of wet-rice cultivation in the Irrawaddy–Sittang Delta had been transforming Burma's once subsistence-based agricultural areas into a vibrant market economy geared toward exports. Rice production quickened the economic life of Lower Burma and increased population mobility. Internal migrants from the dry zones of Upper Burma moved south—often pushed by drought, food shortages, and unrest and pulled in by new opportunities for work and profit—while foreign laborers, merchants, and money lenders from India and southern China also entered the country.[24] People moved more efficiently with improvements in transportation, especially as the Irrawaddy Flotilla Company started to navigate fluvial routes in 1868 and new railroad lines opened to connect Prome (1877) and Toungoo (1884) to Rangoon.[25] Many migrants entered Burma through this port, as well as Akyab and Bassein, where work could be found in the wharfs, rice mills, industries for logging and mining, as well as in building railways.[26]

Social changes accompanied these economic developments. The population of the Delta area grew dramatically and by the 1880s, more than 10 percent of its enumerated population was born outside of Lower Burma.[27] Urban towns had higher shares of migrants, both internal and foreign, whose influx was especially visible in those with major ports. Rangoon was "well on its way to becoming an Indian city," as the population share originating from India increased from around 26 percent in the 1870s to 48 percent by the early 1890s.[28] The ports of Akyab and Bassein were also busy, as incoming migrants gained greater mobility with the trains and steamboats moving between heartland and coasts. The Chief Commissioner of the colony noted with satisfaction that with "the great progress, which Burma has lately made in population and revenue, [which made it] necessary that the administrative machinery should grow in proportion."[29] Yet, with such great progress came social instability, both real and perceived by local administrators of the British colonial state. In Lower Burma, increases in murder, *dacoity* (armed banditry), and robbery, along with crimes against property were reported. Relatedly, many noted outbreaks of cholera in different parts of the colony, surmising that the illness had traveled due to coolies moving both inland north to military cantonments in Thayetmyo and Mandalay abroad "ordinary boats and steamers which ply upon the [Irrawaddy] river and south to Rangoon along the Sittang Railway."[30] The 1885 war sent more people fleeing from unrest in the north into Lower Burma, which intensified the felt social disorder, associated with population movement. The jails and prisons saw much overcrowding by refugees and resistant individuals newly labeled as criminals. By the 1890s, Burma was on its way to claiming the dubious honor as "the most criminal province of British India."[31]

During these decades, opium consumption was frequently associated with disease, crime, and mobile populations in the official mind of the British colonial state. Administrative ambivalence attached in diverse ways to opium eating Indian dockworkers and Chinese opium smokers laboring in the tin mines for whom consuming the drug seemed both injurious and necessary for their arduous work. Myriad assumptions were made about whether opium helped or harmed the ill, whether it served as a painkiller or weakened the immune system, alongside conjectures about the varied forms of criminality and stigma that accompanied those who ingested opium in Burma. Bureaucratic actors sometimes invoked the Buddhist religion (and translated strictures condemning opium) to denounce the drug's alien place in Burmese society, but would also turn to religion to argue for opium's traditional place in Burma (as monks used opium for ritual tattooing practices). Conflicting narratives about opium consumption as both indicative of and disruptive to the progress and uplift of a colony under British rule prevailed among local administrators.

From a bewilderingly diverse array of opinions and perspectives regarding opium consumption in Burma emerged a very specific narrative. It had a distinctive arc that centered on opium consumption as a cause of nonviolent forms of crime, which were limited to Burmese people residing in Lower Burma. This narrative also used the term "moral wreckage," paired with a Burmese term of *beinsa*, to refer to an odd sort of opium-caused individual injury that was not reducible to physical forms of damage, but could spread to families. It also claimed a way to calculate the extent of diffusion, which reached approximately 11 percent in the early 1890s. On the one hand, this was a familiar theme about the vulnerabilities of indigenous subjects that the British in Burma had expressed many times before.[32] On the other hand however, the causal narrative and number it invoked was new, precise, and would come to ring persuasively to the ears of authorities in India, enabling the 1894 ban on opium consumption in Burma. To do so, it is necessary to begin specifically. Let us start in 1877, in the jail of Akyab town on the western coast of Burma, close to Bengal.

The Jail of Akyab

The summer of 1877 was an unusually unhealthy one for the Akyab jail. Built in the late 1820s, this jail was one of the oldest in Burma and had long been notorious for high morbidity and mortality rates. Even considering this, more than eighty prisoners died in 1877, a near fourfold increase over the past years.[33]

The death cluster was due to an especially unfortunate confluence of events, according to Dr. Johnstone, the jail's medical officer. A cholera outbreak in Akyab town had spread to the jail, killing forty-five prisoners by the end of July. The doctor explained that his jail had already been overcrowded by prisoners transferred from Kyaukpyu, a neighboring district hard hit by a drought and then famine, pushing desperate people to crime. Kyaukpyu's own jail had been unable to accommodate the influx and sent inmates to Akyab for sentencing. "These prisoners had been without exception opium eaters to excess who had fallen into a bad state of health," because they could not afford opium after paying famine prices for rice, Johnstone explained.[34] He believed that the Akyab jail's "lamentable mortality" was due to these individuals who when "deprived of opium are quite unfit for work and as a means of living, resort to theft; and when they become inmates of a jail, they are strongly predisposed to be attacked by such diseases as diarrhea, dysentery, and a diseased condition called . . . anemia."[35] In other words, according to this local administrator, people who had used opium were especially vulnerable to three diseases, which were responsible for thirty-three deaths in the Akyab jail in 1877, in addition to the forty-five cholera victims.

Johnstone was not the first to see a link between opium consumption and poor health in this particular jail. His predecessor J. W. Mountjoy had made a similar claim that Akyab prisoners suffered from a "general debility" because "most of these men are opium eaters admitted in an emaciated and feeble condition of body."[36] In 1874, Mountjoy had conducted a comparative study of Akyab and Chittagong, a nearby town in Bengal that was "in nearly all respects similar to Akyab . . . situated on a highly malarious coast and at the mouth of a river . . . and under the same influences of climate."[37] Mountjoy identified a correlation between the Akyab jail's higher mortality rates and the larger number of opium addicts in the town, which contrasted with Chittagong's fewer addicts and fewer jail deaths. At the time, the Inspector General of Prisons reviewed Mountjoy's study but dismissed it as mere conjecture, in part because there were "no means of judging whether the Arakanese are as a rule greater opium eaters than the Chittagongians or whether a larger number of opium eaters are admitted into the Akyab jail."[38]

On reviewing these notes in 1877, Johnstone, as he struggled with Akyab jail's high mortality numbers, began to record opium-related morbidity patterns among the inmates. Thus, when another large number of deaths occurred the next year, medical officers were able to count how of the 112 inmates who had died from cholera, "all the first victims came from the part of the jail set apart for reconvicted prisoners, all of whom were opium eaters."[39] Over the next few years, administrators of this jail continued to collect information that generated more fine-grained pictures of opium and illness. For instance, in 1881 civil surgeon Dr. Foster counted "350 Burmans, 4 Hindus, 12 Mussulmans, 1 Christian (Armenian), 1 Eurasian" who had admitted to "excessive use of opium prior to imprisonment" and were responsible for many of the jail's

TABLE 4.1. Prison Population and Estimated Opium Consumers in Lower Burma's Prisons, 1881

	Total jail population 13/12/1881			Number who were smokers or eaters of opium when they came into jail		Number who have apparently suffered in health or constitution in consequence of indulgence in opium	
	Natives of Burma	Natives of India	Chinese and others	Natives of Burma	Natives of India	Natives of Burma	Natives of India
Akyab	300	12	4	117	2	33	1
Kyoukphyoo	70			59		4	
Sandoway	15			2			
Rangoon	1,367	152	272	350	18	62	3
Maoobin	54		3	3			
Bassein	338	7	1	109		33	
Henzada	82		1	33		9	
Myanoung	15	3	5	8	2		
Thayetmyo	40	2	5	6			
Moulmein	1,012	102	54	93	2	9	1
Tavoy	82	4	4	8	1	6	
Mergui	3	1		1			
Toungoo	211	19	3	38		10	
Shwaygyin	44	5		8	2	3	1
Total	3,633	307	307	835	27	169	6

Source: RPAB 1881, p. 42.

deaths.[40] Other jails in Burma began to follow Akyab's lead, reporting the number and nature of those "suffering in health or constitution in consequence of indulgence in opium."[41]

The opium statistics that the prison administration of Burma would later show that Akyab's worrisome reputation was actually at odds with recorded reality, as it had neither the largest number nor most unhealthy inmates among the colony's eleven jails. Table 4.1 illustrates. Yet Akyab jail's administrators remained vigilant and by way of continuing to describe and explain the immediate circumstances that worried them, these actors set the foundations for later arguments about moral wreckage, which would move from identifying opium consumption as a secondary cause of inmate morbidity to the primary source of imprisonment.

One of the early pivots toward crime and criminality occurred in an 1881 study by the Akyab jail's civil surgeon O. Baker. By this time, the prison's medical community subscribed to a hypothesis that opium eating was causing a high rate of dysentery. Baker was dissatisfied with existing studies and decided to examine broader patterns across the colony. In the process, he noted that "among the 4,000 criminals jailed under the Indian Penal Code in Burma in 1881, 1,764 were opium smokers, but of violence-related crimes—'hurt, affray, and assault'—only 5 were opium smokers."[42] Although officials working with prisoners were surely not unaware of the difference, hitherto studies had assumed that all incarcerated opium consumers were criminals of similar stripes. Baker's findings suggested that those habituated to opium were perhaps prone to a particularly docile type of crime, while giving reason to question how exactly such opium-related crimes arose. The Inspector General of Prisons now found the medical officer's note "very suggestive and interesting" and mused: "[i]t would be interesting to know whether offenders under the Code were first eaters and then criminals, or first criminals [and] then eaters."[43]

The Town Bazaar

Similar questions were being raised outside of the jail walls, in the town of Akyab. Excise officers tasked with policing local markets and maintaining public order were also puzzling over patterns of opium consumption and associated problems, alongside but not yet together with the officials of the jail. Compared with the quasi-controlled environment of a jail, the town's opium bazaar was a messier world that situated administrators approached with fewer means for direct observation and more opportunity for speculation.

The British in Akyab had often sensed that the seaport's residents tended to consume unusually large amounts of opium. The origins of this "unhappy taste," wrote the head of the Excise Department, could be found between 1857 and 1862, when Bengal had abolished Burma's opium tax farms and opened a competitive sales market.[44] Prior to 1857, opium had been scarce and expensive, but during the few years that liberal sales were allowed, "drinking sprits and smoking opium had become almost universal among the young men of Arakan; and in Akyab alone, which contained almost 20,000 inhabitants, upwards of ninety shops had been established for the sale of intoxicating liquors and drugs."[45] Although Burma soon reinstated a tax farming system that restricted sales under a single licensed vendor, a "new and insatiable demand" had already emerged.[46] Into the 1870s, more town administrators identified interrelated reasons for why high levels of opium consumption were continuing in their jurisdiction.

One had to do with Akyab as a port town on the Naf River, very close to Bengal's Chittagong, where a competitive opium market still remained.[47] As a result of the different sales regimes operating side by side, opium sold in Chittagong was cheaper than in Akyab where an opium tax farmer set prices, so of course, reasoned local administrators, residents bought their opium in the nearby Bengali town. Moreover, illicitly bringing opium across the border was profitable and so "it is no wonder that plenty of people are to be found eager to take a part in the business of smuggling."[48]

The other reason stemmed from the perceived weaknesses of indigenous inhabitants in Akyab compared with foreign populations. "Other races," explained the head of the Excise Department, "might be contented with a moderate enjoyment of such a stimulant, but the Burmese and Arakanese could not resist indulging to excess whenever opium was placed before them."[49] Excise officers encountering the residents of the town opined that such excess

> . . . would assuredly be ill-compensated by the increase of crime, such increased consumption among a race where gambling and dacoities are a past time, would bring in its trail . . . and not only so, but it may assuredly be accepted that every additional man who takes to this insidious drug withdraws not only his atom of industry from the general weal, and consequently contributes less to the general revenue, but an entire family are in all probability influenced for the worse. The total consumption, however much it may be regretted, is steadily advancing.[50]

It is important to note that despite using words such as "race" or "Burmese" and "Arakanese," Akyab's administrators were not articulating stable categories that identified racial attributes and linked them to different physiological dependencies.[51] Rather these were descriptive labels for perceived differences between original inhabitants of Akyab and newcomers in the town. Industrious *laskars* (sailors from India) working at the piers could chew small amounts of opium with little harm, it seemed, as did the "Hindoo" who set up residence in the town, marrying a local woman and sharing his taste for eating opium with her family, as well as the "Chinaman" smoking his pipe around the opium shops that his countrymen owned. The indigenous population of Akyab was seen as weaker, more prone to vice, and vulnerable by comparison.

If such anxieties had been confined to Akyab, they might have remained the alarmism of a few vigilant administrators. But this was not the case. Albert Fytche, the Chief Commissioner of the colony from 1867 to 1871, paid sustained attention to this seaport and others in Arakan "where there is generally a considerable foreign population already accustomed to the use of stimulants."[52]

Perhaps Chief Commissioner Fytche had a personal attachment to this place, as a former member of the Arakan Battalion who had helped transform Akyab from a small fishing village into a productive port.[53] Fytche likely also had political concerns, as his Commissioner in Arakan clashed often with the Bengal authorities over who was at fault for opium smuggling between Akyab and Chittagong. Officials in the border districts were especially critical of Burma's opium farming system, calling it anachronistic and a cause of contraband for which there was "no exaggerated picture of lawlessness," insisted the Collector of Chittagong.[54] Faced with criticism from Bengal, perhaps the new leadership of a young British Burma needed to defend its own provincial authorities and their work. Akyab represented a ready site for demonstrating capable colonial governance.

The ways that local administrators shaped Chief Commissioner Fytche's perspective is significant in several respects. First, they emphasized the peculiarities of an opium bazaar in Burma in light of its social dynamics, as a type of divided market where foreigners might buy and sell opium on equal grounds, but where the same exchange became distorted when native inhabitants of Burma were involved. Hardly rational consumers, the Burmese and the Arakanese in the coastal markets were seen as entering a market where two distinct types of transactions occurred: one between foreigners mutually impervious to the effect of opium, and another more insidious one between foreign and indigenous inhabitants. Given their different capacities for consumption, the latter were necessarily at the mercy of the former in a precarious position that suggested corrupt dynamics of market exchange.

Second and relatedly, as low-level bureaucrats were selectively attentive to certain aspects of their jurisdictions over others, higher administrators such as Fytche and subsequent Chief Commissioners would inherit a focus on specific sites like Akyab, and easily reason that similarly opium-riddled port towns like Akyab existed in and beyond Arakan, "there being many facilities for bringing the drug into the province by means of the crews of the steamers continually trading to Rangoon and Moulmein."[55] Aboard the Calcutta steamers, *laskars* frequently smuggled small quantities of opium, learned Ashley Eden, who replaced Fytche in 1875, while the Chinese who settled in these towns purchased expensive opium sales licenses. Foreignness obtained a clearer referent through the figures of mobile Indians and rich Chinese and their opium dealings, which gave a more vivid sense of inequalities to market transactions and reinforced administrative perspectives about the peculiarity of Burmese opium bazaars. Not only were "natives" more vulnerable to opium use itself, but they were also likely at the mercy of hardier foreigners who might encourage, tempt, and indeed force consumption on them. Akyab itself became firmly established in official accounts as the geographical origin of these social issues. The 1878 Excise Report for the colony stated that "the evil . . . [was] fostered in its infancy by the proximity of Chittagong to Akyab."[56]

Finally, interpretations of Burma's opium markets at once drew upon and reconfigured an existing understanding of a colonial economy for excise as operating according to social logics peculiar to their local contexts. For British India in general, a principled approach to excise administration had long sought "[F]irst, to raise as large an amount of revenue from intoxicating liquors and drugs as is compatible with the greatest possible discouragement of their use, and second, to avoid raising the tax on opium or checking its sales beyond certain limits as experience teaches that, under such circumstances, the people will procure the drug by surreptitious means."[57]

Administrators in Burma were quick to point out a tension between these two aims as policy approaches, as the former set a strong presence of the state while the latter minimized it, alongside different visions of what constituted the public benefit at hand. Albert Fytche argued that while Bengal might embrace the second, in his Burma where there was growing "native" opium consumption "it [has] been found absolutely necessary to give prominence to the first principle, namely that of *raising for the public benefit the greatest amount of revenue with the smallest possible consumption*" [emphasis added].[58] Moreover, opium bazaars worked differently in this corner of the empire, insisted local administrators, and the best way to strike a balance between minimizing consumption while maximizing revenue was to recognize the peculiar social dynamics along which local markets operated in coastal towns in Burma. They reasoned that it made sense to approach the foreign supply and indigenous demand differently and proceeded to raise the license fees for sales in 1872, a reform justified by the assumption that the mostly Chinese vendors would recover costs by selling at more expensive retail prices, which would deter many, including the everyday Burmese and Arakanese from buying opium. Although "[t]he change of system might very possibly lead to a temporary falling off of revenue," it was considered "well worth the risk."[59]

The next years fulfilled neither of the Excise Department's professed expectations—both reported opium revenue and quantities of opium sold increased until the late 1870s. Initially, not all administrators were troubled by these trends, some bluntly welcoming increased revenue or considering it a function of the colony's population growth. Others surmised that it was the foreigners who were consuming more and that a simple taste for a luxury commodity was on the rise. In general however, all dwelled upon what was more immediately visible: the numerous Burmese and "miserable opium-eaters" seen around an increasing number of opium shops in coastal areas—Arakan alone had eleven and added seven more by 1878.[60]

It was yet unclear who exactly was consuming how much opium in Burma because an administrative scheme for categorizing opium consumers as Burmese, Chinese, and Indians would not emerge for another few years. The Excise Department was beginning with the bluntest of estimates, dividing how much opium left the government warehouses by the known total population. By this count, between 1868 and 1878, opium consumption across the colony had more than doubled from 91 to 217 grains per person. "Of course, it is not forgotten that in the same interval the population has considerably expanded," qualified yet another new Chief Commissioner named Charles Aitchison who would review the Excise Department's reports a few years later, but "[s]till, the consumption of opium has increased at a much quicker rate."[61] More troublingly, Aitchison would feel these numbers "leave no doubt that the taste for the drug is rapidly spreading all over the province and among the rural population."[62]

From Coast to Interior

Worries about opium consumption diffused, alongside the improvement of transportation connecting coastal areas to rural towns and villages. For instance, the completion of a railroad line linking Rangoon to inland Prome in 1877 was met with trepidation among excise officials who urged that "[I]t must not be forgotten, too, that the foreign population . . . is ever on the increase . . . [and] are, by the opening of the railway, being more spread over the division."[63] They reiterated earlier concerns about foreigners as supplying opium, while clarifying how "both Chinese and natives of the Madras coast . . . are the principal consumers of the drug" and "with this inroad of opium-using foreigners into the province, the taste for opium is spread[ing] amongst the Burmese."[64]

The mobility of Chinese immigrants also played a key role in refining the local administration's conceptions about how opium consumption was spreading across the colony. There is a striking tension to how centrally the mobile Chinese came to figure in official discourse, not least given how local administrators were also acutely attentive to Indian opium consumption and the relatively smaller number of Chinese who inhabited Burma. Compared with approximately 240,000 Indians counted in Lower Burma in the 1880s (around 6.5 percent of the population), there were fewer than 10,000 Chinese who never rose above 1 percent of the colony's population.[65] The Chinese in Burma were also seen by many British bureaucrats as less mobile than the Indians, with an observed tendency to stay in the major towns and had such "energy in trade and wealth" that made them "no doubt the most valuable class of migrants we get in Burma."[66] Nonetheless, the figure of the roving "China-men" would come to figure centrally in administrative narratives about opium consumption and its diffusion in Burma. A memo penned by the Commissioner of Tenasserim in 1874 presaged such formulations. The alert Commissioner warned how "petty Chinese traders and pedlars . . . will make a tempting offer for an opium license in an out-of-way place."[67] The Chinese migrant community within Burma was small and unevenly distributed, "largest in Tenasserim—the area closest to China—and the smallest in Arakan, the area farthest from China."[68] Administrators here thus encountered more Chinese and their reports made more explicit links between "Chinamen" and "traders and pedlars," clarifying the perniciousness of their work. They informed the Commissioner that "*they* give the people at first, opium for nothing, induce them to use it, and when the habit has been once acquired, *they* trust to their after-profits to repay them all outlay . . . Our greatest difficulty is the *Chinamen*; *they* have combinations among *them*" [emphases added].[69]

The Excise Department learned to fear the plurality of "Chinamen" and perceive their growth in both numerical size and economic prowess. "Chinamen are now over the length and breadth of the province," corroborated another officer from Pegu.[70] The traveling "Chinamen" was a blunt category that ran roughshod over otherwise recognized varieties of Chinese migrants in Burma and their tendency for more sedentary life styles, based in towns where they engaged in trade, leather manufacturing, and some fruit and vegetable cultivation in nearby plots. British administrators intent on understanding already presumed problems about Burmese opium consumption selectively discounted certain details in favor of more sweeping characterizations of a typified China-man. "There are combinations among these men" which are especially dangerous because "do what we can, they will circumvent us," learned yet another new Chief Commissioner named Rivers Thompson.[71] Excise administrators warned him that such combinations reportedly eluded ordinary measures of control ("the small fry are generally caught by the police, while the big fish escape punishment") and circumvented conventional means of discipline ("they or some secret club pay the fine inflicted [on the small fry]" and returned to supplying opium "quite ready to begin again, hoping that with greater caution, they will next time have better luck and evade the law").[72] "The Chinamen should be watched," agreed Thompson.[73]

This clues us to the profoundly impressionistic manner in which official knowledge about opium in British Burma was emerging. The relative strength of this foreign opium-smoker (even though not all Chinese smoked their opium) aligned with the mobility of Chinese "traders and pedlars" (even though such roving tendencies were limited to a small portion of the Chinese population) to bolster a belief in the socioeconomic strength of this group (even though many Chinese migrants were poor) that was reinforced by their demographic growth in Burma (even though the Indians constituted the largest growing minority population in the colony). It was not despite, but rather based on, such inconsistencies that sweeping characterizations of opium consumption's spread across the colony were made. A similar logic of problem construction applied to the indigenous people of Burma as well.

Consumption and Crime

Beginning in the west, a "demoralization of the Arakanese" was progressing with "fearful strides . . . mainly owing to the indulgence of the inhabitants in this vice," wrote one administrator named G. J. S. Hodgkinson, after he toured Kyaukpyu and Sandoway in 1879 and listened to officials who had visited the islands of Sagoo and Ramree off the coast.[74] Hodgkinson reported to the Chief Commissioner that opium smoking was spreading in places of the "most abject state of poverty" where the population lived in "small huts or hovels, in which the people squat in a state of nudity, without a mat to lie upon or a wall to protect them from the outside world."[75] In neighboring Prome, a Deputy Commissioner agreed that a "taste for opium is daily gaining a pernicious ascendancy," associated with indigent and bad characters who were ostracized socially, hearing they were called *beinsa* in Burmese, as a term of opprobrium.[76] Moving further inland, C. J. F. S. Forbes also recognized *beinsa* as referring to an opium using Burmese who "will not work until he gradually becomes poorer, till he is absolutely without means of subsistence, and yet he must obtain his expensive and necessary luxury; or die for want of it." Forbes posed the question that others were already answering: "He obtains it, not by working for it, then how?"[77]

By "regard[ing] other people's earnings as their legitimate prey" replied J. Hind from Kyaukpyu, who had observed Burmese opium consumers "prowl about during the greater part of the night, committing principally petty thefts of anything."[78] Paddy and rice appeared as the common targets, but other articles were also stolen stealthily "however small the amount . . . so long as it will answer for food, for clothing, or is convertible into money," Hind explained.[79] Another administrator named W. W. Pemberton added that he knew some opium consumers, so lucky as to "marry women of indifferent character, as none other will accept them," who would survive on "his wife's earnings, gifts, and thefts from his relations, and theft from the general population."[80] J. Butler surmised that this was a general pattern among the Burmese for whom opium "shatters the [sic] strength, it empties their purse, thus conducing to poverty and destitution; and finally leads to crime, which closes in jail."[81] J. C. Davis from the Salween district concurred: "As regards opium smoking, I can state positively that, as a rule, amongst natives of Burma, it leads to the commission of crime, unless the opium eater be a person of sufficient means to indulge in the drug," which he stated was very rarely true.[82] Indeed, Davis opined that in his land-locked district, opium consumers were not only linked to "nearly every case of petty theft" but in some cases to *dacoity* and robbery as well.[83]

Such extents of Burmese crime, however, were more palpably felt than systematically recorded. Yet, there was an underlying reality that the administrators claimed to know based on proximate experience. Forbes from Tharrawaddy dismissed how "[i]t is sometimes said by those ignorant of the country and the people that it is unjust and illegal to class an opium smoker as a bad character."[84] Butler from Kyaukpyu wrote that "here on this side, everything is different," in "a state of utter moral degradation"—pagodas, *kyoungs* (monasteries), *zayats* (a type of Buddhist pavilion sometime used as houses for travelers) were disappearing, as was a zeal for industry evidenced by the absence of bullock carts from villages where "they scarcely grow more than just enough to keep them from starving, and seem utterly wanting in all life or energy."[85]

And so in 1878, when Charles Aitchison assumed office, he discovered in the administrative records, "a close and direct connection . . . in this province between opium smoking and crime."[86] "When reviewing the Report on the Administration of Criminal Justice for the year 1877, my attention was drawn to the change which was alleged to be gradually coming over the Burmese national character under British rule," he explained.[87] Like many before him, the incoming Chief Commissioner learned from what existing administrators deemed colonial reality. Although Aitchison was new, he was surrounded by longer-serving bureaucrats who attested that such troubling change was due to growing opium use among the Burmese. Aitchison's concerns were confirmed soon after, when he visited Akyab and heard the pleas of so-called influential "natives" to save them from the misery entailed on the population by opium. On consulting "responsible officers in all divisions and districts of the province and natives everywhere," he explained, Aitchison was able to more firmly assert that opium consumption was causing widespread problems of upset social and moral order.[88] Knowledgeable administrators like Butler, Forbes, Davis, Pemberton, Hind, and Hodgkinson had submitted papers that explained how exactly this negative impact occurred:

> [a]mong the Burmans, the habitual use of the drug saps the physical and mental energies, destroys the nerves, emaciates the body, predisposes to disease, indulges indolent and filthy habits of life, destroys self-respect, is one of the most fertile sources of misery, destitution and crime, fills the jails with men of relaxed frame predisposed to dysentery and cholera, prevents the due extension of cultivation and the development of the land revenue, checks the natural growth of the population, and enfeebles the constitution of succeeding generations.[89]

In April 1880, Aitchison drafted a memorandum about opium consumption that gained official and public attention beyond Burma. This document received credit from pious anti-opium activists in London as newly framing opium issues in the Far East as "not of morality but the salvation of a race," by clarifying the sequential decline of Burmese and indigenous opium users—from individual ingestion to poverty to crime to societal injury (in contrast to immigrants from China and India capable of moderate opium use).[90] The Aitchison memo also presented the Government of India with an explicit argument for why the British Empire must take a more aggressive approach against opium consumption among the Burmese.[91]

"Probably a variety of causes have contributed to the spread of this vice," Aitchison began.[92] Some were inevitable: British rule had brought education and emancipated people from despotic rule but with the new sense of personal liberty among an Oriental people came a weakening of religious beliefs and customs that sanctioned improper behavior: "such results ought neither to surprise nor alarms us," Aitchison assured Calcutta, and it was as impossible to "put back the shadow on the sun-dial as arrest the disintegration of old-world customs."[93]

"But there are other causes within our control," the Chief Commissioner continued.[94] He would like to shut down as many shops as possible to put the injurious drug out of the reach of the common Burman, but keep a few open for the non-Burmese. "It is impossible to say precisely what the numbers of the

Chinese and natives of India are, but they are probably not less than 200,000," Aitchison guessed, who were "perhaps the most thriving and industrious section of the population, to whom the drug is a necessary of life and . . . rarely abused."[95] He envisioned two opium markets working side by side: one free for foreigners and the other tightly restricted for the Burmese. Aitchison acknowledged that normally, this type of government involvement risked injuring personal liberties and the growth of smuggling. And because this was true for the Chinese and Indian spheres of commerce, he would leave them undisturbed.

The Burmese realm in Burma, however, operated as an abnormal site in the official mind, as the liberty of a Burman was already precarious as a result of his diminished capacities for opium consumption. Smuggling, "even on a considerable scale, would never lead to the universal consumption of the drug," which was the greater social harm that put the colony at risk, opined the Chief Commissioner.[96] He declared that British India's excise principles were inapplicable to Burma, where "the question has altogether passed beyond the stage at which revenue considerations predominate."[97] The Far East colony represented an extraordinary context where utilitarian market principles for balancing maximum revenue and minimal harm must take secondary place to the state's role in protecting the public from harm. Such action was all the more necessary, urged Aitchison, as on-the-ground officials attentive to native opinion were hearing louder and louder whispers of blame among the Burmese about disorder and crime under British tutelage: that "the evil complained of is an innovation of our own times and our own government."[98]

One year later, Aitchison left Burma for the Punjab, and after retiring from public office in 1888, served as the director of the Church Missionary Society. After he died in 1896, the SSOT remembered him "by his outspoken statement of the evils produced by Opium amongst the Burmese."[99] But he, "like other Christian officials, was not sufficiently emancipated from his official surroundings," regretted the author of his obituary.[100] For ardently pious anti-opium activists, Aitchison had sought insufficient action and was complicit in an imperial agenda for profit-seeking because of his willingness to allow Chinese, Indians, and other indigenous users of opium to continue their habit uninterrupted, while limiting restrictions to the Burmese.

For local administrators who remained in Burma, however, Aitchison's memorandum marked a clear turning point toward a more principled approach to opium regulation that would unfold over the next decade. The colony's opium shops were reduced in number and the retail opium price of opium increased on average by 20 percent. In adopting these measures, the British stood to simultaneously please the many groups that divided colonial society and clarify an agenda for a reformed government. Taking a radical departure from Bengal's regulatory approach, Burma's demonstrable resolve to protect uniquely opium-threatened subjects would not only redeem colonial authority in the eyes of the ruled, but surely, reasoned local administrators, it was the proper thing to do.

Hubris accompanied such sensibilities of righteousness, which in turn hardened expectations within the local administration about how the colony's opium market worked and concomitantly, what regulatory changes were possible, as well as why they had failed in the past. "The extension of indulgence in opium is a growth of recent years, and has been mainly due to our excise system," admitted G. D. Burgess from the Chief Commissioner's office.[101] Restricting Burmese consumption would almost certainly result in a loss of opium revenue, anticipated authorities who estimated a yearly sacrifice between 5 and 13 lakhs of rupees.[102] But, the Chief Commissioner's office comforted itself, "the expectation entertained by many local officers [is] that the revenue will gradually be recouped by the advancing prosperity of the people, by their increased ability to consume and the export duty paying goods, and by enhanced extensions of cultivation."[103] Rangoon assured Calcutta that Burma's provincial budget could handle the loss, and secured approval for higher retail opium prices alongside more shop closures.

However, worried many, opium consumption was still on the rise among the Burmese, taking more illicit forms. Some assessed that foreign smugglers had seized on opportunities arising from restrictions on sales and were moving opium along old routes from Chittagong (into Akyab) and Madras (into Rangoon and Moulmein), as well as from Yunnan. The "Chinamen" of this province were known to bring opium into the Kingdom of Burma, which border officers found trickling into the British-ruled south as well. Anxieties about roving inland Chinese traders became a concern that all the more intensified as the 1885 war led to the conquest of this territory as Upper Burma and a prolonged "pacification" campaign ensued.[104] As migrants fled unrest in the north alongside marauders, jails overflowed with the displaced and resistant alike, while mobile populations visiting towns in the delta area increased. Moreover, the annexation of Upper Burma had administratively complicated the demographic landscape of the colony by bringing the Shan States and other highland area inhabitants who were indigenous populations and who appeared to consume opium without the injurious effects observed in the Burmese. Suspected increases in opium consumption were thus occurring as jail, excise, and town administrators encountered wartime disorder and its long aftermath.

Thus it seemed clear to situated officials that extant restrictions placed on opium shops and price control were inadequate, given widespread crime, *dacoity*, and evident demoralization of the Burmese people, which, as years of experience showed, had opium consumption as its primary cause. To the official mind of British Burma, a more involved approach was now imperative. Indirect restrictions on sales were inadequate, and it was time to take more direct action. In the summer of 1891, yet another new Chief Commissioner named Alexander MacKenzie, submitted a proposal to the Government of India for "the prohibition of sale of opium to, and possession of opium by, Burmans."[105]

Constructing an Official Problem

MacKenzie's request was at first refused. Prohibition was an extreme and controversial measure for British India where the harms of opium consumption on non-European subjects, let alone its criminal impact, were still being debated. D. R. Lyall of the Bengal Board of Revenue captures a key sentiment of British India's imperial authorities at the time when he stated flatly: "[o]pium never leads to crime of any kind . . . . It does not make a man quarrelsome or violent, but calms and soothes him."[106] Apologists for opium dwelled on the 1857 rebellion in India to express great caution toward interventionist measures into colonial society, especially those that risked encroaching upon perceived "native" activities.[107] According to Lyall, "in a political view, total prohibition would be so dangerous, and would alienate so large a body of her Majesty's subjects in India" and "dissatisfaction would be enormous, and . . . fanned as it would be by professional agitators, [prohibition] would . . . amount to disaffection and require the presence of more British troops in India."[108]

To persuade Bengal to sanction such a risky measure as directly prohibiting opium consumption, Burma must provide evidence that "the evil to be removed [was] as great . . . as depicted."[109] More precisely, the Government of India required that MacKenzie and the local administration prove two points: first, the wide prevalence of harmful opium consumption in Burma; and second, that opium injured Burmans more than other races.[110]

This was a tall order for any official organization, let alone one like the colonial administration of Burma, which at the time had 100 commissioned officials spread thin across a territory that had doubled its size with Upper

Burma's annexation.[111] At the same time, perhaps it was more feasible in Lower Burma, where the task was to demonstrate an already shared vision of local opium problems, rather than to newly discover them. The heroic way by which the perceived reality of situated administrators became a verifiable one for those who had never been in the jails, ports, towns, and villages emerges in a report drafted in April 1892 by the Financial Commissioner, Donald MacKenzie Smeaton.[112] Smeaton crafted a systematic picture, estimating the number of indigenous opium consumers in Burma and their criminal presence using two sources of data—statistics and testimonies from jail officials and reports from town and village administrators from across the colony.

On paper, the official problem of opium consumption in Burma finally solidified. Smeaton relied on a sample of roughly 1.2 million Burmans across the four divisions of Lower Burma to identify the share of opium consumers based on which he estimated the general prevalence across the colonial population. For instance, district officials in Arakan division surveyed 54 percent of the division's Burmese inhabitants (285,263 out of 533,000) and identified approximately 8,688 individuals, or 3 percent of this sample population, as notorious smokers or eaters of opium. Given that most of these individuals were adult males, Smeaton reasoned it would be fair to assume that they, in fact, represented the heads of households, which would mean approximately "11% of [families in Arakan] therefore have opium-smoking or opium-eating fathers."[113] Applied across the colony, the conclusions were "startling," opined Smeaton. Over a sample of 1.2 million Burmans in Burma, a total of 85,600 adult males had been identified, which indicated that 2 percent of the entire population or 11 percent of the families in the colony were affected by opium consumption.

One of Smeaton's key assumptions in this assessment was that one Burmese opium user represented one Burmese family composed of at least five people, which quickly amplified the magnitude of opium consumption's impact on colonial society by fivefold. The opium smoker as a father was a particularly powerful image that emphasized the salience of consumption on a microsocial level. Constructed as a matter of the family rather than one of individual misdeed, Smeaton was able to demonstrate empirically the widespread use of opium as a problem across the colony. More importantly, his analysis of the negative impact of opium consumption provided a clear exposition of a theory of moral wreckage.

Smeaton linked opium consumption among Burmans to both bodily injury and criminal tendencies. He first relied on jail statistics that showed that Burman inmates were more likely to suffer from disease and certain types of vulnerability than Indians, Chinese, Europeans, or other groups. This differential effect was best catalogued in the three jails of Arakan that included Akyab, which showed in 1891 that 52 percent of Burmans compared with 31 percent of non-Burman inmates were addicted to opium. Other jails repeated this comparative ratio, which when considering a 22 percent increase in the share of opium-smokers across the entire jail population from 1883 to 1891, Smeaton interpreted as an indication that opium consumption among Burmans with criminal tendencies was on the rise.

In addition, Smeaton reviewed the notes of medical officials in jails who reported two different types of deterioration observed among the addicts. Physically for Burmans:

> [T]he drug exercises a depressing effect on the functional activity of the sympathetic system and destroys nerve force. The internal organs become impaired, the healthy secretions are diminished, and the victim becomes physically weak. He wastes and becomes emaciated, his skin generally turns sallow, his lips and gums turn dark in color, he steadily loses weight and he becomes impotent. He becomes predisposed to fatal diseases induced by trifling causes which, in healthy persons, would have no evil effects at all.[114]

In addition, upon the mind, it appeared: "[T]he sensory nerves are weakened by the action of the drug on the grey matter of the brain, and dullness, melancholy, and loss of memory ensue. These, supervening on great physical languor, result in a complete wreck of the victim."[115]

The civil surgeon for Arakan's jails had referred to this as a state of "moral wreckage," a language that must have left a powerful impression on Smeaton. He introduced it into the administrative reports of British Burma as a category applicable to Burmans outside of the jails and their opium consumption patterns. Using the accounts of district officials who visited villages and spoke directly to elders, opium shopkeepers, as well as reports from local informants for three months in the winter of 1891, Smeaton estimated that across Lower Burma, at least one-fifth of the families had convicted criminals in their midst; and two-thirds had fathers suffering from "physical and moral wreckage."[116]

"Morally wrecked" was at once a novel label that not only caught the attention of metropolitan officials but also contained a strong claim about the effects of opium consumption that had to be defended, as Smeaton was forced to do. On December 19, 1893, Sir James Broadwood Lyall asked Smeaton, "Do you not think that the heading, 'physically or morally wrecked' is sensational?"[117] Lyall was the chairman of a royal opium commission for India that was touring

District.	Extent of Local Inquiry.	Population of selected Localities.	Consumers of Opium.			Percentage of Consumers to Total Population examined.	Number of Consumers physically or morally Wrecked.			Percentage of those physically and morally Wrecked to Total Number of Consumers.
			Smokers.	Eaters.	Total Consumers.		Physically.	Morally (taken to Crime).	Total.	
Akyab -	23 circles, 110 villages.	133,023	1,899	2,643	4,542	3·4	1,969	682	2,651	58
Kyaukpyu -	Greater part of district.	140,000 (approximate).	1,024	2,208	3,832	2·7	2,000 (approximate).	912	2,912	76
Sandoway -	19 villages -	12,000 (approximate).	161	133	294	2·5	Not stated	196	196	67
Total, Arakan Division.	—	285,023	3,684	4,984	8,688	3·	3,969	1,790	5,759	66

FIGURE 4.1. Statistical table of opium consumption, Arakan Division, Lower Burma, c. 1893. (Source: Royal Opium Commission 1894, vol. 2, p. 541.)

Burma; and he had in his hand Smeaton's 1892 report. He pointed to the following table (see Table 4.2) regarding Arakan. Lyall thought there was "a most extravagant assumption" underlying the heading, "that every man who is found to be an opium-consumer and has been suspected or convicted of crime has come to it through opium." The chairman and other members of the opium commission queried: "may it not be the other way?" That is, they wondered whether criminals were simply more prone to using opium and that an established criminal class in Burma—those "law-breaking, and vicious, and self-indulgent people"—were naturally taking to opium.

Smeaton firmly dismissed this counterargument. "What you call the effect is the cause. It is after a man has taken to opium that he takes to crime," he responded to Lyall.[118] In the case of Burma, Smeaton asserted, opium smoking and eating had an injurious effect upon the people of the colony unlike elsewhere in the Indian Empire. Crime was not in the nature of the gentle Burmese, but drugs altered them incomparably: "Whatever may be the effect of opium on other races, there can be only one opinion as to its effects on Burmans. It is damnation to him, body and soul."[119] This effect manifest in a secular fashion as a Burman became an outcast, "he knows he is an outcast, resigns himself to his own fate, rarely if ever tries to recover himself, takes to pilfering, is a pest and byeword [sic] in the neighborhood, and frequently ends in jail."[120] According to Smeaton, it was difficult for those without experience on the ground to comprehend the opium reality of the colony, not least because more familiar European and Indian institutions for collecting information were unavailable and unreliable in Burma as the "petty crime, petty thefts" taken by an opium-ruined Burman "would hardly come within the cognizance of a criminal court at all."[121]

Then, how could Smeaton prove these claims, demanded Lyall. "My evidence is chiefly hearsay," Smeaton responded simply.[122] But, he insisted, the problems caused by opium consumption in Burma were glaringly obvious to those on the ground. The opinions of local administrators who reported conversations with village elders, their cumulated expertise, and fleshing out of statistical returns with words instead of numbers comprised an alternative empirical foundation for knowing colonial circumstance, one for which the standards of necessary evidence varied based on the circumstances.

Smeaton's confidence in deep empiricism and inductive modes of reasoning was not a rogue position at the time. Rather, it reflected a common perspective by a middling official stationed in British Burma. Chief Commissioner MacKenzie, whose proposal for opium prohibition had been initially rejected, also "attach[ed] very minor importance to the collection of statistics at any precise point in time.[123]

"With all deference to the view taken by the Government of India," he tempered, his authoritative objection to opium derived from "the *consensus* [emphasis added] of voices condemning it, extending as this does through a long series of years, and emanating as we know from authorities of every shade of opinion, official and non-official, European and native."[124] Numbers had a trifling value, he opined, "when we have before us indisputable evidence as to the results of the personal knowledge and experience of such a cloud of witnesses."[125]

One knew a "morally wrecked" Burman when one saw one, Smeaton assured those who might doubt his and his Chief Commissioner's expertise. Known "morally wrecked" people included

> Kaing Hla Phru, son of Rhauk Phwe, deceased, was a rich merchant; became an opium-smoker. His father tried all in his power to make him leave off opium, but of no avail. He did no work, and died a confirmed opium-smoker in the lifetime of his father.

> Shwe Tha, aged 23, son of Aung Rhe, advocated, passed his Middle School examination and was preparing for his entrance examination; took to opium smoking and left off all study. His father tried his best to reform his son, but of no avail, and when he could not get any money for opium, he used to take away anything he could lay hold of. The father was obliged to send him away.

Htun Aung Gyaw, son of Ah Thu Ke, merchant; became opium-smoker, and when he could not get money from his parents he commenced stealing from his parents, and when they died he inherited their valuable properties, which he soon squandered; lastly, he sold his house, and became so poor that no one would receive him and was obliged to go away to the district.

Re Phaw, son of Ka La, merchant, deceased, was doing a good business, dealing in piece goods from Calcutta; became opium-smoker, stopped all his work, and devoted all his time in smoking opium, and spent all his money in opium and gambling, and died in a wretched state.[126]

And the list went on. Commonly, these accounts were "the evidence of fathers, which is very clear in establishing opium as the cause" of "doing no work," "(leaving) off all study," "stealing from . . . parents," and "d(ying) in a wretched state."[127] The "morally wrecked" were clearly well known to importune their family and kin.

Modest British officials in Burma thus laid claim to an immodest sort of expertise. They countenanced situated experiences and direct observations as a unique and authoritative form of colonial knowledge, which gained strong credibility at a time when statistical evidence was valued, but the colonial state's infrastructure was yet too weak to generate those numbers. For no one else could quite speak in the same way, for example, about the minute and almost nondescript violations that the Burmans purportedly called *beinsa* and considered crimes of a moral nature. Perhaps no other agent of Empire cared to replicate the minutiae of routine tasks or even lay claim to the mundane details that everyday administration yielded. Still, the consolidated product represented a powerful means for colonial rule in the 1890s, as it persuaded imperial administrators, politicians, and policymakers to acknowledge the special circumstances of British Burma and alter colonial law and policy accordingly. In February 1893, the Government of India approved the Chief Commissioner of Burma's request to ban the possession and use of opium by Burmans.

Lasting Significance

In 1894, British Burma established an opium monopoly with the declared objective of "arrest[ing] the growth of the habit of indulgence by the Burmese and to prevent the rising generation of the race from commencing it."[128] That prohibition began as such in 1890s Burma is remarkable for at least three reasons. First of all, a loss of revenue was expected. This was hardly a shock to the local administration but a reflection of how principles for colonial excise had been reconfigured over the course of two decades to embed a language of sacrifice into the management of local markets. G. A. Strover of Pegu Division regarded this as inevitable: "[t]o strike at the root of the evil of opium consuming, it is obvious that the sacrifice of a large proportion of opium is a *sine qua non*," he reassured his colleagues.[129] In 1891, an administrator stationed in Ma-ubin named S. H. T. de la Courneuve had already provided a template for calculating the estimated loss of annual provincial revenue as he proposed sales restrictions in and a standardized licensing system for vendors with fixed amounts of opium issues.[130] "By doing this a considerable revenue would be sacrificed," de la Courneuve admitted, "but we would show the world that we are earnest in our endeavors to suppress or restrain within proper limits the opium traffic. I have never yet met a member of the general public who believed in the sincerity of our intention with regard to this traffic; the taunt is always that Government is afraid to sacrifice revenue."[131]

Second, social pressures for banning opium weighed lightly upon the colonial administration in Burma. While officials of the Excise Department perceived a general sentiment among those considered respectable portions of the Burmese population in favor of anti-opium measures, there is little evidence to suggest that the administration sought prohibition in response to demands from this community. As one administrator, D. J. A. Campbell, pondered the possibility of indigenous support in enforcing restrictions on sales and consumption, he believed that "[n]otwithstanding the strong feeling of the Burmese against opium, I doubt whether much help can be looked for from the *lugyis* [village elders] to suppress it.[132] *Thugyis* [local headmen] and *ywathugyis* [village headmen] in the exercise of their powers as Excise Officers could do much to stop the use of opium if they are really in earnest about it," Campbell surmised.[133]

Rather, it appears that officials in Burma encountered more pressure from social groups in the colony *after* Mackenzie's 1891 inquisition was launched, which thus refined but did not prompt the 1894 reforms. Members of the Young Arakan Club in Akyab endorsed enthusiastically the measures proposed by MacKenzie at a meeting in November 1891, after his proposal for "stringent" measures were made known publicly through local newspapers.[134] Also, in the summer of 1892, a memorial with 555 "native" signatories and letters from the Burma Branch of the British Medical Association (BBMA) weighed in on a draft of the opium addict registration scheme that had been published in the Burma Gazetteer, requesting that medical practitioners and tattooers be exempt from registration, a demand that the administration accommodated.[135] Members of the SSOT were also enthusiastic about the specific reforms proposed by the local administration, bringing new attention to Burma and its opium problems, which had hitherto been dwarfed by concerns with India and China.[136]

Third, colonial Burma's turn toward banning opium began despite a prior awareness among some high-ranking officials, both in Burma and in India, of greater problems to come. "We fear this measure may be followed by extensive smuggling," worried Lord Kimberley, Secretary of State for India, even as he sanctioned the new system: "It will create a new and artificial class of criminal offences and will afford opportunities for police oppression to an extent constituting a serious evil."[137] The colonial administration was, in effect, formalizing the two different opium markets in Burma that Aitchison had identified in the 1870s: one for Burmans who registered as addicts and another open to all non-Burmans. This dual system had obvious flaws, as any Burman found eating or smoking opium without registration status became an outlaw—literally a figure outside of the administrative definition of legal consumer.

Moreover, added a new Chief Commissioner named Frederick Fryer, surely a new business would emerge to satisfy the now illegal and illicit consumption of most Burmans. It would be nearly impossible to police the boundaries between the two separate markets, Fryer pointed out, without increasing the capacity for surveillance to a dangerous extent. In addition to "the multiplication of petty offences and to increasing the powers of petty officials to harass the people," Fryer predicted, "to employ [the police] to enforce a general prohibition against the use of opium would be to arm them with another weapon of extortion, the use of which would be keenly resented by the Burmans."[138]

Nonetheless, prohibition began. A crucial force behind this bold move was the role of local administrators and their expressions of anxiety, which drew upon a slow accumulation of quasi-ethnographic evidence and partial statistics that portrayed a colony in crisis in ways requiring extraordinary redress by the colonial state. It was from deep within the bureaucratic administration that both the will and means for an anti-opium reform emerged, not least as officials affirmed that more than one-tenth of the people in their jurisdiction were ruined by opium consumption and that an epidemic of crime and social disorder was occurring under their watch. Moreover, by theorizing the causes of "moral wreckage" and demonstrating its specific applicability to Burmans, local administrators helped translate vague concerns regarding the vulnerabilities of non-Europeans into specific agendas for regulation that metropolitan officials from a distance could accept.

There is an irony to how such self-referential expertise and tenuous evidence generated the conditions of possibility for overarching reforms to imperial

governance. The bureaucrats of Burma perceived of opium problems and ascertained their magnitude against the backdrop of administrative categories
and normalcies that they were defining in spite of themselves. Claiming to know
an unfamiliar colonial world was not an easy task: even as officials went about
collecting information on Burmans and propounding causal theories linking
opium consumption to moral wreckage, the very meanings of a "Burman" and
"moral wreckage" were contested. "It is very difficult to distinguish between
physically wrecked and morally wrecked," complained B. A. N. Parrott, the
Commissioner of Arakan who had overseen the 1891 survey.[139] "In fact, many
of the officials have not understood the question," he warned. "Who is a Burman?" asked the Commissioner of Tenasserim as he prepared to order his local
officials to restrict the consumption of Burmans in his division in 1893.[140]
Smeaton quietly responded: "the definition of 'Burmese race' or 'Burman'
for the purposes of the new regulations has not yet been authoritatively decided
on."[141] The official problem of opium in Burma—a social crisis stemming from
more than 11 percent of the colony's indigenous inhabitants affected by the
moral wreckage caused by opium consumption—emerged as a reality of their
own making.

And over subsequent decades, this dynamic recurred as the British in Burma
witnessed the two main problems that administrators had anticipated in the
1890s—namely, the growth of an illicit demand for opium and a rise in reported
crime across the colony. In 1907, yet another Chief Commissioner and his administrators "discovered" a disturbing growth in the number of criminal offences since the late 1880s until the present. It appeared that a 200 percent increase over twenty years had occurred in both the amount of opium sold on
the legal non-Burman market in Burma and number of crime convictions across
the colony. The correlation was suspicious, and another colony-wide inquiry
was launched, asking local officers and jail officials to, again, weigh in on their
"opinion as to the causes of the increase in the number of criminal offenses."[142]
W. H. A. St. J. Leeds requested: "[y]ou will note particularly whether, there is,
in your opinion, any connection between the increase of crime and the increase
in the consumption of opium."[143]

Conclusion

This chapter has traced the bureaucratic construction of an official problem of
moral wreckage in late nineteenth century Burma that guided the British colonial state's introduction of an opium monopoly. From regular work managing opium emerged a shared understanding among local administrators about

the sumptuary practice of opium smoking as a cause of direct injury to families in Burma, in ways that were deemed symptomatic of a broader crisis of social order threatening the stability of colonial rule. Through a slow process of escalation within the colonial bureaucracy, petty opinions and observations about the causal effects of opium consumption on indigenous subjects became taken-for-granted realities that served as an evidentiary basis for this colony's anti-opium turn. Perceived associations between opium consumption and crimes, alongside the economic conditions that constituted their material basis, aroused the anxieties of low-level administrators in Burma. These weak actors in the colony exercised a strong influence over the emergence of one of the first and formal expressions of the British Empire's prohibitionist stance in Southeast Asia.

The next chapter examines British Malaya, focusing on the Straits Settlement of Singapore, which had its own history and set of anxieties relating to opium and prohibition. Other than a very distant shared seat of sovereign authority in London, there is very little that rendered Malaya similar to Burma in terms of their "opium question," i.e., what defined the proper role of a colonial state toward perceived problems relating to opium. The great entrepôt of Singapore hosted a naval base with strategic importance to the external defense of the empire (unlike the modest port of Akyab); the Chinese migrant community associated with opium smoking was large across the Malay Peninsula (reaching more than 50 percent of the local population in the Straits Settlements, compared with less than 1 percent in Burma); and since its inception, this particular British colony had relied heavily on taxes levied on opium consumption. As we will see, from the vantage point of local administrators, these were some of the many aspects of the colony's political economy for opium that they managed. And as there were so many possibilities for problems to emerge in the process of everyday administration over opium, it is again necessary to begin specifically in order to understand how certain tensions emerged and became politically consequential in the ways that they did.

5

Fiscal Dependency in British Malaya, 1890s–1920s

DURING THE 1920S, the British in Malaya created an opium revenue replacement reserve fund. Officially, its declared purpose was to reduce reliance on opium taxes for one of the most fiscally opium-dependent territories of Southeast Asia under European rule, by setting aside a large sum of surplus revenue to which a fixed 10 percent share of subsequent years' revenue would be added.[1] The fund was first introduced in 1925 for the Straits Settlements of Singapore, Malacca, and Penang, as well as the Malay State of Johor, and extended across the Federated Malay States by 1929.

This chapter explores the remarkable public and hidden life of this opium revenue replacement reserve fund. It represented the declared flagship of the British Empire's anti-opium turn before a skeptical international community, not least because the Straits Settlements collected more than 50 percent of its colonial revenue from taxing opium consumption, of which nearly half was used to maintain a crucial naval base near Singapore. From the perspective of metropolitan officials, this opium fund served to signal Britain's honest willingness before peer imperial powers to ban opium.[2] It was also considered novel in the realm of colonial governance, "a financial innovation of a startling nature for which, as far as we know, no precedent exists," according to contemporary observers.[3] In addition, the fund's emergence marked a less openly touted but no less significant shift for British rule across the Malay Peninsula that had global repercussions. Anchored in the Straits Settlements and especially Singapore, the opium fund and derived interest was very large—growing from 30 million Straits dollars to 37 million within the first three years of its operations—and used to finance public infrastructure projects in parts of the British Empire in the Caribbean, Africa, and Oceania.[4]

How did this arrangement emerge and evolve? Despite its multifold significance for the Malay Peninsula under British rule and interwar imperial rule more generally, the opium revenue replacement fund has not been placed front and center in existing studies. Histories of opium and empire have been slow to grapple with the meaning of opium revenue for the British in Malaya, focusing more on the anti-opium movements spurred by social activists, intellectuals in the colony, and merchant communities.[5] The exceptional works of A. J. Stockwell (1980) and Harumi Goto-Shibata (2006) have shed welcome light, showing how opium revenue figured in imperial policy discussions during the 1920s over how much the Straits Settlements should contribute to the Singapore naval base, as well as disagreements among British military officers, bureaucrats, and diplomats about what constituted the Empire's best interest and defense of reputation on the international stage. Both elucidate clearly what heavy demands for reform were being directed from those in high seats of power in London, Calcutta, and Geneva toward those administering in the Straits Settlements. Yet, it is less clear when such external voices were heeded by those on the ground, and to what extent did expressed visions for reform from afar actually matter for regulatory change at an everyday level in the colony.

This chapter argues that local administrators stationed in the Straits Settlements and moving across the Malay Peninsula generated the conditions of possibility for the opium fund to emerge. It traces a slow process through which these actors came to construct the colony's fiscal dependency on opium as an official problem. Although heavy reliance on vice taxes on opium consumption had been a longstanding issue, especially for Singapore founded on a principle of free trade that precluded the collection of customs duties, this had been generally accepted as an inevitable condition of the colony. Around the 1890s, however, this dependency was becoming conceived of administratively as a source of concern relating to the fragile legitimacy of indirect taxes levied on Chinese residents of the colony, and by the 1920s, it escalated into acute anxiety about what legacies British colonial rule would leave. In the process of addressing small challenges arising in the everyday management of opium revenue—ranging from deciphering murky accounts of contracted tax collectors, addressing direct complaints and perceived unhappiness from a diverse opium-consuming constituency and its critics in the colony, policing infractions, and worrying about contraband—local administrators came to construct fiscal dependency as a politically actionable cause and design a form of state intervention that centered on the importance of substituting opium revenue. The way by which they narrowed the scope of possible options for state action and internally justified it enabled the opium fund to emerge as a viable reform in 1925.

Understanding the micropolitics of the colonial bureaucracy gives reason to rethink prevailing narratives about the opium revenue replacement reserve fund as well as the significance of opium prohibition for the British colonial state during the interwar years. The early 1920s marked an eventful moment in the development of international drug control regimes, when the highest of imperial minds were especially occupied with the old European opium colonies in Southeast Asia. The 1924–1925 Geneva Opium Conferences represented an arena for empires to exercise "discretionary publicity," by openly disclosing information about unseemly conducts in ways that could damage each other's reputation and credible standing.[6] Britain stood to face criticism regarding how much and how long it had profited from the opium trade and consumption. "The situation was so embarrassing that Britain decided to reconsider the opium policies of her empire," according to Goto-Shibata, that on January 1925, Viscount Cecil of Chelwood declared Britain's commitment to ban the use of prepared opium altogether in her colonies, upon which "the government of the Straits Settlements decided to introduce new policies" that included the opium revenue replacement reserve fund.[7] Relying primarily on archives of the Colonial Office, its correspondences with the Straits Settlements, and Cabinet meeting records, Goto-Shibata argues that the opium fund was launched in response to metropolitan directives, while situating it amid disagreements between the Colonial and Home Offices, as well as tensions separating the colonial Governor and Legislative Council of the Straits Settlements from the metropolitan government in London.

This chapter reveals that this story is not necessarily incorrect but incomplete, using a diverse set of administrative records including reports of the Government Monopolies Department; commission interviews with opium-related consumers and suppliers across the Malay Peninsula; writings of colonial administrators including the original architect of the opium fund paired with records of metropolitan-based actors in the Colonial, Home, and Foreign Offices, and Treasury; as well as the papers of the Crown Agents who held the opium fund. It traces an ongoing process of problem construction within the colonial bureaucracy, for which external pressures served as important catalysts but do not necessarily explain how the policy solution took the shape that it did as an opium revenue reserve replacement fund. In addition, the hitherto overlooked official records of local administrators show how as opium consumption ceased as a tax base, the accumulated monies it had generated evolved into a source of investment wealth for the British Empire. The emergence of the 1925 opium fund entailed a profoundly transformative process for the colonial state that would integrate the Straits Settlements and indirectly ruled Malay States on issues of opium, while forging financial links among far-flung territories under British rule.

Singapore 1925

The Singapore summer of 1925 was an irritable one. Traffic troubles coupled with complaints about public order arose as rickshaw drivers quarreled on Battery Road and Chinese *samsengs* "terrorized" residents in Cecil Street for money.[8] It was also a sickly time, especially for migrants living in the Tanjong Pagar area slums hard hit by tuberculosis: "As many as 2,000 have died in one year in Singapore and that does not tell the whole sad tale, for a good many spend their last earnings to pay for a passage home so that their bones may rest in the land which gave them birth," reported one local paper.[9] Among the Chinese urban migrant workers who remained, unemployment rates were high while manual labor arduous, and ways for "temporary escape from the embarrassment and horror of life in their society in Singapore" included opium consumption.[10]

It had been the year that urban improvements were supposed to happen, with the Singapore Traction Company scheduled to modernize the city's transportation with new trolleybuses. It was also a year of heightened expectations for wealth and prosperity as Malaya slowly pulled out of its post–World War I slump, thanks to increasing global demand for the colony's main exports—tin, rubber, and petroleum—alongside a boost to Singapore's trade activity with the opening of the Johor Causeway (1923).[11] It was a time of cautious optimism for better years to come, more so as possibilities for the Singapore Improvement Fund were debated, which would hopefully deal with the city's slums that were "death-breeding rat holes which shelter tens of thousands of the people worth of this place."[12] The colony's budget was finally running a surplus and spending was set to increase for urban transportation, housing, and sanitation.

Thus, many were unhappy in August 1925, when the colonial administration announced that the Straits Settlements would set aside 30 million Straits dollars in a reserve fund, to be supplemented every year by 10 percent of the colony's total tax revenue. This was a fund prepared "[i]n the event of the Colony falling upon evil days owing to serious reduction in the opium revenue" at a time when government opium sales represented 75 percent of the Straits Settlement's

excise tax and internal revenue, or 55 percent of total revenue.[13] It was acknowledged in retrospect by metropolitan officials as "a financial innovation of a
startling nature for which, so far as we know, no precedent exists."[14] At the time
in the colony, it dismayed the Singapore Chamber of Commerce, which believed
that "there is no time for hoarding" but that now was "a time for spending."[15]
Tan Cheng Lock, a Malayan member of the Legislative Council, objected that
this measure would withhold "large sums of money required to be spent on such
work as the improvement of the disgraceful slums of Singapore."[16] Others on
the Council agreed: W. H. Thorne called it a "retrograde step to . . . cut down
our budget in such a manner," while for P. Simpson, the reserve fund entailed
"prospective loss to hamper the progress of the Colony and handicap the present for the sake of a distant future."[17]

Despite such objections, the colonial government officially introduced the
Straits Settlement's opium revenue replacement reserve fund in 1925. The proximate impetus came from the international convening in Geneva, when Britain
faced accusations from peer empires as "being influenced by money considerations in postponing a desirable social reform."[18] The British representative
instructed the Governor of the Straits Settlements "to propound a scheme for
building up a fund to replace the opium revenue."[19] The Governor in turn asked
the colony's Treasurer, a man named Arthur Meek Pountney, to design this measure. In this regard, Malaya's opium fund emerged amid reputational pressures
on Britain in a world where anti-opium norms were more firmly expressed in
international arenas compared with what nineteenth-century Burma had faced
(Chapter 4). At this level, the rationale for a revenue reserve fund was simple. It
was necessary to prepare for the possibility that opium revenue might disappear and show "that the local governments on the ground were honestly prepared to meet that situation."[20]

However, the emergence of this opium fund must also be understood in light
of disagreements over public spending and urban order in Singapore, which
drew upon older and unresolved anxieties about revenue and colonial governance across the Straits Settlements and British rule over the Malay Peninsula
more generally. For on the one hand, there had been several occasions since the
1900s when Britain had faced external criticism on matters of opium trade and
consumption in the Far East, without the colonial authorities taking action to
close down the drug's commercial life. On the other hand, for administrators
concerned with 1920s Malaya, the felt pressures of a moralizing world community were real but not urgent concerns. There was not an immediate sense that
Britain's Far East colonies would need to abandon opium revenue any time soon.

For instance, in early 1921, the Colonial Office made a case for Malaya, along with Hong Kong, to receive separate representation at international conferences in light of "special interests" based on their insular location, large share of migrants, risks of native discontent and smuggling from banning opium, as well as high revenue dependency.[21] The Colonial Office reminded the British representative to Geneva that it "deplor[ed] any drastic or ill-considered action in prematurely suppressing the opium traffic in the Eastern Colonies."[22] And after the Geneva Conferences, even once the opium revenue reserve fund was well in place, administrators such as Walter Ellis could confidently state in 1930 that "[m]y own view, based on a long experience with this matter, and a knowledge of the general feeling at Geneva on the subject is that the Straits Settlements will continue, for a very long time to come, to draw a substantial revenue from opium."[23]

The summer of 1925 was thus both a decisive and incomplete moment of change for British Malaya. Administrative resolve for the opium reserve fund was fueled not simply by an urgency pressed from London and beyond, but also alongside a sense of opportunity to address challenges that those stationed across the Malay Peninsula had long struggled with—the tax officials and financial experts, immigration officers, and customs and excise administrators tasked with the colony's everyday management. Their small world of bureaucratic work had moved at a swifter pace than that of the global anti-opium agitators, and by the 1920s local officials had already rehearsed many arguments for and against the defensibility of opium revenue, while considering myriad possible alternatives.

Compared with late nineteenth century Burma examined in the previous chapter, Malaya in the early twentieth century was more alive with official sensibilities about the harms of opium and its debated defensibility. Treasurer Arthur Pountney, as he prepared to announce the revenue reserve fund in 1925, noted that for the past thirty years "reams have been written and volumes spoken on opium smoking as a dangerous vice and almost an equal amount has been written and spoken in the attempt to prove that opium smoking is a relatively harmless relaxation."[24] He was unequivocal: "This is clearly not the time nor the place to debate the question of whether it is necessary on physical, moral, or ethical grounds to put a stop to opium smoking."[25] Rather the question at stake was about fiscal dependency—namely, British Malaya's longstanding reliance on opium revenue that had come to be seen as a problem worth solving by a colonial state. To understand how it emerged, it is necessary to begin with Singapore, the richest of the Straits Settlements.

The Early Years

One of the earliest formulations of Malaya's opium revenue question occurred with the founding of Singapore (1819), between the competing visions of Lieutenant Governor Stamford Raffles and William Farquhar toward taxing vice in the new island colony. Farquhar served as the first Resident of Singapore, the chief administrative officer for the colony; and he introduced a British-run tax farm for opium that followed the East India Company's approach in Penang and Malacca that sanctioned the sale and distribution of opium as a type of local industry along with spirituous liquors and gambling dens.[26] He reasoned that in Singapore, already existing markets for Malays entertained by cockfighting, Chinese who indulged in gaming, as well as established tastes for intoxicants, gave reason to normalize these as economic activities and extract much needed revenue for managing the port. For instance, during Farquhar's tenure, a pauper hospital that cared for the transient and impoverished ill was established in a shed in the Singapore cantonment, using revenue from sales licenses for opium, arrack, and gambling.[27]

Farquhar was dismissed abruptly in 1823 by Raffles who disagreed with what he considered crude pragmatism on part of the Resident: "I have no hesitation in saying that [raising revenue on the retail sale of opium] is highly objectionable and inapplicable to the principles on which the establishment at Singapore is founded," Raffles informed Farquhar.[28] The Lieutenant Governor had dreamed of an "enlightened island experiment" where acting magistrates were to observe a *Law of the Settlements* that would not "endanger the safety or liberty of person or the security of property," and pursue "a public institution or source of expense" only when "the benefit . . . was obvious to the enlightened part at least, if not to the whole body of the community."[29] And this benefit, Raffles decided, was best served by the absence of what he called corrupting vices, such as gaming and cockfighting, that caused fraud, robbery as well as the use of intoxicants, which endangered the "community" because "the indulgence in that vice . . . [led] to acts of dishonesty."[30] The Malays' cockfights and Chinese gaming should be banned, and opium and spirituous liquors repressed through heavy taxes.[31]

Raffles' idealism would fail in the decades to come. Variations on Farquhar's vision prevailed as opium became the most profitable of commodities for British Singapore's tax farming system. In its first few years of operation, the Singapore farm's annual rents from opium fluctuated and officials calculated its share as anywhere between 30 and 49 percent of local revenue. From the 1830s

onward until the tax farming system ended, reported rents stabilized and seldom fell below 40 percent; and at peak years in the 1850s, more than 50 percent
of taxes were collected from opium sales in the Straits Settlements.[32]

During these early years, heavy reliance on opium revenue did not much
trouble local administrators who regarded the drug trade as an inevitable condition of the colony. To woo merchants—British, Dutch, Bugis, and country
traders—to Singapore, Farquhar's temporary replacement in 1823 was urged
to take care not to interfere in "the most perfect Freedom of Trade for this
Article."[33] Successors were sensitive to any semblance of regulatory interference
that might inconvenience and deter traders passing through Singapore, a free
port that did not levy customs duties and limited taxation to levies on houses
in the town of Singapore property and fees collected from licenses to sell liquor,
opium, and operate gambling venues.[34] With regard to opium, particular care
was taken to separate taxes on opium sold and consumed in Singapore from its
movement in and out of the port. However, it was not just Singapore's free port
status that fashioned administrative conceptions of the natural fiscal state of a
colony sustained by opium revenue. There were two additional considerations
that weighed upon local administrators.

Malaya Unlike Burma

One concerned military expenses associated with Singapore. Until the late
1860s, the Straits Settlements was under what administrators called the "Indian
regime"—a jurisdiction under the British East India Company's Board of Direc-
tors until 1830, followed by the Presidency of Bengal until 1851, and thereafter
the Government of India—and paid for the upkeep of a military garrison and
coal station located in Singapore, which ranged between 27 and 67 percent of
local revenue.[35] The Straits Settlements became a Crown Colony in 1867, newly
overseen by the Colonial Office and its military payments were reduced to
17 percent.[36] Still, this remained a substantive amount, not least because Singapore's free port status continued to give limited leeway for raising tax revenue. Local administrators had many reasons to see opium revenue as all the
more necessary, especially after the opening of the Suez Canal (1869) quickened the pace of economic life through the Straits of Malacca, at once inten-
sifying Singapore's strategic value and increasing its naval defense costs.[37] By
the early twentieth century, the Straits Settlements were making the largest contribution to the Imperial Exchequer of all Crown Colonies at 20 percent of its
gross revenue, of which opium revenue accounted for more than half.[38] The

colony's administrators argued frequently that these payments hindered their ability to provide public infrastructure. In addition to claiming exemptions for harbor improvement and telephone- and railroad-related gains, British authorities in the Straits Settlements cited the tendency of opium revenue for violent fluctuations and possibilities of decline under international pressures as reasons to lower military contributions.[39]

A second concern for the local administration was the migrant Chinese. The 1880s had seen a rapid increase in the yearly number of immigrants entering Singapore, doubled from less than 50,000 in 1881 to upwards of 100,000 by the end of the decade, a number that would continue to rise to 214,000 on the eve of World War I.[40] Unlike in Burma, the British in Malaya encountered the Chinese as a migrant majority and created a Chinese Protectorate (1877) and later Chinese Affairs Department that specialized in addressing complaints and welfare issues relating to Chinese residents.[41] Compared with Akyab and Rangoon, where idioms of mobile foreignness had forged anxieties about Chinese traders using opium to prey on vulnerable indigenous populations, in Singapore, administrators saw the "Chinamen" as less strange, their opium entanglements less worrisome, especially for migrant workers engaged in arduous manual labor. Compared with the sustained attention that the Burmese and Arakanese received in Burma, the indigenous Malay figured less centrally in discussions relating to opium consumption.[42] Rather, those managing Singapore and other major ports of the Malay Peninsula focused on opium smoking among the Chinese, but saw it as an issue meriting little official reason for state intervention.

In the previous chapter, when popular opium consumption for Burmans was banned and registration introduced in 1894, British officials were assuming state control over the market without strong pressures from anti-opium groups based in Burma's local society. In contrast, officials in Malaya would face demands from influential Straits Chinese and merchant groups in Singapore, Penang, as well as Kedah, who called for the colonial state to restrict the free opium market and register consumers, citing opium's harms to the Chinese inhabitants.[43] Yet the colonial state would wait until 1909 to centralize control and until the 1920s before starting registration. In 1890s Malaya, the time was not yet right for those on the ground.

Delays in introducing state regulation over popular opium consumption were partly due to a general acceptance of Chinese-specific spheres of commercial activity in the colony, as enclave economies that followed logics unfamiliar to but acceptable for the British official mind and practices of profit-making that included the recruitment, management, and capturing of labor through opium. For instance, the Chinese coolie who bought opium, smoked it, and bought more represented a given fixture on gambier and pepper plantations, and later in the tin mines that employed migrant workers from China. Abuses were the subject of some attention, but administrators considered the management of social ills arising from opium consumption as a distinctive Chinese affair. A certain opaqueness to Chinese ways of overseas social and economic life was accepted, all the more so when it involved activities such as secret societies and informal policing arrangements that were underwriting the very profitable opium tax farms of the Straits Settlements, especially in Singapore.[44]

Throughout the nineteenth century, the Singapore farm was a dynamic institution, both driven by and riddled with competition among groups divided by kinship ties, fictive clans, as well as strategic factions that formed locally over the monopoly privilege to import, sell, and distribute opium.[45] The tax farm was controlled by the Straits-born Chinese until 1843 until they lost their bid to a Hokkien from Penang and then a Hokkien–Teochew syndicate in 1847, which merged the tax farm with Johor. In 1870, a grand coalition was formed and broadened the reach of the Singapore–Johor farm to Riau and Malacca.[46] In 1886, the license was resecured by a Straits Chinese family that also made a successful bid over the Hong Kong farm, launching an "internationalized system of Chinese capital" capable of moving off shore and circulating freely, extending to "farms in Shanghai, Batavia, Deli, Bangkok, and Saigon."[47] The tax farmers maintained order and controlled smuggling by employing a private police force (*chintengs*) and a network of informants that in Singapore in the 1880s numbered approximately eighty.[48] The Singapore farm's geographic expansion was coupled by the enthusiasm of Chinese entrepreneurs across and beyond the Straits Settlements, willing to invest in a lucrative opium business.

In turn, British administrative perceptions of the Chinese were colored strongly through the lens of the Singapore tax farm's profitability, which was ascertained indirectly by the amount that the tax farmer and his competitors were willing to bid for a license to monopolize the market. Local administrators invited tenders "[t]o feel the pulse of the farming community and find out what the approximate value of the farm is."[49] This was an imperfect mechanism, not only for assessing the value of the tax farm but also for gaining information about a Chinese-run opium market in a British colony—what was the nature of demand, who were the consumers, how profits were turned, as well as why did fraud and smuggling occur when they did.[50] Yet, such vagueness was left undisturbed, in part because license fees paid by the Singapore tax farmer generated welcome excise revenue.

Lack of official knowledge about the financial workings of the tax farm also served strategic means for exercising plausible deniability over the colony's limited fiscal basis, especially when administrators faced increasing calls for military contributions. In 1891, for instance, the Colonial Office had sought to double Singapore's military contributions, a measure that met with strong objections by local administrators who cited revenue that was "precarious, depending among other sources, upon the opium farms, which are becoming less and less productive."[51] The relative downward (and upward) trends of tax farm productivity served as a malleable fact for the local administration, as they did not have direct access to the Chinese-run tax farmer's accounting books and could plausibly claim an inability to verify his syndicate's profit margins and expenses.[52] As late as 1903, the colony's Governor Frank Swettenham would acknowledge to the Colonial Office that "no individual and no Department has made any study of the question and there is no one with experience to whom to appeal for advice on the subject."[53] The Secretary for Chinese Affairs who dealt directly with the farm licensing process also acknowledged that "[t]ry as one will, one has only a very hazy knowledge of what the Farms are worth, and it is only when the tenders are in that one gets reliable knowledge of what they are probably worth."[54]

It is difficult to pinpoint a precise moment when permissible haziness became a worry about murkiness concerning the Singapore tax farmer's bookkeeping and Chinese opium business arrangements. However, there were traces of faltering confidence on the part of a few administrators around 1903, when a small change to their usual approach to licensing the Straits Settlements' opium tax farms had unexpected results.

The Discovery

In July 1903, a joint auction for the Singapore and Penang opium tax farm licenses took place. The standard practice had been for the Governor's office to issue a public call for tenders for a three-year license to manage the farms, awarded to the highest bidder. A man named Gan Ngoh Bee was prepared to bid $185,000 Straits dollars per month for the license. Gan was the previous farmer for Penang who led a syndicate of Hokkien investors, in partnership with Foo Choo Choon, the Singapore farmer who commanded a similar group of men from Canton.

Before the auction, however, Gan was called aside privately by George Thompson Hare, the Secretary for Chinese Affairs.[55] Hare promised Gan the Penang farm if he raised his bid to $190,000. Gan agreed. But at the auction, the Governor's office received eight additional tenders, including a very large one that amounted to $260,000 by a man named Chung Thye Phin. Hare thus informed Gan, "Your estimate was not right. The other tenders sent in are very high, and the Government cannot give the Farm to you."[56] Gan complained to William Taylor, the Colonial Secretary who then "asked me [Gan] to furnish him [Taylor] with figures on which my calculations as to the Farm being worth only $190,000 were based."[57] Gan complied: "I furnished him with all my figures, I showed him it was impossible to work the Farm at a profit at any price over $190,000."[58] And in the end, "Mr. Taylor offered me [Gan] half the Farm" for the price of $217,000 while awarding "the other half . . . to Mr. Chung Thye Phin, whose tender had been the highest."[59] Gan thus obtained the Penang farm for $32,000 more per month than he had originally planned and was made to partner with Chung, the new Singapore farmer. Governor Frank Swettenham happily informed the Colonial Office that a near 100 percent increase to the Straits Settlements farm rents could be expected as a result of this successful auction, and how "[i]t [was] cause for congratulation that the Colony had not only obtained such a large increase, but that for the next three years, the farms are in the hands of the men best qualified to hold them."[60]

Gan Ngoh Bee's dealings with William Taylor as such capture a moment when one of the Straits Settlements' most influential Chinese merchants opened his accounting books to the British authorities and the colony's foremost specialist in Chinese affairs, G. T. Hare, interfered in the tax farm auctions.[61] This incident would have unanticipated repercussions.

For soon after reacquiring the Penang farm, Gan wanted to raise the retail price for opium, likely to cover the more expensive rents he owed. The administration agreed and approved a 36 percent price increase for 1904—from $2.20 per tahil to $3—reasoning that "opium was so indispensable to the Chinese that no reasonable increase in price would affect its consumption."[62] To the contrary, however, in 1904, the joint Singapore and Penang tax farm's sales plummeted dramatically by 32 percent, a terrible loss, according to Gan, who declared he was nearly bankrupt and petitioned the Governor's office for a reduction to his monthly rents.

Briskly, the new Secretary for Chinese Affairs, Warren Delabere Barnes, began "enquir[ing] how far the loss of the Farm was real and how far it was fictitious."[63] Initially, Barnes was puzzled as "I could furnish no explanation" for why such a large loss in revenue occurred, "and could only think that some organized smuggling was going on" in response to the raised prices.[64] But this was doubtful, he decided, given the Chinese way of policing contraband in the Straits Settlements: men like Gan had their *chintengs* who were remarkably efficient as revenue peons.

Most of Barnes' twenty years with the Malay Civil Service had been spent managing Chinese affairs, with a special focus on mines.[65] So perhaps it is not surprising that in searching for answers he paid attention to the tin mines where Chinese laborers were known to consume much opium in the western Malay States. Barnes noted that when the Penang–Singapore farm had raised its prices in 1904, Perak, Selangor, and Negeri Sembilan reduced their opium imports that same year. Looking back further to 1898, Barnes saw a similar pattern recur, which seemed applicable to the Straits Settlements as well. In Malacca, where tapioca was a staple good for the Chinese, the opium farm's sales had decreased during months when tapioca prices were high, while in Singapore and Penang, opium sales dropped in the summer because "in July, many Chinese must buy durians instead of *chandoo* [opium for smoking]."[66]

"I have found the true cause," Barnes decided.[67] Opium on the Chinese market across Malaya, he argued, was like that of "any other luxury, when the price is dearer, less is used."[68] Contrary to "the old fallacy that the Chinaman must have his opium," Chinese migrant workers chose to consume opium depending on two factors: its price and their wages. When the price rose, the Chinese opium consumers bought less because they could not afford it, which had happened in an extreme way in 1903. "I am convinced," Barnes informed his colleagues, "that the direct and immediate effect of the increased sales prices ... was not only a reduction of consumption by many habitual smokers but an actual abandonment of the habit by a large number."[69]

Barnes was not alone in this assessment. Working alongside, but not together with him, was another local administrator attentive to patterns of Chinese opium consumption. His name was Arthur Meek Pountney, Selangor's Assistant Protector of Chinese—who would eighteen years later rise to the enviable rank of Colonial Treasurer and design the opium revenue replacement fund—and he had also been watching tin mines and opium purchasing patterns, as well as the movement and behavior of Chinese workers in his jurisdiction with a keen eye. "I am extremely fond of figures," professed the Oxford graduate in mathematics, as he produced what was, in 1908, seen by fellow officials as "the most complete ... the most instructive set of tables and notes" regarding Chinese migrants and opium consumption in the colony's administrative history.[70]

"I am very much a figure man," Pountney emphasized. "It is one of my particular hobbies."[71] His calculations, "all done out of office hours," showed that between 1898 and 1907, Selangor's population had increased by 89 percent but with only an accompanying 27.4 percent increase in opium sales, indicating that general opium consumption had decreased over the past decade.[72] This was a surprising finding, in part because this major tin-producing Malay state attracted large numbers of migrant workers from China and most officials had assumed that 80–90 percent of the tin miners were opium consumers. However, Pountney had sent district officials to different mines, "letting them select at absolute random" and directly count the number of opium using Chinese coolies in each.[73] Selangor's mines varied, he learned, and none reported general use but different proportions of smokers—ranging from 4 to 51 percent—of the total labor force, depending on the type of migrant worker and wage system the mine used. There were five types of workers: the *mandors* and *pong shaus,* the *kong si kong,* the *naichiang* coolies, the *teng kungs,* and the tribute laborers; and a mine using *naiching* labor for instance, would pay very low wages for the first 8 hours of work and then "tremendously high wages for the 2 hours overtime."[74] According to Pountney, a steady supply of opium for the Chinese coolie hardly seemed necessary, as the intensity of his labor was hardly constant. Moreover, certain mines would not supply opium at all, including those located far away from the port of Kuala Lumpur town because of high transportation costs and risks of loss. Contrary to popular myths that mine owners or managers always provided their workers with opium and indeed forced addiction to breed docile and indebted laborers, Pountney argued "they won't let them [workers] run into debt for anything."[75]

Beyond the mines, Chinese opium consumption was driven by supply and demand, elaborated Pountney. In December 1907, he had personally visited 223 shops in Kuala Lumpur and met more than 500 people working in the town.[76] The many foremen, fitters, boiler-makers, engine-drivers, turners, rivetters, blacksmiths, moulders, carpenters, painters, and strikers affirmed that opium was not a necessity for the everyday Chinese: on average, only 9 percent identified as smokers, and across occupations, the range was wide: from carpenters representing fewer than 2 percent to nearly 22 percent of the blacksmiths and boiler makers. The most opium smokers were found among the shopkeepers of blacksmiths (71 percent) and daching makers (67 percent), while the goldsmiths, tin-ore purchasers, fruiterers, and drapers seldom used at all. By Pountney's observations, the town scavengers were the only type of worker in Kuala Lumpur that reached the impossible number of 90 percent as opium smokers;

but he could not find a similar number for the jinrickisha pullers, reputed to be the worst addicts to the habit: of the 7 depôts in the busy Ampang and Batu roads in Kuala Lumpur, among the 116 pullers, only 21 (or 18%) were smokers.[77]

Much like Barnes, Pountney saw opium consumption for the Chinese as not a downward spiral toward addiction but an economic choice. He further analogized opium for the hardworking Chinaman to alcohol for the industrious Englishman, as a substance that both could quit if necessary. He himself had experienced this possibility, as "I objected when I was at Oxford to not being allowed to drink my whisky and soda on going into training, but I did without it."[78] More so than Barnes, however, Pountney expressed skepticism about a hitherto assumed fundamental "Chinese" affinity for opium and the idea of shared Chinese traits that determined individual behavior more generally: "The Chinaman has a very poor power of combination, but he has very fair ideas of the liberty of the subject."[79] According to Pountney "[t]here are so many races amongst them which do not naturally combine; take one mining kongsi as an instance, you will probably find half-a-dozen what one might almost take as totally different races in it, and they do not naturally combine."[80]

By way of explaining the events of 1903 and underlying dynamics of the colonial opium economy, Barnes and Pountney were contributing to a shift in the British official mind regarding Chinese consumption, one that replaced a presumed natural affinity for opium by a foreign collective with a logic of economic rationality exercised differently among its composite members. It was an alternative perspective that was neither carefully planned nor guided by strategic intent, and indeed, its significance was hardly evident to the administrators themselves at the time. Rather, this discursive shift was felt in retrospect, through the constraints it imposed, slowly and steadily, across several domains of colonial opium policy.

First and in the short term, Barnes' assessment affected the operations of the Singapore farm, as he concluded that Gan's losses were real in 1904, resulting from the high prices that had deterred opium consumption among Chinese inhabitants in Singapore and Penang as well as workers in the Federated Malay States. For 1905 and 1906, the British administration for the Straits Settlements reduced Gan's monthly farm rents from $217,000 to $190,000, his original bid.[81]

Second and relatedly, Pountney's account of fractured Chinese migrant groups bolstered the local administration's confidence in doubting the sincerity of social demands for banning opium within the colony and withstanding metropolitan pressures for reform. In 1906, organized protests citing the social injury that the Chinese in the colony suffered due to opium took place in Singapore, Penang, and spread to Kedah. Influential Straits Chinese leaders called on the colonial authorities to restrict opium smoking, ban opium in brothels, as well as abolish the tax farms.[82] Outside of Malaya, Empire's politicians worried about these developments. When the Liberal MP Theodore Taylor learned that "in some places, as many as 2,000 Chinese assembled to aid anti-opium associations," he warned the House of Commons that this could indicate more widespread discontent among the Chinese in this colony.[83] Moreover, he reminded his peers, "[l]ast year saw the beginning of a great reform movement in the East," referring to China's 1906 imperial opium suppression decree.[84] The Foreign Office was about to accept an invitation to Shanghai for the 1909 opium conference at the behest of the United States, whose criticism of the Far East opium trade was increasingly strident. Maybe, worried some in London, these anti-opium movements in Malaya were on the right side of history, the British Empire on the wrong. "I do not see how the introduction of apparently ever-increasing quantities [sic] of opium into a British Colony and Protectorate can any longer be defended," the Colonial Secretary confided to John Anderson, the governor of the Straits Settlements, as he tasked the latter with appointing a commission in 1907 to conduct a "searching enquiry which may, it is hoped, result in pointing out the best steps to be taken under the local circumstances for minimizing and eventually eradicating the evil."[85]

However, many administrators in the colony did not share these anxieties, echoing Pountney's view of the Chinese in Malaya as composed of "totally different races" who "do not naturally combine."[86] "I do not think that either the idea or the movement is indigenous," explained Charles Saunders to the Anderson Commission.[87] Both—the idea and movement—were machinations of "zealous and religious people," he argued, especially two groups in Singapore: the Anti-Opium Society and the Chinese Chamber of Commerce.[88] The former, he believed was led by the Reverend Tay Sek Tin "who is of the same congregation as the Reverend J. A. B. Cook," a Protestant missionary who took strong interest in moral reform through Christian values, while the latter was just a few firms, hardly the entirety of a Chinese community it purported to represent.[89] Indeed, insisted Saunders, the anti-opium movement could hardly "represent the ideas of the entire Chinese community," as "there is no public opinion in our sense of the word in that way amongst the Chinese."[90]

Third and relatedly, on the official "discovery" of rational Chinese opium users, the colonial administration adopted the view that opium consumption across Malaya had been decreasing since 1903, caused by the shock of the Penang–Singapore farm's mismanaged sales. Thus, argued those on the ground, it was unnecessary to officially ban opium because a decline was already in process.

One way to understand this administrative argument is as a defense against social and metropolitan pressures to abolish a system sustaining the commercial life of opium. And indeed, such external criticisms did weigh upon the small set of officials managing the Straits Settlements' opium farms. To appease critics and worried authorities in London, the colony formally ended the opium farming system, and replaced it on January 1, 1910 with a state monopoly in Singapore that was extended to Penang and Malacca as well as the Federated Malay States by 1911. However, local administrators were not guided solely by reputational concerns and little changed in the actual operations of opium sales, which remained in the hands of private distributors licensed to run opium shops. For London was far and the idealism expressed by social reformers, Chinese and British alike, misunderstood the everyday realities of colonial government, opined men like Pountney and Barnes. The more pressing issue, from their perspective, was a foreseeable loss in opium revenue.

During the 1900s, internal estimates placed the yearly rents collected for the opium farms at more than 50 percent of the colony's tax revenue, and of that sizeable share, the Singapore farm loomed largest. If this revenue was lost, how could it be made up for, especially in the untaxable Straits Settlements?[91] How could the Crown Colony pay for its yearly military contributions? With what remaining funds would Singapore and its port operate without the indirect taxes on opium sales that paid for the lighthouse's electricity fees, for the maintenance fees of the docks? As we have seen, these were old questions for local administrators. But now, with the perceived reality of declining Chinese opium consumption, a once necessary reliance on opium revenue was becoming a worrisome problem of fiscal dependency.

Consumption and Revenue

How could British Malaya substitute opium revenue? When the Anderson Commission put the question to forty-two individuals in 1907, several possibilities were identified: stamp fees and kerosene taxes, higher excise taxes on tobacco and alcohol, taxes on inherited estates or "death duties," poll or income taxes, or maybe a state monopoly over pawnbroking and taxing money lenders.[92] However, for the colonial administration, none were viable. A tobacco tax, for instance, would require building new bonded warehouses and risked annoying traders, while taxes on kerosene, stamps, and money lending would be too small to compensate for the large loss of opium revenue.

Several nonadministrators pointed to Chinese-specific taxes, based on the idea that consumers who had generated the revenue bore responsibility for its loss. One explicit formulation of this type of sumptuary obligation came from David Galloway, a British psychiatrist and head of the Singapore Medical Association, who argued that because declining opium consumption would most benefit the health and welfare of the Chinese, they should bear the costs of this effort.[93] Echoed in local newspapers supportive of British merchant interests, this notion of Chinese improvement from decreased consumption translated into reason for gratitude to British rule—directly, by attributing declining opium use to imperial efforts to suppress the drug and more generally, in crediting the improved livelihoods of the Chinese in Malaya to the economic opportunities that the colonial state had provided.

It followed that the Chinese owed a debt to the British that should be squared through opium revenue. For instance, in 1908, an editorial from the *Singapore Free Press and Mercantile Adviser* insisted that it was "clearly . . . the duty of government, through some readjustment of taxation, to secure from that particular section of the population, the proportion of revenue that had failed to be derived from opium."[94] This was, opined the author, a matter of equality, merely requiring the numerical majority of opium consumers across Malaya, who were mostly "Chinese and Chinese alien at that" to pay their fair share of taxes, as did "Europeans in the colony [who] pay excise taxation on spirits and beer, and the native population also contributes to the liquor excise." Public opinion as such, favored revenue substitution measures that included a poll tax on migrants from China, taxes on their remittances and savings, as well as an income tax on wealthy Chinese inhabitants who owned property in the Straits Settlements and "have settled here under the protection of our flag to their own immense advantage."

These were spurious arguments, countered spokesmen for part of the Chinese community in the Straits Settlements. For Lim Boon Keng, the well-respected Peranakan doctor and social reformer, an obvious tension was how the Chinese were being called on to pay for losses in opium revenue.[95] According to proponents of Chinese targeted taxes, a reduced demand for the drug was either a natural decline due to the economic improvement of the colony or the result of government policies to suppress a social evil. If the former, Lim reasoned, one must consider that it was the Chinese migrants, especially the opium-consuming coolies, who had contributed to that economic growth through their labor; and if the latter, the colonial government surely had not acted on behalf of foreigners, i.e., those who were "Chinese and Chinese alien at that." Rather, opium consumption was a general social problem, and thus all inhabitants bore a responsibility to pay for its eradication. "I do not think, for instance, that the Chinese should be taxed because cholera breaks out and extra doctors have to be engaged," explained Lim. Likewise, if the colony was able to eradicate opium consumption it was hardly to the advantage of the Chinese only, but "to the general advantage of the State."[96]

Lim's perspective resonated with others who opposed the idea of opium revenue substitution from Chinese pockets. "From what I have heard from the Chinese with whom I have spoken, they seem to think that they will pay, if Government introduces any new tax. Although they don't say the tax should be confined to Chinamen, I don't think they would like a tax of that nature," warned Ho Siak Kuan, a translator for the Chinese Protectorate in Singapore.[97] From the Selangor Anti-opium Society, Choo Cheng Khay argued that levying a tax on savings sent back to China was unfair because it did not touch all classes alike.[98]

Alien Chinese, coolie workers, the wealth of colonial Malaya, and the British flag. For involved administrators, these issues represented constraints on the possibility of levying Chinese-specific taxes to substitute opium revenue. "[T]o produce anything like the same revenue [from opium], the poll tax would have to be $10 or $15 per head," worried Charles James Saunders, the Acting Secretary for Chinese Affairs from Singapore.[99] William Cowan, the Protector of Chinese in Perak, added that such a poll tax had been attempted twenty years ago in his state, as well as a similar tax called the "hospital dollar," which required Chinese migrants to contribute a dollar to the government hospital that provided care for them.[100] Both had failed "[b]ecause the Chinese did not like the collection of money, as they said, 'on their tails.'" Could Chinese workers be taxed as they exited the Federated Malay States? "No, I do not think so," Cowan replied, pointing out "this would be a poll-tax in a different form."[101]

If practicality hindered a poll tax, politics shaped the everyday administrator's reluctance toward imposing a general income tax that would fall mostly on the wealthy Chinese. This "delicate method of taxation," according to E. M. Baker, the State Treasurer for Selangor, was "fifty if not one hundred years in advance of the times" in a colony where inhabitants lacked the education and had yet to "attain that degree of civilization."[102] It would lead to "dishonesty and deception" and drive away "capital business, trade and people," while the Chinese themselves would certainly evade it, leaving the burden to fall "most unjustly on government officials, salaried men, and property owners."[103] The possibility of a Chinese-specific income tax was also raised but swiftly dismissed because it concerned the basic status of migrant Chinese who were not colonial subjects. To call specifically on the Chinese to pay for lost opium revenue risked officially acknowledging a collective of foreigners who had generated the wealth of the colony by paying indirect taxes through opium consumption. Until World War I, local administrators on the ground sidestepped this thorny issue.

Bureaucratic reluctance contrasted with shrill voices in the English-language press to tax a general Chinese community to pay for opium revenue. In early 1909, a local paper reported a rumor in Singapore that the Straits Chinese had raised 3 million Straits dollars to help the Qing build its navy. "What has the Chinese government ever done for the Chinese in Singapore who are not British-born?" asked the *Singapore Free Press* indignantly.[104] These Chinese residents had enough money; and while they "may retain a sentimental affiliation to their country of origin . . . this material support must be given to the land of their adoption." The Chinese living in the Straits Settlements should pay for what was "morally due" to the colony's coffers that were losing opium revenue, because these wealthy aliens had purportedly "transfer[red] the scene of his life's activity to the shelter of a foreign flag . . . the whole of those personal responsibilities, which can be expressed in taxation or even in voluntary contribution." This perspective aligned with anti-opium agitators writing from London, who believed that British officials in the Straits Settlements were dragging their feet on the British Empire's avowed resolve since 1906 to suppress the Far East opium trade in cooperation with China.

Triumphant members of the SSOT were especially scathing in their public criticism of Governor Swettenham as forestalling the realization of this great agenda with the excuse that opium revenue was hard to substitute. Irritated, Swettenham responded in a widely circulated letter to editor of the *Times* that there was "a moral responsibility resting on those who disturb those revenues to discover some equitable mode of compensation, even if that be provided to themselves."[105] The governor was dismissive of a cheap morality that believed "the pressure of international opinion has compelled England to see the error of her ways and tardily mend them," while failing to grapple with the critical "financial question" at stake. "[I]t need not be considered if the taxpayers of [Britain] are willing to make good of whatever may be lost to India and the Eastern colonies," wrote Swettenham. This, however, was not the case.

Rather, the replacement of indirect opium taxes remained a challenge that remained in the hands of the local administration on the ground, with a targeted tax on a diverse and dispersed Chinese community residing across Malaya seen as simultaneously a most lucrative and least possible way to raise alternative sources of revenue. It was in part due to fears of disrupting in-migration (and the loss of valuable labor) and a weakness of state capacity (to levy fees upon mobile populations). The conundrum for excise authorities also drew on a consolidated assumption and evidence about opium markets in the Straits Settlements and parts of the Malay States as a distinctive realm of the Chinese, governed by their own economic rationality. Officially incorporating this realm into the general colonial economy under British rule required clarifying questions that had been addressed before, including what principles governed the taxation of non-British, nonindigenous subjects residing in the colony, and where Chinese migrants, wealthy and poor, fit into that fiscal scheme of governance.

A Problem of Fiscal Dependency

The search for a solution to this problem of fiscal dependency was long deferred. When the state opium monopoly replaced the opium farming system in 1909, a Government Monopolies Department was established, taking over nearly 400 opium shops and more smoking saloons that had been operated by the opium farmers.[106] Until the mid-1920s, the Monopolies Department licensed private vendors to manage these sales venues, while raising the retail price of opium.[107] In the immediate years after the monopoly came into force, reported revenue collected from within-colony opium sales and distribution increased, which the local administration explained as due to the new price regime. Higher retail prices were generating more revenue, but people were consuming less, reported the Monopolies Department, with less opium leaving government warehouses and the manufacturing facilities—the Singapore factory and a new packing plant in Kuala Lumpur—decreasing production. Until 1914, administrators expressed cautious optimism about a small number of opium consumers able to afford expensive government opium who might sustain the colony's coffers until a suitable fiscal substitute was found. This was a short-lived hope, however, interrupted by the outbreak of World War I, which disrupted trade through the Straits Settlements and reduced world demand for the raw exports of rubber and tin.[108]

Local administrators in the colony continued to puzzle over opium revenue substitution, and the exigencies of the war generated both partial solutions and narrowed possibilities for the future. One way to understand how is through the figure of Arthur Meek Pountney. Much had changed since this number-loving administrator had explained the rationality of Chinese opium consumers in 1908 and presented his "most instructive" descriptive statistics of Selangor's opium economy to the Anderson Commission. Pountney had moved to Singapore in 1910 to oversee the census, joined the Treasury Department in 1913, and during the war accepted the unenviable position of Collector General of War Tax.[109] Interrupted trade and a shortage of silver currency hit the economies of the Straits Settlements especially badly and Pountney opted for a general policy of retrenchment. He introduced an emergency income tax in 1917, which was the first and last time until 1947 that the colony successfully implemented such a measure, not least because it fell heavily on the better-off Chinese residents and some European merchants of the Straits Settlements.[110] After the war ended, the income tax continued, much to the dismay of the Straits Settlements Association (SSA), which represented the colony's mercantile interests. On August 31, 1921 a large group gathered at Victoria Theater in Singapore (in front of which stood a statue of Stamford Raffles) protesting against the income taxes as a "suicidal policy" that was "acting as a deterrent to trade."[111] Pountney, now a financial adviser to the governor, sat in an office where the unhappiness on the streets was audible. His past experiences with the income tax and its controversies likely translated into greater skepticism regarding the possibility of levying direct taxes on the Chinese.

Still an expert in Chinese Affairs and proud of his fluency in Cantonese (having spent two years in Canton learning the language during his early cadet days), Pountney was attuned to the slow postwar recovery of Chinese immigration, trade, and colonial economy. He worried about "abnormal factors" aggravating disrupted migration even after the armistice was signed, and a shortage of rice in the colony occurred alongside a general downturn in tin exports that was experienced as "the worst phase of commercial depression in the history of British Malaya."[112] Pountney also sat amid a brewing power struggle that instrumentalized his adeptness with numbers and finance. He had risen in the administrative ranks as a confidant of Governor Laurence Guillemard, who had arrived in 1921 with great ambitions for centralizing the colony's management and expanding spending for public health infrastructure, public works, irrigation and drainage, as well as salary increases for civil servants.[113] Pountney strengthened the Governor-High Commissioner's hold over the colony's finance; and by 1924, Guillemard was pursuing an active policy for centralizing power across the Malay Peninsula concentrated in the Straits

Settlements. Together, the governor and financial adviser also received much criticism for "extravagance, mismanagement and waste."[114]

In 1924, Guillemard asked Pountney to lead a commission to inquire into the opium question for the Straits Settlements and Federated Malay States together. Pountney's perspectives had changed over the past decades, regarding Chinese opium consumption, its significance in the colonial economy, and indeed the very evidentiary basis upon which such assessments could properly be made.

For one, his enthusiasm for numbers that spoke for themselves had diminished. Pountney expressed exasperation about the vagueness of estimates for the basic count of opium smokers in his final report for the 1924 opium commission.[115] He was also deeply disdainful of what he saw as impressionistic accounts by people based on their local experiences. For instance, to Richard Michael Connolly, who had founded the Ipoh Anti-opium society and professed a great understanding of the Chinese and their hardiness while boasting of having spoken to many Chinese laborers about their opium habits, Pountney asked: "How do you approach the coolie to ask him that? You do it through their kapalas [interpreters]; you don't speak dialects of Chinese yourself?"[116] Then, "how do you know what questions the kapalas asked them?"[117] Indeed, if as Connolly argued, the Chinese were a "remarkable race in Asia . . . most imaginative . . . can adapt themselves to any circumstance, and can . . . easily be brought into a condition of docility towards any Government order," then perhaps, Pountney suggested pointedly: "the coolie . . . is quite capable of imagining the answer you desire to your question . . ."[118]

Second, Pountney shifted away from viewing the Chinese community as fragmented. Rather than "totally different races" that did not combine, he envisioned more systematic ways that patterns of opium consumption varied among migrants. Pountney articulated a notion of tribal differentiation that drew direct links from a place of origin in China to degrees of indulgence among the Chinese that explained variations in per capita opium consumption across the colony. Not only did Straits-born Chinese and newcomers from China consume opium differently, but among the latter, "Hokkiens and Tieuchius are the biggest smokers, while the Cantonese and Khehs are the smallest smokers," which in turn mapped onto where they lived and worked.[119]

Finally, Pountney was deeply skeptical of the possibilities of relying on the Chinese to substitute diminishing opium revenue. Previously, he had taken the radically optimistic view toward a poll tax on Chinese migrants, which would maximize the value of Chinese labor for the colony's most productive sectors—raw exports in gambier, tin, and rubber. Previously as Assistant Protector of Chinese in Selangor, Pountney had told Governor Anderson in 1908 that the proper perspective was a "pecuniary one."[120] He had been confident that opium revenue from Chinese consumption could be substituted through careful fiscal reforms and "[a]s long as the wage rates in Malaya "were sufficiently high," making the "country more attractive from a laboring point of view," Chinese migration would not be deterred, as "it is purely a question of money with the Chinese."[121] But now in 1924, Pountney was adamantly against the possibilities of a poll tax on Chinese migrants and more generally, the viability of revenue substitution measures that risked specifically targeting Chinese wealth and merchants. He also strongly opposed levying an income tax and argued for a more general approach that distributed the burden across all inhabitants of the colony.

The Imperial Question of Vested Interests

Pountney's ideas formed the basis for a solution that metropolitan authorities London were seeking. The Geneva Conference was scheduled to begin in late 1924 and Britain's representative Malcolm Delevigne worried especially about the US delegation, which included the famously righteous Bishop Charles Brent who was strongly critical of the European powers that operated opium monopolies. Delevigne (correctly) anticipated Brent's denunciation of Britain's "vested interests" in the Far East—i.e., revenues derived from the sale of opium, and "the Straits Settlements in particular have been singled out for attacks on these lines because for some years past, between 40 and 50 per cent of the gross revenues of that Colony, have been derived from the sale of opium."[122]

Delevigne pressured an interdepartmental committee, assembled to consider the Empire's opium affairs that included the Colonial Office, Home Office, and Foreign Office to address "the question as to what steps could be taken to disarm the attacks to which the British Government were being subjected to on the question of the colonial opium revenues."[123] Despite some reluctance within the Colonial Office, "it was decided as a matter of high Imperial policy" to promise the League of Nations that the British Empire had a plan to reduce opium smoking in her Far Eastern territories.[124] After the fact, Guillemard was informed of this promise by the Colonial Office. Guillemard in turn asked Pountney to lead a small committee of unofficial members of the Legislative

Council who represented merchant interests in the Straits Settlements to design it. The Colonial Office suggested a sort of separate fund to Guillemard. Pountney took it a step further.

The Opium Revenue Reserve Fund

On August 25, 1925, Arthur Pountney put before the full Legislative Council of the Straits Settlements a proposal to set aside $30 million in a reserve fund that could cushion an eventual decrease in opium revenue. "From a purely personal aspect," he announced, "this motion might be termed the apotheosis of that part of my career which has been long and intimately connected with the opium question as it affects Malaya."[125] This fund was at once a clear answer to the Colonial Office's question and also a solution to what had long been considered the impossible problem of the colony: how to substitute opium revenue.

The initial funds would come from the currency surplus of the Straits Settlements, which were at "a position of almost impregnable strength" and could be safely added to the colony's revenue, part of which would then be transferred to an investment fund that "after 5 years . . . give 4 percent interest, an annual income of $1,460,000."[126] However, this interest alone would not be terribly large, yielding "an income of less than one and quarter of the present year's opium revenue," acknowledged the treasurer.[127] Thus, Pountney's proposal included a yearly supplement of 10 percent of the colony's total revenue, which, "[a]ssuming that the fund was left absolutely intact, and growing at compound interest, it would amount in 5 years," he calculated, "to a sum which would give an annual income of $2,050,000; in ten years the income would be $3,100,000; in fifteen years $4,360,000; and 20 years $5,900,000."[128] The accumulated funds, Pountney explained, would then produce an income "within a reasonable period . . . [that] might come to something approximating the revenue from opium."[129]

According to Pountney, a "principle of voluntary curtailment" guided his proposal for the colony's finances, one that did "not want to leave to posterity an annual bill which it cannot meet without a very great reduction of efficiency or a drastic reduction in the maintenance and upkeep of the systems and institutions of Government."[130] Whose posterity did Pountney have in mind? He spoke of the colony's many inhabitants and their future livelihoods for at least the next 20 years. Time was running against legal opium in the colony, to the detriment of the projects that the British had purportedly begun to improve the welfare of indigenous populations and economic progress across the Malay Peninsula.

The treasurer articulated a vision of the colonial state as a frugal entity, "schooling ourselves to a reduced revenue [that] will react in schooling us to a reduced expenditure" for which the opium reserve fund played a crucial instrumental role that "would, in fact, be a direct assistance to posterity, in that it prevents us from presenting posterity with a bill they could not foot."[131] Pountney sidestepped the question of acknowledging the Chinese basis of opium revenue, by looking to future spending rather than the present state of revenue collection. Chinese migrants were recognized as fiscal subjects and taxpayers, and thus the opium revenue they had generated through consumption was deemed substitutable through a fund that would be used to manage public infrastructures—urban development and railroads—that they would also benefit from.

Pountney's proposal did not easily pass the Legislative Council, which was divided on multiple fronts. Some, such as E. S. Hoses, the Officer Administering the Government, admired the treasurer's proposal as anchored in considerations of "both honour and prudence":

> [O]f *honour*, because it is a matter of first importance that we should give tangible proof to all the world that no question of dependence on opium revenue will be allowed to interfere with an honest and sustained endeavor to overcome the evil of consumption within our borders, [and] of *prudence*, because it is desirable to make financial provision for the eventual replacement of our opium revenue in such a manner and at such time as will avoid the imposition of an unduly heavy burden of fresh taxation upon the people of the Colony [emphases added].[132]

J. Mitchell in the Legislative Council agreed, adding that "the time to make reserves is when you have something to make them with and now—if ever—is that time."[133] He argued that "In the event of the Colony falling upon evil days owing to serious reduction in the opium revenue . . . the right thing for us to do is to build up [a] reserve as much as we can."

Others, however, had reservations. P. Simpson felt that "it does not seem that the time has yet arrived to make a further sacrifice, and there appears to be a danger of allowing this prospective loss to hamper the progress of the Colony, and to handicap the present for the sake of a distant future."[134] Malaya had "just recovered from the worst slump in the history of the Colony," agreed W. H. Thorne. He opined that "it would . . . be a retrograde step to endeavor to cut down our budget in such a manner as to provide for the 10 percent now and in order to arrive at that, omit essential services."[135]

Criticisms extended beyond official circles, echoing in public commentary. "We have some admiration on a small scale" for Mr. Pountney, but he is hardly a "Geddes, or Inchcapes, Levehulmes, or even Keynes," sniffed one contributor to the *Singapore Free Press* with the pseudonym Simple Simon.[136] "We used to look to Mr. Pountney as the due successor to the late Mr. Hare and Mr. Pickering," agreed another disappointed reader, "but . . . Mr. Pountney escaped from the Chinese Department of Government . . . into that of High Finance."[137] The reserve fund was a form of "Prussianized Finance," he complained and "[t]o be plain, Sir, I smell a rat, not perhaps, to mix species, so active as a musang or so penetrating as a durian, but still a rat."[138]

Pountney's "indulgence of posterity" was also criticized sharply by the Singapore Chamber of Commerce, whose members felt "there is no time for hoarding . . . but that [it was] a time for spending."[139] The Singapore branch of the SSA assembled a committee to review Pountney's report and saw "no justification for the creation of a Fund permanently to endow the Colony with a perpetual income for the benefit of posterity."[140] Not only was it reckless "to tax the present generation for the benefit of posterity that was without precedent in the finance of the Great Nations of the world," but also, the SSA argued, "the existence of so large a fund . . . will tend towards profligate expenditure on the part of the Government spending departments" and the surplus is "liable to be diverted to other uses."[141]

The SSA further disagreed with Pountney that the fund would evenly distribute fiscal burdens across the general population. It drafted a memo complaining of how the measure "imposed on the present generation of taxpayers throughout Malaya, sacrifices which the entire unofficial community regard as not only uncalled for but also calculated to retard and possibly prevent the necessary development of local resources."[142] The SSA memo referred to the Chinese as "a section of Malaya that constituted the Colony of the Straits Settlements," with the vaguer term "contributed" crossed out in favor of "constituted," to explicitly clarify the significance of this constituency. It continued to explain that

the question arises whether His Majesty's Government shall seek to make a profit out of their policy by levying toll on the interest of the funds which the Colony is accumulating in order to make the policy possible, by insisting on treating it as present revenue, and therefore liable to the one-fifth contribution to His Majesty's Government, the interest on the fund which will merely pass through the books of the Colony on its way to re-investment for the purposes of the fund without reaching the Colonial treasury. There can be little doubt but that a claim to levy toll on this interest would be intensely resented by unofficial opinion in Malaya and would produce a rankling sense of injustice among all classes.[143]

Nevertheless, the reserve fund had already begun its operations for the Straits Settlements and Johor, and was extended across the Federated Malay States by 1929. The funds were entrusted to the Crown Agents, a quasi-governmental office of the British Treasury, independent of the Colonial Office which managed the $30 million endowment and yearly 10 percent transfers from the colony's general tax revenue.[144]

Lasting Significance

The problem of fiscal dependency in British Malaya was thus solved internally, and swiftly; the colonial administration introduced a set of reforms that demonstrated the British Empire's resolve to suppress opium consumption in accordance with the 1925 Geneva Convention. In 1926, the Straits Settlements' Monopolies Department declared the end of its licensing system for opium smoking shops and assumed control over the colony's opium retail shops, reducing the number from more than 500 to 70.[145] These remaining shops were to operate under close government supervision, selling opium only to Chinese users who would voluntarily register as habitual consumers with the Monopolies Department. By 1929, this registration system became mandatory, and coupled with a rationing system, it strictly limited the quantity that an individual could obtain.[146] Non-Chinese inhabitants were required to seek special permissions for registration—in 1929, there were approximately 40,000 registered users, of whom fewer than 150 were Malays and Indians; the rest were of Chinese origin.[147]

However, the rise of opium prohibition across the Malay Peninsula through these restrictions on opium consumption was also a limited process. On the one hand, the international pressures in the mid-1920s had provided an opportunity for metropolitan authorities to address abstract problems of reputation on a diplomatic stage, dealing with embarrassing criticism of their vested interests in the Far East trade. As officials in the Colonial Office later acknowledged, "[w]hile of course, the mere existence of these Funds can do nothing to affect the problem of reducing the consumption of opium, it is believed that the fact that they have been set up has already done much to remove the unfounded impression . . . that the Malayan Governments have been deterred by financial considerations from adopting such measures of control and repression as may be practicable."[148] Diplomats at Geneva now had sufficient evidence to demonstrate the British Empire's resolve and practical plans to reduce reliance on opium revenue across Malaya.[149]

On the other hand, for some local administrators on the ground, anti-opium reforms in the 1920s represented necessary inconveniences accompanying their solution to the long enduring problem of fiscal dependency in the colony. The opium revenue reserve fund was used to request reductions to the Straits Settlements' military contributions. Pountney and Guillemard argued that the sort of "voluntary curtailment" that these funds brought were analogous to "taxation imposed to build railways and other productive works," specifically to raise loans to pay for permanent public works.[150] Although he thought it was a tenuous analogy, the Secretary of State for the Colonies Leo Amery nonetheless asked the War Office to approve the reduction.[151]

Yet, at the same time, this was a solution that all had agreed to but one that pleased no one. Officials in both the metropole and colony complained about the state of opium prohibition and the reserve funds that they had achieved together. "Hope you will realise [sic] what a difficult position I am in," Governor Guillemard complained to Amery: "Malaya has accepted on Imperial grounds an opium policy which on local grounds is considered unnecessary and likely to cause trouble."[152] Guillemard added that opium consumption was not at all detrimental to the colony's progress and that its inhabitants would consider a ban as unwelcome interference: "[h]ope that the British representative(s) at the Assembly of the League of Nations will bear this in mind."[153] In turn, the Colonial Office was displeased with the growth of the reserve fund that Pountney had designed. One officer believed "the local financial authorities have somewhat exaggerated ideas of the size of the funds which it would be necessary to accumulate."[154] In its first year of operation in 1926, the opium revenue reserve fund amounted $34,000,000 and increased to $37,000,000, and in 1928 was "nearly 35 millions [which] although less than 1927, this is 2 million more than the original estimate . . . and if previous experience can be trusted, the actual results will probably be even better."[155] Another wondered about impure intents on part of Pountney and the governor: "It actually seems to have been their intention to build up a fund so large, that the interest upon them would equal the opium revenue which is to be lost and the Governments would then live like rentiers upon their savings."[156] The suspect regard of Whitehall officials was matched by worries in the colony about accountability. Based on explicit

STATEMENT OF INVESTMENTS OF THE OPIUM REVENUE REPLACEMENT RESERVE FUND ON 31ST DECEMBER, 1934

Description of Stock			%	Nominal Value of Stock			Market Value on 31st Dec., 1934		
				£	s.	d.	£	s.	d.
Br. Guiana	Stock	1949/69 ...	5	111,614	8	8	133,658	5	8
Br. Honduras	"	1941/71 ...	4	1,308	13	5	1,305	8	0
Canada	"	1950/55 ...	3½	100,000	0	0	104,750	0	0
Canada	"	1940/60 ...	4	17,277	1	10	18,443	5	11
Canada	"	1953/58 ...	4	99,730	7	9	112,446	0	3
Ceylon	"	1936/51 ...	6	1,896	4	2	1,986	5	7
Ceylon	"	1959 ...	3½	28,939	10	3	29,735	7	0
do.	"	1939/59 ...	4	11,732	11	3	12,289	17	2
do.	"	1960/70 ...	5	59,825	4	11	74,033	14	10
do.	"	1965 ...	4½	36,931	2	3	44,594	6	4
Cyprus	"	1956/66 ...	4	100,600	0	0	110,408	10	0
Conversion	"	1944/64 "A" ...	5	54,293	10	4	67,120	7	2
Consolidated	"	1957/or after ...	4	1,522,019	1	1	1,790,274	18	3
Commonwealth of Australia	"	1945/75 ...	5	1,794	13	9	2,023	10	2
Federated Malay States	"	1960/7	3	8,840	17	7	8,818	15	6
Fiji	"	1946/53 ...	5	9,500	0	0	10,996	5	0
Gold Coast	"	1945/70 ...	6	44,085	13	0	54,996	17	0
do.	"	1939/59	4	21,412	16	10	22,001	13	11
do.	"	1927/52 ...	3	14,267	0	8	14,374	0	9
do.	"	1954/59 ...	3	15,707	1	6	15,514	11	8
do.	"	1956 ...	4½	305,226	2	0	356,351	9	5
do.	"	1960/70 ...	4½	58,994	16	11	69,466	8	7
India	"	1931/or after ...	3½	136,741	16	1	135,203	9	2
do.	"	1942/47 ...	5	51,532	18	2	60,229	1	9
do.	"	1950/55 ...	4½	69,352	0	6	78,974	12	4
do.	"	1958/68 "B" ...	4½	81,548	12	7	94,902	4	4
do.	"	1948 ...	3	2,855	5	7	2,651	16	10
Jamaica	"	1941/71 ...	4½	2,500	0	0	2,668	15	0
do.	"	1952/62 ...	4	47,349	19	1	50,072	11	6
Kenya	"	1946/56 ...	6	144,838	15	9	183,583	3	3
do.	"	1948/58 ...	5	100,983	2	3	118,907	12	4
do.	"	1950 ...	4½	224,395	17	0	257,494	4	9
do.	"	1961/71 ...	4½	227,886	11	3	268,336	8	7
New South Wale	"	1945/65 ...	5	44,981	12	2	50,716	15	3
do.	"	1947/57 ...	5½	30,882	11	7	35,746	11	9
New Zealand	"	1946 ...	5	28,772	9	8	32,728	14	0
do.	"	1944 ...	4½	82,958	3	9	91,876	3	10
do.	"	1955/60 ...	3½	9,007	12	9	9,525	11	6
do.	"	1943/63 ...	4	16,083	19	3	17,169	12	7
do.	"	1947 ...	4½	81,917	14	5	90,723	17	6
do. Inscribed	"	1949 ...	5	70,115	16	4	81,159	1	2
do. "	"	1935/45 ...	5	22,926	13	7	23,327	17	11
do.	"	1945 ...	4½	34,798	9	9	38,539	6	6
do.	"	1948/58 ...	4½	63,448	11	2	70,903	15	3
do.	"	1956/71 ...	5	46,279	15	9	55,882	16	10
Nigeria	"	1949/79 ...	6	83,424	1	10	108,242	15	2
do.	"	1936/46 ...	6	6,710	6	7	7,230	7	7
do.	"	1947/57 ...	5	312,224	5	1	367,644	1	2
do.	"	1963 ...	4	221,163	10	4	251,573	10	0
do.	"	1950/60 ...	5	341,530	5	10	405,567	4	5
do.	"	1955 ...	3	68,895	2	6	50,219	5	3
N. Rhodesia	"	1950/70 ...	5	66,525	7	9	77,668	7	10
do.	"	1955/65 ..	3½	20,000	0	0	21,150	0	0
Queensland	"	1940/60 ...	5	13,913	7	0	15,130	15	4
do.	"	1940/50 ...	4	26,510	7	11	27,504	10	9
Straits Settlements	"	1937/67 ...	3½	217,235	8	7	218,864	13	11
Sierra Leone	"	1938/63 ...	4	3,881	1	1	3,987	15	8
do.	"	1955 ...	4½	27,314	15	9	30,797	8	5
Trinidad	"	1958/68 ...	3½	10,000	0	0	10,475	0	0
Tanganyika	"	1952/72 ...	4	1,200	0	0	1,378	10	0
do.	"	1948/68 ...	4½	7,000	0	0	8,111	5	0
do.	"	1951/71 ...	4	162,316	15	6	188,084	11	3
Uganda	"	1951/71 ...	5	77,213	0	8	91,690	9	6
do.	"	1955/65 ...	3½	5,000	0	0	5,137	10	0
Union of South Africa	"	1940/60 ...	5	4,500	0	0	4,983	15	0
do.	"	1945/75 ...	5	100,489	6	8	116,316	8	1
do.	"	1950/70 ...	5	34,212	14	9	41,654	0	2
do.	"	1943/63 ...	4	21,817	18	10	23,727	0	3
Victoria	"	1940/60 ...	4¾	15,904	5	1	16,818	14	11
do.	"	1945/75 ...	5	11,272	9	11	12,597	0	3
War Loan (Converted into 3½%) 1952 or after	"	1929/47 ...	5	193,129	4	7	209,786	12	6
				6,301,539	2	10	7,223,255	14	6
On deposit with Joint Colonial Fund and Balance ...				17,887	10	0	17,887	10	0
TOTAL ...			...	6,319,426	12	10	7,241,143	4	6
				(*a*) Net value in dollars ..			$62,066,941 98		

(*a*) At exchange 2*s*. 4*d*. to the Dollar

THE TREASURY,
SINGAPORE, 31*st May*, 1935.

H. WEISBERG,
Acting Treasurer, S.S.

FIGURE 5.1. Straits Settlements' opium revenue replacement reserve fund's investments, 1934–1935. (Source: Straits Settlements Blue Book for the Year 1934, p. 173.)

concerns that "[o]ne day this accumulated fund, if not required to replace opium revenue, may be diverted to some imperial purpose," unofficial members of the Straits Settlements' Legislative Council on behalf of the merchant community threatened to block the annual budget's approval in 1928, unless assurances were given that the opium revenue funds were not diverted without a majority approval from the unofficial members.[157]

Nevertheless, the opium revenue replacement reserve fund flourished for decades to come. Under the purview of the Crown Agents, the Straits Settlements' opium money was invested all over the world, helping sustain the financial structure of the British Empire.[158] Beginning in 1926, the $34 million generated nearly $4 million in net value through purchasing colonial stock ranging from Nigeria, Jamaica, Nigeria, Sierra Leone, and the Union of South Africa to Ceylon, Hong Kong, and Canada.[159] By 1935, the investments could be found in nearly all British territories, as Figure 5.1 illustrates, with a total net value amounting to $62 million. It was seen as a fairly stable fund: "[m]y own view," wrote a Colonial Office officer in 1930, "is that the Straits Settlements will continue, for a very long time to come, to draw a substantial revenue from opium."[160] In the Federated Malay States, the opium revenue reserve funds were used to support the Perak Electric Power Company, which had long supplied electricity to the Kinta Valley, one of the main tin mining areas of the Malay Peninsula.[161] In 1930, the fund amounted to $20 million and was estimated to grow to $23.5 million by the end of 1931, accruing 4.75 percent investment gains each year. The government had previously granted a loan to the Perak Company but was afraid it would default; thus, the opium revenue reserve funds were used to transform the initial loan into an investment to avoid losses from the company's possible liquidation or restructuring.[162]

Opium prohibition thus began in British Malaya under a state monopoly, with the promise of restricting opium consumption through a registration system for users, alongside funds that took as their basis the very large amounts of revenue raised from opium over the past decades, which were remade respectable and public as wealth for the colony's benefit of posterity.

Conclusion

This chapter has traced the slow birth of British Malaya's opium revenue reserve fund. When formally introduced in 1925, this policy was both much lauded and much maligned as an anti-opium reform that dealt squarely with the colony's fiscal dependency on opium revenue. It was also a shift in colonial opium policy that followed the demands of British politicians and diplomats to enact demonstrable evidence of efforts to prohibit opium, amid worries about imperial reputation and accountability before peers at the League of Nations' Opium Advisory Committee. However, as this chapter has argued, even this most seemingly obvious instance of a metropole to colony dictate required the work of local administrators in order to manifest, when it did, the way it did. It was possible for the opium revenue reserve fund to emerge, because of an already established set of administrative sensibilities about the necessity and viability of such a reform and long accumulated precedents for defining problems of fiscal dependency.

The broader significance of the experience of British Malaya lies in how deeply reliant the Straits Settlements were on opium revenue, more so than any other colony in Southeast Asia throughout the era of opium monopolies. The opium revenue reserve fund was an incomplete policy solution to a problem of fiscal dependency that administrators had constructed officially. It also rendered invisible, by a sleight of one administrator's pen, a large sum of still remaining revenue raised from opium sales. In this regard, the introduction of this much touted measure that gave evidence to the outside world of British resolve toward opium prohibition also marked a new beginning for hidden finances and a colonial bureaucracy tasked with its management.

The next chapter explores a similarly secretive world that local opium administrators in Indochina fashioned through their everyday work and its cumulative problem-solving logic. In a different colony, of another empire, a familiar sort of tragic comedy of repetitive errors was taking place around the same time in the 1920s, under the purview of the French opium monopoly.

6

Disastrous Abundance in French Indochina, 1920s–1940s

BY THE 1930S, most European opium monopolies in Southeast Asia were restricting popular opium consumption and making demonstrable efforts to reduce their colonial state's reliance on opium revenue. However, the French colony of Indochina was slower to introduce regulatory reforms along these lines. Although the French Indochina opium monopoly collected a large share of local tax revenue from opium sales, much like in British Malaya, comparable efforts to substitute this fiscal base such as an opium revenue replacement fund did not occur. And it was not until the late 1940s that the French authorities declared the end of legal opium sales in this colony.

What explains French Indochina's late turn to opium prohibition? Like other opium monopolies operating during the first half of the twentieth century, the French institution was a vexed entity, riddled with myriad challenges inherited from early moments of state building based on vice taxation. As previous chapters have shown, the micropolitics of colonial bureaucracies were consequential for when and how anti-opium reforms took place, because local administrators defined the necessity and viability of regulatory changes. In the case of Indochina, a complex set of challenges rooted in the opium monopoly's accumulated debts and murky accounting practices rendered radical bans on opium consumption or revenue substitution measures implausible to officials situated in the colony. By the 1930s, the opium monopoly of French Indochina was effectively bankrupt, and local administrators were struggling to recover losses and regain basic solvency. Grand initiatives for substituting opium revenue or banning opium consumption made little sense for this bureaucratic hand of the colonial state.

This chapter traces the process through which the precarious finances of the French opium monopoly in Indochina emerged as an administrative problem. It began with a fateful moment in 1924, when the French in Indochina made a decision to purchase opium supplies from a warlord in China that launched a downward spiral of debt that would bedevil the colonial bureaucracy over the next decade. The first part of the chapter situates this specific decision in the general context of the French opium monopoly's operations since the nineteenth century, elucidating precedents of imperfect bureaucratic reform and tensions with metropolitan authorities over the colony's debt financing. It underscores the considerable discretionary power that local administrators managing the opium monopoly exercised over accounting and bookkeeping to foreshadow the second part of the chapter, which explains how the purchasing episode of 1924 escalated into an internal crisis of the French colonial state in Indochina. I demonstrate how the opium monopoly's administrators overpaid for the Chinese opium and addressed what was at first a small problem by using fictitious sales transfers (called *cessions fictives*), a measure originally designed to achieve temporary liquidity for purchasing opium during the 1900s.

While at first a minor accounting practice within the legal boundaries of colonial administration, *cessions fictives* were repeated in following years and became an entrenched mechanism for balancing the colony's budget. By the eve of World War II, a cycle of overdrawn spending accounts, overdue payments for foreign opium, and more fictitious sales had crossed into the realm of illegal conduct, while posing acute challenges to the financial integrity of the colonial state. Local administrators struggled to procure and pay for opium supplies, while disguising the bankruptcy of the opium monopoly. They pursued a spate of policies to adjust retail prices for opium and organize sales, anxious to find ways to address accumulated problems; and in the process, they limited the conditions of possibility for the colony's anti-opium reforms.

The approach that this chapter takes to reveal the inner tensions of the French Indochina opium monopoly, as deeply mired in a problem of precarious finances of its own making, is significant in several respects. First, it utilizes a set of records from the Vietnamese National Archives that were written by the colony's financial officers and administrators specializing in opium with the Department of Customs and Excise, as well as audit reports by metropolitan inspectors that give privileged insight into the secretive struggles of the French opium monopoly in Indochina during the late interwar period. Into the 1930s, official documentation on the opium monopoly's fiscal and financial practices became more discrete under the glare of international scrutiny.[1] Yet, local administrators in the colony also selectively disclosed certain aspects of the opium monopoly's operations to external observers while burying other forms of information, in ways that are instructive for understanding what anxieties, what perceived problems, troubled those most intimately involved in the colony's everyday administration.

Second and relatedly, understanding the micropolitics of the French colonial bureaucracy regarding opium in Indochina sheds new light on extant understandings of the opium monopoly's interwar life and eventual demise. By the 1930s, many have argued, this institution had become a relic of the past, "morally dubious, an embarrassment" for French authorities under the glare of international scrutiny, which endured, according to Philippe Le Failler for instance, because the French colonial state's fiscal framework was too rigid to allow for substituting revenue collected from opium sales and consumption.[2] Following Le Failler, many locate the enabling conditions for the monopoly's demise in Indochina's booming economy during the late 1930s that allowed the state to mobilize alternative sources of revenue and naturally usher out an institution that had outlived its utility for colonial rule. By contrast, this chapter demonstrates how the end years of the French opium monopoly in Indochina followed a more tortured and delayed process in which involved officials worried not so much about replacing opium revenue collected from indirect taxes but more about how to deal with a considerable backlog of payments for opium supplies, caught in a recursive cycle of debt and overdrawn spending accounts.

Finally, the everyday work and ideas of administrators involved in operating the French opium monopoly in Indochina give reason to rethink the meaning of bureaucratic discretion. Corruption is too blunt a word to capture the invention of fictitious sales transfers for opium and flexible accounting practices employed by local administrators, although their actions clearly defied the expectations of metropolitan officers. The legal environment and international norms surrounding the opium monopoly's everyday operations shifted more quickly than the ability of involved officials to adjust, update, and comply with new and artificially declared standards for moral and legitimate colonial governance. Rather, these state actors were caught amid a sea change of activities that reconfigured the terms on which importing opium was permissible and remade tacitly authorized ways of spending government funds into explicitly interdicted activates. Not only did dividing lines between the legal and illegal shift, but such divides were also clarified as a product of, rather than a precondition to, what local administrators said, perceived, and did. The discretionary power these modest officials exercised as such was not necessarily a guided pursuit of alternatives to given dictates from metropolitan superiors or the public interest, but an ability to define imperatives for state action that was wielded in spite of themselves.

A Fateful Purchase

In 1924, the French opium monopoly bought seventy-five tons of Chinese opium.[3] The seller was a man named Tang Ji Yao, a powerful warlord ruling over Yunnan, the southern province of China that bordered the French protectorate of Tonkin, along the northernmost edge of Indochina. Yunnan had extensive poppy fields that yielded a lucrative harvest that Tang sought to sell. He found a buyer in Marie-Alphonse Kircher, the director of Indochina's Department of Customs and Excise, who paid 2 million piastres for the warlord's opium.

At one level, this transaction was about a political initiative that went awry and nearly became a major diplomatic embarrassment for metropolitan France. Earlier in 1922, the French consul in Yunnan and Governor General of Indochina had struck a deal with Tang, authorizing the warlord's agents to transport opium through French territory to access Tonkin's port of Haiphong.[4] Yunnan was landlocked, and Tang had much to gain from being able to export his opium overseas. In exchange, the French in Indochina secured Tang's commitment to pay for repairs to a damaged railroad linking Tonkin and Yunnan, installing infrastructures for radio-telegram communication along the border, as well as police forces. There were also nonmaterial benefits from gaining Tang's goodwill, not least because the Yunnan–Tonkin border was a fraught site where contraband abound, always busy with anticolonial dissidents fleeing to China. Moreover, it was likely that Tang would find ways to smuggle the opium through Tonkin anyways, reasoned the local French authorities.[5] The Minister of Colonies in Paris agreed and approved the transaction.[6]

However, the British soon caught wind of this agreement and accused the French of violating its international anti-opium obligations and conspiring with Chinese opium traffickers.[7] Worried about France's reputation before peer empires, Paris ordered the Governor General of Indochina to cancel the deal in early 1924.[8] By this point, however, a quarter of the promised sales amount—75 tons of Yunnan opium—had already been sent to the port of Haiphong. The Minister of Colonies ordered the French Consul in Yunnan to explain the situation to Tang, the impossibility of shipping the opium due to British scrutiny, while assuring the Yunnan ruler that he would not incur any financial losses because the French would buy all of the unsold opium sitting in a warehouse in Haiphong.[9] Thus, the opium monopoly paid 2 million piasters for the seventy-five tons of opium.

At another level, the 1924 transaction was a normal affair for local administrators in Indochina. This was neither the first nor the last time that the French colony had procured opium from China. Managing the opium monopoly was a constant task of creating and revising arrangements for buying opium, absorbing risks, and adjusting to exigencies of the moment. The significance of this particular event arose because of what happened after the monopoly spent 2 million piasters to buy the seventy-five tons of Yunnan opium.

It was a large sum of money for a large amount of opium that the monopoly found difficult to sell. Not only did Tang's opium deteriorate in quality from prolonged storage in Haiphong, but the Chinese product was also less popular among opium consumers in Indochina, who generally preferred the taste of Indian opium. In effect, the monopoly had spent nearly half of its annual budget for purchasing opium on a product it did not need, which in turn left the monopoly short of funds to buy the Indian opium it did need to supply the colony's many retail opium shops and smoking dens. Director Kircher faced a predicament: how could the monopoly procure foreign opium that it could not pay for?

Kircher's solution involved a practice of fictitious sales (*cessions fictive*) that would become suspect and quasi-illegal in retrospect, but at the time constituted a normal administrative procedure with established precedents. To understand what Kircher did, it is necessary to begin by understanding the nature of the opium monopoly that he acted on behalf.

The Birth of the French Indochina Opium Monopoly

The French Indochina opium monopoly was created on February 7, 1899, when Paul Doumer, a newly arrived Governor General for the colony, decreed a uniform framework for regulating opium markets across five territories comprising the Union of Indochina—the directly colonized Cochinchina and the protectorates of Annam, Cambodia, Tonkin, and later Laos.[10] Since the beginning of French territorial expansion over the Indochinese peninsula during the early 1860s, each territory had fashioned disparate arrangements for taxing opium consumption and collecting revenue from sales. Over the course of three decades, the geography of French Indochina's political economy of opium developed to resemble a patchwork quilt of opium tax farms mixed with local state monopolies.[11]

After the conquest of Saigon, the French began levying a 10 percent duty on opium entering the port city and established an opium tax farm in 1862 extending to its environs of Cochinchina.[12] At the time, officers of the French Navy oversaw local administration and modeled the tax farm on British Singapore's approach to taxing the everyday vices of local inhabitants.[13] Many saw parallels between the two ports, Saigon and Singapore, in light of Chinese migrants of diverse classes entering through and residing in urban areas, and saw an opportunity to levy indirect taxes. As postmaster of Saigon in 1868, Charles Lemire described the bustling life of the Chinese suburb of Chôlon, a mere 5 kilometers from Saigon's main wharf, with its own quays, roads, markets, bridges, as well as "bright streetlights along roads [where one could find] a pharmacist, a barber, and under an awning, a pastry confectioner. Then a gambling house, a dying workshop, an opium den, a goldsmith's shop, and a large store selling manufactured goods in Europe."[14] Early military administrators regarded opium as part of the everyday life of those residing in this relatively well-off part of the colony.[15] For the first decade of the opium tax farm's operations from 1861 to 1871, opium accounted for 75 percent of indirect taxes and more than 30 percent of total revenue for the budget of Cochinchina.[16]

The Cochinchina opium tax farm was an object of competition among merchants who bid for the right to operate it and supply opium locally, struggling to balance profit with the costs of operation.[17] For some, opium tax farming was a new venture that they were ill prepared for; for others, it was an old business laden with power struggles. The first tax farmers were private French businessmen who were found guilty of forging their accounts and misreporting profits; their immediate successors were influential Chinese merchants based in Saigon representing different migrant communities originating in Fujian and Canton who competed.[18] In 1881, the first civilian governor of Cochinchina, Charles Le Myre de Vilers, abolished the opium tax farm—deemed a "source of contestation and judicial struggles"—replaced by direct management under an office for customs and excise.[19] This Cochinchina-specific opium monopoly, called the *régie directe*, claimed an exclusive right to import opium, and appointed an intermediary who oversaw foreign purchases while contracting a former Chinese tax farmer to oversee manufacturing in the Saigon factory.[20] It assumed management over the Saigon opium factory in 1881 and organized wholesale directly through opium warehouse managers (until 1884) and then issued licenses for individuals to sell in bulk (1885–1890), with separate set of licensing arrangements for retail sales.[21]

"Cochinchina was a laboratory" for Indochina, as "[o]n the spot adminis-trators . . . extend[ed] a system built in Saigon more than 20 years ago to newly annexed territories."[22] In Cambodia, claimed as a protectorate in 1867, the royal tax farms were de facto controlled by neighboring Cochinchina's Chinese tax farmers; and during the early 1880s, King Norodom agreed to contract these tax farms to the French, which were directly supplied by the Saigon factory and incorporated under the Cochinchina *régie directe*.[23] For Tonkin, where the Nguyen dynasty had already established opium tax farms, the French local ad-ministrators instituted a quasi-monopoly in 1883 that shared control over opium imports, manufacture, and sales, but delegated the management to a French entrepreneur who effectively controlled the entire chain of supply and extended it to Annam.[24]

In 1899, these multiple arrangements were integrated under a general opium monopoly encompassing the entirety of French Indochina. This shift was part of a sweeping set of colony-wide administrative reforms launched by Gover-nor General Doumer. "Workaholic, ambitious, energetic, and highly compe-tent," Doumer was a man of many hats: a former mathematics teacher from the rural south of France, who became an important figure in the Radical Party, treasurer of one of the main branches of French Freemasonry, Minister of Fi-nance (1895–1896, 1925–1927), and briefly President of France until his assas-sination in 1932.[25] Doumer's own interests in fiscal and financial reforms shaped the forceful approach he brought to Indochina to promote economic develop-ment, by consolidating a centralized political-administrative structure.[26] Es-pecially pertinent to matters of opium was the introduction of a unified Depart-ment of Customs and Excise, and a general budget. The former was tasked with implementing a divided taxation system that the latter established, which left direct taxation to the protectorates of Annam, Cambodia, and Tonkin, while claiming control over customs duties and indirect taxes, most of which came from opium, followed by alcohol and salt. Together, these three sources of rev-enue, calculated Doumer, would contribute respectively "about one-quarter, one-seventh, and one tenth" of the colony's total tax revenue, laying the native population's "vice of opium, habit of drinking rice alcohol, and need for salt" as the fiscal basis of the French colonial state, known as the "three beasts of burden" (*bêtes de somme*) for the colony.[27]

A key consideration in the Governor General's decision to institute a general opium monopoly was private investment in the colony. Doumer had arrived in Indochina with a vision for building a self-sufficient colony and promoting development, by issuing bonds and securing capital needed to build public infrastructure.[28] The French Empire's creeping process of territorial conquest and pacification in Indochina had incurred high military costs and large accumulated deficits to the metropole, which the colony's fragmented administrative and budgetary structure was ill equipped to pay off.[29] A formidable obstacle to the colony's economic development, in Doumer's opinion, came from the richest part of the Union in the south, where French settlers and merchant communities based in urban areas were unwilling to yield their autonomy over the local budget. To address their concerns, Doumer designed a new budgetary framework that gave the Union full control over indirect tax bases including opium but yielded control over sources of direct taxation to governing bodies of the Union's composite protectorates.[30] Known as the common budget, this balancing mechanism also enabled Doumer to positively signal the colony's stability to external investors by allowing significant discretionary power over calculating net revenue collected from indirect taxes on opium, as well as alcohol and salt, in ways that overreported "imaginative figures."[31]

The birth of Indochina's opium monopoly as such, was the product of a newly arrived Governor General's grand ambitions. For the many administrators in the colony already involved in taxing and reporting on the commercial life of opium, it represented a distinctive nightmare. Over the previous three decades, officials had struggled with myriad problems arising from applying the Cochinchina-centered approach—a state monopoly over opium imports, distribution, and sales—to other protectorates. For instance, in Annam, the French opium tax farmer proved a powerful figure with political and economic clout beyond the protectorate and thus local administrators hesitated to end his contract.[32] In Tonkin, customs and excise officials had long struggled with basic task of transporting opium manufactured in the Saigon factory located in the far south to the northernmost protectorate at the opposite end of the Indochina peninsula.[33] In 1890, the high resident for Tonkin and Annam had complained about a monopoly system as an "unfortunate institution," ill-suited for areas beyond Saigon-Chôlon where "territory was vast and French personnel sparse" and suggested alternatives in the form of levying direct village tax on "Annamites" who consumed opium and a capitation tax on individual Chinese.[34]

In other words, the sweeping reach of French Indochina's opium monopoly outpaced the practicalities of administrative integration. As Le Failler notes, the 1899 law that formally created it marked "no real break [with] the previous laws; rather, it marked an effort to create a homogenizing perspective over the different systems."[35] Similarly at the level of everyday administration, this reform merely paved over existing arrangements, while igniting an uneasy process of integration with many loose ends. It effectively brought Saigon and Hanoi, at opposite ends of the Indochina peninsula within a common regulatory framework, which aggravated already complicated issues of distribution and led to increased incidents of reported smuggling, not least because official definitions of internal and cross-province transit were not yet well defined. The newly fashioned common budget began collecting opium revenue before local administrators had done the footwork for centralizing collections, reorganizing accounting procedures and paperwork for calculating returns and expenditures, as well as assessing profits.

Indochina Unlike Burma and Malaya

The French opium monopoly for Indochina acquired several characteristics that set it apart from opium monopolies in Burma and Malaya examined in previous chapters. First, unlike in Burma, where the monopoly was introduced amid the local administration's concerns with social problems caused by opium consumption, the Indochina opium monopoly assumed an agnostic position about the negative repercussions of opium upon colonial society. In 1902, the general opium monopoly's director André Frézouls assumed comfortably that "[t]he consumption of opium does not seem destined to disappear with the progress of civilization, and the populations of the Far East will not for a long time renounce their vices, as tenacious as those of the countries of the West."[36] In other words, what opium smoking prevailed among French subjects and protégés—the "Annamites, Cambodigiens, Thais, Indonésiens, Muongs, Mans, Meos"—did not escalate into the perceived crises of moral wreckage as it had for the Burmese.[37]

When the Indochina opium monopoly did adopt measures addressing popular opium consumption, they were half-hearted efforts fashioned to address external complaints. For instance, in September 1906, metropolitan politicians called upon Paul Beau, Doumer's successor as Governor General, to consider ending opium market activities under the general monopoly's supervision.[38] The proximate impetus came from Chinese diplomats who had approached the French Ministry of Foreign Affairs, asking for cooperation in controlling the border with Tonkin. Beau explained that the opium's financial importance was too great to change the current system: "this drug and its monopoly currently accounts for around a fourth of the colony's budget."[39] Instead, a spate of decrees was introduced for raising sales prices, banning the sale of dross, adding new curriculum in native schools about the dangers of opium use, and no longer opening new smoking dens.[40] As anti-opium reforms with shallow reach, they reflected shared sensibilities among administrators involved in the *régie's* everyday taxation and accounting activities, skeptical of the necessity of state intervention, not least because of how most opium smokers were Chinese, with few French or indigenous Vietnamese, Cambodian, or Laotian users of the drug. In striking contrast to British Burma, where ideas about injured opium consumers emerged and escalated to become part of official lexicon despite the small number of known Burmese smokers, a key element of administrative discourse in French Indochina centered on small numbers as reason for the limited extent of opium-related consumption problems and rationale against unnecessary interference in colonial society. French administrators tended to firmly assert that "in this country, more than for any other, the question of opium is a specifically Chinese one," as consumption was neither widespread nor obviously harmful to colonial subjects and protégés.[41] Lower administrators served such held opinion as given fact for higher figures in the colony. "Indochina consumes very little opium and the share of addicts is extremely small; opium smokers account for only three out of one thousand of the general population, and nine per thousand of adult males," explained Governor General Ernest Roume, who successfully secured Indochina's exemption from the imperial scope of France's 1916 antinarcotic law, which included opium.[42]

Second, compared to Malaya, where fiscal dependency on opium revenue worried local administrators, less anxiety colored the ways that those in Indochina regarded taxes collected from opium. Officially, both colonies reported exceptionally high shares of revenue from opium, which were acknowledged as collected predominantly from Chinese migrants and diaspora communities. Into the mid-1920s, 30 to 45 percent of French Indochina's annually collected tax revenue came from opium sales, comparable to 40 to 50 percent for British Malaya. Around the time in 1925 when Arthur Pountney was designing the Straits Settlements' opium revenue replacement reserve fund (Chapter 5), his counterpart in Indochina was writing about the inconvenience that ending taxes on opium would bring as "[w]e would need to raise taxes on alcohol, tobacco, matches, fuels, card-playing, mineral oils, sugars . . . rice exports, and create new taxes on consumption, raise tariffs . . . be they Indochinese, French, or foreign."[43] Whereas opium officials in Malaya acknowledged challenges in finding substitutes for lost opium revenue but deemed them reasons to pursue more alternatives, those in Indochina accepted reliance on opium as an inevitable state of the colony, noting that "we cannot hide the fact that whatever happens, we will never be able to replace taxes on opium."[44] Whereas in Malaya, administrative debates over opium revenue substitution had centered on the rights and obligations of the Straits Chinese as fiscal subjects, in Indochina, tax revenues generated from selling opium to the Chinese was treated as voluntary contributions of foreigners residing in the colony.[45]

Finally, the Indochina opium monopoly obtained opium from multiple suppliers, unlike both Burma and Malaya, which almost solely sold opium from India. Whereas the British dependencies—Burma as a province of British India until 1935, the Straits Settlements as a Crown Colony, and the Malay States as indirectly ruled territories—were obligated to import Indian opium and received preferential purchasing rates, this French colony was subject to neither the same legal constraints nor economic benefits. Indeed, Indochina was embedded in an imperial regulatory framework for opium that placed it alongside French settlements in India and the distant protectorate of Oceania in the South Pacific, requiring flexibility for imports. Throughout the first half of the twentieth century, opium shops across Indochina sold, in addition to Benares product—the famed high-quality opium grown in the poppy fields of Bengal and manufactured in Patna factories—opium imported from Persia, Turkey, China, as well as locally grown poppy by the Hmong. This diversity of sources reflects the greater complexity of issues that local administrators in Indochina faced when procuring opium compared with their counterparts in Burma and Malaya.

In particular, the ways in which monopoly officials in Indochina dealt with opium from China and poppy grown within the colony contrast with the experience of Burma, as seen in Chapter 4. Recall that British Burma also shared a border with Yunnan, the southern province of China, and dealt with poppy cultivation among "ethnic minority" inhabitants of highland areas such as the Shan. Unlike how the Burmese opium monopoly generally treated all opium from China as contraband and administratively separated the Shan poppy cultivating areas from Burma proper, the Indochina monopoly periodically imported and purchased opium from Yunnan as well as highland areas inhabited by the Hmong. The French approach was rooted in pre-1899 arrangements that local administrators in the northern protectorates developed to deal with opium-related exigencies in areas located so far from Cochinchina and Saigon's opium factory.

Such myriad accommodations by local administrators made for complicated regulatory regimes for opium with perverse consequences. One example relates to the opium monopoly's approach to Hmong opium production, which underwent several shifts that at once reflected and stoked administrative problems.[46] Initially, local administrators left alone the poppy growing areas of Laos, along with northern Tonkin, treated as "regions too remote for us to supervise."[47] However, in the 1910s, administrators began to buy opium from this highland area, following a spate of revolts attributed to Chinese opium smugglers who were purchasing Hmong opium and stoking unrest against the French.[48] The monopoly's purchasing campaigns from the northern highlands continued sporadically until 1925, when twenty-two tons of opium purchased in Laos were found to be adulterated with sand and cow excrement. Into the 1930s, as Ami-Jacques Rapin has demonstrated, the makeshift measures for purchasing opium that local administrators had been using came under intense political and media scrutiny, which culminated in a scandal in metropolitan France about corruption and fraud in Indochina. The blowback for the colonial administration further entailed a loss of autonomy for the Department of Customs and Excise, which was placed under the Department of Finance, both curtailing the ability of administrators to procure opium and giving reason to disguise their activities from official sight.[49] Such dynamics of borderland problem-solving and escalation recurred throughout the first half of the twentieth century, underlying the operations of the French Indochina opium monopoly. The next section examines one particularly consequential case for its eventual demise.

Borderland Problems

French Indochina shared a long border with China. Porous territorial lines separated the northern protectorates of Tonkin and Laos from the southernmost province of Yunnan, and in this interstitial area, poppy cultivation and opium trades prevailed. The Laos–Tonkin–Yunnan borderland as such represented a site of both anxiety and opportunities. On the one hand, the overlapping frontiers of the French and Qing empires since the mid-nineteenth century rendered it a place of interimperial tensions over the definition of political boundaries and establishment of military presence and border policing. In 1912, the fall of the Qing opened a tumultuous warlord period of political fragmentation for China that added to the volatility of this borderland, not least because Yunnan's political economy for opium represented a lucrative economic base which local strongmen and warlords fought to secure. In addition to poppy cultivation that spilled across the border, opium smuggling abounded from the landlocked province of Yunnan into Tonkin, which enjoyed generous coastal access and the port of Haiphong.[50]

On the other hand, the Laos–Tonkin–Yunnan border also served as a promising place of proximate access into China and a wealth of political and economic opportunities. The same poppy cultivation territories and channels for opium trade that worried the French official mind for Indochina could also excite it, by bolstering opportunities for cooperation with authorities in Yunnan, secure lacking resources for border policing, as well as ways to entice entrepreneurs to invest in the colonial state. The Lyonnais merchant house of Ulysse Pila represented one such group, which initially focused on trading in Chinese silk and during the 1880s sought to export Yunnan's opium, famously helping build the Haiphong harbor infrastructure and linking it through inland riverways and a transborder railroad line to Kunming, the capital of Yunnan.[51] The poppy grown in Yunnan could also serve as a local supply source for the Indochina monopoly, as a welcome alternative to overseas imports from British India. In sum, from the perspective of local French administrators, this borderland was a lively and complicated place of governance. Prior to 1899, local administrators overseeing opium tax farms in Tonkin and Laos had managed cross-border opium flows and taxation flexibly, through periodic arrangements with local authorities in Yunnan and merchants, French and Chinese alike. Some arrangements were formalized, such as an 1887 convention defining the boundary between Tonkin and Yunnan that included permission for the French to purchase poppy from growers in Mengzi, Manhao, and Longzhou in southwest Yunnan or an 1888 decree banning opium imports from China.[52] Other agreements were informal, including tacit permission for poppy cultivation on the French side of the border as well and quiet agreements to allow Yunnan opium to transit through Tonkin.[53]

But with the 1899 introduction of the general opium monopoly, French colonial administration in the northern protectorates of Indochina began to change. While the borderland remained a terrain subject to the vicissitudes of a local political economy of opium, Doumer's reforms were incapable of fully accommodating such local exigencies.[54] In a sense, whereas officials involved in taxing, regulating, and policing opium in Tonkin and Laos continued as they always had, the new regulatory framework pathologized the fluidity and occasional ambiguities that had long enabled their work.

Over the next two decades, administrators of the Department of Customs and Excise, which oversaw the opium monopoly's operations, continued to address border problems, developing myriad solutions that were adjusted and reconfigured. At first, most remained within a realm of permissible arrangements known by metropolitan authorities, deemed lawful if somewhat irregular. For instance, in 1901, the possibility of creating a joint French–Chinese monopoly for importing Yunnan opium was explored and disregarded the next year in favor of granting a six-month import permit to a former French military commander for supplying consumers in Tonkin. In 1903, Pila's company was allowed to take over this quasi-trade monopoly.[55] French administrators also sporadically permitted merchants to transport Yunnan opium through Haiphong port to Hong Kong and foreign markets overseas.[56] Regulatory approaches evolved, matching the rhythm of borderland change. Between 1908 and 1912, Yunnan opium imports into Indochina were banned, following a Qing imperial anti-opium edict in 1906 that raised the price of frontier opium.[57] In tandem, the monopoly temporarily imported opium from Burma and granted a special indemnity for purchasing raw opium to the collector of Lai Chau, on the border with Yunnan.[58]

Blurred lines between lawful irregularities and exceptional necessities prevailed. Attentive to political circumstances in Yunnan following the 1906 edict, the French established a special purchasing account for opium supplies in 1908, which would allow the monopoly to purchase reserve opium and sell when prices were too high.[59] A supplementary contingency account was created in 1911 for making emergency purchases of raw opium.[60] Together, these two accounts, known as the reserve and procurement accounts, enabled the Department of Customs and Excise to make quick payments for foreign opium that would later be recovered by transferring funds from the colony's general budget. These were officially sanctioned arrangements, with regular records kept of the quantity of opium in stock, available credit for purchases, as well as advanced spending amounts.[61] If there was perhaps something unusual about them, it was the sheer size of the funds that that local administrators could mobilize. In 1909 for instance, 1.2 million piastres were charged to the reserve fund to build a stockpile of opium amounting to fifty-two tons; in 1911, 1.6 million piastres were authorized to the supplementary fund. However, from the vantage point of those familiar with the monopoly's everyday operations, such flexibility seemed only reasonable. It was only later that these practices would become viewed in a suspect light, as clearer divisions between official and unofficial, permissible and inappropriate, legal and illegal acts relating to opium trade, sales, and production emerged to define the discretionary power of local administrators as bureaucratic corruption in retrospect.

In the spring of 1922, the implications of this shift became apparent. Tang Ji-Yao became the governor of Yunnan and inherited a large stock of roughly 400 to 500 tons of raw opium from his predecessor that he sought to sell.[62] The French consul for Yunnan, Jean Bodard, agreed to allow the transport of the Chinese opium through Tonkin to Canton and Hong Kong, following established precedents of the Indochina opium monopoly. Bodard reasoned that in addition to signaling goodwill to the powerful warlord, allowing the opium trade would invigorate commerce to the advantage of local poppy growers in the north, while also undermining smuggling across the border. In addition, explained the consul to the Governor General of the colony, this arrangement with the leader of Yunnan could potentially lead to joint investments in building communication lines connecting Indochina to China, cooperation in repairing the Tonkin–Yunnan railway line, buying arms, as well as stabilizing Tang's rule, which would also make the borderland of Yunnan–Tonkin–Laos more predictable.[63]

In the meantime, Governor General Henri Merlin had newly arrived in Indochina with a lack of knowledge about the complex political, economic, and strategic interests intersecting at the China–Yunnan border, and willingly listened to Bodard. Merlin sought approval from the Minister of Colonies in France and authorized the transit of Tang's opium through Tonkin.[64] At the time, one foreseeable complication was sending the opium to Canton and Hong Kong, where British opium exports from India prevailed and might raise objections from British merchants and possibly lead to diplomatic tensions. Thus, French administrators in Tonkin decided to label this flow of opium, not as a reexport of foreign (Chinese) opium, but as an inland transit of moving opium from one part of China to another. It was also decided that the opium should not go to Canton and Hong Kong (where British surveillance was intense), but instead shipped from Haiphong to Shanghai and Tientsin without a French flag.[65] In January 1923, the French authorities agreed to allow 100 tons of Tang's Yunnan opium to enter Tonkin, moving by train to Lao Kay and then the port of Haiphong: seventy-five tons would go to parts of China beyond Macao, while twenty-five tons would be sold to the Indochina opium monopoly at a preferential rate. In addition to the supply of cheaper Chinese opium, the French obtained an advance payment of 50,000 piastres for repairs to the Yunnan–Tonkin railroad.[66]

Complications arose as the British learned of the French–Chinese deal and delays occurred in the process of delivering from Yunnan to Haiphong. Quickly, the Minister of Colonies and Minister of Foreign Affairs ordered Indochina to halt the transactions, and Bodard was instructed to explain to Tang the risks of continuing to transport the opium because the British would likely seize it as soon as the ships traversed waters near Hong Kong.[67] However, at this point, seventy-two tons of Tang's opium had already arrived in the port of Haiphong and was being stored in a French monopoly warehouse awaiting shipment overseas. It was unfeasible to send this product back to Yunnan, not least because the raw opium would soon deteriorate. Thus, offered the French high imperial authorities, the colony of Indochina would buy all of the Yunnan warlord's unsold opium, making a financial sacrifice and liquidating the matter. Tang accepted. And Director Kircher of the Department of Customs and Excise made arrangements to purchase the seventy-two tons of opium sitting in the Haiphong warehouse. He complained about the arrangement, noting that "I do not want my name to be compromised in the least for a matter that I have agreed to 'unravel' only to save the honor of the French government and [colonial] government of Indochina."[68] Yet, Kircher proceeded, following existing precedents for managing opium purchases from Yunnan and using funds from the reserve and procurement accounts.[69]

A Disastrous Abundance

It began with just a few numbers. For the upcoming fiscal year of 1925, Kircher reported a few more chests of opium sold than had actually occurred, using funds from the emergency procurement and reserve accounts created in 1908 and 1911. These "fictitious sales" (*cessions fictives*), in effect, allowed the Indochina opium monopoly's officials to treat unsold opium sitting in a Saigon warehouse *as if* it had already been sold.[70] It served as a mechanism for advance reimbursement; the general budget was to be paid back after actual sales were made. Given how well Indian opium usually sold in Indochina, the director reasoned that this transfer of funds was hardly a risky measure. Surely, the accounts would soon be solvent next year, prayed Kircher.

His optimism would prove wrong. The Indian opium sold more poorly than expected that year, and thus the monopoly quickly raised the retail price for Indian opium in June 1925, seeking to recoup the funds used to buy Tang's opium. But sales plummeted further, and the monopoly remained unable to pay back the general budget. To make matters worse, the Yunnan product was also selling poorly, and therefore a large amount of already old opium remained in the monopoly's warehouses, which would only deteriorate over time. As the situation repeated, administrators explored solutions. In 1928, they introduced a new, enticingly branded "star" (*étoile*) blend of opium, a mix of 90 percent Indian opium with 10 percent "local" product, which likely included some of the Yunnan stock.[71] But neither this blended product nor the pure 100 percent Indian opium sold well. Thus, the monopoly reported fictive sales for 1929 again and purchased more Indian opium that was sold at an even higher retail price on the Indochina opium market for 1930. This resulted in the largest drop in official opium sales in the history of the monopoly's operations since 1899. Only 10,000 tons of Indian opium were sold across the colony, and sales plummeted further to less than 7,000 in 1931, 4,600 in 1932, and to little more than 1,000 tons in 1933.[72] For each year, administrators used the fictive sales mechanism, reporting more Indian opium than actually sold and overdrawing the monopoly's procurement account. The administrative practice outlived the individual who launched it: Kircher's successor Joseph Ginestou authorized another *cession fictive*, reporting an additional 2,000 tons of opium as sold, followed by another 3,400 tons of *cessions fictives* the next year.

It is worth clarifying why the Indochina opium monopoly continued to procure the Indian product despite struggles to sell it and overdraw the procurement accounts, because this aggressive optimism sheds light on how what would later be deemed irrational and thus corrupt conduct by metropolitan inspectors made sense for local administrators at the time. Recall that the the British Empire announced in 1926 that it would incrementally reduce India's opium exports for nonmedical purposes and completely halt the trade by 1935 (Chapter 3). The French authorities received this notice on July 1, 1926 from the Government of India.[73] With a clear and looming deadline in mind, the Indochina opium monopoly's administrators reasoned it was worth buying and stocking as much raw opium as possible. There was a sense of a real end to this foreign supply of opium, which had long dominated the colony's market. There was also a sense of anxiety because Indian opium represented more than 90 percent of the raw product manufactured in the Saigon factory, and consumers buying from the French opium shops across Indochina were accustomed to the smoother taste of this product compared to other foreign sources.

Local administrators opined that anticipated shortages of this desired product were problems that could be solved by stockpiling. To be clear, it was hardly the case that these actors were dismissive of or deaf to the international politics of anti-opium causes at the time, nor were they necessarily trying to continue to sell opium. But at the level of everyday work, they had short time horizons, oriented first toward preventing any sudden disruptions to the opium monopoly. While higher minded reformers worried about the morality of colonial rule and baser motives of profit certainly colored their ways of viewing the world, the monopoly's administrators were also busy, tasked with the nitty-gritty work of managing existing opium distributors, communicating with shopkeepers, setting sales prices, keeping track of how much opium was being sold and where, calculating the costs and returns of these activities, as well as recording and reporting all that had been done. From their everyday perspective, ensuring the basic stability of the monopoly's operations was foremost on their agenda, for which securing a stable supply of opium was necessary.

However, purchased Indian opium continued to sell poorly and began to accumulate in large quantities in the Saigon opium factory's warehouse. The Indochina opium monopoly's outstanding payments rose from 760,000 piasters due at the end of 1931 to a cumulative 5 million piasters owed by 1934. To deal with such ballooning debts, administrators further overdrew the procurement accounts.

When exactly did these makeshift measures of fictitious opium sales and advance payments cross into the realm of illegality? In 1935, the monopoly's spending practices caught the attention of a financial controller who noted a 1.2 million piaster difference in the value of opium stock reported by the Saigon opium factory and amounts in the colony's general budget. This official informed his superiors in Paris of troubling irregularities and began an internal investigation.[74]

The procurement accounts were in "entirely false positions," and "I cannot determine the totality of the *cessions fictives*," despaired the financial controller.[75] He identified a paper trail of yearly transfers amounting to roughly 2,000 ton of opium that had been overreported as sold between 1930 and 1934, as shown in Table 6.1. But, according to the financial controller, "these excesses, in fact, do not even account for the totality of the *cessions fictives*."[76] He found many subaccounts within the procurement accounts, with different labels for emergency funds transferred through local banks across locations including Saigon, Haiphong, and Calcutta with calculations that he struggled to make sense of. On paper, it appeared as if the value of the Indian opium stocks had increased from 8 to 12 million piastres since 1929 and had been sold, with the procurement accounts maintaining a healthy balance of approximately 4 million piastres by 1935. However, the financial controller discovered that the accounts were actually empty, and Indian opium that should have been long sold remained in the Saigon opium factory's warehouse. The advance payments had generated a dangerously artificial liquidity and made it appear as if the monopoly was more solvent than it actually was, inflating the actual value of existing opium stocks and enabling reckless spending behavior. Moreover, the way that the monopoly officials had been transferring funds between a department's account and the general budget was also illegal, deemed the financial controller, invoking a 1921 law that declared such accounting practices void.[77] Thus, a once officially sanctioned administrative practice became illegal, with an acquired clarity on the risky and dangerous nature of past decisions, which had at the time served the pursuit of flexibility and ensuring stability.

The hidden inner life of the Indochina opium monopoly became further exposed in illegal and troubling terms to external observers. For instance, in

TABLE 6.1. The Financial Controller's Calculation of Fictitious Opium Sales by the Opium Monopoly of French Indochina, 1930–1934

Exercice budgétaire d'imputation	Catégorie d'opium	Quantités cédées fictivement	Valeur	Observations
1930	Indien 351 et 361	240 caisses	799.004$	Rembourées au compte approvisonnements généraux
1931	Indien lot 2i 1930 Indien lot 4i 1930	200 caisses 200 caisses	752,322$ 754,058 1,506,380$	
1932	Indien lot 5i 1930	200 caisses (soit 8,400 kg)	754,075$	Les cessions fictives semblant avoir éte beaucoup plus importante (voir p. 24)
1933	Indien lot 6i 1930 Opium local saisi PV 16 à 25 1932	200	750,580$ 5,620 806,830$	
1934	Indien 7i 1930 8i 1930 10i 1931 Opium local saisie PV 9–10 11-12-13-19 de 1933 Lot 27 L. 1933	200 caisses 121 caisses 130–5,160 kg	750,590$ 455,805 489,519 50,956 58,274 1,805,274$	Lots 8i et 10i rachetés par l'exercice 1934 au compte approvisionnement généraux dont $740,290 non réintégrées.

Source: Report by le Directeur du contrôle financier, undated likely 1937, VNA1/DFI/1746.

January 1936, a customs inspector visited the Saigon warehouse and found Indian opium bought five years earlier bearing traces of termites and other insects, and clearly rotting.[78] In turn, the opium monopoly officials gained more reason to hide, or at least obscure from metropolitan scrutiny, an escalating problem. By the next year in 1937, more than 20,000 tons of Indian opium had accumulated, and were further deteriorating. The monopoly ran out of warehouse space and resorted to stashing the opium in a shop on the premises of the Saigon factory and even in the cellar of the Bank of Indochina. It lacked funds to build a proper facility, for neither had proper insulation or ventilation, which further spoiled the precious stocks.[79] Moreover, not only was there a direct loss in value from acquiring such large sums of Indian opium, but the monopoly had also "frozen considerable sums for several years and burdened public finances," with indirect costs of foregone interest on the value of the Indian opium stocks," according to one local administrator in the Department of Customs and Excise.[80] And yet again, Indian opium continued to sell poorly, with reports from the monopoly's licensed sellers indicating that consumers had been steadily turning to cheaper, lower-quality opium from the Laos–Tonkin–Yunnan borderland ever since 1925, when the monopoly had raised retail prices for the Indian opium.

Thus, the Indochina opium monopoly officials now encountered a difficult reality produced by the choices they had made over the past decade: creating blends to dispose of Tang's Yunnan opium, raising the prices of Indian opium, and overdrawing procurement accounts. The 1935 deadline for British India's promised halt of opium exports had passed. French Indochina had successfully acquired large quantities of this valuable opium, which they no longer needed. And in the process, new tastes for Chinese and domestic opium had been fostered, which the Indochina monopoly neither had available nor could afford. The procurement account was empty, and the warehouses were overflowing with rotting opium.

An Old Beginning

This bleak impasse, however, did not spell the end of the Indochina opium monopoly. On May 27, 1935, the new director for the Department of Customs and Excise Joseph Ginestou had already requested an advance of 6.3 million piasters from the Treasury to open a new account, promising to repay the full amount within ten years.[81] The request was approved four months later by the colony's treasurer, the director of public accounting, and the Governor

General. With the replenished funds, the monopoly was able to start afresh, selling opium across Indochina and procuring supplies.

A month after receiving this new cash infusion, a new brand of opium called the "dragon" blend was launched, similar to the "star" blend of the 1920s that mixed Indian and Chinese opium. Like its predecessor, the "dragon" blend also failed to sell widely, prompting officials this time, in late 1936, to lower the retail price.[82] It was a very short-lived measure that was quickly reversed the next year under pressure from Paris, where high officials worried about international criticism if word got out that opium prices were being lowered in Indochina and appearing as if France was blatantly encouraging its colonial subjects to buy opium. However, this short window of cheap opium sales sufficed to spur demand for the "dragon" blend. Sales skyrocketed from 120 kg of dragon opium sold in November 1936 to 400 kg in January 1937, 1,000 kg in February, 1,200 kg in March, and 1,500 kg in April 1937. On the 27th of that month, the monopoly raised the price of this blend again. The new Governor General, Jules Brévié, explained that the higher price reflected rising manufacturing costs, adding that it would have the benefit of curbing outward smuggling from Indochina.[83]

Less publicly acknowledged was the complete exhaustion of the Indochina monopoly stock of Yunnan opium following the quick and spectacular dragon sales in 1936 and 1937. Still, too much Benares opium remained. The opium administrators worried that it "would take at least thirteen years to liquidate."[84] If the monopoly hoped to continue to sell this blend, which Brévié privately agreed was necessary, a viable alternative to Yunnan opium to mix with the aging Indian product was needed.

A new solution emerged again from old precedents. Local administrators turned again to poppy produced in northern Tonkin and Laos. Recall that the opium monopoly had initially purchased from Hmong cultivators, but discontinued the practice in 1925, following the adulteration scandal. Restoring purchasing campaigns with these highland populations required flexibility, insisted Director Ginestou, repeating a now familiar line of reasoning for sanctioning emergency funds and discretionary spending. He explained to Governor General Brévié how these highland populations were "unsophisticated" people, "shy and wary" sellers who would be unhappy with any delayed payments for their opium.[85] Precedents of Hmong uprisings and unrest in Laos showed, according to this administrator, that the French colonial state would risk "encouraging them to sell their opium to smugglers, to the detriment of our revenue." Persuaded, Brévié authorized the use of the monopoly's procurement account to make advance payments to the Hmong.[86]

With confidence, the Governor General explained his reasoning to the Minister of Colonies in May 1938. Past problems had been resolved, according to Brévié.[87] He detailed in a long report how spending practices for customs and excise were now closely monitored by financial experts, and noted improvements in bureaucratic management that rendered future possibilities of spoiled opium or reckless stockpiling unlikely. The balance of Indian opium within the "dragon" blend had also been increased, which would likely enable the department to liquidate the unprofitable stocks "by late 1941 or early 1942."[88] Thus, Brévié reported, all was well. And although the overdrawn funds from the Department of Customs and Excise's spending account had not yet been paid back to the general budget, this would likely occur very soon, promised the Governor General. There were already plans for an initial payment of 1.5 million piasters in the works, Brévié assured the Minister of the Colonies. "If the pace of sales continues at the current pace," he cheerfully declared, "the advance will be cleared within . . . four years."[89]

Perhaps the sanguine outlook of the Governor General had been well warranted. Perhaps the opium monopoly's debts would have been paid off; and there had actually been good reason to place confidence in the inner operations of the Department of Customs and Excise for this French colony for managing opium markets with an eye toward eventually restricting commercial sales. It is difficult to tell. Before the four years that Brévié promised passed, a war broke out in 1939.

The Inheritance

World War II created new exigencies for the colonial administration in Indochina. It interrupted trade routes and the locus of metropolitan authority shifted from the Third Republic's civilian bureaucrats in Paris to officers of the French State based in Vichy, led by Marshal Philippe Pétain. Pétain espoused a National Revolution that asserted paternalistic visions of a hierarchical racialized society and fascist rule, which extended to Indochina under Governor General Jean Decoux, a former admiral in the French Navy. Adding to the challenges of managing a wartime colony, the Japanese Empire invaded Indochina in 1940 and Decoux's military officials administered the colony alongside the Imperial Japanese Army (IJA) until 1945. Decoux pursued a vision of reform infused with Pétain's revolutionary vision, which wrought significant changes on the socioeconomic life of the colony.[90]

However, the war also left many aspects of everyday administration unchanged for those involved in opium affairs. Between 1939 and 1945, the Indochina opium monopoly continued to operate. Disrupted overseas trade intensified struggles to secure supplies and administrators increasingly relied on opium from northern Tonkin and Laos. This shift only made sense, argued the High Resident for Tonkin, who urged authorities in Saigon to encourage the Hmong to increase poppy cultivation within the colony. War represented an extraordinary context, insisted this administrator, in which the international community was falling apart and obligations for drug control were a luxury. "How long is France to stay committed to the Geneva agreements," he asked, "when other powers clearly care little or nothing at all about them?"[91] "The League of Nations is dead; and, right or wrong, we need opium," agreed others in the colony.[92] Thus, in 1940, the Indochina monopoly purchased 7.4 tons of opium from the highland inhabitants.[93]

Governor General Decoux had arrived in Indochina soon after this purchasing campaign had taken place, beginning his tenure with an inheritance from the Third Republic era administration: poppy cultivation in the colony. "The question of local production has been a subject of study since 1900 and forty years later it remains salient," explained one advisor to Decoux, urging the new governor to affirm the Vichy regime's policy in Indochina as continuing to sanction within-colony opium production and operating the Saigon opium factory.[94] Decoux's wartime administration also took over its predecessor's outstanding debts and its accounting practices for creating artificial liquidity and advancing cash payments.

The wartime French Indochina opium monopoly continued as it always had. In early 1942, four senior administrators congratulated each other for their work in organizing yet another purchasing campaign from the highlands of Tonkin and Laos.[95] Georges Gautier, the Governor General's secretary general, informed Eugène Mordant, military commander of Indochina's troops, that Director Ginestou would happily accept the same rates as the previous two years for the military's help in transporting the opium to Saigon. Gautier reminded Mordant that the colony now had nine purchasing centers across the northern expanse of the colony and noted that Ginestou would be grateful for the commander's continued assistance. Mordant replied quickly and positively: the opium monopoly would have as many trucks and men as it needed, at a daily rate of "forty francs per truck and forty francs per driver, plus fuel and insurance."[96]

Around the same time, Ginestou was also corresponding with the colony's Director of Finances, Jean Cousin, asking for money to pay for this transportation.[97] An extra 4,000 piasters or so would also be greatly appreciated, added the Director of Customs and Excise. In the Laos–Tonkin–Yunnan borderland, he explained, Vietnamese mandarins served as intermediaries for reaching the rural poppy growers. These local elites needed money, preferably in cash, to pay the cultivators, arrange local means for transports, and to compete with smugglers, who also sought Hmong opium. Ginestou thus articulated a new reason for advances on monopoly's procurement account.

Ginestou assured Cousin that this advance would not give rise to the type of accounting problems that had occurred in the past. "I'm hoping you'll grant my request," he wrote, "using funds deducted from accounts of the Hanoi customs official, which will be paid from our general supplies account as soon as the opium has been obtained by our agents."[98] According to Ginestou, cash advances were critical to the success of the monopoly's purchasing campaigns and even though "this method was not technically in compliance with regulations, it still seemed the only one capable of rapidly producing a solution."[99] Cousin agreed and authorized, first, the 4,000 piasters for Lao Kay and then an additional 7,000 for a neighboring province. Soon, the Indochina opium monopoly had secured a 5 million piaster advance to purchase opium from the sales centers in Tonkin and Laos, as well as to pay for transportation costs.

There were some internal reservations to these practices. For instance, Decoux expressed skepticism towards further expanding domestic poppy production, wary of the lack of infrastructure and entrenched smuggler networks throughout the highland borderlands. But Ginestou, invoking his knowledge of the opium monopoly's precedents over the past four decades, explained to the new Governor General that interrupted supplies and halting sales would provoke grave financial and social consequences.[100] Reports abound that in the following year, political dissidents, "communists and crackpots," were using Saigon's opium dens as recruiting sites.[101] Anxiously, Decoux's office went beyond Ginestou's recommendation to prepare an executive order to finally ban opium altogether, declaring all consumption illegal, starting with a ban for French citizens and Indochinese state employees. In early January 1942, Decoux sent a draft of the order to Ginestou.

Ginestou responded with a detailed confidential memo that reconstructed the colony's history of opium administration and portrayed exigencies on the ground, in a way that illustrates vividly how the local expertise of a situated administrator shaped the policy direction that higher authorities would pursue.

Apologizing for his memo's length, Gintesou began by explaining that "the question is of such importance to the colony that it deserves to be dealt with fully."[102] Many trends militated against taking official action against opium, Ginestou argued. He argued first, that opium consumption was not growing in Indochina. Yes, opium sales were increasing, but this was misleading, Ginestou claimed. Per capita consumption was actually decreasing relative to the colony's population growth, which had increased from eighteen to twenty-five million individuals over the previous decade, in addition to a growing number of migrant Chinese. Harmful excesses due to opium use were rare among the French and Indochinese in Indochina, Ginestou continued. For the period of the late 1930s when sales had increased, he explained, it was not that people were consuming more opium, but that they were hoarding what had become a valuable good, not least because the price of "dragon" blend opium was high and nonsmokers could use the drug as a form of currency. Put differently, opium had taken on an alternative economic life in the colony, which did not relate to its widespread consumption, insisted the director.[103]

Ginestou's second argument was that a ban was not feasible given the opium monopoly's current finances. Opium revenue generated from commercial sales remained important. Even if the ban were limited to French citizens and Indochinese functionaries, "a very large and important basis of clientele disappears," he wrote.[104] Ginestou distinguished between addicts who consumed to harmful excess and those who casually indulged in the habit among the French, Chinese, and native inhabitants of Indochina. The latter were the important clientele; if their habit was officially curtailed, the colonial government would in turn risk losing between 20 and 25 percent of its current receipts. "The greater the scope of the ban, the greater the gap to fill," Ginestou pointed out. "I am well aware that financial objections should not get in the way of actions inspired by lofty ideals of morality and dignity," he said, but balancing the colonial budget and replacing the foregone millions of piasters entailed its own set of obligations toward taxpayers in the colony. Indeed, if one stepped back for a moment to reflect, as Ginestou advised Decoux to do, "for centuries many nations had combatted social ills, including prostitution, drinking, drug addiction, and gambling," yet none had succeeded. The reason was simple: "Nations have indeed made decisions. But there are two steps in a decision: first, resolve; then, action. The nations concerned have never gone past the first step, likely because they consider that life, or reality, escapes all man-made legislation, and it is thus better to safeguard morality by channeling and containing vices, rather than trying to destroy them."[105]

In other words, banning opium would be fundamentally futile. Imagine, he implored the Governor General, the social repercussions that would follow from a failed attempt: intensified contraband, popular discontent expressed in public criticism, anonymous letters, and an "overflow of rancor and hate" against the regime. "The Annamites, like the French, are a passionate people, as we have seen from their support of our National Revolution, but such passion also invites criminal tendencies exemplified by dissidents [from the Vichy cause]." Now was not the time to test these people, which would risk "instability, both intellectual and moral disequilibrium, and social convulsion."

Finally, warned Ginestou, whether a ban on opium consumption was limited to French citizens and Indochinese officials was irrelevant. The selective application of any official interdiction would invite legal inconsistencies and political problems concerning the status of indigenous civil servants. Ginestou offered Decoux two alternative drafts of a proposed ban that avoided targeting French citizens and Indochinese officials. Formally, argued the Director of Customs and Excise, the Governor General would risk introducing a law that violated French civil and criminal codes that established distinctions based either on nationality or on all inhabitants of a territory.[106] Yet from his perspective, declared Ginestou, these legalistic inconsistencies were problematic but hardly insurmountable. What was truly unjustifiable, and indeed hypocritical, was making a vice into a crime for a Frenchman in Indochina, while letting nationals of foreign countries free to continue a practice condemned in the name of morality. With regard to other vices—public drunkenness, gambling, and incitements of morality, a general approach was taken. Why was opium an exception? Why did the protection for French in Indochina not extend to foreigners in this specific case?

Ginestou pointed to the lack of answers to these questions, and counseled Decoux to take caution before stepping into these murky areas of colonial regulation, especially, he emphasized, since any ban on opium consumption would surely fail, as had been the case across the world—in China, in India, in South America, and in Canada—in addition to the instructive histories of alcohol prohibition in the United States and Switzerland.[107] For Indochina, the proposed ban would create new categories of *opiophages*, namely, "eaters" (*mangeurs*), "drinkers" (*buveurs*), and "chewers" (*chiqueurs*) of opium "amongst the poorest classes and drug addicts" as well as spur "consumers of black and red narcotic pills, of morphine, of heroin, of cocaine, of laudanum, of hashish." The French colony did not have an opium problem yet, but if Decoux pursued this course of action, a drug problem would surely emerge, concluded Ginestou.

It is unclear which of these arguments persuaded Decoux, but the proposed ban on opium consumption failed to materialize. The wartime opium monopoly continued to purchase opium from northern Tonkin and Laos while the monopoly continued to use variants of fictitious sales to sustain this practice. Old problems recurred, as did pursuits of new solutions. "The Director of Customs and Excise has informed me of your objections to his plan to use advances from the provincial budgets [for Laos and Tonkin] to pay premiums to opium sellers," wrote Decoux to the colony's treasurer in 1943.[108] The treasurer had pointed out the lack of legal basis for such use of such funds. Decoux replied that there were political reasons to avoid drawing too much publicity to this measure or to give it a paper existence. He urged the treasurer to approve the funds.

Lasting Significance

World War II ended in 1945, and both Japan and Vichy France withdrew from Indochina. French presence was reestablished, however, through a colonial security and federal police service under the purview of a High Commissioner based in Saigon. In 1946, the French authorities officially ended the opium monopoly.[109] A federal ordinance declared the end of legal opium sales and banned opium shops and smoking dens in French territory.[110] Instead, the state would provide limited supplies for medical and pharmaceutical uses of opium and open clinics for addicts where they could seek detoxification and treatment under the supervision of a doctor. The clinics would keep a registry of the people they treated and issue medical certificates and the ordinance further decreed its oversight by a commission composed of public health, customs, and excise administrators.

However, according to Pierre Perrier, the director of the federal police at the time, actually ending the operations of the opium monopoly was an impossible task. Not only was the "strict sense" of the 1946 ordinance's text difficult to follow, but problems arose as the specific task of procuring necessary opium for the clinics and supplying the detoxification centers was being done by the Department of Customs and Excise.[111] "The police currently have more important tasks to perform," Perrier explained to the High Commissioner of the colony, adding that overseeing detoxification clinics in Saigon and Chôlon and detecting clandestine smoking facilities required manpower he did not have.[112] Rather, the task fell on the customs and excise administrators who, as the police director acknowledged, were making a mess of the new medical regime.

Of course, Perrier had his own agenda. In March 1948, an American agent from the Federal Bureau of Narcotics had been in Saigon collecting information about opium use and had written a scathing report criticizing French administrators on the ground as collecting bribes from the clinics and effectively running a quasi-legal market for the drug.[113] Perrier's men had intercepted the report and the director sought to explain to the High Commissioner how facts on the ground differed from the somewhat "fanciful" account of this foreign observer.[114]

Perrier explained his reality on colonial ground: since 1946, most smoking dens had only changed their signs and reopened as detoxification centers, while new Chinese hotels had emerged in Saigon that specialized in secretly supplied their guests with medical opium bought from the clinics, resold at nearly twice the price set by the government. Local administrators were overburdened, not only failing to control such illicit activities, but also unable to supply registered individuals with medical certificates and thus pushing them towards the black market. Demand in the colony was high, the police director informed the High Commissioner, but "opium is missing."[115] Thus, to solve this official problem of procurement, Perrier concluded, an official from the customs department had just been sent to the Middle East to place orders for new supplies.

Conclusion

This chapter has examined the stubborn resilience of the French opium monopoly of Indochina and the nature of its prohibition politics. Recurrent attempts to purchase and pay for imported opium—that were short-sighted in retrospect but deemed reasonable at the time by those most intimately involved—escalated into an acute crisis of debt that the colonial bureaucracy struggled to manage throughout the first half of the twentieth century. Local administrators at once defined and addressed problems tied to procuring opium to supply to domestic consumers, which were rooted in antecedent tensions embedded in the colony-wide regulatory framework instituted during the late nineteenth century. While everyday work continued over the course of the next three decades, the legal environment and world around local administrators changed, reconfiguring the terms on which once vaguely permissible forms of importing opium were made illegal, altering the meaning of once tacitly authorized ways of spending. In this evolving context, local administrators exerted increasingly less control over the outcomes of their actions yet were propelling the opium monopoly toward more illegal transactions and secretive financing.

The larger theoretical significance to understanding the experience of French Indochina lies in rethinking the meaning of bureaucratic discretion and its effects on the colonial state. Understanding the microlevel processes and inner anxieties of French local administrators further sheds alternative light on common historical understandings of the life and eventual fate of the Indochina opium monopoly. Its operations carried on during World War II and soon thereafter, sustained by the outstanding obligations of its administrative past, which were passed on to future state builders of the post–World War II era. This lasting legacy is the subject of Part III.

Part III

7

Colonial Legacies

OPIUM PROHIBITION ACROSS Southeast Asia under European rule marked a dramatic reversal of the economic bases of governance on which colonial states were built and officially justified rule over others. Yet, the extraordinary nature of this change is often overlooked, because in retrospect, ending the commercial life of opium seems like such an obvious thing to have happened. So deeply etched in our current imaginary are the dangers of drug trafficking and harms of opiate addiction that a state's imperatives for restricting these activities seem self-evident.

This book has revealed the myopia of this presumption. For the many European powers that divided Southeast Asia since the nineteenth century, establishing the state as the sole locus of control over opium-related economic activities and asserting authority to intervene into society was not an inevitable outcome. Rather, it constituted a slow, hesitant, and difficult process of administrative reform. In Part I, I located the beginnings of this process in early moments of territorial conquest, when local administrators began to regulate opium's commercial life through vice taxation, despite a great deal of ambiguity about what exactly defined its consumption as a colonial vice. Unlike modern states that puzzle over the people they govern before powering over society, colonial states did the opposite.[1] They powered before and puzzling, borrowing regulatory rationales from other colonies, developing ad hoc templates for categorizing people, as well as collecting revenue and claiming just reasons for doing so, while clarifying in retrospect why the colonial vice of opium consumption constituted an object of taxation at all. Such early overreach cast a long shadow of the work of subsequent administrators who at once addressed and reproduced myriad problems anchored in imperfect and vaguely justified arrangements of the past for regulating opium consumption. The era of the opium monopolies from the 1890s to 1940s was a period of recurrent struggles within the bureaucracies of colonial states.

Part II took a fine-grained lens to the experiences of British Burma, Malaya, and French Indochina, exploring the administrative anxieties that bedeviled different opium monopolies. Each case demonstrated the bureaucratic construction of opium problems by tracing how small inherited tensions escalated over time into large challenges that local administrators defined officially as problems and in turn committed to solving. Through everyday work, seemingly minor officials of empire generated the conditions of possibility for major shifts in regulatory approaches toward a direction of expanding the scope of state involvement in opium markets and clarifying the permissible boundaries of opium-related commercial activities. The rise of opium prohibition as such entailed a process of colonial state transformation from within. And it unfolded unevenly across Southeast Asia, at different moments in time and through policies that took varied forms, depending on the ways by which local administrators gave official reality to perceived problems, defining the necessity and viability of anti-opium reforms.

Existing histories have often viewed the opium monopolies of Southeast Asia in light of revenue collected from and injury occasioned by opium consumption and thus discern the intent of colonial states through the depredations its institutions caused. But the story becomes more complicated when we look deep inside of the bureaucracy. With a shift in perspective comes an alternative interpretive stance: one that requires taking seriously what actual work involved administrators were doing and the languages of prohibition they wrote. It also requires questioning straight lines drawn between what the colonial state sought and how its actions impacted subject populations. Attending to the stories that emerge from within the state does not change the fact that opium monopolies profited grossly from a drug sold to the detriment of colonized subjects. What it alters is the way we understand how the power of rulers was organized and the nature of colonial governance.

There is something distressingly pedestrian about how colonial states governed in the ways they did, under the sweeping rubric of opium prohibition. Along with an unsatisfying absence of straightforward revenue imperatives or clear-cut intent for social control, it also becomes difficult to dismiss the narratives about harm, profit, and morality that involved administrators told as the alibis of official actors hiding base motives of exploitation and domination, or as mere performances of moral respectability before external audiences. Rather, what we better see is an ill-planned, uneasy process of change, riddled with inconsistencies in policy and language that were not reflections of simple hypocrisy, but expressions of deeper underlying tensions in bureaucracies that had slowly built up over time.

Colonial opium prohibition as such, has left lasting imprints on contemporary Southeast Asia. Part III turns to these colonial legacies. This chapter traces the stubborn endurance of the opium monopolies during and after World War II, showing how these colonial institutions have shaped the punitive approaches toward drug offenders that states adopt today. It also dwells on what has become invisible and taken for granted about the power of the state in the realm of opium and drug addiction, through illustrative photographs of colonial life under opium monopolies in Burma, Malaya, and Indochina and their afterlives. The final chapter concludes by addressing the analytical and normative implications to understanding the colonial administrative state in light of its fragilities and reinterpreting bureaucratic discretion as a creative act of problem solving.

I have argued throughout this book that the anti-opium reforms that local colonial administrators pursued were always imperfect, with myriad perverse effects. As seen in British Burma (Chapter 4), the 1894 ban on popular opium consumption was followed by an official "discovery" of increased crime in the colony, in part because the illegal and illegitimate nature of opium consumption became more clearly defined by the colonial state. In Malaya (Chapter 5), while the opium revenue replacement reserve fund of 1925 enabled the British to demonstrably reduce their reliance on opium in the Straits Settlements, it also established illicit government finances by reconfiguring profits raised from opium sales into a form of imperial investment wealth with limited public accountability and visibility in official records. In Indochina (Chapter 6) during the 1930s and 1940s, French efforts to reduce the colony's dependence on foreign opium imports and adjust retail sales prices for opium spurred poppy growing among the highland minorities along the northern border with China.

Crime, secretive finances, and large-scale poppy cultivation. Such were the inheritances that the newly independent countries of Southeast Asia carried into the second half of the twentieth century. The results of bygone colonial policies were presumed as a fait accompli by postcolonial state builders. Given an existing opium economy associated with crime and already coupled in murky ways with government funds, how should a state govern? With ongoing and expanding agricultural bases for opium production in territories where issues of border insecurity and social disorder prevailed, what should a state do? New rulers did not pursue utopian visions of a world without dangerous drugs, but took an already existing problem of illicit drug economies as their point of departure. And amid the exigencies of postwar reconstruction and decolonization, new rulers formulated solutions similarly to how their colonial predecessors had once done: by powering first and puzzling later. Quick money could be found in the excess stocks of opium in government warehouses and underground drug markets around former government retail shops; politicians could secure off-the-book funds and buy allies in a volatile new political order, while urgent efforts to stabilize unrest in both urban areas and borderlands could utilize the ties and networks that had once interwoven the colonial state with opium suppliers, armed actors, as well as poppy growers in frontier borderlands. By the 1960s, colonial-era opium monopolies had become reconfigured into the invisible sinews of power, money, and patronage of postcolonial states.[2]

World War II and the Afterlives of Colonial Opium Monopolies

World War II swiftly interrupted the imperial world that European powers had fashioned for Southeast Asia. In September 1940, Japan's armed forces invaded French Indochina, and within six months conquered parts of British Malaya and Burma as well as the Dutch East Indies and American-ruled Philippines. The Japanese occupation lasted until August 1945. It was a brief yet profoundly disruptive period to many existing European arrangements for colonial governance.[3] The IJA and Navy instituted military administrations across Southeast Asia that reconfigured local political economies and societies to serve wartime needs for supplies, labor, as well as secure the cooperation and allegiance of local elites and populations.[4] Not only did the Japanese introduce centralized planning systems within conquered territories in ways that promoted self-sufficiency, but they also pursued a regional approach to economic autarky that severed transport in and out of colonies once deeply interwoven through trade and well-connected to metropolitan areas of Europe.[5] Moreover, as civilian authorities retreated from the region, new officers of the Allied forces—namely, the American–British–Dutch–Australian forces until August 1943 and the combined South East Asia Command (SEAC) thereafter—also developed new arrangements for mobilizing support, securing resources, and fighting enemies.

For the global political economy of opium, World War II also ushered in radical changes, because of a growing need for opium and its alkaloids for medicinal purposes. Most significantly, India temporarily reversed its nonexport policy for opium, becoming the main supplier of opium for the Allied countries east of the Suez Canal.[6] Emergency wartime exigencies sanctioned a new abundance of opium production and trade that in turn fostered new contraband flows. Following the virtual closing of the Mediterranean Sea to Allied forces after the fall of Yugoslavia to Axis powers in 1941 and interruptions to trans-Pacific mercantile shipping, the business of smuggling Indian opium into Europe and into North America flourished.[7] In other words, the direction of illicit opium trades became reversed during the war. As Figure 7.1 illustrates, prior to 1939, contraband opium from India flowed to the east, through ports like Singapore, Hong Kong, Shanghai, and Yokohama to cross the Pacific Ocean and enter Vancouver, Seattle, and San Francisco. But from 1941 to 1945, smugglers of Indian opium were moving westward, circling the Cape of Good Hope or risking passage through the Suez Canal and Mediterranean to reach Europe and then traverse the Atlantic Ocean to enter major ports like New York and Montreal.

Yet, amid such changes, the opium monopolies across Southeast Asia continued to operate as they always had. Wartime dynamics that altered the imperial political order and global opium economy outpaced change within the region. Across Japanese occupied territories, Allied and Axis forces alike preserved and rebuilt opium shops and factories, while also making use of opium's utility for local populations. In Burma from 1943 to 1945, for instance, the Japanese used opium to pay workers conscripted to build wartime infrastructure, including an aerodrome and a railroad linking Bangkok to Rangoon.[8] British and American officers in Burma also turned opium into a type of currency, especially in areas where paper money could not buy the cooperation of Burmese and Chinese populations.[9] In the Straits Settlements as well, the Japanese assumed control over the opium monopoly, continuing to sell and distribute opium; they also repaired the opium factory in Singapore, which had been partially destroyed during bombings in December 1941. "Currently," reported a Japanese research bureau in 1943, the Singapore opium factory was operating at one-third of its previous capacity, yet still able to supply "three million tubes for roughly 70,000 opium smokers in Malaya and Sumatra."[10] In Indochina, as we have seen in Chapter 6, the Vichy regime upheld existing contracts with Hmong poppy growers to purchase their product and transport it to Saigon for sales and export. Alongside the Japanese until early 1945, the French colonial opium monopoly's ties to local growers and key distribution networks linking the far northern Laos–Tonkin–Yunnan border and urban south also remained intact.[11]

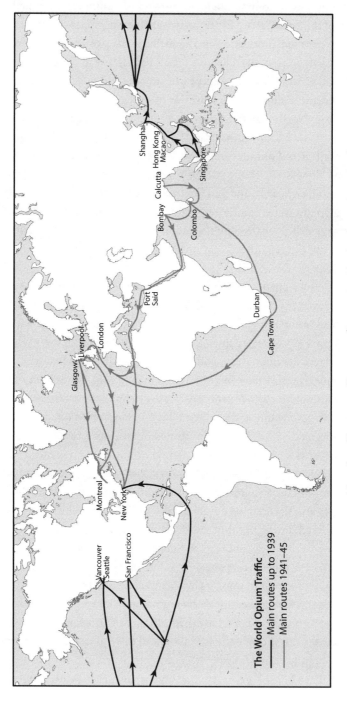

FIGURE 7.1. Map of world opium traffic, c. 1946. (Source: British Library, IOR/L&E/732.)

World War II did not interrupt the colonial worlds that European opium monopolies had made since the late nineteenth century. Rather, opium-related administrative activities were continued under the purview of wartime authorities, following new political and territorial boundaries that blurred the jurisdictions that had divided European colonies. One example concerns the territorial expansion of poppy cultivation at the border between Burma and Thailand. Prior to the war, the British permitted limited quantities of poppy cultivation at the far northeastern edge of Burma for the Shan States, which were principalities ruled indirectly under indigenous rulers called *sawbwas*, while the Thai monarchy banned local production altogether.[12] In 1942, the Japanese occupied one of the Shan States called Kengtung, which was placed under the administration of the Japanese-supported Thai National Army (TNA or *Phayap* army). The TNA encouraged poppy growing in Kengtung to supply the opium factory in Bangkok, which had the effect of fostering cultivation across this territory which, after the war, would be returned to Burma. In other words, the Japanese acquired a frontier site for poppy cultivation that was significantly expanded into an illicit opium production economy straddling the borders of Burma and Thailand.[13]

Another illustrative example of the wartime catalysis of colonial opium policies concerns the policy of SEAC regarding opium monopolies in Japanese occupied territories. While the war was still ongoing in 1943, the British, French, and Dutch agreed to not resume opium monopolies on the end of hostilities. The driving force behind this initiative came from the United States, which asked European powers to close opium shops in their colonies where US troops were fighting the Japanese, citing need to protect the health and morals of military men.[14] Formally, the Allied forces agreed. The British Empire was eager "to take advantage of the opportunity offered by the complete break with the past," declared the Foreign Office, and on November 10, 1943, the British announced the prohibition of opium smoking in its colonial territories in the Far East, along with the French for Indochina and Dutch regarding the East Indies.[15] Officially, upon war's end, opium monopolies would cease to exist.

In effect, however, this wartime policy enabled opium monopolies to continue to operate into the postwar era. It not only deferred the actual implementation of significant anti-opium reforms, but also, the SEAC grouped together British-ruled Burma, Malaya, Borneo, and Ceylon, northern Sumatra, as well as Siam and parts of the Dutch East Indies and the south of French Indochina for the purpose of military operations, giving an arbitrary unity to colonies with otherwise very different histories with opium. The regional scope on which the future abolition of opium monopolies was declared clashed with local realities, real and perceived, by wartime authorities, who gained reason to stress the peculiarities of colony-specific circumstances.

The British, for instance, explicitly exempted Burma from the scope of the 1943 prohibition declaration. Lord Louis Mountbatten, the Chief Commander for SEAC, heeded the opinions of British Civil Affairs officers accompanying the military forces in Burma who inherited the lexicons of local administrators that cited the unique vulnerabilities of this colony, where opium consumption, crime, and social disorder so famously intertwined.[16] For Burma, "[i]t has been pointed out to me that it is not a practical proposition to attempt to enforce an immediate and rigid prohibition," explained Mountbatten, and "we may have to acquiesce temporarily in extended local cultivation and consumption."[17] When the war started, Burmese armed resistance units had reportedly assumed control over the government's opium shops, while people in the Kachin Hills had taken to poppy growing.[18] According to those based in Japanese-occupied Burma, to suddenly prohibit cultivation, interrupt opium sales, and "the refusal to provide addicts with opium may cause serious unrest and may make the reoccupation and pacification of Burma more difficult than it otherwise would be."[19] Mountbatten assented. Thus, after the war officially ended in August 1945 and the Japanese withdrew, the British returned to Burma and by October of the same year, the Excise Department had purchased twenty tons of opium from India and resumed state-controlled licit sales in the colony.[20] Opium was also resold by the British in Malaya after 1945, as the British Military Administration temporarily sanctioned the use of opium for issue, cited as a "military necessity."[21]

In other parts of postwar Southeast Asia as well, the European colonial opium monopolies endured. In Indochina, although French civilian authorities officially shut down government-run shops and remade them into detoxification clinics for addicts, they were forced to quickly reverse this approach. After the Japanese left, Saigon and the southern part of the colony were almost immediately engulfed in armed conflict between French forces and the Viet Minh, the Indochinese Communist Party (ICP)-led alliance of independence-seeking groups, which became the First Indochina War (1946–1954).[22]

Historians have demonstrated the role that opium revenue played in financing the armed struggles of the Viet Minh, French, as well as early Democratic Republic of Vietnam (DRV) during this period, which marked Vietnam's protracted decolonization process.[23] Alfred McCoy has famously shown how French counterinsurgency approaches during the Vietnamese revolution were developed utilizing opium production economies in northern Vietnam and Laos and distribution networks for transport and urban sales into South Vietnam.[24] Christian Lentz's valuable recent study demonstrates how the French opium monopoly's infrastructure endured into the early 1960s, as the cash-strapped DRV built on late colonial and wartime arrangements to make "revolutionary exchanges" with poppy-producing highland minorities including the Hmong, Thai, Lao, Khmu, Mien—state-led barter systems that aimed to absorb all forms of material exchange—that gave way to taxation systems for postcolonial state.[25]

In the immediate wake of World War II, French intelligence and paramilitary forces had limited funds and struggled on at least two fronts. First, the Viet Minh had already established bases in the rural north and effectively mobilized peasants for guerrilla warfare, especially as wartime famines and continued food shortages strengthened the appeal of national independence.[26] The Laos-Tonkin–Yunnan borderland where the Hmong grew poppy (Chapter 6) represented especially fraught sites where the French external intelligence agency (*Service de documentation extérieure et de contre-espionnage* or SDECE) strived to prevent the Hmong from joining the Viet Minh. The director of the SDECE approached Hmong leaders who had previously organized poppy purchasing campaigns for the prewar and wartime opium monopoly under both the Third Republic and Vichy regime, and renewed old agreements as new political bargains: the SDECE would provide the manpower and means to transport Hmong-grown poppy and raw opium to sell in Saigon, in exchange for promises not to join the Viet Minh and cooperation in organizing Hmong villages into counterinsurgency units.[27] Opium also played a key role in securing border security in northwest Tonkin, where the French established an autonomous Tai federation (1948–1953) with a budget that relied on opium from Hmong and Chinese traders.[28]

Second, the Viet Minh also extended reach into the south with a branch called the Southern Regional Resistance Committee (SRRC) that infiltrated the French stronghold of Saigon. The French Far East Expeditionary Corps (*Corps expéditionnaire français en Extrême-Orient* or CEFEO) were tasked with defending the city and its environs and built strategic alliances with an armed group called the Binh Xuyen, by granting them control over the Saigon opium factory and its network of detoxification clinics/former opium shops in exchange for support quelling the urban communist insurgencies.[29] The CEFEO's efforts to stabilize and resume French control over Saigon and South Vietnam eventually relied heavily on the existing urban system for opium distribution and associated black markets, which, as McCoy has shown, enabled "a combination of crime and counterinsurgency: control over the municipal police allowed systematic exploitation of the vice trade: the rackets generated large sums of ready cash, and money bought an effective network of spies, informants, and assassins."[30] As in the north, the opium monopoly's infrastructures in the south of Indochina served as an asset for French forces lacking funds and capacity to tame postwar socioeconomic disorder and rebuild political authority.

Postwar revivals of key sinews of the opium monopolies were not practices unique to returning colonial powers. In the East Indies after 1945, the Republic of Indonesia fought for four years against the Dutch for independence. Robert Cribb's pioneering study has shown that during this postwar period of conflict and social revolution, the Republic lacked viable tax structures and thus used opium to raise revenue as well as secure a source of foreign exchange, under an institution called the *Djawatan Tjandoe* (or Opium Agency). "In its personnel, organization, and equipment, the Republic's Djawatan Tjandoe was a direct continuation of the colonial Opium-Regie," according to Cribb, explaining how opium helped finance the nascent independent government. During the Japanese occupation, the Dutch-established opium distribution network to government shops in Java continued to operate, and approximately twenty-five tons of raw and refined opium remained in the Salemba opium factory when the Japanese surrendered in August 1945.[31] It was a public affair: "within Jakarta, the Republic sold opium . . . both to predominantly Chinese addicts and to pharmaceutical firms. These sales were apparently quite open and price rises were recorded in the local Indonesian press."[32] Building on existing infrastructure and using surplus stocks of opium, the Republic was able to swiftly raise money from opium sales, which served both internally to build an effective army and military expenditure, as well as externally to secure foreign currency and finance the Republic's diplomatic and trade activities overseas.

Postcolonial Southeast Asia:
From Prohibition to Punishment

The act of reviving opium monopolies was a short-lived solution that postwar state-builders, colonial and independent alike, embraced to secure emergency sources of financing and as a means for taming social disorder. By the late 1940s, it became difficult for rulers, old or new, to cite exceptional circumstances, such as pacifying acute unrest or the special needs of a war-torn colony, as a reason to openly sell opium or operate government-run shops and factories. Within countries struggling to transform subject populations into a society of citizens, there was a decided taint to overtly continuing a colonial institution in an era of decolonization. Internationally, clearer lines were drawn separating opium as a dangerous drug and its harmful consumption from legitimate medical uses under the purview of the United Nations, which inherited and gave more forceful expression to the League of Nations' aspirational frameworks for narcotic control. The United Nations created a Commission on Narcotics that met in late 1946 to discuss possibilities for limiting raw materials, illicit traffic, as well as ending the opium monopolies in the Far East.[33] Commitments to multilateral cooperation were enabled by India's earlier declaration the same year to prohibit opium smoking and restrict cultivation and manufacture, which was significant given how its former status as the main wartime opium supplier for Allied forces had expanded global supply.[34] In March 1947, the United Nations Economic and Social Council adopted a resolution for abolishing opium smoking, which officially rendered the key activity of opium monopolies verboten in the eyes of an international community that denounced opium's commercial life, and affirmed a state that condoned nonmedical forms of consumption, sales, and trade as violating the terms of membership within a world society composed of nation-states.[35]

However, the categorical clarity with which an international community could denounce Southeast Asia's opium economies was not a luxury that countries of the region could afford. Rulers struggling to establish political order did not start from blank slates but a postwar reality that had linked opium to key state-building tasks, including securing territorial borders in poppy growing areas, quelling social unrest, and building political alliances using funds from and distribution networks for opium sales. Blurred lines abound, often rendering crude corruption with elites indistinguishable from reasonable patronage, blatant collusion with criminal organizations indistinguishable from necessary cooperation, and government-sponsored extortion rackets indistinguishable from the official provision of protection.

For instance, in Indochina, where the French remained until 1954, the remnants of the opium monopolies continued to figure centrally in counterinsurgency campaigns and postcolonial state building. In northern Vietnam and Laos, high financial and strategic value continued to attach to the Hmong poppy-cultivating areas and their connecting routes to the Saigon opium economy, which enabled the French to sustain alliances with peasants and armed groups against the Viet Minh resistance.[36] The DRV competed with the French to secure control over opium, for both strategic and fiscal reasons, and instituted a "temporary opium regime" in 1952 that recognized smallholding farmers as legal opium producers and levied taxes, collected by cadres of State Shops.[37] On the departure of the French, the DRV established monopoly control over opium production in formerly contested territories, while using euphemized terms such as "local agroforestry product" and "special product" to disguise the revenue source that filled government coffers.[38]

Secretive arrangements relating to opium's production, trade, and taxation also prevailed in the southern reaches of Vietnam, where overlapping efforts at postwar pacification, decolonialization, and postcolonial state building continued. The French CEFEO in Saigon maintained its partnership with the Binh Xuyen for counterintelligence and urban security, initially delegating control in 1948 over a few blocks in the southern part of Chôlon and eventually yielding the position of Director-General of Police of Saigon-Chôlon to a Binh Xuyen military commander as well as "control . . . [over] the capital region and the sixty-mile strip between Saigon and Cap Saint Jacques," encompassing the river waterways linking the city to the coast.[39] Organized rackets over opium sales, along with gambling concessions and prostitution, served as a key economic base for the Binh Xuyen, enabling them to build "a multi-faceted business enterprise whose economic potential constitutes . . . one of the most solid economic forces in South Vietnam," in the words of one CEFEO officer.[40] The French gave unbridled permission to the Binh Xuyen's racketeering because it not only paid for the thousands of informants and intelligence needed to combat the Viet Minh, but also served to "create a political counterweight to Vietnamese nationalist parties gaining power as a result of growing American pressure for political and military Vietnamization" that would replace the French.[41]

In Malaya as well, the vestiges of the opium monopoly had accompanied the British as they returned and established the Malayan Union in 1946, combining the Malay States and Penang and Malacca under one administration, with Singapore as a separate Crown Colony. Since the war, the opium revenue replacement reserve fund had been invested in sterling securities in London, amounting to 58 million Straits dollars and carried over to the Union Government and its successors until independence in 1957.[42] During the 1940s and 1950s, the opium fund evolved into a profoundly controversial source of revenue, not least because of a near absent public accountability regarding how it was spent and raised interest. For instance, in 1947 a committee report of the Singapore Association estimated that approximately 9 million Straits dollars that should have accrued as interest during the war was missing.[43] In 1949, around

45 million Straits dollars from the opium fund was invested again in the Perak River Electric Power Company, which as seen in Chapter 5, had already received a bailout from the British in 1930 using these same funds.[44] Once officially defined as a means to provide direct assistance to posterity, the opium revenue replacement reserve fund's legitimate purposes became increasingly ambiguous. In 1952, when legislative councilors for Singapore asked to use the fund—which had since grown to 55 million Straits dollars—for the medical treatment of opium addicts and their registration and rationing, the British chose not to.[45] These legacy funds were further concealed in the budgets of the independent governments for Malaysia and Singapore, as after 1957, the opium revenue reserve fund—which reached an unprecedented high of 65 million Straits dollars—was merged into the general revenue surplus.[46]

Political power struggles became anchored firmly in illicit opium economies. In Burma after the British withdrew, near anarchy prevailed and the sinews of the colonial opium monopoly persisted as contested sites for building financial and popular support among groups challenging the new independent state. In 1949, the fledgling government led by a coalition of political parties called the Anti-Fascist People's Freedom League (AFPFL) immediately assumed control over the opium shops, and U Aye, the head of the Excise Department announced an Opium Den Suppression Act for Rangoon, while opening an anti-opium clinic appended to a mental hospital in the nearby suburb of Tadagale.[47] However, efforts to extend the anti-opium law beyond the capital were thwarted by leftist and separatist militias and insurgents that organized local protection rackets over opium-entangled illicit economies throughout the country.[48] This was not a strategy limited to insurgent groups, but one that militias aligned with the fledgling AFPFL-led government and Burmese military also pursued. Mary Callahan's lucid analysis of post-1948 period has noted how the army's field commanders waging upcountry counterinsurgency campaigns lacked support and oversight from central authorities in Rangoon, and became involved in large-scale opium trade with professional smugglers.[49]

For Burma, the political stakes to controlling the remnants of the colonial opium monopoly were perhaps most heightened along the north and northeastern frontier areas with Yunnan China where poppy cultivation prevailed and opium had served as form of currency during the war. After their defeat by the Communists in 1949, soldiers of the Chinese Nationalist Party (Kuomintang or KMT) fled across the border into the Shan State of Kengtung, building up a base from which to launch rearguard offenses against the Communists. Opium became central to the KMT's operations, as one of its generals explained: "We have to continue to fight the evil of communism and to fight you must have an army, and an army must have guns, and to buy guns you must have money. In these mountains, the only money is opium."[50] Into the 1950s, as the KMT established a more permanent presence in the northern reaches of Burma along borders with Laos and Thailand, it threatened the popularity of the central government, while also receiving support from the United States for anticommunist operations in Southeast Asia.[51] As a result, control over opium production and distribution acquired heated security-related and ideological stakes that would only intensify in the coming years.

The postwar era of opium-entangled counterinsurgency and political struggles was simultaneously the age of drug wars and criminalization of activities relating to the transport, distribution, and sales of opium. It was a world in which too many promises for social stability, control over government, as well as profit-sharing had become anchored in the spoils of drug-related economic activities. Competition abounded over the stubborn remains of the colonial opium monopolies among groups striving to carve out a place in the new political order, ranging from military officers and the police to bureaucrats, politicians, as well as their financial and electoral brokers. The greater political utility of illicit economies went hand in hand with more assertive expressions of a state's imperative to punish. Given how so many powerful figures were implicated, forcefully denouncing another and launching antidrug campaigns could serve as a means for undercutting a competitor's power base. Such was the case, for instance, in Saigon-Chôlon in 1948, when the municipal police launched a series of raids against the detoxification clinics in the city that operated as opium shops and arrested smugglers in river routes under CEFEO-Binh Xuyen protection.[52] This antinarcotic campaign, namely, postwar Vietnam's first "drug war," took place amid divisions between the French civilian authorities and paramilitary officers over pacifying the city, as the former sought to enervate the strong arm of the latter. This dynamic would recur into the post-independence period as the Saigon opium economy and its transportation links to poppy cultivation and opium production in the north evolved into high-stakes arenas for illicit finance and patronage-building that powerful political actors sought to monopolize and thus displace rivals from.[53]

Criminalizing opium-related activities could enable those in official seats of power to undermine potential challengers. In Malaysia, antinarcotic campaigns accompanied the postwar British authority's efforts to quell the Malayan Communist Party (MCP) and its military arm, the Malayan National Liberation

Army (MNLA), during the Emergency (1948–1960).[54] The British worried about, and sought to weaken, the MCP's ties with secret societies and Chinese gangs with suspected control over opium trades by arresting opium sellers and smugglers.[55] Especially vigorous anticommunist, counterinsurgency campaigns were waged between 1952 and 1954, under the brief tenure of Gerald Templer, the British High Commissioner who famously electrified every aspect of counterinsurgency in Malaya through tactics for winning "hearts and minds" that would deprive the MCP of popular support.[56] By the time Templer left Malaysia, emergency measures for targeting drug offenders with suspected ties with the communists were formalized, including Section 39B of the 1952 Dangerous Drugs Ordinance that sanctioned the death penalty.[57]

In Burma, loudly official antidrug positions could both delegitimize rivals while help disavow the complicity of state actors. After the 1962 military coup, the country's north and northeastern area where opium production and trade had increased under the KMT became a refuge for myriad groups challenging the Rangoon-based junta. General New Win adopted an ambivalent approach that on the one hand, declared a complete ban on opium sales in the Shan States, which was "a move targeting the major income source for anti-Rangoon insurgents and Nationalist Chinese alike."[58] On the other hand, as Pierre-Arnaud Chouvy has shown, Ne Win also encouraged private militias called *Ka Kwe Ye* (KKY) to take local law and order into their own hands, while "tacitly authoriz[ing] the KKY militia to engage in all types of business and trade, including . . . opium and heroin trafficking."[59] While the KKY successfully destabilized insurgents challenging Ne Win's regime, many also developed their own fiefdoms in the north "due to ceaseless internecine feuds, largely sparked by the very competitive opium business."[60] Unable to control these militias, he disbanded the KKY in 1973, and anti-narcotic campaigns recurred targeting refineries, torching poppy fields, and arresting the leaders of these private militias. Soon after, Ne Win's government issued the Narcotics and Dangerous Drugs Law and Rules, a measure that introduced capital punishment for drug trafficking.[61]

Punishment displaced prohibition as the common language by which rulers across Southeast Asia affirmed their proper role concerning opium. In a familiar shadow of the near past, an official vocabulary congealed, one through which actors in privileged positions of government arrogated an authority to wield extraordinary powers, citing exceptional obligations to protect people. Declared penal imperatives did not serve to merely mask or distract attention from simple corruption. Rather, they gave expression to unresolved inconsistencies and deep tensions that those tasked with governance inherited, struggled with, and reproduced constantly. Otherwise very different governments across the region similarly formulated questions of governance in ways that presupposed the impossibility of doing away with political economies of opium already entwined with the coercive and fiscal arms of fledgling state apparatuses. Viable answers were in turn articulated in terms of compromises. What constituted permissible forms of collusion between the state and groups specializing in illicit drug activities? What were tolerable violations of law and order for those tasked with their maintenance? How could an already complicit state best manage its opium-entangled secretive finances, with what sort of presentation of self before others, including the international community and citizens on behalf of whom it professed to govern? This narrowed problem space, with its curtailed imagination for possible alternatives to rigidly state-centered governance, remained the most stubborn of colonial legacies from the opium monopolies, proving especially difficult to shake in the decades to come.

For, moving into the second half of the twentieth century, states across Southeast Asia, postcolonial and otherwise, continued to puzzle over these questions and pursued imperfect answers. And, once again, actors involved in actual administration across the region felt the weight of, but did not necessarily follow, the dictates of an evolving global world of ideas and interests. While the United Nations and other observers from afar worried about how to bridge new humanitarian ideals and reality, guiding problematics for those on the ground concerned how to deal with an accomplished fact of drug economies entangled with power and profit. The forces of the Cold War, as ideological blocs supplanted old imperial divides, with new centers of metropolitan power consolidating in the United States, Soviet Union, and China, would continue to shape but not determine how states dealt with a messy reality of armed groups, politicians, military elites, and police, as well as ethnic minorities, with respective stakes in illicit poppy production, opium smuggling, and profit-sharing arrangements. This fraught political economic landscape represents one of Southeast Asia's most vexed inheritances from European colonial opium prohibition. It was more than a failed utopian project of moral reform or a tragic episode of domination over subject populations. Colonial opium prohibition constitutes an unwieldy and incomplete process of state transformation that continues today.

An Invisible History

A final and perhaps most striking legacy of colonial opium prohibition is contemporary myopia toward the remarkable transformation through which the state has come to dominate how we understand imperatives for punishing drug offenses and the regulation of vice more generally.

There is a very familiar scene that mention of the history of opium and vice typically evokes, as illustrated in Figure 7.2. This is a photograph of an opium den taken by Harrison Forman, the renowned American photographer and journalist, likely during his visit to Malaya in November 1950.[62] We see a crowded space, packed with men smoking opium. Poverty and ill health are in palpable evidence in the emaciated figures, lying down on unclean wooden surfaces, surrounded by peeling wallpaper that reveals the building's skeletal base. This is a dark space, only briefly illuminated by the flash of the photographer's gaze, which manages to capture the partially obscured face of one man, looking directly into the camera as he grips his opium pipe. We do not see the faces of the other opium smokers. One looks away, while the others remain prostrate with only their bare feet and skeletal legs in sight. This is a familiar and upsetting scene, centered on the tragic figure of an opium addict and his pitiable circumstances. It typifies the sort of "spectacle of a human being obtruding on our notice his moral ulcers or scars" in ways that upset the viewer, not least by "tearing away that 'decent drapery' which time or indulgence to human frailty may have drawn over them."[63] Entitled "Singapore, view inside opium den," this photograph renders visible a poignant and deeply troubling aspect of opium's social life in the British colony, which represents one of the most common and most easily recollected visions of opium's history in Asia.

The view from inside an opium den is one among many vantage points from which to reflect on the past. Yet, this single perspective claims a near monopoly over our historical imaginary, in ways that give hypervisibility to the debilitated opium addict, at the risk of foreclosing inquiry into others who also consumed opium. Our relative unfamiliarity with another scene that Forman photographed just a few years earlier, also in Singapore, illustrates this point. Figure 7.3 depicts the British government's opium retail shop. The words "2 hoon tubes at 26 cents" on the wall explains how much a standard retail unit of opium costs in both printed English and hand-painted Chinese characters. The man exiting the shop is a registered Chinese opium consumer.[64] As a drug addict, he is part of the same world as those lying listless in the dark opium den in Figure 7.2. But it is lighter outside, and this man's slender frame appears sturdier; he walks erect.

FIGURE 7.2. Malaya. View inside opium den in Singapore, c. 1950. Photograph by Harrison
Forman. (Credit: From the American Geographical Society Library, University of
Wisconsin–Milwaukee Libraries.)

His eyes are also averted from the photographer's camera, but less to avoid its
gaze; he is looking down at a booklet. Compared with how easily we might sur-
mise about the unhappy plights of the men inside the Singapore opium den,
it is much harder to grapple with this particular figure.

Understanding the colonial history of opium prohibition across Southeast
Asia as an imperfect and incomplete process of colonial state transformation
provides a new perspective through which to see the less familiar past. Look
again at Figure 7.3. The presence of the colonial state is overwhelming. The government opium shop is a well-guarded establishment with metal bars covering
the window and door. The booklet that the Chinese opium consumer holds is
a registration card, issued by the Government Monopolies Department, which
contains his personal information and an identifying photograph, and affirms
his addict status and how much opium he is permitted to purchase per visit to
the shop: a 2 hoon tube for 26 cents. Behind this man, there is a caged wall that

FIGURE 7.3. Malaya. Man walking out of building of opium seller in Singapore, c. 1941. Photograph by Harrison Forman. (Credit: From the American Geographical Society Library, University of Wisconsin–Milwaukee Libraries.)

protects local administrators who will check each registration card, issue the standard tube containing opium, and accept money in exchange. This man steps outside of the opium shop as a ward of the state, with a sumptuary habit defined officially as permissible and legal.

The readily visible past of opium is accompanied by an invisible history of a colonial state. This duality is well captured by two additional images, of yet another type of opium addict in Singapore. They were publicity photographs produced by the British Central Office of Information in 1957. Two years earlier, a rehabilitation center for opium addicts had been established with much fanfare on St. John's Island, six miles off the shore of Singapore.[65] According to one administrator involved in launching this initiative, the island was beautiful and green, and the patients would sleep in comfortable beds, live in airy dormitories, and eat well-prepared food. While their families were looked after by rehabilitation officers, the patients would receive "occupational therapy" including tailoring and wood and rattan work for furniture.[66]

There was, of course, an invisible side to St. John's. The first cohort totaled merely eighteen individuals who had been remanded in the opium ward of a prison in Singapore and approved by the General Hospital as suitable for treatment and not "beyond redemption."[67] They represented a specific class of vulnerable yet treatable figures recognized by the British state, based on inner administrative criteria and ideas about what defined the state's proper involvement. There had been a much larger number of individuals rejected as unworthy of admission to St. John's.[68] From the outside, the system made little sense, opined one Singapore magistrate, on reviewing the complaint of one addict named Lye Ah Lam who had been medically certified but rejected by the opium treatment center's superintendent. "I consider this extremely funny," the magistrate remarked without humor.[69]

This "funny" past is rendered visible through the two photographs in Figures 7.4 and 7.5, which show us only the fortunate: one (Figure 7.4) depicts a patient who adopted a pet bird when it was a fledgling, according to the caption provided by the Central Office of Information. The other (Figure 7.5) presents three men preparing bamboo to make sturdy woven baskets, like the ones stacked in the corner, as part of their occupational therapy. However, these are also portraits of the colonial state in different guises. The Central Office of Information's caption for Figure 7.4 adds, "Up to date, there have been 932 patients, 765 of whom have been released as cured. So far there have been only 30 known failures, all of whom have been re-arrested. There is no second chance given to men rearrested after treatment on the Island."[70] The basket-weaving men sit with their backs to the camera, sitting close to the ground, before a man in a white suit standing with his hands on his hips, a smile on his face. This is Robert Black, Singapore's penultimate British colonial Governor.

Why is the plight of the opium addict so visible to us, but the presence of the colonial state less immediately so? What renders the opium den so familiar as a site of vice, troubled morals, and human vulnerability, while masking the corresponding role of the state in defining these terms? The answer, at least in the context of Southeast Asia, lies with the very incremental nature of historical change. For the period throughout the half-century this book has examined, it is difficult to pinpoint decisive turning points that mark when opium prohibition began and ended. The process through which colonial states reconfigured their complicated fiscal and symbolic relationships with opium was choppy, with many reversals and inconsistencies in how it unfolded. Such a slow-moving process of change lends especially well to selective recall, as we tend to dwell on certain sites, eventful moments, and more sensational figures that reaffirm our current anxieties and help fashion clean and efficient narratives about how we have arrived at where we are. In this sense, today's alarm over the profoundly aggressive ways by which states across Southeast Asia punish drug offenders,

FIGURE 7.4. Malaya. Photograph of St. John's Island opium addict rehabilitation center, c. 1957. (Credit: The National Archives, Kew, INF 10/315/18.)

to the detriment of the security and dignity of so many people, has had the effect of muting curiosity about why the state occupies such a central role in this aspect of social life in the first place. It is not that a modern state conceals its terrible powers from public view, but rather that we tend not to look for, ask about, and puzzle over a wider variety of activities that comprise a state's manifest presence over time. Put differently, the way by which the state recedes from our view lies with the eye of the beholder.

FIGURE 7.5. Malaya. Governor of Singapore Sir Robert Black visits opium addict rehabilitation center on St. John's Island, c. 1956. (Credit: Ministry of Information and the Arts Collection, courtesy of National Archives of Singapore.)

Recall again the first photograph of opium addicts in the Singapore opium den from 1950 (Figure 7.2). This is a crowded tableau that immediately concentrates our attention on the numerous decrepit figures, suggestive of insidious forces that drained the health, energy, and life out their bodies. At the time, however, this fixed scene also conceals, without providing context of what happened before and after this particular moment, precluding inquiry into the world that created this image and how it has shaped subsequent societies. Excavating the hidden sinews of power that structure social life under the state and articulating its presence requires renewed curiosity about how change happened the way it did and developing new vocabularies about the state capable of describing nitty-gritty realities of its presence without resorting to presumed intentions or fixed goals. The next two figures of government opium shops in British Burma, one from the 1890s and the other from the 1920s, help illustrate.

The first opium shop in Figure 7.6 foreshadows the changes that took place after the opium monopoly's introduction in 1894, as examined in Chapter 4.

FIGURE 7.6. Burma. View of opium shop and dwellings on the Irrawaddy River, 1880s.
(Credit: The British Library Board, P/2664.)

Sitting on the banks of the Irrawaddy River, this establishment is in plain public sight and bears a rickety sign with hand-painted white letters that declare it
an "opium shop." A dark-skinned barefooted man in a white head-cloth is standing in front of the shop, likely its proprietor, one of thirty men authorized by
the British to openly operate such an establishment at the time.[71] He is looking
into the distance. Perhaps he is waiting for clients. After 1894, when the colonial state banned popular opium consumption in Burma, citing the problems
of "moral wreckage" among the Burmese, the number of people visiting retail
shops in the colony's capital did not decrease. Rather, by limiting Burmese access to the opium shops, the new policy encouraged hawking around the
shops, as the many other non-Burmese inhabitants of the colony bought opium
legally and sold it furtively to those newly denied entry into the shop.[72] Perhaps
the proprietor looks into the distance, stern-faced in his watchfulness against
those violators. With the 1894 ban on indigenous opium consumption emerged
a shadow economy around the monopoly's opium shops.

Figure 7.7 shows another opium shop in Rangoon during the 1920s. It illustrates what changed in British Burma over the course of three decades, as the
opium monopoly continued to confront problems of illicit sales and consumption. Signs for retail opium shops now bore clearly printed labels announcing

FIGURE I — Government opium retail shop at
Rangoon (Burma)
with two Indian opium-consumers.

FIGURE 7.7. Burma. Government opium retail shop in Rangoon, with two Indian opium
consumers, 1920s. (Source: League of Nations 1930.)

the location, license number, as well as the name of the licensed vendor. O. G.
Dover, likely a member of the Dover family who were well-established chemists
in Burma, who held opium shop no. 1, located on busy Canal Street away
from the docks.[73] The two unsmiling men standing under the sign are registered
Indian opium consumers, who represent the unhappy byproducts of the colonial state's recurrent struggles to resolve problems of opium hawking and
illicit consumption that followed the 1894 ban. Identifying non-Burmese who
were exempt from the general ban as the cause of growing illicit drug economies,
the opium monopoly created a separate consumption registration system

for non-Burmese foreigners, which restricted the amount of opium they could purchase while labeling them as the legal clients of government opium shops. An explicit double standard was encoded in these regulatory approaches to opium consumption in Burma—the registered Burmese smokers were morally wrecked individuals, while the registered non-Burmese were legitimate clients. By 1929, there were 235 Burmans, 12,619 Chinese, and 365 Indians enumerated in the monopoly's registration lists.[74] Thus, the two men centered in this second photograph are members of a cohort of state-authorized opium consumers in British Burma, decades after the monopoly began prohibition. It is tempting to view them as captured by a project for social control through racialized categorization schemes or a top-down attempt to register a problematic population of drug addicts in Burma. However, as we have seen, the story behind how they became rendered "legible" to the state is more complicated.

Common narratives about criminality are also unsettled as we begin to pay more attention to the less visible presence of the state, and ask more questions about when and how it recedes from view. Figures 7.8, 7.9, and 7.10 help to illustrate this point. All three photographs were produced by the French colonial authorities during the 1920s in reference to opium smuggling in Tonkin.

At first glance, all the images are about law-breaking individuals in relation to opium. However, there is much more going on. Figures 7.8 and 7.9 are photographs that center the figure of a smuggler, but they are neither about the individual nor his criminality. Rather, the first is about a vest; the second is about a raincoat. These photographs represent descriptive statements on the part of the colonial state about the paraphernalia that smugglers use to evade policing and surveillance. "A vest with multiple pockets worn by smugglers who are part of a convoy. Each vest holds an average of 10 kilograms of raw opium," explains the caption under Figure 7.8.[75] "A double-layered raincoat made of latanier palm leaf. Raw opium blocks are hidden between the coat and the lining," reads the caption for Figure 7.9.[76] These photographs were illustrations for a booklet circulated among colonial administrators, with an explicit intent to share information on the many ways that opium could illicitly traverse the politically fraught borderland of Laos–Tonkin–Yunnan, which we examined in Chapter 6.[77] In addition to vests and raincoats, the visible objects capturing the colonial state's attention included a metal hat (made of "zinc or brass" with a hidden lid), a shoe sole, a teapot, a bamboo basket, a box of candy, a bicycle, as well as a porcelain toilet. Strikingly, in these captioned images, the smuggler who violated the law is absent, despite his hypervisibility. Indeed, it is unclear

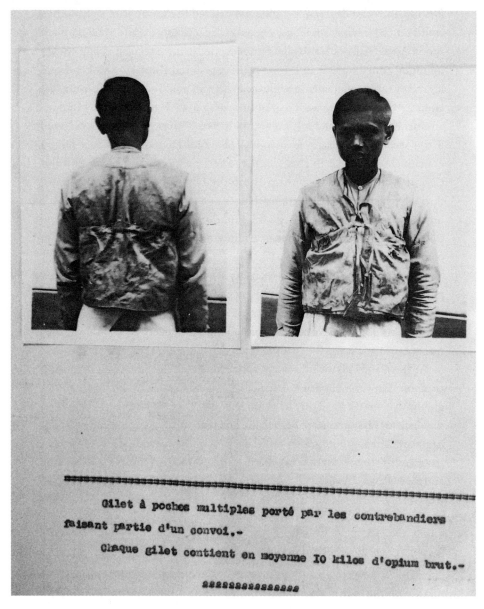

FIGURE 7.8. Indochina. Opium smugglers and their disguises: Man wearing a vest with multiple pockets, c. 1924. (Credit: Archives nationales d'outre mer, France, FM/ AFFPOL/3262.)

Manteau de pluie doublé en feuille de latanier.-

Des pains d'opium brut sont dissimulés entre le manteau
et la doublure.-

FIGURE 7.9. Indochina. Opium smugglers and their Disguises: Man wearing a Raincoat, c. 1924. (Credit: Archives nationales d'outre mer, France, FM/AFFPOL/3262.)

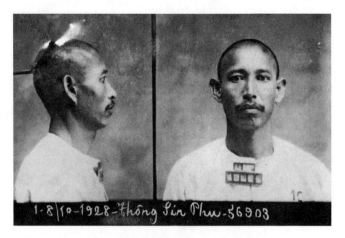

FIGURE 7.10. Indochina. Photograph of Thông Sin Phu, a Chinese man arrested in Tonkin for opium smuggling, c. 1928. (Credit: Archives nationales d'outre mer, France, INDO/RSTNF/02138.)

whether the man photographed was a smuggler at all or a man summoned before the state to pose as one.

In contrast, the criminality of the subject of Figure 7.10 is obvious. This is a police photograph following a typical two-part arrangement, of a side view and front view of his person from the waist up. According to the caption, this is a man named Thông Sin Phu, now identifiable to the state by a number: 56903. Thông Sin Phu was a Chinese man living in French Tonkin, who had been arrested in 1928 on discovery of 122 kilograms of opium in his house.[78] He was sentenced to one year in prison and later expelled to China, as his smuggling activities led to suspicions that he was also involved in illicit arms trades and spreading political propaganda across the Tonkin–Yunnan border. Later in the 1930s, this photograph was shared among customs officials, amid worries that he might have reentered the colony under a pseudonym and was continuing to acquire, sell, and transport opium in the northern borderlands with China. This image and the way in which it circulated, reappeared, and aroused anxieties for local administrators alerts us to how there was never one but always multiple processes through which the colonial state saw individuals defying the terms through which it defined their behavior, identity, and activities. Even when a law-breaking individual is most visible, as in this police photograph of Thông Sin Phu, the corresponding regard of the state that defines those terms is never stable. And we risk attributing an arbitrary coherence to the state's relationship with the illicit, illegal, and indeed criminal, and missing an opportunity to question why this relationship appears in the ways it does.

So, let us return to the opium den. And puzzle over, rather than presuppose, what is disturbing about the experiences of others who bear the weight of a colonial past in Southeast Asia, once ruefully described as a "history . . . strewn with the wrecks of control schemes, of one kind of another, as regards opium."[79] Figure 7.11 is a photograph taken in December 1972, by the Pulitzer Prize–winning French photographer Raymond Depardon in Saigon.[80] The opium den is a dark room lighted by a lamp that allows the three men, who are lying horizontally in a circle, to vaporize opium in the long smoking pipe they are passing around. What is this form of sociability? What about it eludes ready narrative arcs about addicts in need of rescue or criminals to be punished? For the everyday lives of people continue to misalign with the official problems that states define. For instance, "[a] villager belonging to the Meo [Hmong] tribe, smokes opium in his hut," reads the caption of Figure 7.12, which was taken in 1975 in Laos by A. Abbas, with the French photo agency Gamma. Another opium lamp lights this private place of rural abode, illuminating the face of a man whose attention is focused intensely on his pipe. An open rucksack hangs on the wall above this Hmong tribesman. Perhaps the opium he smokes is a source of comfort after a long day of physical work; perhaps it is the cause of ill health, debt, and misery. But surely, the ways that we, as products of the same past that has obscured how profoundly the state has asserted its presence over our lives, regard him are yet too blunt to capture his lived reality.

Conclusion

This chapter has explored the afterlives of colonial Southeast Asia's opium monopolies. It identified how these institutions survived World War II and persisted into the second half of the twentieth century. During the war, both Allied and Axis forces stationed across the region used opium as an emergency form of currency to secure the labor and loyalty of local populations, directly utilizing existing infrastructures for opium sales, production, and distribution, which included material forms of retail shops, factories, and transportation means as well as more abstract purchasing arrangements with poppy growers in highland frontier areas. In the immediate wake of the war, returning European colonial powers and new independence-seeking rulers alike restored these infrastructures as expedient fiscal, financial, and coercive means for postwar reconstruction and decolonization struggles. Postcolonial states across

FIGURE 7.11. Indochina. Men smoking opium in an opium den in Saigon, c. 1972.
(Credit: Raymond Depardon/Magnum Photos.)

FIGURE 7.12. Indochina. Man smoking opium in a Meo (Hmong) village in Laos, c. 1975.
(Credit: A. Abbas/Magnum Photos.)

Southeast Asia continued to build on these already existing opium-entangled foundations for key tasks of collecting revenue, quelling violence from competitors, and policing borders.

Contemporary Southeast Asia bears two interrelated legacies stemming from the postwar continuity of the colonial opium monopoly's infrastructures. The first is the emergence of highly politicized illicit drug economies. Into the late 1940s and 1950s, while state involvement in opium-related commercial activities was officially disavowed, the extent to which boundaries separating the legal from illegal, permissible from criminal, legitimate from illegitimate activities were defined by the very same states with deep opium debts, creating a capacious realm of compromises interweaving myriad groups with shared stakes in defending and sustaining the postcolonial state. A second legacy concerns the ways by which we, as observers from the present day, misunderstand this historical process and remain captured within an imaginary of the colonial state that rendered its own involvement in the social lives of putatively vulnerable and marginal people as seemingly obvious and inevitable, masking what was in fact the product of human action.[81]

8

Conclusion

WHAT ANIMATES the most grandiose acts of statecraft may come from the more pedestrian of places. Throughout this book, this theme has recurred in several guises. Underwriting Empire's dramatic volte-face on opium—from an openly defended source of colonial revenue to an officially denounced danger-ous drug—was a plodding world of bureaucratic puzzling and problem-solving. Immodest interventions into society emerged from the activities of modest administrative actors. Institutions centralizing control over society took dynamism from highly ambivalent positions regarding state action. Outwardly confident expressions of authority were products of inward-looking struggles by official actors quelling their own misgivings about the basic viability and jus-tifiability of a system they were tasked with managing. The public transcripts of a state that laid arrogant claim to know the lives of others and its self-aggrandizing rhetoric took material from records written in many moments of anxiety.

Understanding this bureaucratic dynamic in the historical context of South-east Asia provides a theoretical opportunity for scholars of colonialism and the modern state to rethink some of our basic assumptions about why and how rulers govern. We are more familiar with an image of the state as a bold and often audacious entity. An impulse to monopolize control over violence, physical and symbolic, has famously guided the ways that modern states have expanded ter-ritorially and controlled society.[1] Hunger for wealth and power are best known to animate top-down interventions to extract resources and tame unruly be-haviors. Perhaps one the most poignant formulations of the audacity of the state comes from James Scott's *Seeing Like a State* (1998), which elucidated the misplaced confidence of states pursuing projects of administrative, economic, and cultural standardization anchored in brittle forms of official knowledge and schemes for social engineering that exceeded their abilities to comprehend complex local realities. His depiction of the ideologues of high modernity brings the arrogance of power into sharp relief, through figures who sought to render society legible in the positive names of progress, science, and civilization but with detrimental consequences for the societies that states professed to improve.[2]

Yet the powerful are not always confident nor do they always enact power in the same ways. The deeper one looks into the administrative apparatus of a state, the more clearly do the anxieties of those who govern appear, struggling to solve problems of their own making with a tragic ineptness. What the inner lives of opium-entangled colonial bureaucracies in Southeast Asia have revealed is the extent to which even the most seemingly obvious acts of levying taxes and regulating people's behavior cannot always be seen as straightforward projects for revenue extraction and social control. What guided, for instance, Donald Smeaton's resolve to restrict Burmese opium consumption in 1894 and register individuals was hardly a grand design to impose a standardizing grid over colonial society. Nor, as we have seen in Malaya and Indochina, were there clearcut aspirations for improved efficiency when collecting opium revenue, whether actual or fictitiously recorded. Instead, there was a bewildering array of problems to solve with varying degrees of felt imperatives, scattered across different realms but with linked repercussions. If there was a logic to how the European states regulated opium in colonial Southeast Asia, it was more one of localized problem solving, animated by uneasy resolve rather than unbridled confidence.

There are interrelated analytical and normative implications to this alternative understanding of the everyday administrative state, which orients attention away from the loud hubris of power toward the quiet trepidations of those who govern. To begin by thinking along with welcome approaches to reconceptualizing the state in light of its complexity and "many hands, functions, and forms of power," political scientists gain reason to assume less coherence behind motivations for bureaucratic projects that adjust and advance the state's fiscal reach.[3] If, as this book has hopefully persuaded, there are context-specific regulatory histories and ambivalent administrative actors, then rationales for policies altering the scope of taxation and depth of social control must differ depending on how bureaucracies reflect on their own pasts and construct problems internally. It follows that retrospective assessments, ways of archiving official records, and interpretation by low-level administrators may define reasons that higher officials take for granted as imperatives for state action. This approach also underscores the value of empirically exploring rather than presuming a priori the motivations and goals of specific actors involved in the design, drafting, presentation, and defense of policies, while inviting more inquiry into the everyday politics of the bureaucratic realm, through the question of who does what, when, and how, to reformulate Harold Lasswell's classical definition of politics.

Second and relatedly, sustained focus on quotidian administrative practices and bureaucratic worlds opens a broader vantage point from which to theorize the nature of authority and meaning of legitimacy that distinguishes the state, colonial and modern alike. The state is "a foundational concept in the social sciences, one that cannot be replaced by governmentality or governance or institution," Kimberly Morgan and Ann Orloff remind us, because states "signify forms of power that differ from those found in other arenas . . . [and] while taking varying forms in different places and time periods, [the distillation and concentration of power in states] generates a distinctive and often potent organizational form."[4] As we have seen throughout Part II of this book, the recursive nature of bureaucratic work and incremental processes of knowledge accumulation generated taken-for-granted sensibilities among administrators about official problems relating to opium consumption worth solving through state intervention, which served to justify the role of European colonial states (or lack thereof) in non-European societies. The invention of grandiose claims to legitimate rule over others as such emerges from concrete tasks of everyday governance.

While analytically invaluable, there is something discomforting about linking the concrete tasks of petty bureaucrats to the abstract mentality of what we called "the State," not least because it provides a visceral encounter with people who wielded enormous power despite themselves. In order to span spectrums ranging from the microlevel individual to macrostructural forces, it is necessary to parse out what individuals meant to do, how they acted, and what happened as a result of what they did. Intentionality, action, and effect. On the one hand, as we learn to recognize how one connected to another in diffuse and circuitous ways, we gain a richer understanding of agency in historical context and the complexity of the social world. On the other hand however, a sense of unease may also obtain. The absence of straight lines connecting intentions, to action, to their effects is troubling, especially when such effects are about the wrongs of colonialism and its lasting legacies. The burden of retrospective judgment becomes complicated; it becomes hard to locate the onus of responsibility for wrongdoings of the past even as we recognize their manifest legacies today.

To return once more to the colonial opium monopolies of Southeast Asia, it is helpful to recognize how they instantiate what Ranajit Guha has called colonialism's paradox of dominance without hegemony.[5] As an alien form of rule imposed upon a society with its own history and politics, colonialism represented an absolute externality, according to Guha, fundamentally incapable of assimilating the people it purported to rule for, and in the interests of. Through the experience of British-ruled India, he argued that unlike the metropolitan state that could dominate civil society through persuasion, the colonial state in India relied on coercion, a way of exercising authority that came to rely on fear than consent. Guha identified the roots of this difference in how the colonial state "did not originate from the activity of Indian society itself," and thus sidestepped a formative process by which a ruling class emerged from civil society first and then separated itself from that society in order to stand above it.[6] Instead, the inception of the colonial state in India began with an already existing separation between ruler and a society that she did not represent or speak on behalf of, which was overlaid by a second separation between foreign and indigenous populations. The colonial state was "thus doubly alienated—in becoming as well as in being."[7] It was a despotic entity, with its nineteenth century form resembling ancient and medieval precursors with "no mediating depths, no space provided for transactions between the will of the rulers and that of the ruled," argues Guha, stressing a "sense of isolation that haunted the regime."[8]

Dividing lines between colonial state and society, foreign and indigenous, alien and already belonging at once drew upon and refracted many other separations along lines of class, status, gender, and race both among those who ruled and those who were subject to rule.[9] Separations also abounded between theory and practice, law's ideal and reality, colonial policy formation and its implementation, as well as immanent tensions within the ideologies and political rationalities for imperial rule.[10] Exploring these many processes that rendered colonial states separate from and yet increasingly intrusive in society is an ongoing task for students of colonial history. Yet, it is also a challenging task, especially for those of us who inherit, but do not inhabit the same intellectual milieu of an earlier generation of scholars writing amidst decolonization struggles with more clearly politicized aims of resistance and critique.[11] Political scientists often follow a standard practice of bracketing normative considerations, deferring the personally uncomfortable or politically incorrect implications that may accompany our analyses. Questions about whether and what sorts of politics, sensibilities, and value judgments animate current modes and methods of inquiry toward colonialism are seldom posed explicitly. For those animated by methods of positive scientific inquiry and its pursuits of objective truth, such truths may reveal that certain aspects of colonial rule caused salutary political and developmental outcomes in the long run.[12] And the modernizing projects of high colonialism form a subject that both fascinates and worries, not least because the richness of archival records produced by obsessive record-keeping bureaucracies generate immense potential for systematic analysis while also clearly transmitting the biases of official actors who recorded and kept such documents. Different but similarly normative stakes linger in the background of analyses for those pursuing other truths, including the agency and lived experience of people, the intimacies of their everyday lives, as well as the nature of power and politics of difference in fundamentally unequal polities.

This book has endeavored to squarely reject an impulse to separate its comparative and historical analysis of opium prohibition in Southeast Asia from felt discomfort with exploring the inner lives of a colonial state through the opium monopolies. While recognizing how such arrangements operated to the detriment of many people at the time and have left negative imprints upon state–society relations and law and order across the region today, I have found neither clean nor direct links from the intentions of involved administrators to bureaucratic action and its lasting effects. It would have been an easier story to tell with the more familiar protagonist of the state as a bold and audacious entity.[13] But this comfortably blameworthy figure disappeared in the process of looking inside the underbelly of its bureaucracy, which revealed a teeming mess of problems that administrators were struggling to solve. The simpler narrative would have risked aggrandizing domination by giving undue credit to this fragmentary nature of everyday administration as driven by a coherent vision when in fact there had been none. The more complicated story takes on a different risk of excusing culpable agents of colonialism for the world that they created, by showing how it was recurrently propelled by their actions, yet always beyond their control.

This leads to a concluding implication of this book's argument about the acute anxieties and inner trepidations of those who wielded power. From within the colonial state, the common and troubling voices that become audible were those of its agents explaining the meaning of their actions. Local administrators often invoked the word legitimacy to affirm precedent, to self-authorize a normative content to policy actions taken and planned, as well as to announce problems solved successfully. They touted the legitimate nature of discretionary decisions made, fretted about weak legitimacy in the process of taxing consumption, and urged better resolve to overcome threats to their legitimate work faced from polemicists and idealistic reformers.

For most scholarship on the modern state that conceptualizes legitimacy along the lines of popular assent toward a leader, as well as studies of the colonial state that recognize its domination without hegemony, the word legitimacy from the mouths of administrative agents must ring hollow.[14] Nonetheless, as an actor's category for bureaucrats across Southeast Asia under European rule, legitimacy existed as a frequently invoked term, as a part of the lexicon of everyday administration and central to the official language of state power. Thus, I have sought to understand what local administrators meant when they claimed legitimacy with a broader aim of differentiating between when such invocations contained a complex set of ideas and beliefs (and when they did not), and to parse out when such expressions of resolve were instrumental to successfully realized ends (and when they were not).

Professing legitimacy was a way for colonial administrators to self-narrate what was appropriate and justified about their own conduct, and thereby a reflexive statement about their own role and place in a narrowly conceived world. It was a means for persuading oneself about the reasonableness of past policy actions that nonetheless caused problems in the present, and also, the other way around: to dwell on the bureaucracy's near and far pasts to locate once misguided causes of today's ills. This felt necessity to tell a causal story, attribute responsibility, or make bluntly apologist claims did not reflect the intentionality of any single individual, but sparked from small fissures arising from everyday administrative work. Such narratives were profoundly inward-looking as actors enacted scripts that were *not* always meant to address, impress, and assuage external audiences.

George Orwell's 1936 essay "Shooting an Elephant," set in Burma under British rule, is often invoked to illustrate the theatrical imperative that colonial officials internalized and performed before colonized subjects.[15] Despite personal ambivalence about shooting an elephant that had ravaged the bazaar in Moulmein and killed an Indian, Orwell's protagonist had felt compelled to do so because of the crowd's expectations: "Here I was, the white man with his gun, standing in front of the unarmed native crowd, seemingly the leading actor of the piece; but in reality, I was only an absurd puppet pushed to and fro by the will of those yellow faces behind." The hollowness, futility of the white man's dominion in the East was made obvious in this moment, from the perspective of Orwell as a colonial police officer surrounded by "an immense crowd, two thousand at the least and growing every minute." It was a moment of crisis, distressingly public. It was also, however, in Orwell's own words, "a tiny incident in itself."

More illuminating of the day-to-day of a British colonial administrator is Orwell's description of "A Hanging" in Burma, written in 1931, five years before "Shooting an Elephant."[16] An early morning execution of a Hindu man had been scheduled. It was already 8 a.m. "For God's sake hurry up, Francis" says the British superintendent of the jail with irritation to Francis, the Dravidian head of the jail: "The man ought to have been dead by this time." Nonetheless, once the noose is fixed around the prisoner's neck, the superintendent pauses, as the condemned man "began crying out to his god. It was a high, reiterated cry of 'Ram! Ram! Ram! Ram!,' not urgent and fearful like a prayer or a cry for help, but steady, rhythmical, almost like the tolling of a bell." The superintendent waits: "his head on his chest . . . slowly poking the ground with his stick; perhaps he was counting the cries, allowing the prisoner a fixed number—fifty, perhaps a hundred." Finally, the superintendent orders the execution, pokes the dead body with a stick, and blows out a deep breath. "The moody look had gone out of his face quite suddenly. He glanced at his wrist-watch. 'Eight minutes past eight. Well, that's all for this morning, thank God.'" Orwell conveys the macabre nature of the whole situation, as with the dead man dangling a mere hundred yards away, the white administrators and "native" executioner and jail officials proceed to laugh, joke, and have a drink together. "Even the superintendent grinned in a tolerant way" and provided alcohol to everyone, saying "You'd better all come out and have a drink . . . I've got a bottle of whisky in the case. We could do with it."

This episode captures the significance of the everyday work of minor administrators and inner anxieties of the colonial state that this book has sought to convey. Away from the crowds, Orwell's jail superintendent enacted a script that did not perform the might of Empire, a Briton, or a white man before darker-skinned subordinates. He also neither followed nor deviated from the orders of superiors in Calcutta or London. There was a certain way of doing things, away from the crowds, for a task of "unspeakable wrongness, of cutting a life short when it is in full tide" that was nonetheless a regular job for a small number of men.[17] The European colonial superintendent's inward pursuit of legitimacy was one of a person with power who needed to find reasons for wielding it, based on what he conceived of as appropriate, decent, and perhaps even right. He had his own theory of what he should do, which was not personal and volitional, but shaped incrementally through precedents of and experiences with past executions and many more to come. Secular criminal law in the Burmese colony neither made room for a Hindu's expression of piety during such final moments at the gallows, nor was there clarity about the social significance of a call that was "not urgent and fearful like a prayer or cry for help." Uncertainty abounded within the grand script of Empire that purported to deliver justice, which men like the superintendent of the jail both reinforced and reconfigured, by way of pausing briefly to allow the condemned to speak. Perhaps it was deliberate, a sort of magnanimous hubris that respected another's last rites. Perhaps it was less thoughtful, a way to briefly delay a distasteful task. Either way, what the superintendent did shaped the process of the hanging.

Similarly, there were no procedural formalities for using a stick to poke a dangling body to confirm a prisoner's death. Rules and norms existed neither for nor against the specific act of white administrators drinking together with the "native" officers early in the morning, after a successful hanging. It was successful in the sense that it was not disagreeable. As Francis reminded the superintendent: "Well, sir, all hass passed off with the utmost satisfactoriness. It wass all finished—flick! Like that. It iss not always so—oah, no! I have known cases where the doctor wass obliged to go beneath the gallows and pull the legs to ensure decease. Most disagreeable!" This uneventful episode was much more common than the spectacular shooting of a valuable elephant, and more generally represents the sort of scene at which men like the superintendent could enact an enormous number of discretionary acts. And it was hardly the regard of Francis and the few other "subaltern" officers at the jail that propelled the superintendent to do what he did. His own anxieties, in official capacity for an empire ill-equipped to wield the terrible power that it did, shaped the process by which the hanging unfolded, with an irritable punctuality, moody patience with the last prayer of the condemned man, and dark conviviality at its end.

What compels people who dominate others to find meaning in their actions and self-narrate why they did so? I conclude with an invitation, for those who venture to theorize and understand historical and ongoing processes of state transformation, to pose and ponder questions that have been as unsettling as this particular one has been for this book. It is tempting to disclaim the normative implications of an answer that finds some introspection and creativeness in places where, and at times when, the positive connotations of such aspects of human agency are unwelcome. Such has been the context of colonial Southeast Asia, at the height of European rule, when formal political inequality and blatant sanction of social discrimination prevailed to the detriment of so many people's dignity, welfare, and survival. There is something distressing about acknowledging a disjuncture between what local administrators—those most proximate to the everyday execution of extractive, coercive, and disciplinary practices—did, and why they did it. However, what I hope this book has persuaded the reader of is the value of feeling uncomfortable, because it suggests that our easy recourse to either blaming or pitying cogs in a bureaucratic machine no longer exists.

APPENDIX

TABLE A.1. Volume and shares of Indian opium exports to China and Southeast Asia, 1870s–1920s

	Indian opium exports (chests)	Indian exports to China	Indian exports to Southeast Asia	China's share of Indian opium exports (%)	SEA's share of Indian opium exports (%)
1870	88,500	77,100	8,300	87	9
1875	88,400	77,200	11,000	87	12
1880	92,200	83,000	9,600	90	10
1885	88,000	76,000	11,700	86	13
1890	85,800	70,900	14,400	83	17
1895	60,900	45,600	14,800	75	22
1900	69,700	49,800	19,100	71	27
1905	62,900	48,000	13,700	76	22
1910	43,900	31,300	12,200	71	28
1915	11,400	0,(800)	7,100	0	62
1920	10,500	0,(900)	8,560	0	82
1925	5,700	0	4,700	0	82

Source: Richards 2002, p. 156.

FIGURE A.1. Ekstrand Commission's maps of opium sale zones: French Indochina, c. 1929.
(League of Nations 1930.)

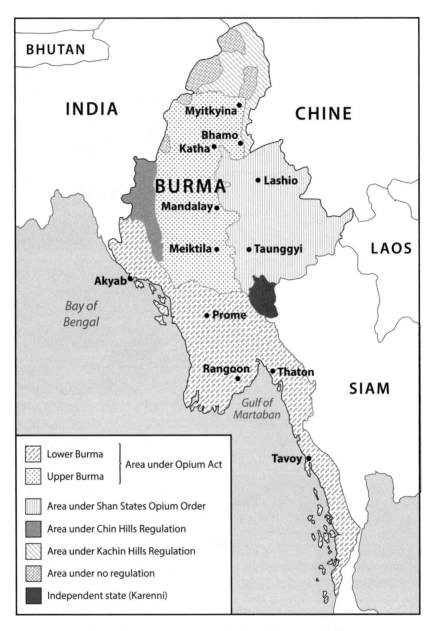

FIGURE A.2. Ekstrand Commission's maps of opium sale zones: British Burma, c. 1929.
(League of Nations 1930.)

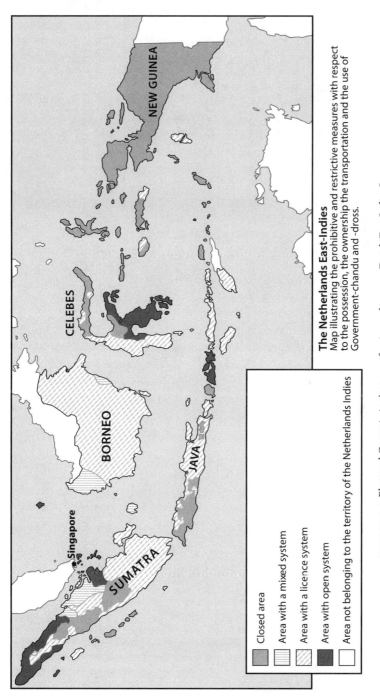

The Netherlands East-Indies

Map illlustrating the prohibitive and restrictive measures with respect to the possession, the ownership the transportation and the use of Government-chandu and -dross.

Closed area

Area with a mixed system

Area with a licence system

Area with open system

Area not belonging to the territory of the Netherlands Indies

FIGURE A.3. Ekstrand Commission's maps of opium sale zones: Dutch East Indies I, c. 1929.

(League of Nations 1930.)

TABLE A.2. Comparing shares of Chinese population and number of opium shops in Burma, Straits Settlements, Indochina, 1890s and 1920s

	Total population		Approximate share of Chinese population		No. of opium shops For 1920s, before/after Geneva Convention (no. of registered users)	
	1890s	1920s	1890s	1920s	1890s	1920s
Burma	8 million	13 million	<1%	1.2% (149,000)	20 (7,500)	125/120 (13,000)
Straits Settlements	500,000	880,000	56% (280,000 in 1901)	57% (500,000)	740 (n/a)	500/70 (40,000)
Indochina	15 million	20 million	<2%	2% (400,000)	>680 for Tonkin (n/a)	3,000/2,300 (n/a)

Sources: For total population for Burma, Mahajani 2001, p. 179; Straits Settlements, Manderson 1996, p. 3, Census of British Malaya 1921; Indochina, Banens 2009, p. 45. For approximate share of Chinese population for Burma, Ritchell 2009, p. 2; Straits Settlements, Manderson 1996, p. 41 for 1901; Indochina, ANOM/GGI 43089. For official number of opium shops and consumers for Burma, MNA/01/15 (b), 390; Straits Settlements, 1908 Commisison Report, vol. 3, p. 81; Indochina (Nankoe, H., Gerlus, J.-C., & Murray, M. 1993, p. 194).

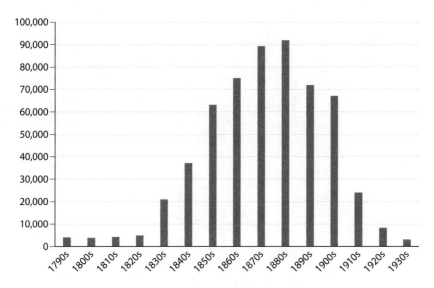

FIGURE A.4. Changing volume of India–China opium trade, 1790s–1930s (number of chests exported from India). (Source: Richards 2002, p. 156.)

TABLE A.3. Timeline of key colonial, metropolitan, and international opium-related reforms

	World/Europe	British Burma	British Malaya	French Indochina
Pre-1900s	**1846**: France, Poisonous Substance Law **1868**: Britain, Pharmacy Act **1874**: Britain, Creation of Society for Suppression of Opium Trade	**1826**: Introduce opium tax farming in Arakan and Tenasserim **1893**: Abolish opium tax farming, Create opium consumer registration **1894**: Introduce opium monopoly, with government-owned shops and auctioned sales licenses	**1819**: Introduce opium tax farm in Straits Settlements (SS) **1894**: Chandu and Liquor Ordinance strengthens government control over opium sales, limiting to male Chinese **1896**: Creation of Federated Malay States (FMS) and assumed control over existing tax farms	**1861**: Introduce opium tax farm in Cochinchina **1881**: Introduce opium monopoly for Cochinchina, Government control over Saigon opium factory **1881–1889**: Introduce opium monopoly for Cambodia, Annam, Tonkin **1899**: Introduce opium monopoly for Indochina
Early twentieth century and World War I (1900–1919)	**1907**: Anglo-Chinese Agreement for Opium Suppression **1908**: France, Anti-Opium Law **1909**: Shanghai Opium Commission Meeting **1912**: Hague Opium Convention **1916**: Britain, Defense of the Realm Act, 40B **1916**: France, Anti-Opium Law **1919**: Versailles Peace Treaty	**1902**: Reform opium sales system. Creation of resident excise officer in government opium shops **1909**: Strengthened police powers for excise officers **1910**: Reforms to licensed sales system. Creation of Chinese opium consumer registration system **1917**: Creation of Chinese advisory committees for opium regulation	**1900–1902**, FMS, Restrict opium tax farms sales and government control over opium imports **1909–1910**: SS, FMS, Abolish opium tax farms Introduce opium monopoly Create mixed government shops and licensed vendor system	**1903–1905**: Create differential sales pricing zones **1907**: Ban on opium use by government employees **1914**: Introduce opium monopoly for Kwang-chou-wan **1916**: Create uniform pricing zone for Indochina, exempting Laos

Interwar period (1919–1939)	**1920**: Britain, Dangerous Drugs Act **1925**: Geneva Opium Conventions **1931**: Bangkok Agreement for Suppression of Opium Smoking **1936**: Geneva Trafficking Convention	**1920**: Abolish government opium shops, replaced by licensed shop system **1923**: Shan State Opium Order **1925**: Myangmya experiment **1930**: Introduce Dangerous Drugs Act **1937**: Expand control over Shan State opium	**1925**: Abolish government-run shops, replaced by licensed vendor **1925–1926**: Create opium revenue replacement reserve fund **1927**: Abolish licensed opium vendors **1928–1929**: Create opium consumer registration system **1933**: Create opium rationing system	**1921**: General reform to opium monopoly **1922**: Re-create differential sale zones **1924–1927**: Create anti-opium curriculum in schools **1930**: Reform licensed wholesale system, increased penalties for opium-offenses
World War II and after	**1943**: Britain, France, Holland, declare end of opium monopolies **1946**: Lake Success Protocol **1947**: UN resolution for abolishing opium smoking	**1948**: Ban on opium sales Abolition of opium monopoly	**1946**: Ban on opium consumption Abolition of opium monopoly	**1946**: Ban on opium sales **1951**: Abolition of opium monopoly

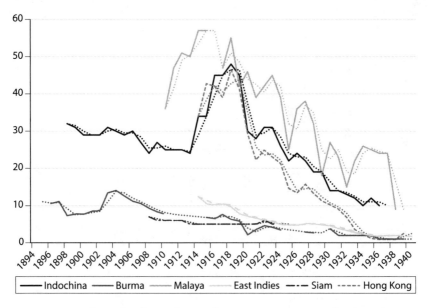

FIGURE A.5. Comparing shares of reported net opium revenue across Southeast Asia, 1890s–1940s (% of total colonial tax revenue).

ABBREVIATIONS

The following abbreviations are used in the Notes and Bibliography.

AFPFL	Anti-Fascist People's Freedom League
ANOM	Archives nationales d'outre-mer (Aix-en-Provence, France)
AREAB	Annual Report of Excise Administration in Burma (post-1889)
AREABB	Annual Report of Excise Administration in British Burma (pre-1889)
BL	British Library
BMOC	Opium Committee for British Malaya
CAC	Corps d'administrateurs coloniaux
CEFEO	Corps expéditionnaire français en Extrême-Orient
DFI	Direction de Finances de l'Indochine
DRV	Democratic Republic of Vietnam
GGI	Gouvernement général de l'Indochine
ICS	India Civil Service
IOR	India Office Records
KMT	Kuomintang, Chinese Nationalist Party
MNA	National Archives Department of Myanmar (Yangon, Myanmar)
NAC	National Archives of Cambodia (Phnom Penh, Cambodia)
NARA	National Archives and Records Administration, United States
ROC	Royal Opium Commission of Britain
RPAB	Report on the Prison Administration of Burma
SDECE	Service de documentation extérieure et de contre-espionnage
SNA	Singapore National Archives
SRRC	Southern Regional Resistance Committee
SSA	Straits Settlements Association (Singapore Branch)
SSOC	Opium Commission for the Straits Settlements and Federated Malay States
SSOT	Society for the Suppression of the Opium Trade

TNA The National Archives of the United Kingdom (Kew Gardens, London, United Kingdom)

UNODC United Nations Office on Drugs and Crime

VNA1 National Archives of Vietnam, Center No. 1 (Hanoi, Vietnam)

NOTES

Notes on Terms Used

1. Although opium-related administrative discussions during the late nineteenth and first half of the twentieth century overlapped with considerations of cannabis, cocaine, and methamphetamines, this book centers attention on raw and prepared forms of opium. For influential books on cannabis, see Mills 2003; on cocaine, see Gootenberg 1999; on heroin, see McCoy 1972; on methamphetamines, see Chouvy 2002. Unless otherwise indicated, I focus on opium smoking because it was the prevalent approach across Southeast Asia and thus preoccupied the colonial administrators I examine. I also generally adopt the terms of *habitual consumption* and *daily use* that these actors used at the time, and avoid using words like addict and addiction because today they are laden with a negative connotation that risks misrepresenting the diverse range of past perspectives regarding opium smoking.

2. On Southeast Asia as a geographic container and analytical category, see Smail 1961; Emmerson 1984; Kratoska, Raben, & Nordhold 2005. The widespread use of the label occurred during World War II, when Allied forces established a Southeast Asia Command that mirrored the geographic scope of Japanese occupation, while the current political and territorial boundaries that separate Southeast Asia from East and South Asia followed the 1967 creation of the Association of Southeast Asian Nations (ASEAN) and rise of area studies during the post-World War II era.

1: Introduction

1. House of Commons, June 25, 1875, vol. 225, col. 601.

2. On the French Cochinchina opium tax farm's reported share of net revenue at 60% during the 1880s, see Descours-Gatin 1987, p. 179. On the British Singapore opium tax farm as accounting for about half of Singapore's total local revenue throughout the nineteenth century, see Trocki 1993, p. 166.

3. Fytche to Government of India, March 31, 1870, British Library (BL)/India Office Records (IOR)/P/2780.

4. Wertz 2013, p. 485; *Les Annales coloniales*, January 7, 1925.

5. Levi 1988; Scott 1998; Tilly 1992.

6. Berridge 1999; Courtwright 2001; Winther 2003; Tyrell 2010; Rimner 2018.

7. D. Smeaton to J. B. Lyall, December 19, 1893, Final Report of Royal Opium Commission (ROC) vol. 2, p. 538.

8. Hesnard 1930, p. 78. On Hesnard's career in French Indochina, see Turbiaux 2009.

9. Ghosh 2008, p. 439.

10. Warren 1985, p. 12.

11. Cogent overviews of debates over conceptualizing the modern state include Nettl 1968; Evans, Rueschemeyer, & Skocpol 1985; Mitchell 1991; Steinmetz 1999; King & Lieberman 2009; Morgan & Orloff 2017. On scholarship challenging fixed intentions on the part of rulers for monopolizing violence or seeking territorial expansion, see Corrigan & Sayer 1985; Centeno 2002; Slater 2010; Naseemullah & Staniland 2016; Wyrtzen 2017; on how the concept and operationalization of state capacity risks oversimplifying the varied ways that states actually exercise power, see Boone 2003; Soifer & vom Hau 2008; Centeno, Kohli, & Yashar 2017; and on the analytical problems of reifying boundaries that arbitrarily separate domestic and international politics, state and society, public and private spheres of life in ways that run roughshod over more overlapping and complex relationships, see Migdal 1988; Htun 2003; Adams, Clemens, & Orloff 2005; Canaday 2009.

12. Weber 1979 [1923]; Downs 1967; Wilson 1989.

13. Dixit 1996; Svensson 2005; Gailmard & Patty 2012.

14. Blau 1956; Goodin 1988; Huber & Shipan 2002.

15. This alternative understanding of low-level bureaucratic discretion has been explored in studies of policy implementation among frontline service providers and street-level bureaucrats, which focus on citizen–administrator interactions. I am especially indebted to works by Lipsky (1980), Dubois (1999), and Zacka (2017) that have elucidated the agency and normative judgments that low-ranking police officers and social service providers, counselors, and educators make in challenging environments with limited resources that pose trade-offs and moral dilemmas on the part of these actors. My account of minor administrators in colonial contexts differs in that their discretionary power emerges, not through encounters with ordinary citizens or society writ large, but in an insular fashion as they dwell on administrative precedents, a point I elaborate on in the text that follows.

16. Alonso & Starr 1980; Bourdieu 1999, 2014; Steinmetz 1999; Kertzer & Arel 2002; Gorski 2003; Loveman 2005, 2014; Morgan & Orloff 2017.

17. Existing literature on vice taxation has focused mostly on metropolitan Europe, where such fiscal arrangements have been famous objects of public controversy and popular discontent; and states could flourish or flounder, depending on how rulers justified the revenue they collected. In eighteenth-century Britain for instance, excise duties on spirituous liquors and beer were extended amid expressed concerns that excessive consumption ruined the health of the common people and corrupted morals. While taxing stimulants enriched the state and enabled unprecedented debt financing that helped the early modern British state wage wars and build administrative capacity, the fiscalization of consumption was also deeply unpopular, alienating large swaths of the intoxicant-consuming public. See Brewer 1989; Ashworth 2003. Old regime France introduced levies on tobacco, labeling its consumption a luxury rather than necessity of life, redefining indirect taxes as a voluntary contribution that subjects made to the king. The tobacco tax was at once lucrative and stoked widespread fiscal rebellions and powerful critiques of a despotic monarchy that contributed to the French Revolution. See Johnson 2006; Kwass 2013a, 2013b, 2014. Exceptional studies that acknowledge the colonies in relation to vice taxation include

Brewer & Porter 1993; Courtwright 2001 (p. 5), who notes that vice taxes formed the "corner-stone of the modern state, and the chief financial prop of European colonial regimes."

18. Cooper 1996, p. 1135.

19. Brubaker & Cooper 2000, p. 16.

20. Bourdieu 1991, p. 170.

21. For a sustained critical examination of bellicist and Marxist theories of the modern state, see Gorski 2003.

22. See Loveman 2005, pp. 1655–1657 for a cogent definition of symbolic state power, and how it relates to but differs from conventional definitions of cultural power and ideology. Loveman, following Bourdieu, stresses a distinguishing attribute of symbolic state power in how it operates through misrecognition and reifying reality, generating "the appearance that no power is being yielded at all" and "making appear as natural, inevitable, and thus apolitical, that which is a product of historical struggle and human invention." Unlike Weberian forms of legitimacy that require explicit recognition of the validity of the state's authority or ideological forms of state power that command collective sentiments that overtly acknowledge the loci of the state, symbolic state power relies on masking the very presence of its carrier. Symbolic state power is a subcategory of cultural power, which can deploy certain symbols, scripts, and performances with the effect of inculcating shared values, beliefs, and meaning-making practices among people. More generally, this line of inquiry stresses that categories and classifications about, for instance, citizenship and nationhood, the economy, or race and ethnicity are constructed (rather than natural) and meaningful in context (instead of divorced from the social practices and historical processes that produce them). Hall 1985; Mitchell 1991; Bourdieu 1999; Steinmetz 1999; Wedeen 1999; Lara-Millán 2017.

23. Loveman 2005, p. 1653. Also see Torpey 1999; Diamant 2001; Telles & Paschel 2014; Hunter and Brill 2016.

24. Anderson 2001; Loveman 2014.

25. Scott 1998, 2009.

26. Adler & Pouliot 2011, p. 4.

27. McNamara 2015.

28. Pressman & Widalvsky 1973; Rudolph & Rudolph 1979; Carpenter 2001. See Pepinsky, Pierskalla, & Sacks 2017, pp. 250–257 for a review of existing scholarship on bureaucratic politics. See Hollyer, Rosendorff, & Vreeland 2018 on the politics of administrative information.

29. Bergson 1959[1900], p. 3b.

30. Warren 1985; Stoler 1989, 1995; Bankoff 1991; Levine 2003; Mills and Barton 2007; Saha 2013.

31. For instance, within Southeast Asian colonial history, on tensions within white settler communities and problems of "mixed" children, see Stoler 1989; Saada 2011. On the fluidity of intra-Asian intimacies and creole diasporas, see Loos 2008; Walker 2015.

32. Important works in this vein identified myriad repertoires through which subjects engaged with and resisted authorities who deemed them pitiable, deviant, and debated their terms of rescue, reform, or repression, while also situating these local encounters in broader contexts of immigration flows, legal structures, global political economies, and colonial capitalism. See Warren 1985, 1990; Spivak 1988; Rafael 1993.

33. Burchell, Gordon, & Miller 1991. Following Foucault, students of the colonial state have come to think along the lines of "state effects" by which disparate practices of governance embed complex constellations of power struggles that generate the impression of an already existing, clearly delineated state structure external to this inner process. Archival energies have also been directed toward unveiling internal conflicts among those who ruled, within communities of white colonizers and settlers, and identifying inconsistent strategies for governing in ways that make assumptions about straightforward goals or single-minded visions driving state action untenable. See Mitchell 1991; Stoler 1989, 1995.

34. Lessard 2009; McClintock 1995; Stoler 1995, 2010; Tracol-Huynh 2010; Reyes & Clarence-Smith 2012.

35. Levine 1998, p. 290. Levine's nuanced study of the British Empire's nineteenth century regulation of prostitution through the Contagious Disease Acts shows how local authorities in the colonies of Hong Kong and the Straits Settlements held countervailing concerns with Chinese prostitutes because of their ties to Asian male laborers who were viewed simultaneously as essential to the colony's economic prosperity and threats to social stability. Nancy Rose Hunt's work also illuminates the many contradictions of purpose that motivated taxes levied on polygamy in Belgian Congo: to avoid risks of backlash from an overt attempt to control society, to eradicate deep rooted customary practices, to police morals, and to extract revenue "from those who were assumed to have greater wealth and wealth gained and expressed immorally in the colonial sign, polygamy/wealth /slavery/prostitution." Hunt 1991, p. 474. Within European communities as well, as Ann Stoler has shown, ambdivalence abound over the status of the white male in ways that informed regulations toward concubinage that at once condoned and abhorred interracial and same sex intimacies. See Stoler 1989, 2010.

36. On gambling, see Bankoff 1991; Saha 2013; Davis 2013; Warren 2017. On drinking, see Korieh 2003; Peters 2004; White 2007; Sasges 2017.

37. I draw inspiration from Morgan and Orloff (2017, p. 3) in approaching colonial and nation-states within a common analytical framework, agreeing that "widening our lens beyond nation-states to include empires and other forms of governance enriches understandings of the multiple levels at which governing authority operates, processes of internal and external boundary formation, and how the 'rule of difference' operates in both imperial and state contexts."

38. Tilly 1985, p. 169.

39. Ibid.

40. On the role of the Quaker-led Society for the Suppression of the Opium Trade in lobbying Parliament to end the British Empire's practice of exporting Indian opium to China, see Brown 1973; Berridge 1999. On American evangelical reformers who galvanized an international order in which civilized empires embraced the suppression of opium as a universal humanitarian cause, see Tyrell 2008. On international norm changes and the rise of global prohibition regimes during the late nineteenth and early twentieth centuries, see Nadelmann 1990. On developments within metropolitan Europe that spurred legislation against nonmedical uses of opium, including the growth of the medical profession, recognition of addiction as a disease, popular and nationalistic associations of opiate use with lower classes, racial minorities, and presumed subversive individuals, see Yvorel 1992; Courtwright 2001; Padwa 2008; Black 2016. On multilateral cooperation through international conferences and conventions, especially under the auspices of the League of Nations, see McAllister 2000.

41. On the role of the United States in international drug control regimes, see Stein 1985; Walker 1991; McAllister 2000; Wertz 2013.

42. Trocki 1999.

43. Le Failler 2001.

44. Décamps 1909; LaMotte 1920; McCoy 2000.

45. Opium Revenue Replacement Reserve Fund, June 22, 1936, The National Archives of the United Kingdom (TNA)/Colonial Office (CO) 273/616.

46. I draw inspiration from the work of Thelen and Mahoney 2010 in understanding gradual institutional change as animated by the internal contestation of agents and inherent ambiguities to institutions.

47. Heclo 1974, p. 305.

48. McCoy 1972; Rush 1990; Trocki 1999; Tagliacozzo 2005; Tagliacozzo, Perdue, & Siu 2015, p. 6.

49. Alfred McCoy (1972) has famously demonstrated the extent to which the grievances and exploitation experienced by inhabitants of highland poppy-growing areas of Burma and Indochina under European rule set the stage for Cold War–era drug trafficking. Eric Tagliacozzo's works (2002, 2008) have shown how smugglers in maritime Southeast Asia were adept at avoiding and circumventing the colonial state's gaze, spurring European authorities to adjust and innovate control strategies while also developing more agile legal administrative infrastructures for policing, surveillance, and collecting intelligence.

50. Since the late 1980s, a new wave of abolition reversed the global distribution of countries retaining the death penalty, which has become increasingly uncommon, and reserved mostly for intentional homicide, treason, and espionage. On Asia's relatively slow turn to abolition, see Johnson & Zimring 2009. In 2018, around 30 countries include executions in sentencing guidelines for drug offences; eight are in Southeast Asia. See Girelli 2019; Amnesty International 2019.

51. Chin 2009; Chouvy 2010.

52. Sewell 1996, p. 843.

53. Go 2011, pp. 240–241. I also follow Cooper and Stoler 1997; Crooks and Parsons 2016 for comparative approaches to empires and bureaucracy that extend beyond metropolitan-colony divides and explore concrete practices of governance across different times and places.

54. Skocpol & Somers 1980; Geddes 2003; Mahoney & Rueschemeyer 2003; Slater & Ziblatt 2013; Goertz 2017.

55. Hussin 2016. On ecologies as a set of actors, locations, and their relationships, see Abbott 2005; on imperial and transnational "fields" that extend from Bourdieu's notion of a "structured space of objective oppositions that operate as a universe of possible stances," animated by competitive struggles over unequally distributed forms of capital, see Steinmetz 2008, p. 591; Go 2008.

56. Ibid.

57. World Peace Foundation 1925, p. 94.

58. On opium monopolies under mercantile companies prior to the mid-nineteenth century, see Prakash 1988; Markovits 2009, 2017 on the British East India Company; Souza 2009 on the Dutch East India Company; Bisiou 1995 on the French East India Company.

59. For example, see Nankoe, Gerlus, & Murray 1993 (p. 195) on the Dutch colonial administrator W. P. Groeneveldt sent to French Cochinchina in the late 1880s to study its opium

monopoly; Le Failler 2001 (pp. 97–102) on how the Saigon opium factory of French Indochina and its dross control system was inspired by the Dutch in Java.

60. Stoler 2010, p. xi.

61. See Bell 2006; Benton 2008 for critiques of biased reconstructions of imperial discourses that rely heavily on a small circle of unrepresentative canonical figures.

62. See Rothschild 2012, pp. 6–8 on approaches to a "history of the inner life" with a micro-level focus on the ideas and sentiments of people.

63. Hevia 1998; Scott 2009; Stoler 2009.

64. Smith 1985; Hull 2012; Raman 2012.

65. Rush 1985, 1986; Warren 1985; Trocki 1990; Fee & We 2004; Frost 2005; Tagliacozzo 2005.

66. Coleridge 1853, vol. 2, p. 175.

2: A Shared Turn

1. La Motte 1920, p. xi.

2. Ducourtieux et al. 2008, p. 159.

3. McCoy 1972, p. 90.

4. *Friend of China* 1875, pp. 143–144; Scheltema 1907; Rowntree 1905, pp. 163–164; Lecoq 1913; Trocki 1999, p. 161; Rush 1990, pp. 217–241.

5. Descharmes 1855; Braddell 1857; Descours-Gatin 1987, pp. 227–229; Berridge 1999.

6. See Heclo 1974.

7. Owen 1934; McAllister 2000; Rimner 2018.

8. Geertz 1981; Anderson 2001; Wedeen 1999; Loveman 2005, 2014; McNamara 2015.

9. Gusfield 1963; Devlin 1965; Musto 1987; Stigler 2003; McGirr 2015.

10. Prakash 1988; Bisiou 1995; Markovits 2009; Souza 2009; Wolf 2010, pp. 232–261.

11. On the economics of the India-China opium trade, see Chaudhuri 1966. On the opium trade as *casus belli* between China and the Western powers, see Chang 1964; Wong 2002.

12. Hamilton 1727, cited in Trocki 1999, p. 37; Owen 1934, p. 8.

13. Hell 2007, p. 86; Le Failler 2001, p. 61; Tran 2017, p. 29. On precolonial bans on opium in Burma, see Sangermano 1969[1833], p. 66.

14. Trocki 1999, p. 56.

15. Descours-Gatin 1987, p. 16.

16. For this general description of opium tax farms, I rely on Rush 1990; Descours-Gatin 1992; Butcher & Dick 1993; Nankoe, Gerlus, & Murray 1993; Trocki 1999, 2002;Descours-Gatin 1987, 1992; Bisiou 1995. For a vivid account of precolonial opium tax farms, see Wahid 2013, pp. 25–30 on the Sultanate of Mataram before the Dutch in Java.

17. On the varieties of opium tax farms, see Rush 1990, pp. 43–69. Trocki (1999, pp. 142–159) identifies three general types of opium tax farms across Southeast Asia: the urban opium tax farm existed in all major cities with clients of diverse ethnic and racial backgrounds; the Malayan system that catered mostly to Chinese consumers (which extended beyond the Malay Peninsula and archipelago to parts of Sumatra, Borneo, Australia, and the Philippines); and the Javanese system that had more Southeast Asian consumers (which applied to Java, the central Siam, and Cochinchina).

18. In Indochina, French businessmen also bid for and acquired the contracts for tax farms. On the Mssrs. Ségassie and Télésio who held the first contract of Cochinchina in the 1860s, see Descours-Gatin 1992, pp. 43–48 and Sasges 2015; on Vandelet and Dusstur who operated the Cambodia tax farm in 1881, see Descours-Gatin 1992, p. 70. On imperial labor demands that invited Chinese migration and settlement patterns across Southeast Asia, see Ken 1965; McKeown 2010. On the strength of nineteenth-century Chinese entrepreneurs in Southeast Asia, the existing literature is vast, identifying the role of family networks, business acumen, as well as coethnic ties with Chinese migrant laborers that contributed to lowered costs compared with competitor European enterprises, see Campbell 1923; Purcell 1948; Cushman 1986; Reid 1996.

19. Rush 1990, p. 44.

20. Trocki 1999, p. 140; Inspector General of Police, British Burma to Chief Commissioner, May 24, 1873, BL/IOR/P/4.

21. Descours-Gatin 1992, p. 70; Proceedings of Finance and Commerce Department, British Burma, November 1893, BL/IOR/P/4281.

22. Trocki 1999, 2002.

23. See Appendix Table A.2 for more details.

24. An exception was the Dutch East Indies where the indigenous Javanese population who consumed opium outnumbered the Chinese. See Wiselius 1886; Rush 1990; Chandra 2002.

25. Little 1848, pp. 20–21.

26. Cited in Wright 2014, p. 1.

27. International Labor Organization 1935, pp. 15, 34, and 48.

28. Trocki 2002.

29. Trocki 2002, p. 331.

30. Rush 1990, p. 104.

31. Trocki 1999, pp. 158 and 138.

32. Straits Settlements Blue Book 1893; Descours-Gatin 1987, pp. 179–180.

33. Report from Colonial Military Contributions Committee, Hong Kong Opium Revenue," April 9, 1914, TNA/T1/11642/11908.

34. Cited in Victoria 2015, p. 143.

35. Report by M. Moretti, Inspecteur de 3ème classe des Colonies on "la question de l'opium" (Moretti Report), April 5, 1926, Vietnamese National Archives, Center 1, Hanoi (VNA1)/ Fonds de la Direction des finances de l'Indochine (DFI)/1746.

36. On the general economic impact of opium, and debates regarding whether opium sales served as an indicator of or actually caused prosperity in the colonies by improving worker productivity in labor intensive sectors of colonial economy and stabilizing financial contracts between merchant capitalists and planters, see Bailey & Truong 2001. On the relationship between opium and growth of the Chinese middle class and purchasing power, see Trocki 2002. On the broader significance of Chinese immigrants in terms of class formation and sociopolitical integration across colonial Southeast Asia, see Sidel 2008.

37. Scott 1906, p. 269.

38. Report by the Opium Commission for the Straits Settlements and Federated Malay States 1908 (SSOC 1908), vol. 2, p. 92. On opium as considered less harmful than alcohol in the Dutch East Indies, see Rush 1990, pp. 234–235.

39. Rush 1990, p. 28, citing P.A. Daum, *Ups and Downs of Life in the Indies* 1892.

40. Chinese Gambling and Lottery in Bassein, November 10, 1873, BL/IOR/P 780/5.

41. Audience de M. Chauvin, December 21, 1929, Archives nationales d'outre-mer (ANOM)/ INDO/GGI/43079.

42. Pannier 1911, p. 21.

43. On theological conceptions of vice as sins against divine orders, see Bloomfield 1952. On "ordinary vices" that offend liberal sensibilities about freedom and public–private distinctions, see Shklar 1994. On vice according to the law as victimless crimes that do not involve direct injury upon an individual based on purposive intent, recklessness, or negligence, see Harcourt & Zimring 2014.

44. Bray 1995, pp. 14–17; Jordan 1997.

45. Bebbington 1982, p. 22. Both Protestant and Catholic religious workers abroad made pious conceptions of vice portable, notwithstanding competing visions of doctrine and goals of evangelism. On British missionaries across Africa and Asia, see Hilton 1988; Comaroff & Comaroff 1999; Porter 2004. French Catholic missionaries also conceived of vice in terms of sin, while seeing themselves as "soldiers of God" who would save the souls of heathens through conversion. Daughton 2006, p. 12; Tuck 1987; Prudhomme 2007.

46. Reyes & Clarence-Smith 2012, p. 4; Also see Atkinson & Errington 1990; Andaya 1994; Hansen 2007; Peletz 2009; Turner 2014.

47. Didérot 2003 [1765].

48. On modern vice as a secular "perspective beset with anxiety about the governability of urbanized masses living without any evident structure of rule under conditions where traditional authorities, such as the Church or a visible dominant class, [were] weakened or no longer present," see Hunt 1996, pp. 10–11. On the vice of gambling in terms of an immoral activity due to heavy risk-taking, which incurred greater pains from losing that would exceed the pleasure of winning, see Bentham 1843; Laplace 2009[1825], 1912. On vice as self-regarding harms, see Mill 1909[1848]; on vice as immoral violations of a society's collective sensibilities of good, see Stephen 1993[1873].

49. Mehta 1999; Pitts 2005.

50. Kidd 1879, p. 353; Korieh 2003.

51. Logre 1924, p. 78, citing Jeanselme 1907.

52. Anderson 2006; Amrith 2010.

53. Pick 1993, p. 15.

54. Hobson 1905.

55. On urban vices and fears of degeneracy in terms of venereal diseases, see Warren 1990 on prostitution in British ruled Singapore. On the British Empire more globally and moral regulation, see Levine 1998, 2003; Korieh 2003; Howell 2009; Heath 2010; on the French colonial conceptions of urban vice, see Proschan 2002 on pederasty and opium addiction; Tracol-Huynh 2010 on prostitution. On scientific racism in colonial policy, see Ballhatchet 1980; McClintock 1995; Tilley 2011.

56. Long 1924, cited in Le Failler 1993, p. 513.

57. Furnivall 1944, p. 304.

58. Stoler 1995, 2010; Saada 2011; Walker 2012; Firpo 2016.

59. In British Burma until the 1880s, the core group comprised the Financial Commissioner at its head and Assistant Commissioners by major division, who were graduates of the

Imperial Service of the Indian Civil Service, while the secondary group were generally district officers in major towns. On the general organization of colonial administration in Burma, see On the Burma Commission, June 28, 1887, BL/IOR/L/P&J/216/2018; Donnison 1953. For the nineteenth-century Straits Settlements, the core group included Resident Councilors for Singapore, Penang, and Malacca, and later the Protector of Chinese (and Secretaries for Chinese Affairs), who were selected through the Far Eastern Cadet Service, while the secondary group included an Excise Licensing Officer and Import and Export Officers. In 1910, a Government Monopolies Department was established with a Departmental Office-in-Charge and Chief Superintendent based in Singapore, Assistant Superintendents for Penang and Malacca, and expanded ranks that included Chief Accountants, Controllers and their Assistants, as well as a Preventive Service. See Annual Records Straits Settlements 1910, 1915. French Cochinchina under the military government had a Commissioner for Farms, who was replaced in 1898 by a general Director of the Customs and Excise Department who, along with an Under-Director for the protectorates and their High Residents formed a core group with graduates from the *École coloniale* in Paris with a secondary group of low-level *fonctionnaires*. See Galembert 1924.

60. Descours-Gatin 1992, p. 29.

61. Annual Report on Excise Administration of British Burma (hereafter AREABB) 1872. Also see ROC 1894, vol. 2, p. 516.

62. Rush 1990; Trocki 1990.

63. Tagliacozzo 2005 demonstrates a "paradoxical dynamic" to state formation through which borders were simultaneously strengthened and undermined through the interaction of states and smugglers, a dynamic that was especially pronounced for the drug trade adept at evading state authorities. By way of policing, the insular Southeast Asian states developed legal edifices with strong powers of search, witness protection, recruitment of spies and informants, as well as procedures to prosecute illicit traders in opium, morphine, and ganja (pp. 196–202). However, smugglers still traversed the vast Anglo-Dutch frontier while also carving out spaces of resistance against colonial hegemony. Such threats that secret trades and porous borders posed to the colonial state in turn required responses by authorities—"contraband was whatever those in power said it was, and these designations sometimes changed quickly"—and "attempt[s] to stamp out smuggling and unrestricted movement along the frontier required processes of imagination and identification on the part of colonial Europeans" (pp. 364 and 367).

64. To be sure, the topic of opium sales in Burma, Malaya, and parts of Indochina did occur in nineteenth century Britain and France, but usually at eventful junctures, amid wars, scandals, and during electoral struggles when the overseas reach of empires became subjects of public and political controversy. Moreover, metropolitan authorities tended to focus on the opium trade and smuggling occurring in major ports such as Singapore and Batavia controlled by mercantile companies, with less interest in the consumption of local inhabitants.

65. Ludden 1993, p. 252.

66. Ibid., p. 259.

67. Mantena 2010, p. 155; Mamdani 2012.

68. On the Third Republic's approach to the colonial sciences and their cultural and academic institutions, see Singaravélou 2011; Conklin 2013.

69. Scott 2004, p. 4.

70. India Office List 1893, p. 62; Allen 1970, p. 159; Sager 2016, p. 157; *Annuaire Statistique de l'Indochine* 1923, p. 248 ; Isoart 1961, pp. 199–200. Contrast the French in Indochina who employed more than 5,000 customs and excise officers for a population of 30 million, to the British in India who had fewer than 5,000 to govern over 325 million. Among top functionaries, the French had studied law and were trained in a Colonial School in Paris and then directly joined a Colonial Administrator Corps (CAC), whereas the British passed general exams for the India Civil Service (ICS) or Far Eastern Cadet Service under the Colonial Administrative Service (CAS). Galembert 1924; Kirk-Greene 2000, pp. 100–160. On the emergence and evolution of French training for colonial administrators, see Thomson 1937, pp. 58–87; Sager 2014, pp. 129–151.

71. On the ideologies of the French colonial empire, see Thomas 2011; on the British in India, see Metcalf 1994. For canonical formulations of French assimilation and British indirect rule, see Boutmy 1895; Lugard 1922. For comparisons of British and French colonial services, see Lowell 1900; Dimier 2004. On the British, see Mason 1954; Glass 1985; Gardiner 1998; Kirk-Greene 2000. For the French, see Chailley-Bert 1903; Maspero 1929; Suignard 1931, Cohen 1971; Sager 2014.

72. Although there were French Protestants who also criticized the opium trade (see Bisiou 1995, p. 65), their organized activities were weaker compared to those of the British. The French Empire had an office of civilian inspectors with the Ministry of Colonies that externally audited the colonial administration and their finances, and a strong commercially oriented colonial lobby in the national legislature during the early twentieth century. The British had no equivalent to the French inspectors inside the imperial bureaucracy scrutinizing revenue raised from opium but had an Office of the Crown Agents independent of the Colonial Office that oversaw the financial transactions of the empire across colonies and a powerful religious lobby for social reform in Parliament, the Society for the Suppression of the Opium Trade (SSOT). On the French Missions of Inspection, see see Girault 1943; Sasges 2017, pp. 59–60. On the French colonial lobby see Andrew and Kanya-Forstner 1971, 1974; Persell 1983; Lagana 1990. On the British Crown Agents see Ponko 1966; Kesner 1977; Sunderland 2007. On the SSOT, see Brown 1973; Johnson 1975.

73. Go 2011, p. 102.

74. Influential studies on colonial policy for land and property, education, law, and religion have stressed the extent to which official opinion developed through interactions with local elites and communities(Guha 1963; Wilson 2011; Hussin 2016) or accommodations of metropolitan knowledge communities (Sibeud 2002; Singaravélou 2011), and how policies relating to medicine and hygiene were deeply informed by expert professions including indigenous healers, Anglo-European medical scientists, and their transnational networks (Arnold 1993; Edington & Pols 2016).

75. Kelsall 1955; Robson 1956; Cohen 1971.

76. Woodruff 1954, p. 270.

77. Trevelyan 1942.

78. Cohen 1971.

79. Kirk-Greene 2000, p. 22.

80. Mamdani 1996, p. 77.

81. Mahoney 2010.

82. Barkey 2008.

83. Adams 1996, p. 17.

84. Scott 1969, p. 1145.

85. Orwell 1974 [1934].

86. Mantena 2010.

87. McBride 2015.

88. Steinmetz 2007.

89. Ibid., p. xiv.

90. Steinmetz 2008, p. 61.

91. Ireland 1907; Galembert 1924; Maspero 1929; Donnison 1953.

92. Bernard Cohn's influential works on the "investigative modalities" of the nineteenth-century British Empire that collected and officialized facts about indigenous cultures show how these entailed disjunctures between constructed taxonomies of difference and the realities they purported to represent. Focusing more locally on the transmission of information, works by Christopher Bayly and Martin Thomas have respectively elucidated the worries of British and French Empires with intelligence provided by "native" informants that colored the ways by which colonial administrators came to craft narratives about security threats. Jon Wilson's work stresses the formative influence of unease with strangeness, and intersubjective experiences with foreign people in lands far from home. He brilliantly captures the felt distance and deep suspicion that unhappily estranged officials of the eighteenth-century British East India Company experienced and how they shaped the disposition of colonial governance, with a "mood of anxious detachment [that] dominated the way officials privately discussed their lives." See Wilson 2008, p. 66.

93. Brubaker & Cooper 2000, p. 16.

94. Tilly 1985, p. 169.

95. I am grateful to Andrew Abbott for this formulation.

96. Finnemore and Sikkink 1998, pp. 897–898. Seminal studies in the sociological literature on moral panics focus on the role of religious groups, the media, experts and activist networks in fashioning new common senses that animate bottom-up pressure for legislative and administrative reform. See Gusfield 1963; Cohen 1972. Scholarship on the criminalization of vice shows how prohibitionist laws reflect social norms and community standards, and may assume instrumental value for politicians and legislators seeking electoral and popular support. See Harcourt and Zimring 2014. On constructivist approaches in political science on the evolution of international norms and global prohibition regimes, see Nadelmann 1990. More recent literature on transnational activism that centers attention on the role of networks and international practices include Adler & Pouliot 2011; Carpenter 2014; McNamara 2015.

97. Bernard 1901, p. 72.

98. Ibid.

3: The Different Lives of Southeast Asia's Opium Monopolies

1. League of Nations 1930, vol. 1, p. 13.

2. Réponse au questionnaire de la Commission d'enquête sur le contrôle de l'opium à fumer en Extrême-Orient, ANOM/INDO/GGI/43078.

3. League of Nations 1930, vol. 1, p. 4.

4. Ibid., p. 39.

5. Ibid., p. 19.

6. Ibid.

7. Audience de M. Chauvin, December 21, 1929, ANOM/INDO/GGI/43079.

8. Ibid.

9. Ibid.

10. League of Nations 1930, vol. 1, p. 21.

11. Ibid.

12. Scott 1896, p. 110.

13. Ibid., citing Cook 1772, vol. 1, p. 288. The term "amok" was not specific to opium consumption, but translated more generally as a condition of rage relating to violent individual behavior. For the significant literature on "amok" as a trope among colonial officials of Malaya, see Swettenham 1903; Spires 1988. I am grateful to an anonymous reviewer for this clarification.

14. During the 1650s, merchants of the Dutch East India Company (Vereenigde Oost-Indische Compagnie or VOC) began to transport opium grown in Bengal to Batavia and Canton. The British East India Company (EIC) entered the trade in 1708, and in 1775, the Governor General of Bengal Warren Hastings declared a monopoly over the production and sale of opium in Bengal. Hastings established a "contract" system that granted contracts to British entrepreneurs for delivering certain amounts of opium to the EIC, which was sold to private merchants who exported the drug. Due to the exploitative rent-seeking behavior of contractors toward poppy growing peasants, the contract system was replaced by an "agency" system through two reforms under the purview of the new Governor General Charles Cornwallis, respectively in 1789 and 1797, which together created an opium agency with paid employees of the EIC overseeing Bengal's opium industry. Until 1857, the EIC's opium agency (also called the opium department) purchased poppy grown in the eastern Ganges River plains, processed it in opium factories in the towns of Ghazhipur or Benares in Bihar and Bengal, which was in turn transported to Calcutta and sold through public auctions to merchants who exported it overseas. After 1857, the Government of India replaced the EIC and continued this approach until 1935, when India declared the halt of its opium exports for non-medical use, effectively ending the commercial trade. For details on the organization of the Bengal opium economy, see Chaudhuri 1966; Richards 1981; Cassells 2002. Indian opium also included poppy cultivated in the Western Princely states, which was shipped through Bombay under what was called the "Malwa" system. On the Malwa system, see Farooqui 1995, 2005.

15. I follow Richards 1981 in focusing on the flow of India's opium exports between 1789 (when the first Cornwallis reforms took place) to 1935. Also see Appendix Table A.1 for India's opium exports to China and Southeast Asia (1870s-1920s) and Figure A.4 for India's exports to China (1780s–1930s) based on Richards 1981, pp. 154–162.

16. Greenberg 1951, p. 104; Richards 2002a, p. 377.

17. Cited in Scheltema 1910, p. 224.

18. Marx 2007[1858], p. 24.

19. *Journal des économistes*, December 5, 1860.

20. Gide 1910.

21. House of Commons, May 6, 1908, vol. 188, col. 369.

22. Pannier 1910, pp. 376–377. This was hardly a universal sentiment of his time, according to Jacques Pannier, a Protestant pastor in France, who insisted that news of the Anglo-Chinese agreement was received with a "skeptical smile" and cynicism of its sincerity let alone God's attention

to the movement against opium. Pannier 1911, p. 31. But see Chailley-Bert 1908, p. 177 and commentary in *la Quinzaine coloniale*, April and May 1908. For a brilliant account of the diverse coalition of transnational activists and public opinion debating opium during this period, see Rimner 2018, especially chapters 2, 4, and 6.

23. Owen 1934, p. 332. For contemporary accounts see Rowntree 1905.

24. Lowes 1981, p. 83.

25. Johnson (1975) and Brown (1973) demonstrate how the SSOT emerged in the 1870s and paved the way for later anti-opium movements to gain influence in Westminster and Whitehall, especially after the Liberal Party's victory in 1906 and rise of John Morley as Secretary of State for India. On tacit agreements among policymakers in London, Calcutta, and Beijing preceding 1906 who shared beliefs about the opium trade's indefensibility, see Newman 1989, pp. 532–535.

26. Lodwick 1996.

27. Parssinen 1983; Roth 2002; Foxcroft 2007; Mills 2003, 2014.

28. Taylor 1969, p. 29.

29. On international drug diplomacy, see Taylor 1969; McAllister 2000, 2007. On domestic politics and society, see Courtwright 2001; Ahmad 2007.

30. Chang 1964; Spence 1975; Zhou 1999; Thai 2018.

31. Brook & Wakabayashi 2000, p. 19; Baumler 2007.

32. Wong 2002, pp. 190–199.

33. Bello's focus on the landlocked western provinces revises histories of opium prohibition that generally focused on elite decision-making and factional politics centered in Beijing and Sino-Western diplomatic conflicts on the eastern coast. See Bello 2005, 2013. For an overview of the historiography of Qing opium prohibition, see Bello 2005, pp. 8–16.

34. Zheng 2005, p. 78. Also see Dikötter, Zhou, & Laamann 2004. On how practices of smoking opium and tobacco aligned, see Benedict 2011, p. 79.

35. Foster 2000, 2010.

36. Wertz 2013, p. 476.

37. Ibid., p. 469.

38. Markovits 2009, 2017.

39. Richards 1981.

40. Richards 2002a, pp. 168–173. See Winthers (2003) on how British reformists critical of opium's economic life in India espoused an enthusiastic program of empire, using the rhetoric of science and authoritative claims to medical expertise.

41. Farooqui 1995, 2005.

42. For exemplary recent studies, see Baruah 2016; Rimner 2018.

43. *Journal des économistes*, December 5, 1860.

44. Lucy was the English interpreter for General Cousin de Montauban, who led the French forces in China alongside the British in the last battles that had ended the Second Opium War. He wrote to his father from the battlefield, "They [the British] are masters of the Yangtze River all the way into Nanking, China's main trade port . . . they impose their supremacy, their protectorate." And of course, Lucy added, "we know what that word protectorate means in the language of British power. Simply ask the Ionian Islanders (the British conquered these Greek Islands until 1862) or the Rajas of India (the rulers of the Princely States of India who were subject to British indirect rule). Lucy 1861, p. 193.

45. Ibid.

46. Ibid. On Catholic missionaries in China and the French "religious protectorate," see Brandt 1936; Young 2013.

47. On the rich traditions of literary commentary on opium use in nineteenth-century Britain and France, see Milner 2002; Boon 2002; Padwa 2012.

48. Pannier 1911, p. 8.

49. Pila 1925, p. 3. Also see Budistéanu 1929.

50. See Lowes 1981, pp. 112–114 on the general reluctance of French diplomats to partake in 1907 discussions; Bisiou 1995 on opium in French India; Yvorel 2012 on the anti-opium position of Senator Joseph Catalonia, who urged France's more active participation in the 1909 Shanghai conference. Xavier Paulès' works on French drug detoxification clinics in China during the late Qing and Republican periods represent a recent and welcome development. See Paulès 2008, 2010.

51. Delrieu 1988; Yvorel 1992; Bergeron 1999.

52. Yvorel 1992, 2012; Retaillaud-Bajac 2009, 2011.

53. Descours-Gatin 1987, 1992.

54. Le Failler 1993, 1995, 2001; Rapin 2007.

55. Compared with Descour-Gatin and Le Failler, Bisiou approaches the drug monopolies from a more legalistic perspective, viewing the pressures of reputation and prestige from a moralizing international community and its drug control conventions as weak. He identifies the two world wars and the Indochina war as pivotal events that contributed to the eventual demise of the French drug monopolies. See Bisiou 1995, pp. 448–452.

56. Wakabayashi 2000, p. 57; Yang 2012.

57. Jennings 1995, 1997; Goto-Shibata 2002; Kingsberg 2011, 2013; Hsu 2014.

58. Kingsberg 2013.

59. Robins 2015, p. 11.

60. Kozma 2013.

61. Gingeras 2014.

62. Schayegh 2011. For an exemplary study of transnational smuggling that links the Middle East to South and Southeast Asia, see Mathew 2016.

63. Beyond the region, the United Kingdom and Mauritius were the largest importers from India, but in very small quantities that seldom rose above an annual 100 chests combined. The UK imported record amounts in 1915 owing to an increase medical demand for heroin during World War I.

64. Report by M. Merat, Inspecteur de 2ème classe des Colonies regarding "la vérification de M. Deyme, Directeur des Douanes et Régies" (Merat Report), February 18, 1930, ANOM/ FM/INDO_NF/282/2481; Memorandum on opium for the use of India's Representative on the United Nations Narcotic Commission, 1946, BL/IOR/L/E/9/732.

65. When India announced its planned halt to all opium exports in 1925, there was a temporary upward trend in opium imports across the region, as colonies began to stock Indian opium in their warehouses, anticipating future shortages.

66. McKeown 2010, p. 98. Chinese traders from diverse subgroups settled across the region as merchants, compradors, tax revenue farmers, as well as agriculturalists and miners. See Purcell 1948; Brown 1993; Tagliacozzo & Chang 2011.

67. Retaillaud-Bajac 2009.

68. Berridge 1999, pp. 251–264. The 1920 Dangerous Drugs Act limited the production, import, export, possession, sale and distribution of opium, cocaine, morphine or heroin to licensed persons. On its key concerns with forged prescriptions relating to cocaine, see Mills 2003, pp. 192–193.

69. Bisiou 1995, p. 475.

70. Report to the President of the Republic, *Journal officiel de la République française*, March 14, 1917. The promulgated version of the 1916 law for Indochina distinguished opium sold in the colony from narcotics in general (through a *décret d'applications* dated March 14, 1917). The original proposal of this law in 1911 by Senator Catalonia bracketed the question of its application to the colonies. On debates between Catalonia and Marius Moutet centering on the special circumstances of Indochina, see Bisiou 1995, pp. 476–480; Yvorel 2012.

71. Padwa 2008, 2012.

72. Padwa 2008, p. 170.

73. Opium's "association with poor citizenship and treason gave [opiates] a special place within France's wartime anti-intoxicant crusade" and the 1916 law on poisonous substances rendered drug control "a police matter more than a public health initiative." Padwa 2012, p. 128. On interwar France's drug regimes, see Retaillaud-Bajac 2009.

74. Padwa 2012, p. 191. On Britain, see Mills 2005 about DORA as related to military discipline concerns, especially opium and cocaine use among off-duty soldiers in London.

75. British Burma's opium monopoly was formally placed under colonial laws for India—the 1878 All India Opium Act that centralized state control over the subcontinent's opium economy and the 1930 Dangerous Drugs Act for India—but the Chief Commissioner of Burma and later governor exercised considerable discretion in adjusting policies to local circumstances. For British Malaya, the Legislative Council for the Straits Settlements, and in French Indochina, the Governor General of the colony issued ordinances and decrees that gave legal effect to opium-related decisions.

76. Wright 1924, p. 283.

77. "Décret du 23 juin 1922," *Journal officiel de l'Indochine française*, November 22, 1922.

78. McAllister 2000; Mills 2014.

79. Brook & Wakabayashi 2000, p. 4. While Brook and Wakabayashi focus on national and imperial systems for opium control, opium regimes also capture the workings of on-site colonial bureaucracies.

80. Warren 1985, p. 61.

81. Ibid., p. 50.

82. *L'Écho annamite*, January 5, March 27, April 3, June 27, December 8, 1925.

83. Zinoman 2001, p. 147.

84. Goto-Shibata 2006, p. 61.

85. Trocki 2002, p. 300.

86. Trocki 2005, p. 156.

87. Le Failler 2001, p. 346.

88. Proschan 2002, p. 636.

89. McCoy 1972, 2000; Cohen 1984; Maule 1991, 2002; Chin 2009; Chouvy 2010.

90. Culas 2000; Rapin 2007.

91. Williams 1961, p. 39. Rush (1990) clarifies the tensions that riddled Chinese-run opium tax farms, dividing elites as they competed to control not only the profits generated from opium sales but also the policing and patronage networks that sustained tax farms. Also see Diehl 1993; Chandra 2002; Trocki (1999) has advanced a powerful thesis that the emergence of capitalism in nineteenth-century Southeast Asia was made possible through opium tax farms, which enabled the primitive accumulation of Chinese capital. See Wahid 2013 for an excellent recent study of the Dutch opium tax farms and monopoly in the growth of the East Indies' colonial political economy.

92. Kenji 2012, p. 96. For contemporary perspectives on the anti-opium issue in the Straits Settlements as a distinctively Chinese identity issue, see Lim Boon Keng 1906; Wen 1907.

93. Phung Nhu Cuong to Decoux, November 13, 1944, ANOM/INDO/RSTNF/4175.

94. Ho Chi Minh 1960, p. 17.

95. Mills and Barton 2007, p. 13.

96. Wright 2008, p. 621.

97. Goto-Shibata 2006; Miners 1983, p. 275.

98. Descours-Gatin 1992. See Brocheux & Hémery (2009, p. 81) on the significance of the opium monopoly for introducing a general colonial budget subsidized by indirect taxes and financing expenses for building public infrastructure.

99. SSOT 1891, p. 3.

100. LeGrain 1925.

101. Phung 1937; Nguyen-Marshall 2008, p. 127; Zinoman 2014, p. 136.

102. Avis présenté au nom de la commission des affaires extérieures . . . par Marius Moutet, March 7, 1916, ANOM/AMIRAUX/ 43013.

103. Despatch by High Commissioner of Federated Malay States, July 24, 1929, TNA/CO 717/66.

104. Proceedings of Legislative Council, February 28, 1883, TNA/CO 273/119.

105. On anticipated diminishing revenue from the Singapore tax farm, see November 16, 1889, TNA/CO 273/162. On the Chinese-run tax farms and estimated losses from opium duties, see January 1, April 28, July 15, November 12, 1897, TNA/CO 273/232.

106. Descours-Gatin 1992, pp. 44–48.

107. Le Failler 1993, p. 471.

108. Goto-Shibata 2006. For the East Indies, the Dutch opium monopoly also saw a decline in the profitability of opium revenue during the Great Depression. See Chandra 2002, p. 105. During this period of economic downturn, the Dutch claimed 64 percent of its annual opium revenues as profit, which was still a significant windfall, according to Chandra. However, compared with the pre-Depression years, when the profitability reached 80 to 90 percent, this constitutes a decrease of nearly 20 percentage points.

109. See Chapter 7 on the end of the opium monopolies.

110. I relied on annual reports from the Excise Department for British Burma, British Malaya's government Monopolies Department, and French Indochina's Department of Customs and Excise, general budget as well as retrospective assessments from metropolitan auditors. For the Dutch East Indies, I relied on data made available by Siddhartha Chandra from 1914 to 1941. See Appendix Figure A.5 for details on sources consulted. These types of official records, which include statistics on opium revenue and calculations of profit, must be interpreted with caution.

Especially in the case of French Indochina, official numbers overestimate net opium revenue. With these caveats in mind, patterns in available data demonstrate a declining profitability to opium revenue after the introduction of the monopolies. In British Burma, opium revenue was a combination of indirect taxes collected through licensed opium vendors who paid sales duties and license fees to the colonial government (under the category of excise revenue) and receipts based on the value of opium sales that the Excise Department made to these vendors (under a separate category of opium revenue). Ireland 1907, vol. 2, pp. 574–575. Customs duties on Indian opium imported into Burma were minimal, because it was administered as a province of British India (until 1935). Throughout the period examined, Burma's provincial contract with the central government of India generally allowed Burma's administration to retain one-half of its collected excise revenue, which included license fees and sales duties on opium. Opium revenue itself was classified as imperial revenue that was wholly remitted to the Government of India, but because it was, in effect, a small share of the revenue that the Burma Excise Department collected. For instance, in 1905, the category of opium revenue amounted to 650,000 rupees while opium's share of excise revenue totaled 4.8 million rupees (AREABB 1905, p. 37). My estimates for British Malaya are limited to the Straits Settlements, in part because it is difficult to combine opium revenue collected for this Crown Colony with the Federated and Unfederated Malay States' opium revenue collections that included import duties. Opium revenue in the Straits Settlements was an indirect tax that combined license fees collected from opium vendors and sales duties. Beyond opium revenue, local tax revenue for the Straits Settlements was collected from dues on the Straits lighthouse and wharves; a variety of licenses on arms and ammunition, fisheries, and liquor vendors; and petroleum and stamp duties.

111. *Straits Times*, October 6, 1925.

112. Ibid.

113. Report of the Chief Commissioner of Burma to Government of India, March 31, 1870, BL/IOR/P/2780.

114. C. J. Saunders, September 8, 1907, SSOC 1908, vol. 2.

115. Dumarest 1938, p. 97.

116. Le Failler 2001, p. 84.

117. On the Opium Question in Relation to Burma, July 5, 1892, ROC. vol. 2, pp. 624–628.

4: "Morally Wrecked" in British Burma, 1870s–1890s

1. Wertz 2013, p. 469. During the first decade after 1898, the Americans in the Philippines considered and revised several regulatory approaches including high tariffs on opium imports, legal opium sales under a monopoly, and restoring the opium tax farm. See Foster 2010.

2. Foster 2000, 2010; Wertz 2013.

3. On anti-Chinese sentiments based on opium-smoking among Chinese migrant workers, see Rush 1985 on the Dutch East Indies; Goto-Shibata 2006 and Kenji 2012 on the British Straits Settlements.

4. Richards 2002b; Wright 2008.

5. For the first year of prohibition, the Government of India's Finance and Commerce Department estimated "an annual loss of revenue to the amount of 15 lakhs of rupees." Landsowne to Earl of Kimberley, March 22, 1893, ROC, vol. 2, p. 631.

6. Note by the Financial Commissioner on the Extent to Which Opium Is Consumed in Burma and the Effects of the Drug on the People (hereafter Smeaton 1892), April 27, 1892, ROC, vol. 2, p. 544.

7. D. M. Smeaton to J. B. Lyall, Question 8089, December 19, 1893, ROC, vol. 2, p. 230.

8. Ibid.

9. Ibid.

10. J. Butler to Commissioner of Irrawaddy Division, December 5, 1891, Myanmar National Archives (MNA)/1/15 (e), 9094.

11. S. C. F. Peile to Chief Secretary to the Chief Commissioner, January 22, 1892, ROC, vol. 2, p. 605.

12. Smeaton 1892, p. 539.

13. Dalzell to Financial Commissioner, December 2, 1891, ROC, vol. 2, p. 605.

14. D. M. Smeaton to J. B. Lyall, December 19, 1893, ROC, vol. 2, p. 230.

15. Ibid.

16. Statistics of Opium Consumers, March 1, 1898, MNA/1/15 (b), 390.

17. Prohibition of possession and use took force under Sections Three and Five of the Opium Rules to the 1895 Burma Amendment to the 1878 Indian Opium Act. See *Burma Opium Manual 1904*, p. 5.

18. Bengal Board of Revenue to Government of Bengal, November 10, 1870, BL/IOR/P/2780.

19. On opium regulations under the East India Company rule, see Cassels 2010, chapter 5. On the Government of India's opium laws, see Deshpande 2009.

20. British Burma referred to the western and southern coastal provinces of Arakan, Pegu, and Tenasserim, which were also called Lower Burma. After the Third Anglo-Burmese war, the British annexed the remaining northern territories, referred to as Upper Burma. On the annexation of Upper Burma and its consequences, see Webster 2000. The 1878 India Opium Act took force in Lower Burma in 1879 and was extended to Upper Burma in 1888. See *Burma Opium Manual* 1904.

21. See Report of the Chief Commissioner of Burma, March 31, 1870, BL, IOR/P/2780; Note by F. W. R. Fryer . . . Officiating Chief Commissioner, Burma, on the Opium Question in Relation to Burma (Fryer 1892), July 5, 1892, ROC vol. 2, pp. 624–628.

22. Kim 2018.

23. For instance, the total number of opium shops in Lower Burma was fifty in 1875 and grew to sixty-seven in 1878, but reduced to twenty-seven in 1881. See AREABB 1889.

24. Adas 2011.

25. Ibid., p. 35.

26. On the organization of Indian labor migration in Burma, see Kaur 2006, pp. 432–438. On Tamil migrants, see Amrith 2009.

27. According to Adas 2011, the population grew at an estimated 3.4 percent annually between 1852 and 1881. . Ritchell 2006 estimates a lower rate for Burma at 1 percent between 1826 and 1891, comparable to India and other Southeast Asian countries at the time except for Java (pp. 16–17).

28. Adas 2011, p. 53; Ritchell 2006, pp. 45–47.

29. Assistant Secretary to the Chief Commissioner of British Burma to the Secretary to the Government of India, March 1874, BL/IOR/P/5.

30. See reports on cholera outbreaks in Rangoon, November 1873; Thayetmyo, October 8, 1874, BL/IOR/P/4 and 5.

31. See Saha 2013, p. 656 on debates regarding whether crime rates post-annexation reflect an increase in real instance of criminal behavior or perceptions of greater violence and improved reporting.

32. See Wright 2014, pp. 23–29.

33. *Report on the Prison Administration of Burma* 1878 (RPAB). The annual reports included the Chief Commissioner's summary and a longer report by the Inspector General of Prisons, accompanied by special reports for specific jails. See Special Report of Akyab jail 1874, MNA/01/02, 209.

34. RPAB 1878, p. 45.

35. Ibid.

36. Ibid., p. 47.

37. Ibid. Mountjoy's argument and approach was novel against the backdrop of conventional wisdom among local administrators in Burma regarding cholera epidemics that stressed seasonal factors and water supplies to explain different outbreaks of the disease in cantonments and local villages. For an example of such received wisdom among local administrators, see "Sanitary Measures for Prevention of Cholera and Other Epidemics at Thayetmyo," May 1874, BL/IOR/P/5.

38. Ibid.

39. RPAB 1878, p. 25.

40. RPAB 1881, pp. 42–43.

41. RPAB 1893, p. 29. In 1883, the Inspector General of Prisons ordered that all jails should register inmates who appeared or self-avowed as opium consumers.

42. RPAB 1884, pp. 30–31.

43. RPAB 1884, p. 31.

44. Report of the Chief Commissioner of Burma to Government of India, March 31, 1870, BL/IOR/P/2780.

45. Ibid.

46. Fytche to Government of India, March 31, 1870, BL/IOR/P/2780.

47. For more detail on the nineteenth-century Akyab-Chittagong differences, see Kim 2018.

48. Commissioner of Arakan to Chief Commissioner British Burma, February 26, 1886, BL/IOR/P/2780.

49. Report of the Chief Commissioner of Burma to Government of India, March 31, 1870, BL/IOR/P/2780.

50. AREABB 1867, section 25.

51. On the contested status of scientific knowledge on causes of opium addiction and its disputed harms in South Asia during this time period, see Winther 2003. For an alternative account that emphasizes the stability of racial categories regarding Burman opium consumers in the late nineteenth century, see Wright 2014.

52. AREABB 1867, section 5.

53. Fytche 1878, vol. 1, pp. 86–107.

54. Consultation with Board of Revenue, November 10, 1870, BL/IOR/P/2780.

55. AREABB, 1870, section 12.

56. AREABB, 1878, section 7.

57. This utilitarian approach to excise administration in India was made clear during debates over the 1856 *Abkaree* Act, as the Chief Justice of Bengal framed his objections to a new set of legal rules by reminding the Legislative Council of Samuel Johnson's definition of excise from the second edition of the Dictionary of the English Language (1776): "a hateful tax levied upon commodities and adjudged, not by the common judges of property but wretches hired by those to whom excise is paid." Legislative Proceedings, September 6, 1858, BL/IOR/V/9/2. The excise related administrative manuals circulated in Bengal echoed John Stuart Mill's *Principles of Political Economy* to articulate the objective of excise administration in Bengal: "No tax should be kept so high as to furnish a motive for its evasion to be too strong to be counteracted by ordinary means of prevention, and especially no commodity should be taxed so highly as to raise up a class of lawless characters, smugglers, illicit distillers, and the like." Mill 1848, vol. 6. "Comparison between Direct and Indirect Taxes."

58. Report of the Chief Commissioner of Burma to Government of India, March 31, 1870, BL/IOR/P/2780.

59. Others were reassured that "[t]he loss of revenue will not be heavy as Burma does not grow opium for home consumption, but obtains a supply by diverting a portion of the Indian produce from the China market." See AREABB 1871, section 10.

60. AREABB 1875, section 14.

61. House of Commons 1880, Memorandum by Charles Aitchison on the Consumption of Opium in British Burma, April 30, 1880 (Aitchison 1880).

62. Ibid.

63. AREABB 1872, section 20.

64. Ibid.

65. Ritchell 2006, p. 2. On the Indian population in Burma, see Kaur 2006, p. 431.

66. Crosthwaite 1912, p. 40.

67. AREABB 1873, section 10.

68. Siegelman 1962, p. 85.

69. AREABB 1873, section 10.

70. AREABB 1874, section 7.

71. AREABB, 1874, section 7.

72. Ibid.

73. AREABB 1873, section 10.

74. G. J. S. Hodgkinson, March 12, 1879, Aitchison 1880, p. 9.

75. Ibid.

76. W. C. Plant, August 28, 1878, Aitchison 1880, p. 10.

77. C. J. F. S. Forbes, undated, Aitchison 1880, p. 10.

78. J. Hind, January 18, 1879, Aitchison 1880, p. 12.

79. Ibid.

80. Memorandum by Pemberton, Deputy Commissioner, Kyouk-pyoo, February 6, 1879, Aitchison 1880, p. 11.

81. J. Butler, July 31, 1878, Aitchison 1880, p. 10.

82. J. C. Davis, March 24, 1879, Aitchison 1880, p. 12.

83. Ibid.

84. Forbes, undated.

85. J. Butler, July 31, 1878.

86. Aitchison 1880.

87. Ibid., p. 1.

88. Ibid.

89. Ibid., p. 2.

90. *Friend of China*, June 1891.

91. See Wright 2008, pp. 631–634 for an alternative interpretation of Aitchison's memorandum.

92. Aitchison 1880, p. 3.

93. Ibid.

94. Ibid.

95. Ibid., p. 6.

96. Ibid. But see Birla 2009 on the legal production of the market in Bengal.

97. Aitchison 1880, p. 6.

98. Ibid., p. 5.

99. *Friend of China*, April 1896. On Aitchison's missionary affiliations and earlier political career, see Smith 1897; Wright 2008.

100. Ibid.

101. G. D. Burgess to Government of India, December 30, 1880, Aitchison 1880, p. 16.

102. de la Courneuve to Commissioner of Irrawaddy Division, December 2, 1891, MNA 01\15 (b), 40.

103. Ibid.

104. Crosthwaite 1912.

105. Minute by Alexander Mackenzie, April 30, 1892, ROC vol. 2, p. 537.

106. D. R. Lyall to J. B. Lyall, Question 3184, November 24, 1893, ROC vol. 2, p. 64.

107. On the post-Mutiny shift in colonial native policy and the broader tension to liberal ideologies of indirect rule for the British Empire during the late nineteenth century, see Mantena 2010.

108. D. R. Lyall to J. B. Lyall, Question 3191, November 24, 1893, ROC vol. 2, p. 64.

109. Proceedings of the Chief Commissioner in the Financial Department, August 29, 1891. MNA 01\15 (e), 9094.

110. Ibid.

111. Proceedings of Department of Finance and Commerce, Government of India, November 1, 1887, BL/IOR/L/P&J/20/216.

112. Smeaton 1892. On Smeaton's trajectory within the ICS, beginning as an Assistant Magistrate and Collector in Allahabad in 1867, becoming Financial Commissioner and officiating Chief Commissioner for Burma until 1896, returning to India as an Additional Member to the Council of the Governor General of India until 1901, see History of Services of Gazetted and Other Officers in Burma 1902, pp. 11–15, BL/IOR/V/12. On Smeaton's personal background and social and political activities, see Prior 2004.

113. Note by the Financial Commissioner on Opium Dens in Burma, January 5, 1892, ROC vol. 2, p. 543.

114. Ibid., p. 551.

115. Ibid., p. 539.

116. Ibid., p. 547.

117. J. B. Lyall to Smeaton, Question 8092, December 19, 1893, ROC, vol. 2, p. 230. All quotes in this paragraph from Questions 8090 and 8092.

118. J. B. Lyall to Smeaton, Question 8090, December 19, 1893, ROC, vol. 2, p. 230.

119. Note by the Financial Commissioner 1892, ROC vol. 2, p. 609.

120. Ibid.

121. Smeaton to J. B. Lyall, Question 8095, December 19, 1893, ROC, vol. 2, p. 230.

122. Ibid., Question 8090.

123. Minute by Alexander Mackenzie, Chief Commissioner, Burma, April 30, 1892, ROC vol. 2, p. 537.

124. Ibid.

125. Ibid.

126. Aung Rai, Tun Chin, Maung Zan U, and Maung Chin Htun Aung to Commissioner of Arakan Division, ROC, vol. 2, p. 554.

127. Ibid.

128. Chief Commissioner of Burma, Financial Department, March 1, 1898, MNA 01\15 (b), 390.

129. G. A. Strover to Secretary of Chief Commissioner, November 30, 1891, ROC, vol. 2, p. 556.

130. de la Courneuve, December 2, 1891, MNA 01\15 (b), 40.

131. Ibid.

132. D. J. A. Campbell to Commissioner of Irawaddy Division, November 27, 1891, MNA 01\15 (e), 9094.

133. Ibid.

134. Maung Hla Paw U to Financial Commissioner, November 16, 1891, ROC vol. 2, p. 604.

135. Memorandum of the Burma Branch of the British Medical Association, August 12, 1893, ROC vol. 2, p. 499.

136. Pease to Earl of Kimberley, 1886, MNA 01\11\270; *Mandalay Times*, April 28, 1892.

137. Government of India to Secretary of State for India, February 9, 1893, ROC vol. 2, p. 628.

138. Fryer 1892, p. 627.

139. Parrott to Financial Commissioner, December 3, 1891, ROC vol. 2, p. 547.

140. Commissioner of Tenasserim to Financial Commissioner, March 22, 1893, MNA 01\15 (b), 116.

141. Financial Commissioner to the Commissioner of Tenasserim, April 7, 1893, MNA 01\15 (b), 116.

142. Untitled Report, 1907, MNA 01\15 (e), 15982.

143. Ibid.

5: Fiscal Dependency in British Malaya, 1890s–1920s

1. Memorandum Regarding the Straits Settlements Opium Revenue Replacement Reserve Fund, October 1926, TNA/CO 273/534/9.

2. Despatch by High Commissioner of Federated Malay States, July 24, 1929, TNA/CO 717/66.

3. Report of Opium Revenue Replacement and Taxation Committee, January 1928, TNA/CO 273/550/8.

4. Variants of the opium revenue replacement reserve fund were also introduced for Brunei and Portuguese Macao. Colonial Office to Clementi, January 25, 1934, TNA/CO 273/588/3; Goto-Shibata 2006, p. 51; Horton 1994, p. 63.

5. Wen 1907; Cheng 1961; Trocki 1990; Kenji 2012. See Bailey and Truong 2011 for an excellent study of the economic impact of opium for Southeast Asia, which addresses fiscal dependency on opium for British Malaya but does not address the question of revenue legitimacy.

6. McAllister 2000, p. 84. See Chapter 3 on the post-World War I international convenings that took place under the purview of the League of Nations' Opium Advisory Committee.

7. Goto-Shibata 2006, p. 65.

8. *Straits Times*, July 9, 1925.

9. Ibid, August 29, 1925.

10. Warren 1985, p. 59.

11. *Straits Times*, October 1, 1923; June 28, 1924; Turnbull 1989, pp. 140–141.

12. *Singapore Free Press and Mercantile Adviser*, August 15, 1925; *Straits Times*, August 29, 1925.

13. In 1921, the Straits Settlements' next largest sources of revenue were from license fees and excise taxes collected on liquor sales (3 million Straits dollars), land rents (1 million Straits dollars), and petroleum (700,000 Straits dollars). See Straits Settlements Blue Book 1921; *Straits Times*, October 6, 1925.

14. Report of Opium Revenue Replacement . . . , January 1928, TNA/CO 273/550/8.

15. *Malayan Saturday Post*, October 23, 1926.

16. *Straits Times*, October 6, 1925.

17. Straits Settlements Legislative Council Proceedings 1925, CO 275.

18. Memorandum Regarding the Straits Settlements . . . , October 1926, TNA/CO 273/534/9.

19. Ibid.

20. Despatch by High Commissioner of Federated Malay States, July 24, 1929, TNA/CO 717/66.

21. Opium Trade in the Eastern Colonies, February 10, 1921, TNA/CAB 24/119/55.

22. Ibid.

23. Minute by Ellis, October 28, 1930, TNA/CO 717/76.

24. Straits Settlements Legislative Council Proceedings, 1925.

25. Ibid.

26. Cowan 1950.

27. Lee 1975, p. 79.

28. Logan 1855, p. 446; Chew 1991, p. 38.

29. Egerton 1897, p. 222.

30. Ibid., pp. 5–6; Turnbull 1989.

31. Regulations IV and V of 1823 Prohibiting Gaming Houses and Cockpits; and Preventing Slave Trade in Singapore; see Raffles 1823.

32. Trocki 1990, pp. 96–97.

33. Mackay 2005, p. 126.

34. Trocki 1990; Knapman 2016, pp. 131–134. Public works using opium revenue included harbor improvements, the Singapore River works, and railways. On the oppositions of European merchants that extended to regulatory efforts aimed at helping navigation and trade such as

lighthouses, suppressing piracy, or fees for port maintenance, see Turnbull 1989, p. 188 and pp. 194–195 on controversies over the Horsburgh Lighthouse in 1846 and 1854.

35. Share for the Government of India, between 1858 and 1866. See House of Lords, July 24, 1891, vol. 356, cc. 214–234.

36. Report from Colonial Military Contributions Committee, Hong Kong Opium Revenue, April 9, 1914, TNA/T1/11642.

37. This intensified concerns over of how to divide growing expenditure for defending Straits Settlements, which was a broader question about how to distribute responsibility between Imperial Government and Crown Colony, metropolitan taxpayers and overseas inhabitants.

38. Report from Colonial Military Contributions Committee . . . , April 9, 1914, TNA/T1/11642.

39. The War Office disagreed with this position, maintaining that "without imperial protection such improvement [in Singapore] would not be possible." See Report from Colonial Military Contributions Committee, Minority Report by Mr. Perry and Mr. Hewby, April 9, 1914, TNA/T1/11642.

40. Willcox 1929, p. 913.

41. Y. Li 2016, p. 141. In Burma, the post of Adviser on Chinese Affairs was established in 1891 and abolished in 1904; and a post for Examiner in Chinese and Chinese Advisory Board was established in 1909. On intercolony learning between Burma and the Straits Settlements in creating these specialized positions, see Noriyuki 2014. On Singapore, see Ng 1961.

42. Swettenham 1903, p. 3.

43. Cheng 1961; Goto-Shibata 2006.

44. On Chinese secret societies in the Straits Settlements, see Freedman 1960; Purcell 1948; Lee 1978; Trocki 1990.

45. On the Singapore opium tax farm, see Trocki 1990, 1993.

46. Trocki 1990, p. 118.

47. Ibid., p. 179.

48. Trocki 2002, p. 310.

49. W. D. Barnes, February 8, 1908, SSOC 1908, vol. 2, p. 931.

50. The official distance kept from the opium farms was also a subject of criticism from European merchants, and in certain instances, the colonial administration opted to restrict trade over controlling the farms directly. For instance in 1883, Governor Weld placed extraordinary restrictions on trade to the Netherland East Indies owing to fears of an opium smuggling conspiracy that injured the Singapore opium farmer and his syndicates. Unofficial members of the Legislative Council complained on the inconveniences to their trade and criticized the Government for "taking for granted that the farmer's interests are identical with its own, [when] we have seen the farm may be a house divided against itself." February 28, 1883, TNA/CO 273/119.

51. House of Lords 1891. In 1895, as the Straits Settlements requested a shift to the military contributions to the 20 percentage system, the volatility of the opium revenue was cited as a reason and became a recurring argument. See Report from Military Contributions . . . , April 9, 1914, TNA/T1/11642.

52. The professed lack of official knowledge about the tax farms' internal workings was an established trope. In 1883, while addressing merchant complaints about the privileged treatment of Chinese tax farmers, Governor Weld informed the Legislative Council "that we did not know

into whose hands the Spirit Farm went. We know now that the name given was not that of the real moneyed man." The year 1904 was the first time that the colonial administration gained direct access to the tax farmer's books through the Protector of Chinese, making it possible to monitor the finances of the syndicate, which included the estimated sales of chandu and costs, as well as the net profit and losses of the Straits Settlements farms (and Johor and Kedah). Trocki 1990, p. 201. Even then, Swettenham would despair that "there is no individual who knows the farms." Swettenham to Secretary of State for the Colonies, October 9, 1904, TNA/CO 273/292.

53. Ibid.

54. Barnes, February 8, 1908, SSOC 1908, vol. 2, p. 931.

55. Swettenham to Secretary of State for the Colonies, October 9, 1904, TNA/CO 273/292.

56. SSOC 1908, vol. 2, p. 530.

57. Ibid., p. 531.

58. Ibid.

59. Ibid.

60. August 17, 1903. TNA/CO 273/291.

61. On Gan Ngoh Bee's influence in Singapore, see Wright 1908, pp. 716–721.

62. Undated 1904, TNA/CO 273/292/40854; Note, September 10, 1904, TNA/CO 273/300/41171.

63. Barnes, February 8, 1908, SSOC 1908 Report, vol. 2, p. 945.

64. Ibid.

65. Barnes, February 8, 1908, SSOC 1908, vol. 2, p. 929; *Singapore Free Press*, October 30, 1911.

66. Memorandum . . . to the Straits Settlements and Federated Malay States by Mr. Warren Barnes, SSOC 1908, vol. 3, p. 165.

67. Barnes, February 8, 1908, SSOC 1908, vol. 2, p. 945.

68. Ibid.

69. Ibid.

70. A. M. Pountney, January 7, 1908, SSOC 1908, vol. 2, p. 907.

71. Ibid.

72. He compiled descriptive statistics from the official census of Selangor (1891, 1901) and sea returns from district officers in coastal districts and harbor master at Port Swettenham of migrations to the Chinese protectorate to estimate the population and used returns from the customs department and registrars of imports and exports (for prior to 1901), and then the Gazettes and "certain private records" to estimate the number of chests of opium imported. SSOC 1908, vol. 2, pp. 872–873.

73. Pountney, January 7, 1908, SSOC 1908, p. 892.

74. Ibid., p. 891.

75. Ibid., p. 896.

76. Return Showing the Number of Opium Smokers Amongst the Jinkirisha Coolies in Seven Depôts in Kuala Lumpur, Selangor, December 26, 1907, SSOC 1908, vol. 3, p. 156.

77. Ibid.

78. Pountney, January 7, 1908, SSOC 1908, vol. 2, p. 900.

79. Ibid., p. 897.

80. Ibid.

81. Annual Department Reports for the Strait Settlements 1905. Straits Settlements Blue Book 1904–1907.

82. In Singapore, two doctors—Amoy-born Suat Chuan Yin and the much-respected Peranakan Lim Boon Keng—had reopened their opium refuge for addicts on Tank Road, which offered free "cures" of the habit and herbal remedies, hypnotic drugs and tonics to ease the curative process. The refuge was called "the Anti-opium Smoking Lodge of the Charitable Institution for the Fostering of Virility" and launched along with the Singapore Anti-Opium society, led by Tan Boon Liat. See Cheng 1961, pp. 56–57.

83. House of Commons, March 18, 1907, vol. 107, p. 524. On Theodore Cooke Taylor as a strong partisan of anti-opium reforms, who saw China's willingness to restrict the harmful drug as a lynchpin for the cross-empire cooperation necessary to end opium's commercial life, see Taylor 1910; Greenwood 1957.

84. House of Commons, March 18, 1907.

85. Colonial Office to Anderson, April 25, 1907, TNA/CO 273/325.

86. Pountney, January 7, 1908, SSOC 1908, p. 897. Pountney himself was also skeptical of the anti-opium movements, believing that Chinese public opinion was highly fragmented. Regarding the anti-opium society that led mobilization in 1906, he told the Anderson Commission: "Probably amongst a considerable portion of the people, the idea that opium is deleterious and the determination to stop it was the origin of the society," but also, "in others of the supporters, I doubt whether the same thoroughly honest motives were existent." Regarding the regulation of the opium market for Selangor, Pountney was also skeptical of the involvement of state, believing that opium consumption was "a personal matter and not a matter for legislation." He formulated the question of banning opium as "a question of the amount of interference with the liberty of the subject." (p. 907).

87. C. J. Saunders, September 8, 1907, SSOC 1908, vol. 2, p. 100.

88. Ibid.

89. Ibid., p. 96. On Cook's anti-opium activities in the Straits Settlements, see Cook 1907.

90. Others disagreed about who exactly the ringleaders were: one surmised that it was actually the former Consul-General for China at Singapore, a "Cantonese man" who was stirring up local unrest. Some were more sympathetic than Saunders about the sincerity of anti-opium societies, especially in light of their social reform efforts. See Barnes, February 8, 1908, SSOC 1908, vol. 2, p. 954. They "are doing such grand work, and in proof of their grand work, they have paid out money cure of these people," observed the Protector of Chinese in Perak. See W. Cowan, January 3, 1908, SSOC 1908, vol. 2, p. 798. In general, however, administrators were skeptical toward the Chinese anti-opium societies as reflecting widespread discontent and therefore not serious reasons to restrict opium consumption, let alone abolish the tax farms.

91. On possible losses of revenue for the Federated Malay States as relatively less worrisome, see Cowan, January 3, 1908, SSOC 1908, vol. 2, p. 838.

92. For example, on stamp fees and taxes on money lenders see Cowan, January 3, 1908; death duties, see Cook, October 12, 1907; poll and income taxes, see Saunders, September 8, 1907, SSOC 1908.

93. Galloway 1923.

94. *Singapore Free Press*, March 4, 1908. All quotes in this paragraph from this source.

95. Lim Boon Keng, August 17, 1907, SSOC 1908, vol. 2, p. 51.

96. Ibid.

97. Ho Siak Kuan, September 28, 1907, SSOC 1908, vol. 2, p. 149.

98. Choo Cheng Khay, November 23, 1907, SSOC 1908, vol. 2, p. 441.

99. Saunders, September 8, 1907, SSOC 1908, p. 98.

100. Cowan, January 3, 1908, SSOC 1908, vol. 2, p. 848.

101. Ibid.

102. *Straits Times,* January 28, 1911.

103. Ibid.

104. *Singapore Free Press,* March 12, 1909. All quotes in this paragraph from this source.

105. *The Times,* May 13, 1908. All quotes in this paragraph from this source.

106. Cheng 1961, p. 140.

107. Straits Settlements Blue Book 1906, 1910, 1920.

108. On imperial preference and Malaya's persistent maintenance of a primary commodity export driven economic structure, see Leng 2002, pp. 247–249.

109. Straits Settlements Records of Service 1926, pp. 154–155. I am grateful to Dorian Leveque for help identifying Pountney's record.

110. See Turnbull 1989, pp. 88–89, 141, 238, on Orfeur Cavenaugh's failed proposal in 1863 and John Anderson's attempt in 1906, which was thwarted by the protests of unofficial legislative councilors and European and Asian businessmen. See *Straits Times,* May 1, 1917 for a public complaint that the interest on investments made on the war loan was not exempt from income tax.

111. *Straits Times,* September 1, 1922.

112. Great Britain 1924, Proceedings of the Committee Appointed . . . to Inquire into Matters Relating to the Use of Opium in British Malaya (British Malaya Opium Committee Report 1924), p. ix.

113. Wah 1981; Leng 2002. In doing so, Guillemard sought to bring the Federated Malay States under the fold of the Straits Settlements, and found opportunity to override the objections of established high administrators including George Maxwell, the Chief Secretary of the Federated Malay States. "[F]inance is Maxwell's weakest point," he argued and during the postwar trade slump that hit the Malay States badly, Guillemard appointed Pountney as Financial Adviser in return for the Straits Settlements' floating a 10 million pound loan to the Federation. Guillemard tried again in 1922 to pass an income tax ordinance for the Straits Settlements, which was eventually withdrawn and in May 1923, the post of a Collector General for Income Tax was also abolished. *Straits Times,* November 28, 1922; December 29, 1923.

114. Wah 1981, p. 49.

115. British Malaya Opium Committee Report 1924, p. A9.

116. Ibid., p. C163.

117. Ibid.

118. Ibid.

119. Ibid., p. A61.

120. Pountney, January 7, 1908, SSOC 1908, vol. 2, p. 900.

121. Ibid.

122. Memorandum Regarding the Straits Settlements . . . , October 1926, TNA/CO 273/534/9.

123. Ibid.

124. Ibid.

125. *Straits Times*, August 24, 1925.

126. Ibid.

127. Ibid.

128. *Straits Times*, October 6, 1925.

129. Ibid.

130. Ibid.

131. Ibid.

132. *Straits Settlements Legislative Council Proceedings* 1925.el

133. *Straits Times*, October 6, 1925.

134. Ibid.

135. Ibid.

136. *Singapore Free Press*, August 26, 1925.

137. *Singapore Free Press*, October 7, 1925.

138. Ibid.

139. *Malayan Saturday Post*, October 23, 1926.

140. Report of the Subcommittee appointed by the Straits Settlements Association, April 6, 1926, TNA/CO 273/534/9.

141. Ibid.

142. Guillemard to Amery, September, 21, 1926, TNA/CO 273/534/9.

143. *Straits Times*, October 19, 1926.

144. On the role of the Crown Agents, a quasi-public but essentially private firm in the service of the Colonial Office that managed its public works projects for colonies and after World War I, expanded to issuing loans, managing investments, and supervising development projects, see Ponko 1966; Kesner 1977.

145. League of Nations 1930, vol. 2.

146. Registration of Opium Smokers, 1929, TNA/CO 273/555/5.

147. *Singapore Free Press*, April 21, 1931; Goto-Shibata 2006. The League of Nations observed in 1929 that there was no rationing system of opium-smokers per se, but a maximum quantity set for registered consumers in Malaya. League of Nations 1930, vol. 2, p. 51.

148. September 16, 1927, TNA/CO 273/537/6.

149. The High Commissioner of the Federated Malay States argued that opium formed only 17 percent of total revenue and taxation was very light, and thus requested to reduce the revenue contributions to the reserve fund from 15 percent to 7 percent. Unlike the Straits Settlements, the Malay States had loans amounting to 80 million Straits dollars used for capital works to develop the railways, public infrastructure, and the electrical services, post office, and telegraphs department ("of which some $72 millions have been spent on works of development to date, and for the redemption of which our Sinking Funds will amount to over $9 millions at the end of 1929," explained the High Commissioner). Despatch by High Commissioner . . . , July 24, 1929, TNA/CO 717/66.

150. Guillemard to Amery, August 13, 1926; Report of the Subcommittee . . . , April 6, 1926, TNA/CO 273/534/9.

151. Colonial Office to War Office, October 26, 1926, TNA/CO 273/534/9.

152. Guillemard to Amery, September 21, 1926, TNA/CO 273/534/9.

153. Ibid.

154. Despatch by High Commissioner . . . , July 24, 1929, TNA/CO 717/66.

155. Unnamed, 1928, TNA/CO 273/508.

156. Ibid.

157. Guillemard to Amery, September 21, 1927, TNA/CO 273/537/6.

158. See Federated Malay States: Opium Revenue Replacement and Special Reserve Funds for 1925, 1930, 1935, 1940, TNA/CAOG/9/193; Clementi to Passfield, September 11, 1930; Crown Agents to Colonial Office, April 2, 1931, TNA/CO 717/76.

159. Straits Settlements Blue Book 1926. On the Crown Agents and public flotation of colonial stock, see Sunderland 2007.

160. Campbell to unnamed, 1930, TNA/CO 717/66.

161. Clementi to Passfield, September 11, 1930, TNA/CO 717/66.

162. Note by J. A. Calder, October 16, 1930, TNA/CO 717/66.

6: Disastrous Abundance in French Indochina, 1920s–1940s

1. Le Failler 2001.

2. Ibid., pp. 325–326.

3. Le président du Conseil for Ministry of Foreign Affairs to Ministry of Colonies, May 16, 1923, ANOM/Fonds ministériel (FM)/Direction des affaires politiques (AFFPOL)/3251.

4. Report by A. Bodard, consul de France au Yunnan, November 23, 1923, ANOM/GGI/42972.

5. Report by Bodard, August 16, 1923, ANOM/FM/AFFPOL/3251.

6. Ministry of Colonies to Government General of Indochina, October 11, 1922, ANOM/INDO/GGI/42972.

7. Moretti Report on "la question de l'opium," April 5, 1926, VNA1/1746.

8. Fabry to Governor General of Indochina, undated likely 1924, ANOM/INDO/GGI 43054.

9. Ibid. For an overview of this situation from the Ministry of Foreign Affairs' delegation in Yunnanfou, see Report by Bodard, August 16, 1923, ANOM/FM/AFFPOL/3251

10. "L'arrêté concernant le régime de l'opium en Indochine, " February 1899, no. 2, *Bulletin officiel de l'Indochine française* p. 171.

11. Report by M. Rigaux, Délégué de l'Annam au Conseil supérieur de la France d'outre-mer on "la Régie de l'opium," August 18, 1937, ANOM/FM/INDO_NF/374.

12. Descours-Gatin 1987, p. 463.

13. Denis 1965, p. 29. On the protracted annexation of Cochinchina, see Brocheux & Hémery 2009, pp. 25–27.

14. Lemire 1869, p. 3.

15. Peyrouton 1913, pp. 138–139.

16. Descours-Gatin 1992, pp. 101 and 39.

17. Ibid., pp. 48–49.

18. On the first tax farmers Ségassie and Télésio and their malfeasance, see Descours-Gatin 1992, pp. 43–48. On the Chinese tax farmer in Cochinchina, Wangthai, the head of the Canton congregation and wealthy financier, see *Journal officiel de la Cochinchine française,* February 19, 1881; on the Chinese tax farmer Ban Hap, who originated from Fujian and took over the Cochinchina farm in 1865, see Descours-Gatin 1992, pp. 54–63; Goscha 2016. On the transnational connections of Ban Hap, see Trocki 2004, pp. 159–174.

19. The office for customs and excise was initially under the director of interior but separated into an autonomous office in 1888. See Descours-Gatin 1992, p. 89.

20. From 1888 to 1892, the colonial administration decided to limit the intermediary opium purchasing role to French traders. Before and after, however, all traders were eligible for this role. See Descours-Gatin 1992 (pp. 92–93) on the major merchant houses that held this position, including Robert and Charriol (1881–1886), Denis Brothers (1886–1892), and Grunberg Brothers (1893–1898).

21. Dumarest 1938, pp. 24–27.

22. Le Failler 2001, p. 68.

23. *Journal officiel de la Cochinchine française*, February 10, 1881. On the Cambodian tax farms under Kings An Dong and Norodom, see Forest 1979, p. 215. On the strength of the Chinese in Cambodia, see Moura 2015[1883], pp. 448–451. On tax farmer competition and alliances involving French and Chinese merchants in Cambodia and Cochinchina, see Descours-Gatin 1992, pp. 67–85.

24. LeFailler 2001, pp. 68–70. The French opium tax farmer for Tonkin was a man named René de St. Mathurin who obtained contracts on behalf of the Société fermière de l'opium au Tonkin with the backing of the Lyonnais merchant house of Ulysses Pila that sought commercial opportunities from opium sales and potential poppy cultivation in these northern areas. On the strength of de St. Mathurin's collective and conflicts with the French colonial administration, see Décamps 1909, p. 119; on Pila and Lyonnais economic interests in Indochina, see Klein 1994. For an overview of the legal administrative reforms integrating these territories, see Dumarest 1938, pp. 44–53.

25. Brocheux & Hémery 2009, p. 80.

26. Fourniau 2002; Lorrin 2004.

27. Sasges 2012, p. 133.

28. Doumer 1902.

29. Brocheux & Hémery 2009, pp. 78–82.

30. Existing obstacles against centralizing fiscal management were objections from French settlers in the south and merchant communities based in urban Cochinchina. See Isoart 1961. To the extent that opium revenue chiefly affected the Chinese community who controlled mostly rural trade and usury, it represented a relatively less controversial fiscal base. See Brocheux & Hémery 2009, p. 92.

31. Sasges 2017, p. 54. Gerard Sasges' important work on the alcohol monopoly demonstrates how Doumer's calculations for the combined net revenue for opium, alcohol, and salt revenue in his general budget were based on gross numbers, using constant rates of taxation for sales, rather than the actual margin between the rates at which excise authorities purchased the products and sold to their distributors.

32. Ibid., pp. 51–52.

33. Dumarest 1938, pp. 50–51.

34. Rodier to Nam Dinh, December 31, 1890, ANOM/INDO/GGI/25374.

35. Le Failler 2003, p. 90.

36. Doumer 1902, p. 162.

37. "Note pour Monsieur le chef du Service des affaires extérieures," December 9, 1929, ANOM/INDO/GGI/43089.

38. "Mesures prises en vue de la suppression de l'usage de l'opium," 1907, ANOM/FM/AFFPOL/2418.

39. Ibid.

40. These reforms were recommended by a commission inquiring into the extent of opium-related social problems in Indochina, led by the Consul-General of France, C. Hardouin in 1908. See ANOM/AMIRAUX 43000 and 43003; "Un questionnaire rédigé par la Commission . . . , ANOM/INDO/GGI 43089.

41. "Note sur la situation de l'Indochine au regard de la question de l'opium," October 31, 1929, ANOM/AGEFOM/726. Classified as "Asian foreigners" (*Asiatiques étrangers*), individuals of Chinese origin were administratively distinct from what the French called "Asian subjects" (*Asiatiques sujets*) or protégés, which referred to indigenous inhabitants of Annam, Cambodia, Thais [*sic* Tai], Indonésiens, Muoungs, Mans, Meos, and others. "Note pour Monsieur le Chef du Service . . . ," December 9, 1929, ANOM/INDO/GGI/43089. Yann Bisiou's careful work has demonstrated that this was a prevailing discourse for French opium monopolies that stressed the limited responsibility of the colonial project to intervene in the habits of foreigners in the colony, as long as the harms of opium consumption did not affect indigenous populations, an open position stated explicitly by one member of the colonial council for French Oceania who exclaimed during a council meeting that "if the Chinese want to poison themselves, let them do so! I do not care, so long as the natives do not imitate them." See Bisiou 1995, p. 84.

42. "Au sujet de la suppression de l'usage de l'opium," May 16, 1916, ANOM/FM/AFFPOL/2418; "La question de l'opium: Application de la loi du 12 juillet 1916 en Indochine," *Journal officiel de la République française*, January 28, 1916.

43. Kair to Minister of Colonies, May 21, 1925, ANOM/FM/AFFPOL/3156.

44. Ibid.

45. Such conceptions of state–Chinese community relationships relating to opium were embedded in broader fiscal and economic arrangements. The French exercised more direct social and economic controls over Chinese merchants and laborers, requiring mandatory affiliation in congregations and levied direct fees and taxes that the British did not. See Sambuc 1909. Marie-Paule Ha notes that within Indochina, taxes on the Chinese were twice as high as that on the French, "under the pretext that in their different bookkeeping methods, Chinese merchants would more likely underreport their profits," Ha 2009, p. 194. Also see Boudet & Coulet 1929.

46. Le Failler 2001; Rapin 2014.

47. Rapin 2014, p. 1.

48. Gunn 1986.

49. Le Failler 2001, p. 290.

50. For an excellent study of the turbulent politics and security concerns along the Tonkin-Yunnan border see Grémont 2018. On poppy cultivation in Tonkin and Laos, see Rapin 2000.

51. On the rich literature discussing the Lyon business community's vested interests in Indochina's economic development and colonial exploration, see Klein 1994.

52. Le Failler 2001, pp. 110–111.

53. For instance, in 1889, French diplomatic authorities sought to allow opium to transit through the Red River. French consul in Canton to Stephen, October 21, 1889, ANOM/INDO/GGI/24882.

54. Some informal arrangements were included and refined within the framework of the 1899 law: for instance, article 87 of the 1899 decree allowed special treatment of the Yao and Miao to cultivate poppy, which was formalized in 1905 as permission for poppy cultivation in four provinces in Laos—Muong Sing, Luang Prabang, Muong Son, and Tran Ninh—and avowed resolve on part of the French to purchase opium produced in excess of their local demand for opium smoking.

55. Descours-Gatin 1992, p. 240.

56. For example, see requests and permissions granted for opium transport in ANOM/INDO/GGI/42911–42914.

57. Newman 1989, p. 531.

58. Bisiou 1995, p. 169.

59. "Mesures prises ou à prendre pour remédier aux irrégularités ou en empêcher le retour," VNA1/DFI/1746; Report by M. Devouton, Inspecteur de 1ère classe des Colonies regarding "la vérification de M. Prats, Directeur des Douanes et Régies de l'Indochine à Hanoi" (Devouton Report), June 1937, ANOM/Fonds privés, Émile Devouton.

60. Ibid. This emergency fund was embedded within the general procurement accounts, allowing a Saigon-based administrator to authorize local banks to transfer money quickly in order to make quick payments on behalf of the opium monopoly with a promise of later regularization.

61. Ibid.

62. Tang Ji-Yao (1881–1927) was one of the warlords who emerged triumphant from the fall of the Qing order, and became the military governor of Yunnan in 1913. He was an antimonarchist with ambitions for a "greater Yunnan" who had invaded Sichuan in 1917 as well but lost power to a civilian in June 1920 and was ousted from Yunnan in February 1921. His return to power as Yunnan governor in May 1922 incurred expenses, which amounted to roughly 6 million piasters for military expenses and 2 million for civilian administration. On Tang's involvement in opium trades, see Le Failler 2001, p. 262; Meyer & Parssinen 2002.

63. Scalla to Governor General of Indochina, June 14, 1922, ANOM/INDO/GGI/42919.

64. Albert Sarraut later explained to the President of the Conseil in Paris that "to refuse Indochina the possibility of obtaining opium supplies in those areas where the influence of Peking is a mirage and its sovereignty a fiction, is to consecrate the monopoly of India. To prevent, on the one hand, the colony from allowing opium to pass through out, makes it almost impossible to consolidate order within our own confines, and is to limit the role that South China can play as a barrier to total anarchy." Sarraut to President of Conseil, May 29, 1923, ANOM/INDO/GGI 42973.

65. Sarraut to Governor General of Indochina, October 11, 1922, ANOM/INDO/GGI 42972.

66. The railway had been damaged in 1921, and the French and Yunnan authorities had been disagreeing over who would pay for repairs. Bodard to Yunnan-fou, November 23, 1922, ANOM/INDO/GGI 42972. See Le Failler 2001, p. 266 on additional gains for the French including reorganization of police forces, major contract for installation of TSF, as well as reduced poppy cultivation.

67. Le Failler 2001, p. 267; Fabry to Governor General of Indochina, April 15, 1924, ANOM/GGI/43054.

68. LeFailler 2001, p. 270. This note of annoyance was also voiced by the captain of the ship that had been transporting the opium overseas, who stated "he had only done what all the boats of Indochina do; that there were now more than 100 cases of this opium from Yunnan waiting for their turn in Haiphong, and if there was a culprit, it was the Government of Indochina itself. It would seem that this shameful traffic was the sole *raison d'être* of our Indochinese commercial flotilla and constituted its sole source of profits." Tulasne to Fleuriau, January 14, 1924, ANOM/ INDO/GGI/43054.

69. On the media attention surrounding this event, by *L'Éveil économique* de l'Indochine and *L'Écho de Chine* against the general government of Indochina and Consul Bodard, see ANOM/ INDO/GGI/42926. According to press reports, French missionaries were also financially involved in this affair.

70. "Rapport sur les comptes administratif des budgets généraux, 1934," VNA1/1746. For the Missions of Inspection's assessment of the emergence of the cessions fictives, see Devouton Report, June 1937.

71. Bisiou 1995, p. 178; Report by the Directeur du contrôle financier, undated likely 1937, VNA1/DFI/1746.

72. Ibid.

73. Merat Report, February 18, 1930, ANOM/FM/INDO_NF/282/2481.

74. Report by the Directeur du contrôle financier, undated likely 1937, VNA1/DFI/1746.

75. Ibid.

76. Ibid.

77. "Rapport sur les comptes administratifs relatifs au budget général, 1931," VNA1/DFI/1746.

78. Governor General of Indochina to Minister of Colonies, September 2, 1938, VNA1/ DFI/3354.

79. Ibid.

80. Under-Director of Customs and Excise Department in Cochinchine to Director of Customs and Excise for Indochina, July 5, 1934, VNA1/DFI/1746.

81. The request was approved by the Director of Public Accounting on September 16 and formally authorized in July 1936. See VNA1/DFI/3354.

82. The label for "dragon" opium had existed sporadically since the 1910s. See Le Failler 1993, p. 321.

83. Moreover, Brévié, who had replaced Robin after Léon Blum's Popular Front assumed power in Paris and was keen to distinguish his administration from the republican imperial predecessors, avowed that higher prices were necessary to combat smuggling out of Indochina that had arisen as a result of the low opium prices. It also likely served as a means to signal outwardly, to the League of Nations and other great powers, France's commitment to anti-opium efforts and thus, cooperative international stance.

84. Brévié to Minister of Colonies, September 2, 1928, VNA1/DFI/3354.

85. Untitled report in file entitled "Achats et régie d'opium en Indochine 1938," VNA1/ DFI/3354.

86. Ibid.

87. Ibid.

88. In April 1937, the dragon blend contained 50 percent of Indian opium, and after its price was increased in November 1937, the percentage was increased to 60 percent.

89. Brévié to Minister of Colonies, September 2, 1928, VNA1/DFI/3354. Reasons for Brévié's optimism include improvements in the colony's economy and the population's purchasing capacity because of rising prices in rice exports following the devaluation of the piastre that year. Chinese immigration had also increased, making an expected sales growth for Indian opium in the major ports and Chinese communities reasonable.

90. On the wartime context of French Indochina, see Jennings 2001; Thomas 2001.

91. On outstanding orders for opium from Persia and worries about its on-time delivery, see confidential note for the Governor General, June 13, 1941; Ginestou to Decoux, September 20, 1940, VNA1/DFI/14628.

92. Ginestou to Decoux, September 20, 1940, VNA1/DFI/14628.

93. On the volume of opium purchased from Tonkin and Laos since the end of World War I, see Ginestou Report 1940.

94. Ginestou to Decoux, September 20, 1940, VNA1/DFI/14628.

95. Gautier to Mordant, March 16, 1942; Mordant to Ginestou, March 23, 1942, VNA1/DFI/3952.

96. Ibid.

97. Ginestou to Cousin, January 17, 1942, VNA1/DFI/3952.

98. Ibid.

99. Ibid.

100. Ginestou to Decoux, September 20, 1940; Ginestou to Decoux, February 24, 1942, VNA1/DFI/14628.

101. Ibid.

102. Ginestou to Decoux, February 24, 1942. All quotes in this paragraph from this source.

103. Ginestou's arguments mainly applied to Cochinchina, because Decoux was mainly concerned with this part of the colony. However, opium-related debates informed by extant administrators also prevailed for other parts of the colony. See report sent by the High Resident of Laos on Laos where problems of inflation and contraband were attributed to overuse of silver for cash payments to the Hmong and their intermediaries, May 15, 1941, VNA1/DFI/3952.

104. Ginestou to Decoux, February 24, 1942, VNA1/DFI/14628. All quotes in this paragraph from this source.

105. Ibid.

106. "French citizens and Indochinese officials" was an ambiguous category, he argued, as not only did a French citizen refer to an adult male, enjoying his civil and political rights, which would effectively exclude French women and children from the ordinance, legally allowing them to smoke opium, but there were also Indochinese officials neither French nor assimilated, yet the proposed legislation sought to treat the two as the same. On nationality, Ginestou pointed to the decree of February 16, 1921, which applied the criminal code to the colony for the French and assimilated subjects; and on residency, Article 3 of the Criminal Code.

107. Ginestou to Decoux, February 24, 1942, VNA1/DFI/14628. All quotes in this paragraph from this source.

108. Decoux to Treasurer General of Indochina, Undated (in file containing correspondences relating to purchasing advances, dated 1943), VNA1/DFI/6705. On uses of advances from provincial budgets, see Ginestou to Decoux, June 20, 1943.

109. Prior to 1946, during the war, the Allied powers of Britain, France, and Holland made official declarations to abolish their colonial opium monopolies and prohibit opium smoking in the Far East territories upon the defeat of the Japanese. See Chapter 7 for details. The French wartime declaration was made in early 1944, by the French Committee of National Liberation led by Charles de Gaulle's government in exile. From Government of the French Republic to League of Nations, July 25, 1945, BL/IOR/L&E/9/732.

110. "Ordonnance fédérale . . . portant sur la suppression de la vente libre de l'opium de monopole," June 20, 1946, *Journal officiel de la Fédération indochinoise.*

111. "Note sur le régime de l'opium en Indochine," March 9, 1948, ANOM/HCI/CONSPOL/83.

112. Ibid.

113. Perrier to High Commissioner for Indochina, March 9, 1948, ANOM/HCI/CONSPOL/83. See Collins 2015, pp. 180–181 on the U.S. government's reception of this document, known as the Tollinger Report.

114. Perrier to High Commissioner for Indochina, March 9, 1948, ANOM/HCI/CONSPOL/83.

115. At the time, French Indochina had approximately 1,000 clinics for opium detoxification and an estimated 100,000 opium smokers. See Fay 1947.

7: Colonial Legacies

1. Heclo 1974.

2. In thus considering the political origins of Southeast Asia's complicit states in the realm of drugs, I am indebted to Deborah Yashar's recent book (2018) on "homicidal ecologies" and drug violence in Latin America. For an especially insightful approach to the complex relationship between drugs and state building, see Andreas 2019.

3. Benda 1972; Tarling 2001. For a critique of the Japanese wartime occupation as a radical rupture for Southeast Asia, see McCoy1980.

4. Cheah Boon Keng 1983; Kratoska 1997; Clancey 2002; Huff and Majima 2013; Huff and Huff 2015.

5. Kratoska 1997.

6. Memorandum on Opium for the Use of India's Representative on the United Nations Narcotic Commission, 1946, BL/IOR/L/E/9/732.

7. The Opium Traffic in the United Kingdom, October 1946, BL/IOR/L/E/9/732.

8. Extract from Burma General Administration, April 1944, TNA/FO 371/50654.

9. Note from the United States Government on Opium Policy in Burma, August 8, 1945; Alleged Use of Opium by American Forces in Burma in Payment for Goods and Services, July 31, 1945, BL/IOR/L/E/9/732. The opium in circulation during World War II was seized contraband from India, Iran, Turkey, and Afghanistan that squeezed past the embargo, as well as imports from Inner Mongolia.

10. Opium Factory Managed by the Financial Department, February 24, 1943, cited in *Chosabu* Reports on Syonan, Huff & Majima 2018. I am grateful to Paul Kratoska for identifying and sharing this source. On the close relationship between the Chosabu, a research bureau, and the military administration, see Akashi & Yoshimura 2008, p. 13.

11. Mordant to Ginestou, March 23, 1942, VNA1/DFI/3952.

12. Maule 1991.

13. On prewar production limitations in the Shan States and their continuity during the war, see Maule 2002. On the Phayap army, see McCoy 1972, pp. 104–106.

14. Foreign Office to Washington, October 31, 1943; Annan to Taylor, February 1, 1944, BL/ IOR/L/E/732; Policy as Regards Opium in Burma, 1945, TNA/FO 371/50654. On the role of the American Foreign Policy Association in pressuring the US government for this approach, see Unnamed, E&O 6558/43, 1943, BL/IOR/L/E/9/732. High British officials were skeptical toward the US intentions. S. W. Harris with the Home Office "doubted whether the danger to U.S. troops was real reason behind the U.S.A. argument, and thought the opportunity was being taken to press for an ideal." See Minutes of the Thirty-Eighth Meeting of the Interdepartmental Committee, September 20, 1945, TNA/FO 371/50654.

15. The Dutch government-in-exile in London had decided to close down its opium monopoly in the East Indies before the British, but delayed its publication in order to allow the British to make a simultaneous announcement. See Miners 1983, p. 295; From Foreign Office to Washington, November 9, 1943, BL/IOR/L/E/732. On the American influence over the 1943 decision, see Collins 2017.

16. CAS(B) Proposals for Opium Policy in Burma, July 1945, TNA/FO 371/50654.

17. Mountbatten to Amery, August 21, 1944, TNA/FO 371/40510.

18. Report of the Committee Appointed to Consider the Opium Problem in Burma, November 29, 1943; Memorandum on Policy as Regards Opium in Burma, undated, 1945, BL/IOR/ L/E/9/732; Cusack to H. Anslinger, March 1, 1962, NARA/RG 170. On the use of opium to pay Kachin soldiers, see Lintner 1999, pp. 70–71.

19. Privately, Mountbatten had reservations against carving out such an exception for Burma, worrying "whether the period of military administration that I am responsible for is not being made use of for economic and sociological experiments which may be called into question by persons having, perhaps, little regard, either for the truth or my good name." Mountbatten to Amery, October 12, 1944, TNA/FO 371/40510.

20. Speer to Anslinger July 26, 1954, in Red China and the Narcotic Traffic-Burma," NARA/ RG 263.

21. Bayly & Harper 2010, p. 106.

22. Marr 2013.

23. On the Viet Minh, see McAlister 1972; Windle 2012. On opium and the DRV, see Lentz 2017.

24. McCoy 1972.

25. Lentz 2017, p. 22. While identifying continuities over time, Lentz stresses the unintended consequences following the colonial opium monopoly's revival for the French in terms of strengthening the Viet Minh's anticolonial, nationalist cause by provoking smuggling and "feeding an underground market endowed with alternative moral and political significance," as well as exacerbating the felt economic inequality and oppression of Hmong poppy growers (p. 16). In addition, the postcolonial state of Northern Vietnam faced difficulties with establishing and popularly legitimating fiscal arrangements relying on opium revenue, not least because of the ways that nationalist leaders formulated anticolonial critiques centered on the injustices of French

opium taxation and peasant hardship. See Edington 2015 on the legacies of the colonial opium monopoly for drug detention centers in Vietnam.

26. On extant grievances among Hmong cultivators and other inhabitants of highland Laos and Tonkin against the French due to the opium monopoly, see Gunn 1986, 1990; Stuart-Fox 1997.

27. On Operation X and its logic, see Trinquier 1961; McCoy 1972, pp. 131–146; Pottier 2005. On the Hmong leader Touby Lyfoung and his involvement as an opium broker, see McCoy 1972. On Lyfoung's personal and political career, see Lee 2015.

28. Project de budget 1947 pour les régions thais, October 30, 1946, ANOM/HCI/CONSPOL/214.

29. On the Binh Xuyen, see Darcourt 1977; K. Li 2016; on its opium involvements, see McCoy 1972; Régime de l'opium en Indochine, April 5, 1948, ANOM/HCI/CONSPOL/83.

30. McCoy 1972, p. 161.

31. Cribb 1988, p. 703.

32. Ibid., p. 704.

33. Moorehead 1947, p. 55.

34. Prohibition of Opium Smoking, November 20, 1946, BL/IOR/L/E/9/732.

35. Abolition of Opium Smoking . . . , March 28, 1947, BL/IOR/L/E/9/732; March 28, 1947, United Nations/E/RES1947/49(IV)D.

36. K. Li 2016. The increased strategic value of these connections raised their costs of maintenance. For instance, by 1954, the SDECE director Roger Trinquier mobilized roughly 40,000 guerrilla fighters in northern Laos and Vietnam, "but he also had to pay dearly for their services; he needed an initial outlay of $15,000 for basic training, arms, bonuses to set up each mercenary unit of 150 men." See McCoy 1972, p. 133.

37. Lentz 2017, p. 17. According to Lentz, in 1952, State shops collected more from taxes on opium production (5.8 billion Vietnamese dong) than tea (3.8 billion VND), the second most valuable crop in northern Vietnam at the time.

38. Ibid., pp. 34 and 39.

39. McCoy 1972, p. 153.

40. Ibid., p. 152.

41. Ibid.

42. *Straits Times*, December 5, 1957.

43. *Malaya Tribune*, October 13, 1948.

44. Also see Exchange of Investments, Perak River Hydro-Electric Power Company, September 11, 1930 to April 2, 1931, TNA/CO 717/76, 1949; Heasman 1947.

45. *Straits Times*, September 17, 1952.

46. *Sunday Standard*, April 15, 1956; *Straits Times*, December 5, 1957.

47. Broadcast by U Aye, Excise Department on the Eradication of the Opium Habit, July 22, 1949. NARA/RG 263. On the limits of the Opium Den Suppression Act, see Thai-Yunnan Project 1992, Newsletter No. 18, pp. 9–17. I am grateful to John Buchanan for insights regarding the limited scope of implementation for 1949 Act.

48. On the People's Volunteer Organizations, a militia organized by nationalist leader Aung San that continued to operate after his assassination, and its rural power bases anchored in gambling and prostitution, see Callahan 2005, p. 111. On the opium ties of factions within this militia

and its ties to the Red Flag branch of the Communist Party of Burma, as well as the Communists' later direct involvement in the opium trade after 1962, see Lintner 1999.

49. Callahan 2005, p. 148.

50. Meehan 2011, p. 381, citing quote by general Tuan Shi-wen from Bertil Lintner, "The Golden Triangle Opium Trade: An Overview," Asia Pacific Media Services, March 2000.

51. McCoy 1972 provides the seminal account of US CIA involvement in the opium trade and support of the KMT during the Cold War.

52. Note sur le régime de l'opium en Indochine, March 9, 1948, ANOM/HCI/CONSPOL/83.

53. For instance, in 1955, a new South Vietnam government led by Ngo Dinh Diem launched several well-publicized crackdowns on drugs that drove out the Binh Xuyen from Saigon. See McCoy 1972 (p. 221) on how Diem and Ngo Dinh Nhu, Diem's brother and political broker, built patronage bases anchored in illicit opium sales and distribution that effectively "reverted to the Binh Xuyen's formula for combating urban guerrilla warfare by using systematic corruption to finance intelligence and counterinsurgency operations."

54. Stubbs 1989, pp. 140–180.

55. Activities of Chinese Secret Society 'Ang Bin Hoay,' TNA/CO 537/2139.

56. Harper 1999, p. 287.

57. Governor of Singapore to Secretary of State for the Colonies, August 27, 1956, TNA/CO 1030/345; *The Morning Bulletin* (December 1, 1952); Harring 1991, p. 371.

58. Gibson and Chen 2011, p. 109.

59. Chouvy 2010, p. 26.

60. Ibid. p. 27.

61. Taylor 2015, p. 426. On the KKY and their commanders who became major warlords including Lo Hsing-han (Luo Xinghan) and Zhang Qifu (Khun Sa), see Lintner 1999; Meehan 2011; Buchanan 2016.

62. Diary 29, Harrison Forman Papers, University of Wisconsin–Milwaukee Libraries.

63. De Quincey 1822, p. i.

64. In 1928, the opium monopoly for the Straits Settlements had made registration a mandatory requirement for all Chinese living in the colony who consumed opium. TNA/CO 273/555.

65. Office of the High Commissioner for Canada to Colonial Office, August 14, 1956, TNA/CO 1030/345; *Newsweek*, July 9, 1956; *Straits Times*, February 5, 1955.

66. TNA/CO 1030/345.

67. Opium Treatment Centre, St. John's Island, TNA/CO 1030/345; Oral History Interview with Saravana Perumal, October 6, 1983, Accessed online at National Archives of Singapore, Oral History Interviews, Reel 11, Accession no. 000335.

68. *Straits Times*, March 25, 1956.

69. Ibid.

70. St. John's Island Opium Addicts Rehabilitation Centre, Singapore, December 1957, TNA/INF 10/315.

71. Instructions for . . . Treasury and Other Officers in the Vend of Opium under the New Opium Rules, 1894, MNA, 01/1 (e), 9606.

72. Report on the Working of the Revised Arrangements for the Vend of Opium in Upper Burma, 1905–1906, BL/IOR/V/24/3127.

73. Proceedings of the American Pharmaceutical Association, 1894, p. 447.

74. AREABB 1930, p. 22.

75. Le trafic illicite de l'opium au Tonkin, May 12, 1924, ANOM/FM/AFFPOL/3262.

76. Ibid.

77. Also see Grémont 2018, pp. 181–192.

78. A.S. du chinois Thoong Sin-Phò, December 20, 1932 ; Renseignements provenant d'un informateur occasionnel sérieux, December 16, 1932 ; ANOM/INDO/RSTNF/2138.

79. Opium Revenue Replacement Reserve Fund, June 22, 1936, TNA/CO 273/616/5.

80. Depardon 2015.

81. Pitkin 1987, p. 277.

8: Conclusion

1. Tilly 1992; Bourdieu 1999.

2. Scott 1998.

3. Morgan & Orloff 2017, p. 7. On the centrality and limited utility of Weberian assumptions about the state, see Boone 2003; Naseemullah and Staniland 2016. Another important line of inquiry in political science concerns state capacity, which grapples with problems that arise from conflating what states pursue (i.e., the reasons and rationales for developing policies and political reform) with what states achieve (i.e., outcomes such as economic growth, democracy, provision of public goods, social inclusion, as well as violence reduction) in ways that misrecognize the actual causes of political and economic development that may not necessarily have to do with the state's involvement or lack thereof; reading the intentionality of the state backwards from policy results that may not necessarily have been intended or foreseeable; underestimating the in-between processes by which policy decisions are implemented on the ground; as well as committing tautologies when measuring and operationalizing the strength of state capacity. See Soifer and vom Hau 2008; Centeno, Kohli, & Yashar 2017; Lee and Zhang 2017.

4. Morgan and Orloff 2017, p. 17.

5. Guha 1997.

6. Ibid., p. 65.

7. Ibid., p. 64.

8. Ibid.

9. Stoler 2010; Wilson 2011; Saha 2013.

10. Wilder 2005; Singaravélou 2011; Hussin 2016.

11. Spivak 1988.

12. Booth 2007; Lange 2009; Mattingly 2015.

13. Scott 1998, 2009.

14. Legitimacy can connote a moral right to rule (that appeals to an external and consensually acknowledged authority by people), be used as a synonym for popularity or perceived appropriateness (by resonating with culturally resonant symbols that are meaningful in people's minds), as well as mean a belief among citizens in the general appropriateness of a regime, practice or leader). Lisa Wedeen has shown how social scientists often use legitimacy a way that "lacks clarity and often obscures the very processes of power, obedience, consent, and acquiescence that it is intended to explain," not least by conflating these three different meanings. Such

conceptual imprecision is problematic, Wedeen notes, because when we say the powerful exercise legitimacy, we end up sidestepping the difficult work of understanding *what* is being considered legitimate *by whom* and *how* to know whether people's expressed consent is voluntary (as opposed to forced or feigned). See Wedeen 1999, pp. xi–xv, 7–18; Lipset 1959; Levi 1988. An alternative conceptualization of legitimacy focuses on horizontal or peer-recognition for a ruler, rather than the assent of the governed. Arthur Stinchcombe argues "the person over whom power is exercised is not usually as important as other power-holders." See Tilly 1985, p 171. Tilly concurs with this more cynical definition of legitimacy that refers to "the probability that other authorities will act to confirm the decisions of a given authority." Rather than focus on society, such minimalist definitions of legitimacy center on "the correspondence between the uses of force and the rules specifying when it can and should be used" (Tilly 1985, p. 141). Also see scholars of international relations who view a sovereign state' claim to legitimacy as attributed by other rulers or the world polity through recognition. See Krasner 1988; Thomson 1996. See Sunshine and Tyler 2003 on legitimacy from a psychological perspective relating to legal and procedural regulation.

15. Orwell 1981 [1936]. All quotes in this paragraph from this source.

16. Orwell 1931. All quotes in this paragraph from this source.

17. Ibid.

SOURCES AND BIBLIOGRAPHY

Unpublished Archival Sources

British Library (BL)
   India Office Records (IOR)
   L/E, Economic Department Records
   L/P&J, Public and Judicial Department Records
   P, Proceedings and Consultations, Government of Burma
   V, Official Publications Series

National Archives of the United Kingdom (TNA)
   CAB 24, Cabinet Papers, Interwar Memoranda
   CAOG, Crown Agents for Overseas Governments and Administrations
   CO 273, Colonial Office, Straits Settlements Original Correspondence
   CO 537, Colonial Office, Colonies General Supplementary Original Correspondence
   CO 717, Colonial Office, Federated Malay States Original Correspondence
   CO 825, Colonial Office, Eastern Original Correspondence
   CO 1030, Colonial Office and Commonwealth Office: Far Eastern Department and
      Successors
   FO 371, Foreign Office, Political Departments: General Correspondence
   INF 10, Ministry of Information, British Empire Collection of Photographs
   T1, Treasury Board Papers and In-Letters

Vietnamese National Archives, Center 1, Hanoi (VNA1)
   Fonds de la Direction des finances de l'Indochine (DFI)

Archives nationales d'outre-mer (ANOM), Aix-en-Provence
   Fonds privés, Émile Devouton
   FM, Fonds ministériels
      AFFPOL, Direction des affaires politiques
      AGEFOM, Agence économique de la France d'outre-mer
      AMIRAUX, Amiraux
      INDO/AF, Indochine, anciens fonds
      INDO/NF, Indochine, nouveau fonds
   GGI, Fonds du Gouvernement général de l'Indochine

RSTNF, Fonds de la de la Résidence supérieure au Tonkin, nouveau fonds
HCI/CONSPOL, Archives du Haut commissariat de France pour l'Indochine, conseiller
   politique

National Archives and Records Administration of the United States (NARA)
   RG 263, Records of the Central Intelligence Agency
   RG 170, Records of the Drug Enforcement Administration

National Archives Department of Myanmar (MNA)
   Colonial Period (01/02, 01/11/, 01/15/15b, 15e)

Newspapers and Periodicals

Friend of China
Friend of India and Statesman
Journal des économistes
La Quinzaine coloniale
La revue du Christianisme social
La Revue indochinoise
L'Avenir du Tonkin
L'Écho annamite
Les Annales coloniales
Malayan Saturday Post
Malaya Tribune
Mandalay Times
Newsweek
Singapore Free Press and Mercantile Adviser
Straits Times
Sunday Standard
The Times

Government Publications Consulted for Select Years

Annuaire Statistique de l'Indochine
L'Atlas Statistique de l'Indochine
Annual Department Records for the Straits Settlements
Annual Report on Excise Administration of Burma
Annual Report on Prison Administration of Burma
Straits Settlements Blue Book
Burma Opium Manual
Budget général de l'Indochine
Journal officiel de la Cochinchine française
Journal officiel de la République française
Proceedings of the Legislative Council, Straits Settlements

Secondary Sources

Abbott, A. (2005). Linked Ecologies: States and Universities as Environments for Professions. *Sociological Theory*, 23(3), 245–274.

Adams, J. (1996). Principals and Agents, Colonists and Company Men: The Decay of Colonial Control in the Dutch East Indies. *American Sociological Review*, 61(1), 12–28.

Adams, J., Clemens, E., & Orloff, A. (2005). *Remaking Modernity: Politics, History and Sociology.* Durham, NC: Duke University Press.

Adas, M. (2011). *The Burma Delta: Economic Development and Social Change on an Asian Rice Frontier, 1852–1941.* Madison: University of Wisconsin Press.

Adler, E., & Pouliot, V. (2011). International Practices. *International Theory*, 3(1), 1–36.

Ahmad, D. (2007). *The Opium Debate and Chinese Exclusion Laws in the Nineteenth-Century American West.* Reno: University of Nevada Press.

Allen, J. (1970). Malayan Civil Service, 1874–1941: Colonial Bureaucracy/Malayan Elite. *Comparative Studies in Society and History*, 12(2), 149–178.

Alonso, W., & Starr, W., eds. (1980). *The Politics of Numbers.* New York: Russell Sage Foundation.

Amnesty International. (2019). Death Sentences and Executions 2018. London: Amnesty International Ltd.

Amrith, S. (2009). Tamil Diasporas across the Bay of Bengal. *American Historical Review*, 114(3), 547–572.

Amrith, S. (2010). Eugenics in Postcolonial Southeast Asia. In A. Bashford & P. Levine (Eds.), *The Oxford Handbook of the History of Eugenics* (pp. 301–314). Oxford: Oxford University Press.

Andaya, B. (1994). From Temporary Wife to Prostitute: Sexuality and Economic Change in Early Modern Southeast Asia. *Journal of Women's History*, 9(4), 11–34.

Anderson, B. (2001). *Imagined Communities: Reflections on the Origin and Spread of Nationalism.* London: Verso.

Anderson, W. (2006). *Colonial Pathologies: American Tropical Medicine, Race, and Hygiene in the American Philippines.* Durham, NC: Duke University Press.

Andreas, P. (2019). Drugs and War: What is the Relationship? *Annual Review of Political Science*, 22, 57–73.

Andrew, C., & Kanya-Forstner, A. (1971). The French "Colonial Party": Its Composition, Aims and Influence, 1885–1914. *The Historical Journal*, 14(1), 99–128.

Andrew, C., & Kanya-Forstner, A. (1974). The Groupe Colonial in the French Chamber of Deputies, 1892–1932. *The Historical Journal*, 17(4), 837–866.

Arnold, D. (1993). Colonizing the Body: State Medicine and Epidemic Disease in Nineteenth-Century India. Berkeley: University of California Press.

Ashworth, W. (2003). *Customs and Excise: Trade, Production and Consumption in England 1640–1845.* Oxford: Oxford University Press.

Atkinson, J., & Errington, S. 1990. *Power and Difference: Gender in Island Southeast Asia.* Palo Alto, CA: Stanford University Press.

Bailey, W., & Truong, L. (2001). Opium and Empire: Some Evidence from Colonial-Era Asian Stock and Commodity Markets. *Journal of Southeast Asian Studies*, 32, 173–193.

Ballhatchet, K. (1980). *Race, Sex, and Class under the Raj: Imperial Attitudes and Policies and their Critics, 1793–1905*. New York: St. Martin's Press.

Banens, M. (1999). Vietnam: A Reconsitution of its 20th Century Population History. Rapport de recherche, *HAL, Centre pour la communication scientifique directe*, 1–47.

Bankoff, G. (1991). Redefining Criminality: Gambling and Financial Expediency in the Colonial Philippines, 1764–1898. *Journal of Southeast Asian Studies*, 22(2), 267–281.

Barkey, K. (2008). *Empires of Difference: The Ottomans in Comparative Perspective*. Cambridge: Cambridge University Press.

Baruah, V. (2016). *Addicts, Pedlers, Reformers: A Social History of Opium in Assam, 1826–1947*. PhD thesis, Cardiff University.

Baumler, A. (2007). *The Chinese and Opium under the Republic: Worse than Floods and Wild Beasts*. Albany: State University of New York Press.

Bayly, C., & Harper, T. (2010). *Forgotten Wars: Freedom and Revolution in Southeast Asia*. Cambridge, MA: Harvard University Press.

Bebbington, D. (1982). *The Nonconformist Conscience: Chapel and Politics, 1870–1914*. East Melbourne: G. Allen & Unwin.

Bell, D. (2006). Empire and International Relations in Victorian Political Thought. *The Historical Journal*, 49(1), 281–298.

Bello, D. (2005). *Opium and the Limits of Empire: Drug Prohibition in the Chinese Interior, 1729–1850*. Cambridge, MA: Harvard University Press.

Bello, D. (2013). The Venomous Course of Southwestern Opium: Qing Prohibition in Yunnan, Sichuan, and Guizhou in the Early Nineteenth Century. *Journal of Asian Studies*, 62(4), 1109–1142.

Benda, H. (1972). *Continuity and Change in Southeast Asia*. New Haven, CT: Yale University Southeast Asian Studies, Monograph Series, No. 18.

Benedict, C. (2011). *Golden-Silk Smoke: A History of Tobacco in China, 1550–2010*. Berkeley: University of California Press.

Bentham, J. (1843). *The Works of Jeremy Bentham*, edited by J. Bowring. Edinburgh: W. Tait.

Benton. L. (2008). From International Law to Imperial Constitutions: The Problem of Quasi-Sovereignty. *Law and History Review*, 26(3), 595–619.

Bergeron, H. (1999). *L'État et la toxicomanie. Histoire d'une singularité française*. Paris: Presses universitaires de France.

Bergson, H. (1959). *Le rire. Essai sur la signifiance du comique*. Paris: Presses Universitaires de France.

Bernard, F. (1901). *Indochine, erreurs et dangers: un programme*. Paris: Charpentier.

Berridge, V. (1978). Professionalization and Narcotics: The Medical and Pharmaceutical Professions and British Narcotic Use, 1868–1926. *Psychological Medicine*, 8(3), 361–372.

Berridge, V. (1999). *Opium and the People: Opiate Use and Drug Control Policy in Nineteenth and Early Twentieth Century England*. London: Free Association Books.

Birla, R. (2009). *Stages of Capital: Law, Culture, and Market Governance in Late Colonial India*. Durham, NC: Duke University Press.

Bisiou, Y. (1995). *Les monopoles des stupéfiants*. PhD thesis, Université de Paris X Nanterre.

Black, S. (2016). Doctors on Drugs: Medical Professionals and the Proliferation of Morphine Addiction in Nineteenth-Century France. *Social History of Medicine*, 1–23.

Blau, P. (1956). *Bureaucracy in Modern Society*. New York: Random House.

Bloomfield, M. (1952). *The Seven Deadly Sins: An Introduction to the History of a Religious Concept with Special Reference to Medieval English Literature*. East Lansing MI: Michigan State College Press.

Boon, M. (2002). *The Road of Excess: A History of Writers on Drugs*. Cambridge, MA: Harvard University Press.

Boone, C. (2003). *Political Topographies of the African State: Territorial Authority and Institutional Change*. Cambridge: Cambridge University Press.

Booth, A. (2007). *Colonial Legacies: Economic and Social Development in East and Southeast Asia*. Honolulu: University of Hawai'i Press.

Boudet, P., & Coulet, G. (1929). Les Chinois en Indochine. *Extrême-Asie, 35*, 457–464.

Bourdieu, P. (1991). *Language and Symbolic Power*. Cambridge: Cambridge University Press.

Bourdieu, P. (1999). Rethinking the State: Genesis and Structure of the Bureaucratic Field, translated by L.Wacquant and S. Farage. In G. Steinmetz (Ed.), *State/Culture: State Formation after the Cultural Turn* (pp. 53–75). Ithaca, NY: Cornell University Press.

Bourdieu, P. (2014). *On the State: Lectures at the Collège de France, 1989–1992*. Cambridge: Polity Press.

Boutmy, E. (1895). *Le recrutement des administrateurs coloniaux*. Paris: Armand Colin et Cie.

Braddell, T. (1857). Gambling and Opium Smoking in the Straits of Malacca. *Journal of the Indian Archipelago and Eastern Asia, 2*(1), 66–83.

Brandt, J. van den. (1936). *Les lazaristes en Chine, 1697–1935*. Pei-p'ing: Imprimerie des lazaristes.

Bray, A. (1995). *Homosexuality in Renaissance England*. New York: Columbia University Press.

Brewer, J. (1989). *The Sinews of Power: War, Money, and the English State, 1688–1783*. London: Unwyn Hyman.

Brewer, J., & Porter, R. (1993). *Consumption and the World of Goods*. London: Routledge.

Brocheux, P., & Hémery, D. (2009). *Indochina: An Ambiguous Colonization, 1858–1954*. Berkeley: University of Califorina Press.

Brook, T., & Wakabayahi, B. (2000). *Opium Regimes: China, Britain, and Japan, 1839–1952*. Berkeley: University of California Press.

Brown, I. (1993). The End of the Opium Farm in Siam, 1905–1907. In H. Dick & J. Butcher (Eds.), *The Rise and Fall of Opium Farming* (pp. 233–245). London: St. Martin's Press.

Brown, J. B. (1973). Politics of the Poppy: The Society for the Suppression of the Opium Trade, 1874–1916. *Journal of Contemporary History, 8*(3), 97–111.

Brubaker, R., & Cooper, F. (2000). Beyond "Identity." *Theory and Society, 29*, 1–47.

Buchanan, J. (2016). *Militias in Myanmar*. San Francisco CA: The Asia Foundation.

Budistéaunu, R. (1929). *L'aspect international de la lutte contre l'opium*. Paris: Librarie générale de droit de de jurisprudence.

Burchell, G., Gordon, C., & Miller, P. (1991). *The Foucault Effect: Studies in Governmentality*. Chicago: University of Chicago Press.

Butcher, J., & Dick, H. (1993). *The Rise and Fall of Revenue Farming: Business Elites and the Emergence of the Modern State in Southeast Asia*. London: St. Martin's Press.

Callahan, M. (2005). *Making Enemies: War and State Building in Burma*. Ithaca, NY: Cornell University Press.

Campbell, P. (1923). *Chinese Coolie Emigration to Countries within the British Empire*. London: P. S. King & Son.

Canaday, M. (2009). *The Straight State: Sexuality and Citizenship in Twentieth-Century America*. Princeton, NJ: Princeton University Press.

Carpenter, C. (2014). *'Lost' Causes: Agenda Vetting in Global Issue Networks and the Shaping of Human Security*. Ithaca, NY: Cornell University Press.

Carpenter, D. (2001). *The Forging of Bureaucratic Autonomy: Networks, Reputations, and Policy Innovation in Executive Agencies, 1862–1928*. Princeton, NJ: Princeton University Press.

Cassels, N. (2010). *Social Legislation of the East India Company: Public Justice versus Public Instruction*. New Delhi: Sage Publications.

Centeno, M. (2002). *Blood and Debt: War and the Nation-State in Latin America*. University Park: Pennsylvania State University Press.

Centeno, M., Kohli, A., & Yashar, D. (2017). *States in the Developing World*. Cambridge: Cambridge University Press.

Chailley-Bert, J. (1903). The Colonial Policy of France. *Fortnightly Review*, 310–323.

Chailley-Bert, J. (1908). L'opium et le Budget de l'Indochine. *La Quinzaine coloniale* (March 10), 5, 177–180.

Chandra, S. (2002). The Role of Government Policy in Increasing Drug Use: Java, 1875–1914. *The Journal of Economic History*, 62(4), 1116–1121.

Chang, H. (1964). *Commissioner Lin and the Opium War*. Cambridge, MA: Harvard University Press.

Chaudhuri, K. N. (1966). India's Foreign Trade and the Cessation of the East India Company's Trading Activities, 1828–40. *Economic History Review*, 19(2), 345–363.

Cheng, U.W. (1961). Opium in the Straits Settlements, 1867–1910. *Journal of Southeast Asian History*, 2(1), 52–75.

Chew, E. (1991). A History of Singapore. In E. Chew & E. Lee (Eds.), *A History of Singapore*. Singapore and London: Oxford University Press.

Chin, K. (2009). *The Golden Triangle: Inside Southeast Asia's Drug Trade*. Ithaca, NY: Cornell University Press.

Chouvy, P. A. (2002). *Yaa baa: production, trafic et consommation de méthamphétamine en Asie du Sud-Est continentale*. Paris: L'Harmattan.

Chouvy, P. A. (2010). *Opium: Uncovering the Politics of the Poppy*. Cambridge, MA: Harvard University Press.

Clancey, G. (2002). The Japanese Imperium and South-East Asia: An Overview. In P. Kratoska (Ed.), *Southeast Asian Minorities in the Wartime Japanese Empire* (pp. 7–20). London: RoutledgeCurzon.

Cohen, P. (1984). Opium and the Karen: A Study of Indebtedness in Northern Thailand. *Journal of Southeast Asian Studies*, 15(1), 150–165.

Cohen, S. (1972). *Folk Devils and Moral Panics: The Creation of the Mods and Rockers*. London: MacGibbon and Kee Ltd.

Cohen, W. (1971). *Rulers of Empire: The French Colonial Service in Africa*. Stanford, CA: Hoover Institution Press.

Cohn, B. (1996). *Colonialism and Its Forms of Knowledge*. Princeton, NJ: Princeton University Press.

Coleridge, S. T. (1853). *The Complete Works of Samuel Taylor Coleridge*. New York: Harper and Brothers.

Collins, J. (2015). *Regulations and Prohibitions: Anglo-American Relations and International Drug Control, 1939–1964*. PhD thesis, The London School of Economics.

Collins, J. (2017). Breaking the Monopoly System: American Influence on the British Decision to Prohibit Opium Smoking and End its Asian Monopolies, 1939–1945. *International History Review*, 39(5), 770–790.

Comaroff, J., & Comaroff, J. (1999). *Of Revelation and Revolution*, vol. 1. Chicago: University of Chicago Press.

Conklin, A. (2013). *In the Museum of Man: Race, Anthropology, and Empire in France, 1850–1950*. Ithaca, NY: Cornell University Press.

Cook, J. A. B. (1907). *Sunny Singapore: An Account of the Place and Its People with a Sketch of the Results of Missionary Work*. London: E. Stock.

Cooper, F. (1996). *Decolonization and African Society: The Labor Question in French and British Africa*. Cambridge: Cambridge University Press.

Cooper, F., & Stoler, A. (1997). *Tensions of Empire: Colonial Cultures in a Bourgeois World*. Berkeley: University of California Press.

Corrigan, P., & Sayer, D. (1985). *The Great Arch: English State Formation as Cultural Revolution*. Oxford: Basil Blackwell.

Courtwright, D. (2001). *Forces of Habit: Drugs and the Making of the Modern World*. Cambridge, MA: Harvard University Press.

Cowan, C. (1950). *Early Penang & the Rise of Singapore 1805–1832: Documents from the Manuscript Records of the East India Company*. Singapore: Malaya Publishing House.

Cribb, R. (1988). Opium and the Indonesian Revolution. *Modern Asian Studies*, 22(4), 701–722.

Crooks, P., & Parsons, T., eds. (2016). *Empires and Bureaucracy in World History: From Late Antiquity to the Twentieth Century*. Cambridge: Cambridge University Press.

Crosthwaite, C. (1912). *The Pacification of Burma*. London: E. Arnold.

Culas, C. (2000). Migrants, Runaways and Opium Growers: Origins of the Hmong in Laos and Siam in the Nineteenth and Early Twentieth Centuries. In J. Michaud & J. Ovesen (Eds.), *Turbulent Times and Enduring Peoples: Mountain Minorities in the Southeast Asian Massif*. Hove, East Sussex: Psychology Press.

Cushman, J. (1986). The Khaw Group: Chinese Business in Early Twentieth-Century Penang. *Journal of Southeast Asian Studies*, 17(1), 58–79.

Darcourt, P. (1977). *Bay Vien: Le maître de Cholon*. Paris: Hanchette.

Daughton, J. P. (2006). *An Empire Divided: Religion, Republicanism, and the Making of French Colonialism*. Oxford: Oxford University Press.

Davis, J. (2013). Cockfight Nationalism: Blood Sport and the Moral Politics of American Empire and Nation Building. *American Quarterly*, 65(3), 549–574.

Décamps, J. (1909). Développement historique de la Régie de l'opium. *Bulletin du Comité de l'Asie française*, 96, 110–123.

Delrieu, A. (1988). *L'inconsistance de la toxicomanie: contribution à l'histoire des discours et des pratiques médicales*. Paris: Navarin Analytica.

Denis, É. (1965). *Bordeaux et la Cochinchine sous la Restauration et le Second Empire*. Artigues Pres Bordeaux: Imprimerie Delmas.

Depardon, G. (2015). *Raymond Depardon: Adieu Saigon*. Göttingen: Steidl.

de Quincey, T. (1822). *Confessions of an English Opium-Eater*. London: Taylor and Hessey.

Descharmes, C. (1855). *Mémoire sur l'opium indigène*. Amiens.

Descours-Gatin, C. (1987). *Opium et finances coloniales: la formation de la Régie Générale de l'Opium en Indochine, 1860–1914*. PhD thesis, Université de Paris VII.

Descours-Gatin, C. (1992). *Quand l'opium finançait la colonisation en Indochine*. Paris: L'Harmattan.

Deshpande, A. (2009). An Historical Overview of Opium Cultivation and Changing State Attitudes towards the Crop in India, 1878–2000 A.D. *Studies in History*, 25(1), 109–143.

Devlin, P. (1965). Morals and the Criminal Law. In *The Enforcement of Morals*. Oxford: Oxford University Press.

Diamant, N. (2001). Making Love "Legible" in China: Politics and Society during the Enforcement of Civil Marriage Registration, 1950–66. *Politics & Society*, 29(3), 447–480.

Didérot, D. 2003 [1765]. *The Encyclopedia of Diderot and d'Alembert*, translated by N. Hoyt & T. Cassirer. Ann Arbor: University of Michigan Library, Collaborative Translation Project.

Diehl, F. W. (1993). Revenue Farming and Colonial Finances in the Netherlands East Indies, 1816–1925. In H. Dick & J. Butcher (Eds.), *The Rise and Fall of Opium Farming* (pp. 196–232). London: St. Martin's Press.

Dikötter, F., Zhou, X., & Laamann, L. P. (2004). *Narcotic Culture: A History of Drugs in China*. London: C. Hurst & Co.

Dimier, V. (2004). *Le gouvernement des colonies, regards croisés franco-britanniques. Gouvernement des colonies*. Bruxelles: Éditions de l'Université de Bruxelles.

Dixit, A. (1996). *The Making of Economic Policy: A Transaction Cost Politics Perspective*. Cambridge, MA: MIT Press.

Donnison, F. (1953). *Public Administration in Burma: A Study of Development during the British Connexion*. London: Royal Institute of International Affairs.

Doumer, P. (1902). *Situation de l'Indochine de 1897 à 1902*. Hanoi: F. N. Schneider.

Downs, A. (1967). *Inside Bureaucracy*. Boston: Little, Brown & Co.

Dubois, V. (1999). *La vie au guichet, relation administrative et traitement de la misère*. Paris: Economica.

Ducourtieux, O., Deligez, F., Sacklokham, S., et al. (2008). L'éradication de l'opium au Laos: les politiques et leur effets sur l'économie villageoise. *Revue Tiers-Monde*, 193, 145–168.

Dumarest, J. (1938). *Les monopoles de l'opium et du sel en Indochine*. PhD thesis, l'Université de Lyon.

Edington, C. (2016). Drug Detention and Human Rights in Post Doi Moi Vietnam. In D. Kim & J. Singh (Ed.), *The Postcolonial World* (pp. 325–342). London: Routledge.

Edington, C., & Pols, H. (2016). Building Psychiatric Expertise across Southeast Asia: Study Trips, Site Visits, and Therapeutic Labor in French Indochina and the Dutch East Indies, 1898–1937. *Comparative Studies in Society and History*, 58(3), 636–663.

Egerton, H. (1897). *Sir Stamford Raffles: England in the Far East*. London: T. F. Unwin.

Emmerson, D. (1984). "Southeast Asia": What's in a Name? *Journal of Southeast Asian Studies*, 15(1), 1–21.

Evans, P., Rueschemeyer, D., & Skocpol, T., Eds. (1985). *Bringing the State Back In*. Cambridge: Cambridge University Press.

Farooqui, A. (1995). Opium Enterprise and Colonial Intervention in Malwa and Western India, 1800–1824. *Indian Economic & Social History Review*, 32(4), 447–473.

Farooqui, A. (2005). *Smuggling as Subversion: Colonialism, Indian Merchants, and the Politics of Opium, 1790–1843*. Lanham, MD: Lexington Books.

Fay, P. (1947). "L'opium." *Revue des troupes colonials, 280*, 52–59.

Fay, P. (1970). The French Catholic Mission in China during the Opium War. *Modern Asian Studies, 4*(2), 115–128.

Fee, L. K., & We, K. K. (2004). Chinese Enterprise in Colonial Malaya: The Case of Eu Tong Sen. *Journal of Southeast Asian Studies, 35*(3), 415–432.

Finnemore, M., & Sikkink, K. (1998). International Norm Dynamics and Political Change, *International Organization, 52*(4), 887–917.

Firpo, C. (2016). *The Uprooted: Race, Children, and Imperialism in French Indochina, 1890–1980*. Honolulu: University of Hawai'i Press.

Forest, A. (1979). *Le Cambodge et la colonisation française*. Paris: L'Harmattan.

Foster, A. (2000). Prohibition as Superiority: Policing Opium in South-East Asia, 1898–1925. *The International History Review, 22*(2), 253–273.

Foster, A. (2010). Opium, the United States, and the Civilizing Mission in Colonial Southeast Asia. *Social History of Alcohol and Drugs, 24*(1), 6–19.

Fourniau, A. (2002). *Domination coloniale et résistance nationale, 1858–1914*. Paris: Les Indes savantes.

Foxcroft, L. (2007). *The Making of Addiction: The "Use and Abuse" of Opium in Nineteenth-Century Britain*. Aldershot: Ashgate.

Freedman, M. (1960). Immigrations and Associations: Chinese in Nineteenth Century Singapore. *Comparative Studies in Society and History, 3*(1), 25–48.

Frost, M. (2005). Emporium in Imperio: Nanyang Networks and the Straits Chinese in Singapore, 1819–1914. *Journal of Southeast Asian Studies, 36*(1), 29–66.

Furnivall, J. (1944). *Colonial Policy and Practice: A Comparative Study of Burma and Netherlands India*. New York: New York University Press.

Fytche, A. (1878). *Burma, Past and Present*, vols. 1 and 2. London: C. K. Paul & Company.

Gailmard, S., & Patty, J. (2012). Formal Models of Bureaucracy. *Annual Review of Political Science, 15*, 353–377.

Galembert, J. (1924). *Les Administrations et les services publiques indochinois*. Hanoi: Imprimerie Mac-Dinh-Tu.

Galloway, D. (1923). Opium Smoking. In *Transactions of the 5th Congress of the Far Eastern Association of Tropical Medicine*. London: J. Bale, Sons & Danielsson.

Gardiner, N. (1998). *Sentinels of Empire: The British Colonial Administrative Service, 1919–1954*. PhD thesis, Yale University.

Geddes, B. (2003). *Paradigms and Sand Castles: Theory Building and Research Design in Comparative Politics*. Ann Arbor: University of Michigan Press.

Geertz, C. (1981). *Negara: The Theater State in Nineteenth Century Bali*. Princeton, NJ: Princeton University Press.

Ghosh, A. (2008). *Sea of Poppies*. New York: Picador.

Gibson, R., & Chen, W. (2011). *The Secret Army: Chiang Kai-shek and the Drug Warlords of the Golden Triangle*. Singapore: John Wiley & Sons.

Gide, P. (1910). *L'opium*. Paris: Thèse, lib de la société du recueil sirey.

Gingeras, R. (2014). *Heroin, Organized Crime, and the Making of Modern Turkey.* Oxford: Oxford University Press.

Girault, A. (1943). *Principes de colonisation et de législation coloniale. Les colonies françaises avant et depuis 1815, notions historiques, administratives, juridiques, économiques et financières.* Paris: Recueil Sirey.

Girelli, G. (2019). *The Death Penalty for Drug Offences: Global Overview 2018.* London: Harm Reduction International.

Glass, L. (1985). *The Changing of Kings: Memories of Burma, 1934–1949.* London: P. Owen.

Go, J. (2008). Global Fields and Imperial Forms: Field Theory and the British and American Empires. *Sociological Theory, 26*(3), 201–229.

Go, J. (2011). *Patterns of Empire: The British and American Empires, 1688 to the Present.* Cambridge: Cambridge University Press.

Goertz, G. (2017). *Multimethod Research, Causal Mechanisms, and Case Studies: An Integrated Approach.* Princeton, NJ: Princeton University Press.

Goodin, R. (1988). *Reasons for Welfare: The Political Theory of the Welfare State.* Princeton, NJ: Princeton University Press.

Gootenberg, P., Ed. (1999). *Cocaine: Global Histories.* London & New York: Routledge.

Gorski, P. (2003). *The Disciplinary Revolution: Calvinism and the Rise of the State in Early Modern Europe.* Chicago: University of Chicago Press.

Goscha, C. (1999). *Thailand and the Southeast Asian Networks of the Vietnamese Revolution, 1885–1954.* London: Curzon Press.

Goscha, C. (2016). *Vietnam: A New History.* New York: Basic Books.

Goto-Shibata, H. (2002). The International Opium Conference of 1924–25 and Japan. *Modern Asian Studies, 36*(4), 969–991.

Goto-Shibata, H. (2006). Empire on the Cheap: The Control of Opium Smoking in the Straits Settlements, 1925–1939. *Modern Asian Studies, 40*(1), 59–80.

Great Britain. (1857). *Papers Relating to the Opium Trade in China, 1842–1856.* London: Harrison.

Great Britain. (1894). *First Report of the Royal Opium Commission on Opium: With Minutes of Evidence and Appendices*, vol. 2. London: Her Majesty's Stationery Office.

Great Britain (1908). *Proceedings of the Commission Appointed to Enquire into Matters Relating to the Use of Opium in the Straits Settlements and the Federated Malay States*, vols. 1 & 2. Singapore: Government Printing Office.

Great Britain. (1924). *Proceedings of the Committee Appointed by His Excellency the Governor and High Commissioner to Inquire into Matters Relating to the Use of Opium in British Malaya*, vols. 2 & 3. Singapore: Government Printing Office.

Greenberg, M. (1951). *British Trade and the Opening of China, 1800–1842.* Cambridge: Cambridge University Press.

Greenwood, G. (1957). *Taylor of Batley.* London: M. Parrish.

Grémont, J. (2018). *Maintenir l'ordre aux confins de l'Empire: Pirates, trafiquants et rebelles entre Chine et Viêtnam 1895–1940.* Saint-Laurent: Maisonneuve & Larose.

Guha, R. (1963). *A Rule of Property for Bengal: An Essay on the Idea of Permanent Settlement.* Durham, NC: Duke University Press.

Guha, R. (1997). *Dominance Without Hegemony: History and Power in Colonial India.* Cambridge MA: Harvard University Press.

Guillemot, F. (2018). *Viêt-Nam, fractures d'une nation: Une histoire contemporaine de 1858 à nos jours.* Paris: La Découverte.

Gunn, G. (1986). Shamans and Rebels: The Batchai (Mèo) Rebellion of Northern Laos and North-west Vietnam (1918–1921). *Journal of the Siam Society, 74,* 107–121.

Gusfield, J. (1963). *Symbolic Crusade: Status Politics and the American Temperance Movement.* Champaign: University of Illinois Press.

Ha, M.-P. (2009). The Chiense and the White Man's Burden in Indochina. In E. Ho & J. Kuehn (Eds.), *China Abroad: Travels, Subjects, Spaces* (pp. 191–207). Hong Kong University Press.

Hall, S. (1985). Signification, Represenation, and Ideology: Althusser and the Post-Structuralist Debates. *Critical Studies in Mass Communication, 2*(2), 91–114.

Hansen, A. (2007). *How to Behave: Buddhism and Modernity in Colonial Cambodia, 1860–1930.* Honolulu: University of Hawai'i Press.

Harcourt, B., & Zimring, F. (2014). *Criminal Law and the Regulation of Vice,* 2nd ed. St. Paul: West Academic.

Harper, T. (1999). *The End of Empire and the Making of Malaya.* Cambridge: Cambridge University Press.

Harring, S. (1991). Death, Drugs, and Development: Malaysia's Mandatory Death Penalty for Traffickers and the International War on Drugs. *Columbia Journal of Transnational Law, 29,* 365–405.

Heasman, R. B. (1947). *Income Tax: A Report to Their Excellencies the Governors of the Malayan Union and Singapore.* Kuala Lumpur: Malayan Union Government Press.

Heath, D. (2010). *Purifying Empire: Obscenity and the Politics of Moral Regulation in Britain, India, and Australia.* New York: Cambridge University Press.

Heclo, H. (1974). *Modern Social Politics in Britain and Sweden: From Relief to Income Maintenance.* New Haven, CT: Yale University Press.

Hell, S. (2007). *Siam and the League of Nations: Modernization, Sovereignty and Multilateral Diplomacy, 1920–1940.* PhD thesis, Leiden University.

Hesnard, A. (1930). La fabrication de l'opium à Saïgon. *La clinique, 140,* 77–78.

Hevia, J. (1998). The Archive State and Fears of Pollution: From the Opium Wars to Fu-Manchu. *Cultural Studies, 12*(2), 234–264.

Hilton, B. (1988). *The Age of Atonement: The Influence of Evangelicalism on Social and Economic Thought, 1785–1865.* Oxford: Clarendon Press.

Hobson, J. (1905). The Ethics of Gambling. *International Journal of Ethics, 15*(2), 135–148.

Ho Chi Minh. (1960). *Selected Works,* vol. 3. Hanoi, Vietnam: Foreign Languages Publishing House.

Hollyer, J., Rosendorff, B. & Vreeland, J. (2018). *Information, Democracy, and Autocracy: Economic Transparency and Political (In)Stability.* Cambridge: Cambridge University Press.

Horton, A. V. M (1994). 'I Have Taken Steps to Ensure that the Utmost Economy Is Exercised': Government Finance in Brunei, 1906–1932. *Journal of the Malayan Branch of the Royal Asiatic Society, 76*(2), 47–92.

House of Commons. (1875). *India and China, The Opium Traffic,* vol. 225, cc. 571–622.

House of Commons. (1880). *Memorandum by C. U. Aitchison, Late Chief Commissioner of British Burma on the Consumption of Opium in that Province, Dated Rangoon, 30th April 1880, with Appended Papers.* Parliamentary Papers, *68*(643).

House of Commons. (1908). *The Opium Traffic*, vol. 188, cc. 339–380.

House of Lords. (1891). The Straits Settlements and Colonial Defense, vol. 356, cc.214–234.

Howell, P. (2009). *Geographies of Regulation: Policing Prostitution in Nineteenth Century Britain and the Empire*. Cambridge: Cambridge University Press.

Hsu, H. Bin. (2014). The Taste of Opium: Science, Monopoly, and the Japanese Colonization in Taiwan, 1895–1945. *Past & Present, 222,* 227–246.

Htun, M. (2003). *Sex and the State: Abortion, Divorce, and the Family under Latin American Dictatorships and Democracies*. Cambridge: Cambridge University Press.

Huber, J., & Shipan, C. (2002). *Deliberate Discretion? The Institutional Foundations of Bureaucratic Autonomy*. Cambridge: Cambridge University Press.

Huff, G., & Huff, G. (2015). Urban Growth and Change in 1940s Southeast Asia. *Economic History Review, 68*(2), 522–547.

Huff, G., & Majima, S. (2013). Financing Japan's World War II Occupation of Southeast Asia. *Journal of Economic History, 73*(4), 938–978.

Huff, G., & Majima, S., Eds. (2018). *World War II Singapore: The Chosabu Reports on Syonan*. Chicago: University of Chicago Press.

Hull, M. (2012). *Government of Paper: The Materiality of Bureaucracy in Urban Pakistan*. Berkeley: University of California Press.

Hunt, A. (1996). *Governance of the Consuming Passions: A History of Sumptuary Law*. London: Macmillan.

Hunt, N. (1991). Noise over Camouflaged Polygamy, Colonial Morality Taxation, and a Woman-Naming Crisis in Belgian Africa. *Journal of African History, 32*(3), 471–494.

Hunter, W., & Brill, R. (2016). 'Documents Please': Advances in Social Protection and Birth Certification in the Developing World. *World Politics, 68*(2), 191–228.

Hussin, I. (2016). *The Politics of Islamic Law*. Chicago: University of Chicago Press.

International Labor Organization. (1935). *Opium and Labor: Being a Report on a Documentary Investigation into the Extent and Effects of Opium Smoking among Workers*. London: P.S. King & Son.

Ireland, A. (1907). *The Province of Burma*, vol. 1. Boston: Houghton, Mifflin, & Co.

Isoart, P. (1961). *Le phénomène national viêtnamien de l'indépendance unitaire à l'indépendance fractionaée*. Paris: R. Pichon et Durand-Auzias.

Jennings, J. (1995). The Forgotten Plague: Opium and Narcotics in Korea under Japanese Rule. 1910–1945. *Modern Asian Studies, 29*(4), 795–815.

Jennings, J. (1997). *The Opium Empire: Japanese Imperialism and Drug Trafficking in Asia, 1895–1945*. Westport, CT: Greenwood Press.

Jennings, E. (2001). *Vichy in the Tropics: Pétain's National Revolution in Madagascar, Guadeloupe, and Indochina, 1940–1944*. Stanford: Stanford University Press.

Johnson, B. (1975). Righteousness before Revenue: The Forgotten Moral Crusade against the Indo-Chinese Opium Trade. *Journal of Drug Issues, 5*(4), 304–326.

Johnson, D. & Zimring, F. (2009). *The Next Frontier: National Development, Political Change, and the Death Penalty in Asia*. New York: Oxford University Press.

Johnson, N. (2006). Banking on the King: The Evolution of the Royal Revenue Farms in Old Regime France. *Journal of Economic History, 66,* 963–991.

Jordan, M. (1997). *The Invention of Sodomy in Christian Theology*. Chicago: University of Chicago Press.

Kaur, A. (2006). Indian Labour, Labour Standards, and Workers' Health in Burma and Malaya, 1900–1940. *Modern Asian Studies, 40,* 425–475.

Kelsall, R. (1955). *Higher Civil Servants in Britain: From 1870 to the Present Day.* London: Routledge and Paul.

Ken, W. L. (1965). *The Malayan Tin Industry to 1914.* Tucson: University of Arizon Press.

Kenji, T. (2012). Anti-Opium Movement, Chinese Nationalism and the Straits Chinese in the Early Twentieth Century. *Malaysian Journal of Chinese Studies, 1,* 85–100.

Kertzer, D., & Arel, D., eds. (2002). *Census and Identity: The Politics of Race, Identity, and Language in National Censuses.* Cambridge: Cambridge University Press.

Kesner, R. (1977). Builders of Empire: The Role of the Crown Agents in Imperial Development, 1880–1914. *The Journal of Imperial and Commonwealth History, 5*(3), 310–330.

Kheng, Cheah Boon. (1983). *Red Star Over Malaya: Resistance and Conflict during and after Japanese Occupation of Malaya, 1941–1946.* Singapore: Singapore University Press.

Kidd, J. (1879). Temperance and Its Boundaries. *Contemporary Review, 34,* 352–358.

Kim, D. (2013). The Story of the Tattooed Lady: Scandal and the Colonial State in British Burma. *Law and Social Inquiry, 37*(4), 969–990.

Kim, D. (2018). A Surreptitious Introduction: Opium Smuggling and Colonial State Formation in Late 19th Century Bengal and Burma. In R. Freedona & S. Reinhert (Eds.), *The Legitimacy of Power: New Perspectives on the History of Political Economy* (pp. 233–252). Basingstoke: Palgrave Macmillan.

King, D., & Lieberman, R. (2009). Ironies of State Building: A Comparative Perspective of the American State. *World Politics, 61*(3), 547–588.

Kingsberg, M. (2011). Abstinent Nation, Addicted Empire: Opium and Japan in the Meiji Period. *Social History of Alcohol and Drugs, 25,* 88–106.

Kingsberg, M. (2013). *Moral Nation: Modern Japan and Narcotics in Global History.* Berkeley: University of California Press.

Kirk-Greene, A. (2000). *Britain's Imperial Administrators, 1858–1966.* New York: St. Martin's Press.

Klein, J. (1994). *Un Lyonnais en Extrême-Orient: Ulysse Pila, 'vice-roi de l'Indochine' 1837–1909.* Lyon: Éditions lyonnaises d'art et d'histoire.

Knapman, G. (2016). *Race and British Colonialism in Southeast Asia, 1770–1870.* London: Routledge.

Korieh, C. (2003). Alcohol and Empire: 'Illicit' Gin Prohibition and Control in Colonial Eastern Nigeria. *African Economic History, 31,* 111–134.

Kozma, L. (2013). White Drugs in Interwar Egypt: Decadent Pleasures, Emaciated Fellahin, and the Campaign against Drugs. *Comparative Studies of South Asia, Africa and the Middle East, 33*(1), 89–101

Krasner, S. (1988). Sovereignty: An Institutionalist Perspective. *Comparative Political Studies, 22,* 66–94.

Kratoska, P. (1997). *The Japanese Occupation of Malaya: A Social and Economic History.* Honolulu: University of Hawai'i Press.

Kratoska, P., Ed. (2005). *Asian Labor in the Wartime Japanese Empire: Unknown Histories.* Armonk, NY: M. E. Sharpe.

Kratoska, P., Raben, R., & Nordhold, H., Eds. (2005). Locating Southeast Asia. In P. Kratoska, R. Raben, & H. Nordhold (Eds.), *Locating Southeast Asia: Geographies of Knowing and Politics of Space* (pp. 1–19). Singapore: National University of Singapore Press.

Kwass, M. (2013a). The First War on Drugs: Tobacco Trafficking, Criminality, and the Fiscal State in Eighteenth Century France. In R. Bridenthal (Ed.), *The Hidden History of Crime, Corruption, and States*. Oxford: Oxford University Press.

Kwass, M. (2013b). Court Capitalism, Illicit Markets, and Political Legitimacy in Eighteenth Century France: The Example of the Salt and Tobacco Monopolies. In D. Coffman, A. Leonard, & L. O'Neal (Eds.), *Questioning Credible Commitment: Perspectives on the Rise of Financial Capitalism*. Cambridge: Cambridge University Press.

Kwass, M. (2014). *Contraband: Louis Mandrin and the Making of a Global Underground*. Cambridge, MA: Harvard University Press.

Lagana, M. (1990). *Le Parti colonial français: éléments d'histoire*. Sillery, Québec: Presses de l'Université du Québec.

La Motte, E. (1920). *The Opium Monopoly*. New York: Macmillan.

Lange, M. (2009). *Lineages of Despotism and Development: British Colonialism and State Power*. Chicago: University of Chicago Press.

LaPlace, P. S. (1912). Sur la suppression de la loterie. *Œuvres complètes de Laplace*, 14. Paris: Gauthiers-Villars.

LaPlace, P. S. (2009). [1825]. *Essai philosophique sur les probabilitiés*. Cambridge: Cambridge University Press.

Lara-Millán, A. (2017). States and a Series of People Exchanges. In K. Morgan & A. Orloff (Eds.), *The Many Hands of the State: Theorizing Political Authority and Social Control* (pp. 81–102). Cambridge: Cambridge University Press.

League of Nations. (1930). *Commission of Enquiry into the Control of Opium-Smoking in the Far East*, Report to the Council, vols. 1 and 2. Geneva: League of Nations.

Lecoq, J. (1913). Un monopole scandaleux. *Le Petit Journal*, 51(18) (April 24, 1913), 1–6.

Lee, M. N. M. (2015). *Dreams of the Hmong Kingdom: The Quest for Legitimation in French Indochina, 1850–1960*. Madison WI: University of Wisconsin Press.

Lee, P. (1978). *Chinese Society in Nineteenth Century Singapore*. Oxford: Oxford University Press.

Lee, Y. K. (1975). Singapore's Pauper and Tan Tock Seng Hospitals. *Journal of the Malaysian Branch of the Royal Asiatic Society*, 49(2), 79–111.

Le Failler, P. (1993). *Le mouvement international anti-opium et l'Indochine, 1906–1940*. Université de Provence, Aix-Marseille I.

Le Failler, P. (1995). Le "coût social" de l'opium au Vietnam: la problématique des drogues dans le philtre de l'histoire. *Journal Asiatique*, 283, 239–264.

Le Failler, P. (2001). *Monopole et prohibition de l'opium en Indochine: le pilori des chimères*. Paris: L'Harmattan.

LeGrain, P. (1925). *Médecine sociale, Traité de Pathologie Médicale et de Thérapeutique appliquée*. Paris: Maloine.

Lemire, C. (1869). Coup d'oeil sur la Cochinchine française et le Cambodge. *Annales des voyages, de la géographie, de l'histoire et de l'archéologie*.

Leng, L. W. (2002). The Colonial State and Business: The Policy Environment in Malaya in the Inter-War Years. *Journal of Southeast Asian Studies*, 33(2), 243–256.

Lentz, C. (2017). Cultivating Subjects: Opium and Rule in Post-colonial Vietnam. *Modern Asian Studies*, 51(4), 1–40.

Lessard, M. (2009). "Cet ignoble trafic": The Kidnapping and Sale of Vietnamese Women and Children in French Colonial Indochina, 1873–1935. *French Colonial History*, 10(1), 1–34.

Levi, M. (1988). *Of Rule and Revenue*. Berkeley: University of California Press.

Levine, P. (1998). Modernity, Medicine, and Colonialism: The Contagious Diseases Ordinances in Hong Kong and the Straits Settlements. *Positions*, 6(3), 675–705.

Levine, P. (2003). *Prostitution, Race, and Politics: Policing Venereal Disease in the British Empire*. New York: Routledge.

Li, K. (2016). Partisan to Sovereign: The Making of the Bình Xuyên in Southern Vietnam, 1945–1948. *Modern Asian Studies*, 11(3–4), 140–187.

Li, Y. (2016). Governing the Chinese in Multi-Ethnic Colonial Burma between the 1890s and 1920s. *South East Asia Research*, 24(1), 135–154.

Lim, Boon Keng (1906). The Opium Question. *Straits Chinese Magazine*, 10, 149–151.

Lintner, B. (1999). *Burma in Revolt: Opium and Insurgency since 1948*. Chiang Mai, Thailand: Silkworm Books.

Lipset, S. (1959). Some Social Requisites of Democracy: Economic Development and Political Legitimacy. *American Political Science Review*, 53(1), 69–105.

Lipsky, M. (1980). *Street-Level Bureaucracy: The Dilemmas of the Individual in Public Service*. New York: Russell Sage Foundation.

Little, R. (1848). On the Habitual Use of Opium in Singapore. *Journal of the Indian Archipelago and Eastern Asia*, 2(1), 1–79.

Lodwick, K. (1996). *Crusaders against Opium: Protestant Missionaries in China, 1874–1917*. Lexington: University of Kentucky Press.

Logan, J. (1855). Notices of Singapore. *Journal of the Indian Archipelago and Eastern India*, 9.

Logre, B. J. (1924). *Toxicomanies*. Paris: Delamain, Boutelleau, et Cie.

Loos, T. (2008). A History of Sex and the State in Southeast Asia: Class, Intimacy, and Invisibility. *Citizenship Studies*, 12(1), 27–43.

Lorrin, A. (2004). *Paul Doumer, gouverneur général de l'Indochine (1897–1902): l'e Templin colonial*. Paris: L'Harmattan.

Loveman, M. (2005). The Modern State and the Primitive Accumulation of Symbolic Power. *American Journal of Sociology*, 110(6), 1651–1683.

Loveman, M. (2014). *National Colors: Racial Classification and the State in Latin America*. Oxford: Oxford University Press.

Lowell, A. (2011). *Colonial Civil Service: The Selection and Training of Colonial Offices in England, Holland, and France*. New York: Macmillan.

Lowes, P. (1981). *The Genesis of International Narcotics Control*. New York: Arno Press.

Lucy, A. (1861). *Souvenirs de voyage: lettres intimes sur la campagne de Chine en 1860*. Marseille: J. Barile.

Ludden, D. (1993). Orientalist Empiricism: Transformations of Colonial Knowledge. In C. Breckenridge (Ed.), *Orientalism and the Postcolonial Predicament: Perspectives on South Asia*. Philadelphia: University of Pennsylvania Press.

Lugard, F. (1922). *The Dual Mandate in British Tropical Africa Public Domain in the United States*. London: Blackwood and Sons.

Mackay, D. (2005). *Eastern Customs: The Customs Service in British Malaya and the Opium Trade*. Bristol: Radcliffe Press.

Mahoney, J. (2010). *Colonialsm and Postcolonial Development: Spanish America in Comparative Perspective*. Cambridge: Cambridge University Press

Mahoney, J., & Rueschemeyer, D. (2003). *Comparative Historical Analysis in the Social Sciences*. Cambridge: Cambridge University Press.

Mamdani, M. (1996). *Citizen and Subject: Contemporary Africa and the Legacy of Late Colonialism*. Princeton, NJ: Princeton University Press.

Mamdani, M. (2012). *Define and Rule: Native as Political Identity*. Cambridge, MA: Harvard University Press.

Mantena, K. (2010). *Alibis of Empire: Henry Maine and the Ends of Liberal Imperialism*. Princeton, NJ: Princeton University Press.

Markovits, C. (2009). The Political Economy of Opium Smuggling in Early Nineteenth Century India: Leakage or Resistance? *Modern Asian Studies, 43*, 89–111.

Markovits, C. (2017). The Indian Opium Economy and the British Empire in the Company Period: Some Additional Reflections Around an Essay by David Washbrook. *Modern Asian Studies, 51*(2), 375–398.

Marr, D. (2013). *Vietnam: War, State, and Revolution (1945–1946)*. Berkeley: University of California Press.

Martin, I., Mehotra, A., & Prasad, M. (2009). *The New Fiscal Sociology: Taxation in Comparative and Historical Perspective*. Cambridge: Cambridge University Press.

Marx, K. (2007) [1858]. *Dispatches for the New York Tribune: Selected Journalism of Karl Marx*. New York: Penguin Books.

Mason, P. (1954). *The Men Who Ruled India*. New York: St. Martin's Press.

Maspero, G. (1929). *Un empire colonial français, l'Indochine*. Bruxelles: Éditions G. Van Oest.

Mathew, J. (2016). *Margins of the Market: Trafficking and Capitalism across the Arabian Sea*. Berkeley: University of California Press.

Mattingly, D. (2017). Colonial Legacies and State Institutions in China: Evidene from a Natural Experiment. *Comparative Political Studies, 50*(4), 434–463.

Maule, R. (1991). The Opium Question in the Federated Shan States, 1931–36: British Policy Discussions and Scandal. *Journal of Southeast Asian Studies, 23*(1), 14–36.

Maule, R. (2002). British Policy Discussions on the Opium Question the Federated Shan States, 1937–1948. *Journal of Southeast Asian Studies, 33*(2), 203–224.

McAlister, T. (1972). Mountain Minorities and the Viet Minh: A Key to the Indochina War. In P. Kunstadter (Ed.), *Southeast Asian Tribes, Minorities, and Nations* (pp. 771–844). Princeton, NJ: Princeton University Press.

McAllister, W. (2000). *Drug Diplomacy in the Twentieth Century: An International History*. London: Routledge.

McAllister, W. (2007). 'Wolf by the Ears': The Dilemmas of Imperial Policymaking in the Twentieth Century. In J. Mills & P. Barton (Eds.), *Drugs and Empires: Essays in Modern Imperialism and Intoxication, c. 1500–1930*. Basingstoke: Palgrave Macmillan.

McBride, K. (2015). *Mr. Mothercountry: The Man Who Made the Rule of Law*. Oxford: Oxford University Press.

McClintock, A. (1995). *Imperial Leather: Race, Gender, and Sexuality in the Colonial Contest*. New York: Routledge.

McCoy, A. (1972). *The Politics of Heroin in Southeast Asia*. New York: Harper & Row.

McCoy, A., Ed. (1980). *Southeast Asia under Japanese Occupation*. New Haven, CT: Yale University Southeast Asian Studies, Monograph Series, No. 22.

McCoy, A. (2000). From Free Trade to Prohibition: A Critical History of the Modern Asian Opium Trade. *Fordham Urban Law Journal, 28*(1), 307–349.

McGirr, L. (2015). *The War on Alcohol: Prohibition and the Rise of the American State*. New York: W. W. Norton.

McKeown, A. (2010). Chinese Emigration in Global Context, 1850–1940. *Journal of Global History, 5*(1), 95–124.

McNamara, K. (2015). *The Politics of Everyday Europe: Constructing Authority in the European Union*. Oxford: Oxford University Press.

Meehan, P. (2011). Drugs, Insurgency and State Building in Burma: Why the Drugs Trade is Central to Burma's Changing Political Order. *Journal of Southeast Asian Studies, 42*(3), 376–404.

Mehta, U. (1999). *Liberalism and Empire: A Study in Nineteenth Century British Liberal Thought*. Chicago: University of Chicago Press.

Metcalf, T. (2004). *Ideologies of the Raj*. Cambridge: Cambridge University Press.

Meyer, K. & Parssinen, T. (2002). *Webs of Smoke: Smugglers, Warlords, Spies, and the History of the International Drug Trade*. Oxford: Rowman and Littlefield.

Migdal, J. (1988). *Strong Societies and Weak States: State–Society Relations and State Capabilities in the Third World*. Princeton, NJ: Princeton University Press.

Mill, J. S. (1909)[1848]. *Principles of Political Economy with Some of Their Applications to Social Philosophy*, edited by W. Ashley. London: Longmans, Green & Co.

Mills, J. (2003). *Cannabis Britannica: Empire, Trade and Prohibition*. Oxford: Oxford University Press.

Mills, J. (2005). Cannabis in the Commons: Colonial Networks, Missionary Politics and the Origins of the Indian Hemp Drugs Commission 1893–4. *Journal of Colonialism and Colonial History, 6*(1).

Mills, J. (2007). Drugs, Consumption, and Supply in Asia: The Case of Cocaine in Colonial India, c. 1900–c. 1930. *Journal of Asian Studies, 66*(2), 345–362.

Mills, J. (2014). Cocaine and the British Empire: The Drug and the Diplomats at The Hague Opium Conference, 1911–12. *The Journal of Imperial and Commonwealth History, 42*(3), 400–419.

Mills, J., & Barton, P., Eds. (2007). *Drugs and Empires: Essays in Modern Imperialism and Intoxication, c. 1500–1930*. Basingstoke: Palgrave Macmillan.

Milner, M. (2002). *L'imaginaire des drogues: de Thomas de Quincey à Henri Michaux*. Paris: Éditions Gallimard.

Miners, N. (1983). The Hong Kong Government Opium Monopoly, 1914–1941. *The Journal of Imperial and Commonwealth History, 11*, 275–299.

Mitchell, T. (1991). The Limits of the State: Beyond Statist Approaches and Their Critics. *American Political Science Review, 85*(1), 77–96.

Moorehead, H. (1947). Narcotics Control under the UN. *Far Eastern Survey, 16*(5), 55–58.

Morgan, K., & Orloff, A. (2017). *The Many Hands of the State: Theorizing Political Authority and Social Control*. Cambridge: Cambridge University Press.

Moura, J. (2015) [1883]. *Le Royaume du Cambodge*, vol. 1. Cambridge: Cambridge University Press.

Musto, D. (1987). *The American Disease: Origins of Narcotic Control.* Oxford: Oxford University Press.

Nadelmann, E. (1990). Global Prohibition Regimes: The Evolution of Norms in International. *International Organization, 44*(4), 479–526.

Nankoe, H., Gerlus, J.-C., & Murray, M. (1993). The Origins of the Opium Trade and the Opium Regie in Colonial Indochina. In H. Dick & J. Butcher (Eds.), *The Rise and Fall of Opium Farming* (pp. 182–195). London: St. Martin's Press.

Naseemullah, A., & Staniland, P. (2016). Indirect Rule and Varieties of Governance. *Governance, 29*(1), 12–30.

Nettl, J. P. (1968). The State as a Conceptual Variable. *World Politics, 20*(4), 559–592.

Newman, R. K. (1989). India and the Anglo-Chinese Opium Agreements, 1907–1914. *Modern Asian Studies, 23*(3), 525–560.

Ng, S. (1961). The Chinese Protectorate in Singapore 1877–1900. *Journal of Southeast Asian History, 2*(1), 76–99.

Nguyen-Marshall, V. (2008). *In Search of Moral Authority: The Discourse on Poverty, Poor Relief, and Charity in French Colonial Vietnam.* New York: Peter Lang.

Noriyuki, O. (2014). Discovery of "Outsiders": The Expulsion of Undesirable Chinese and Urban Governance of Colonial Rangoon, Burma, c. 1900–1920. *The Journal of Sophia Asian Studies, 32*, 80–96.

Orwell, G. (1931). The Hanging. *The Adelphi.*

Orwell, G. (1981). Shooting an Elephant. In *George Orwell: A Collection of Essays* (pp. 148–155). New York: Houghton Mifflin Harcourt.

Orwell, G. (1974). [1934]. *Burmese Days.* New York: Houghton Mifflin Harcourt.

Owen, D. (1934). *British Opium Policy in China and India.* New Haven, CT: Yale University Press.

Padwa, H. (2008). Anti-Narcotic Nationalism in Britain and France, 1866–1916. *Social History of Alcohol and Drugs, 22*(2), 168–189.

Padwa, H. (2012). *Social Poison: The Culture and Politics of Opiate Control in Britain and France, 1821–1926.* Baltimore: Johns Hopkins University Press.

Pannier, J. (1910). Contre l'opium. *La revue du Christianisme social, 23*(10), 704–718.

Pannier, J. (1911). *Mémoire sur la question de l'opium telle qu'elle se présente en France et dans les colonies françaises.* Cahors: Imprimerie de A. Coueslant.

Parssinen, T. (1983). *Secret Passions, Secret Remedies: Narcotic Drugs in British Society, 1820–1930.* Manchester: Manchester University Press.

Paulès, X. (2008). Les institutions de désintoxication pour fumeurs d'opium à Canton entre 1839 et 1952. *Revue Historique, 647*(3), 627–656.

Paulès, X. (2010). *Histoire d'une drogue en sursis: l'opium à Canton, 1906–1936.* Paris: Éditions de l'EHESS.

Peletz, M. (2009). *Gender Pluralism: Southeast Asia since Early Modern Times.* London: Routledge.

Pepinsky. T., Pierskalla, J., & Sacks, A. (2017). Bureaucracy and Service Delivery. *Annual Review of Political Science, 20*, 249–269.

Persell, S. (1983). *The French Colonial Lobby, 1889–1938.* Stanford, CA: Hoover Institution Press.

Peters, E. (2004). Alcohol and Politics in French Vietnam. *Social History of Alcohol and Drugs, 19*, 94–110.

Peyrouton, B-M. (1913). *Les Monopoles en Indochine*. Paris: Émile LaRose.

Phung, Vu Trong. (1937). *Luc Xi: Prostitution and Venereal Disease in Colonia Hanoi*, translated by S. Malarney. Honolulu: University of Hawai'i Press.

Pick, D. (1993). *Faces of Degeneration: A European Disorder, c. 1848–1918*. Cambridge: Cambridge University Press.

Pila, J. (1925). *Le trafic des stupéfiants et la Société des Nations*. Paris: Sirey.

Pitkin, H. (1987). Rethinking Reification. *Theory and Society, 16*(2), 263–293.

Pitts, J. (2005). *A Turn to Empire: The Rise of Imperial Liberalism in Britain and France*. Princeton, NJ: Princeton University Press.

Ponko, V. (1966). Economic Management in a Free-Trade Empire: The Work of the Crown Agents for the Colonies in the Nineteenth and Early Twentieth Centuries. *The Journal of Economic History, 26*(3), 363–377.

Porter, A. (2004). *Religion vs. Empire? British Protestant Missionaries and Overseas Expansion, 1700–1914*. Manchester: Manchester University Press

Pottier, P. (2005). GCMA/GMI: A French Experience in Counterinsurgency during the French Indochina War. *Small Wars & Insurgencies, 16*(2), 125–146.

Prakash, O. (1988). Opium Monopoly in India and Indonesia in the Eighteenth Century. *Itinerario, 12*(1), 73–90.

Pressman, J., & Widalvsky, A. (1973). *Implementation: How Great Expectations in Washington are Dashed in Oakland*. Berkeley: University of California Press.

Prior, K. (2004). Smeaton, Donald MacKenzie (1846–1910). In H. Matthew & B. Harrison (Eds.), *Oxford Dictionary of National Biography*. http://www.oxforddnb.com/ view/article/36124 (accessed November 2, 2018).

Proschan, F. (2002). 'Syphilis, Opiomania, and Pederasty': Colonial Constructions of Vietnamese (and French) Social Diseases. *Journal of the History of Sexuality, 11*(4), 610–636.

Prudhomme, C. (2007). Cinquante ans d'histoire des missions catholiques en France: l'age universitaire. *Histoire et missions chrétiennes, 1*, 11–30.

Purcell, V. (1948). *The Chinese in Malaya*. Oxford: Oxford University Press.

Rafael, V. (1993). *Contracting Colonialism: Translation and Christian Conversion in Tagalog Society Under Early Spanish Rule*. Durham, NC: Duke University Press

Raffles, S. (1823). *Regulations for the Port of Singapore: 1823*. London: Kingsbury, Parbury, and Allen.

Raman, B. (2012). *Document Raj: Writing and Scribes in Early Colonial South India*. Chicago: University of Chicago Press.

Rapin, A. J. (2000). L'introuvable promotion culturale du pavot à opium au Tonkin et au Laos. *Péninsule, 41*(2), 139–166.

Rapin, A. J. (2007). *Opium et société dans le Laos précolonial et colonial*. Paris: L'Harmattan.

Rapin, A. J. (2013). *Du madat au chandu: histoire de la fumée d'opium*. Paris: L'Harmattan.

Rapin, A. J. (2014). The 1925 Opium Purchasing Campaign in Laos: The Anatomy of a Colonial Scandal. Working Paper, Université de Lausanne.

Reid, A. (1996). *Sojourners and Settlers: Histories of Southeast Asia and the Chinese*. Honolulu: University of Hawai'i Press.

Retaillaud-Bajac, E. (2009). *Les paradis perdus: drogues et usagers de drogues dans la France de l'entre-deux-guerres*. Rennes: Presses universitaires de Rennes.

Reyes, R., & Clarence-Smith, W. (2012). *Sexual Diversity in Asia, 600–1950*. London: Routledge.

Richards, J. (1981). The Indian Empire and Peasant Production of Opium in the Nineteenth Century. *Modern Asian Studies, 15*(1), 59–82.

Richards, J. (2002a). The Opium Industry in British India. *Indian Economic & Social History Review, 39*(2–3), 149–180.

Richards, J. (2002b). Opium and the British Indian Empire: The Royal Opium Commission of 1895. *Modern Asian Studies, 36*(2), 375–220.

Rimner, S. (2018). *Opium's Long Shadow: From Asian Revolt to Global Drug Control*. Cambridge, MA: Harvard University Press.

Ritchell, J. (2006). *Disease and Demography in Colonial Burma*. Copenhagen: Nordic Institute of Asian Studies.

Robins, P. (2015). *Middle East Drugs Bazaar: Production, Prevention, and Consumption*. Oxford: Oxford University Press.

Robson, W. (1956). *The Civil Service in Britain and France*. London: Macmillan.

Roth, M. (2002). Victorian Highs: Detection, Drugs, and Empire. In J. Brodie & M. Redfield (Eds.), *High Anxieties: Cultural Studies in Addiction* (pp. 85–94). Berkeley: University of California Press.

Rothschild, E. (2012). *The Inner Life of Empires: An Eighteenth Century History*. Princeton, NJ: Princeton University Press.

Rowntree, J. (1905). *The Imperial Drug Trade*. London: Methuen & Co.

Rudolph, L., &Rudolph, S. (1979). Authority and Power in Bureaucratic and Patrimonial Administration: A Revisionist Interpretation of Weber on Bureaucracy. *World Politics, 31*(2), 195–227.

Rush, J. (1985). Opium in Java: A Sinister Friend. *The Journal of Asian Studies, 44*(3), 549–560.

Rush, J. (1990). *Opium to Java: Revenue Farming and Chinese Enterprise in Colonial Indonesia, 1860–1910*. Ithaca, NY: Cornell University Press.

Saada, E. (2011). *Empire's Children: Race, Filiation, and Citizenship in the French Colonies*. Chicago: University of Chicago Press.

Sager, P. (2014). *Indigenizing Indochina: Race, Class, and the French Colonial Employer-State, 1848–1945*. PhD thesis, New York University.

Sager, P. (2016). A Nation of Functionaries, A Colony of Functionaries: The Antibureaucratic Consensus in France and Indochina, 1848–1912. *French Historical Studies, 39*(1), 145–182.

Saha, J. (2013). Colonization, Criminalization and Complicity: Policing Gambling in Burma c 1880–1920. *South East Asia Research, 21*(4), 655–672.

Sambuc, H. (1909). Notice sur la situation des Chinois en Indochine. *Revue indochinoise, 11,* 1063–1100.

Sangermano, V. (1833). [1969]. *A Description of the Burmese Empire*. New York: Augustus M. Kelley.

Sasges, G. (2012). State, Enterprise and the Alcohol Monopoly in Colonial Vietnam. *Journal of Southeast Asian Studies, 43*(1), 133–157.

Sasges, G. (2015). Scaling the Commanding Heights: The Colonial Conglomorates and the Changing Political Economy of French Indochina. *Modern Asian Studies, 49*(5), 1485–1525.

Sasges, G. (2017). *Imperial Intoxication: Alcohol and the Making of Colonial Indochina.* Honolulu: University of Hawai'i Press.

Schayegh, C. (2011). The Many Worlds of Abud Yasin; or, What Narcotics Trafficking in the Interwar Middle East Can Tell Us about Territorialization. *American Historical Review, 116,* 273–306.

Scheltema, J. F. (1907). The Opium Trade in the Dutch East Indies. *American Journal of Sociology, 13*(1), 79–112.

Scheltema, J. F. (1910). The Opium Question. *American Journal of Sociology, 16*(2), 213–235.

Scott, C. (1896). The Malayan Words in English. *Journal of the American Oriental Society, 17,* 93–144.

Scott, D. (2004). *Conscripts of Modernity: The Tragedy of Colonial Enlightenment.* Durham, NC: Duke University Press.

Scott, J. C. (1969). Corruption, Machine Politics, and Political Change. *American Political Science Review, 63*(4), 1142–1158.

Scott, J. C. (1990). *Domination and the Arts of Resistance: Hidden Transcripts.* New Haven, CT: Yale University Press.

Scott, J. C. (1998). *Seeing Like a State.* New Haven, CT: Yale University Press.

Scott, J. C. (2009). *The Art of Not Being Governed: An Anarchist History of Upland Southeast Asia.* New Haven, CT: Yale University Press.

Scott, J. G. (1921). *Burma: A Handbook of Practical Information.* London: Daniel O'Connor.

Sewell, W. (1996). Historical Events as Transformations of Structures: Inventing Revolution at the Bastille. *Theory and Society, 25*(6), 841–881.

Shklar, J. (1984). *Ordinary Vices.* Cambridge, MA: Harvard University Press.

Sibeud, E. (2002). *Une science impériale pour l'Afrique? La construction des savoirs africanistes en France 1878–1930.* Paris: Éditions de l'EHSS.

Sidel, J. (2008). Social Origins of Dictatorship and Democracy Revisited: Colonial State and Chinese Immigrant in the Making of Modern Southeast Asia. *Comparative Politics, 40*(2), 127–147.

Siegelman, P. (1962). *Colonial Development and the Chettyar: A Study in the Ecology of Modern Burma, 1850–1941.* PhD thesis, University of Minnesota.

Singaravélou, P. (2011). *Professer l'Empire: les "sciences coloniales" en France sous la IIIe République.* Paris: Publications de la Sorbonne.

Skocpol, T., & Somers, M. (1980). The Uses of Comparative History in Macro-social Theory. *Comparative Studies in Society and History, 22,* 174–197.

Slater, D. (2010). *Ordering Power: Contentious Politics and Authoritarian Leviathans in Southeast Asia.* Cambridge: Cambridge University Press.

Slater, D., & Ziblatt, D. (2013). The Enduring Indispensibility of the Controlled Comparison. *Comparative Political Studies, 46*(10), 1301–1327.

Smail, J. (1961). On the Possibility of an Autonomous History of Modern Southeast Asia. *Journal of Southeast Asian History, 2*(2), 72–102.

Smith, G. (1897). *Twelve Indian Statesmen.* London: John Murray.

Smith, R. (1985). Rule-by-Records and Rule-by-Reports: Complementary Aspects of the British Imperial Rule of Law. *Contributions to Indian Sociology, 19*(1), 153–176.

Society for the Suppression of the Opium Trade. (1891). Opium in Burma. LSE Selected Pamphlets.

Soifer, H., & vom Hau, M. (2008). Unpacking the Strength of the State: The Utility of State Infrastructural Power. *Studies in Comparative International Development, 43*, 219–230.

Souza, G. (2009). Opium and the Company: Maritime Trade and Imperial Finances on Java, 1684–1796. *Modern Asian Studies, 43*(1), 113–133.

Spence, J. (1975). Opium smoking in Ch'ing China. In F. Wakeman, Jr. & C. Grant (Eds.), *Conflict and Control in Late Imperial China* (pp. 143–173). Berkeley: University of California Press.

Spires, J. (1988). *Running Amok: A Historical Inquiry.* Athens: Ohio University Press.Stein, S. (1985). *International Diplomacy, State Administrators and Narcotics Control.* Aldershot: Gower.

Steinmetz, G. (1999). Introduction: Culture and the State. In *State/Culture: State Formation After the Cultural Turn* (pp. 1–49). Ithaca, NY: Cornell University Press.

Steinmetz, G. (2007). *The Devil's Handwriting: Precoloniality and the German Colonial State in Qingdao, Samoa, and Southwest Africa.* Chicago: University of Chicago Press.

Steinmetz, G. (2008). The Colonial State as a Social Field. *American Sociological Review, 73*(4), 589–612.

Stephen, J. C. (1993) [1873]. *Liberty, Equality, Fraternity,* edited by Stuart Warner. Indianapolis: Liberty Fund.

Stigler, S. (2003). Casanova, "Bonaparte" and the Loterie de France. *Journal de la société française de statistique, 144*(1–2), 5–34.

Stoler, A. (1989). Rethinking Colonial Categories: European Communities and the Boundaries of Rule. *Comparative Studies in Society and History, 31*(1), 134–161.

Stoler, A. (1995). *Race and the Education of Desire: Foucault's History of Sexuality and the Colonial Order of Things.* Durham, NC: Duke University Press.

Stoler, A. (2009). *Along the Archival Grain: Epistemic Anxieties and Colonial Common Sense.* Princeton, NJ: Princeton University Press.

Stoler, A. (2010). *Carnal Knowledge and Imperial. Power: Race and the Intimate in Colonial Rule.* Berkeley and Los Angeles: University of California Press.

Stuart-Fox, M. (1997). *A History of Laos.* Cambridge: Cambridge University Press.

Stubbs, R. (1989). *Hearts and Minds in Guerilla Warfare: The Malayan Emergency, 1948–1960.* Oxford: Oxford University Press.

Suignard, J. (1931). *Les services civils de l'indochine.* Paris: Larose.

Sunderland, D. (2007). *Managing British Colonial and Post-colonial Development: The Crown Agents, 1914–74.* Martlesham, Suffolk: Boydell & Brewer.

Sunshine, J., & Tyler, T. (2003). Trust and Legitimacy: Policing in the USA and Europe. *European Journal of Criminology, 8*(4), 254–266.

Svensson, J. (2005). Eight Questions about Corruption. *Journal of Economic Perspectives, 19*(3), 19–42.

Swettenham, F. (1903). *Malay Sketches,* 3rd ed. London: John Lane.

Tagliacozzo, E. (2002). Smuggling in Southeast Asia: History and its Contemporary Vectors in an Unbound Region. *Critical Asian Studies, 34*(2), 193–220.

Tagliacozzo, E. (2005). *Secret Trades, Porous Borders: Smuggling and States along a Southeast Asian Frontier, 1865–1915.* New Haven, CT: Yale University Press.

Tagliacozzo, E., & Chang, W.C., Eds. (2011). *Chinese Circulations: Capital, Commodities, and Networks in Southeast Asia*. Durham, NC: Duke University Press.

Tagliacozzo, E., Perdue, P., & Siu, H., Eds. (2015). *Asia Inside Out: Changing Times*. Cambridge, MA: Harvard University Press.

Tarling, N. (2001). *A Sudden Rampage: The Japanese Occupation of Southeast Asia, 1941–1945*. Honolulu: University of Hawai'i Press.

Taylor, A. (1969). *American Diplomacy and the Narcotics Traffic, 1900–1939*. Durham, NC: Duke University Press.

Taylor, R. (2015). *General Ne Win: A Political Biography*. Singapore: Institute of Southeast Asian Studies.

Taylor, T. (1910). *How the Opium Question Now Stands*. London: Society for the Suppression of the Opium Trade.

Telles, E., & Paschel, T. (2014). Who Is Black, White or Mixed Race? How Skin Color, Status and Nation Shape Racial Classification in Latin America. *American Journal of Sociology, 120*(3), 864–907.

Thai, P. (2018). *China's War on Smuggling: Law, Economic Life, and the Making of the Modern State, 1842–1965*. New York: Columbia University Press.

Thai-Yunnan Project. (1992). Report of the Preliminary Joint Survey Team on Opium Production and Consumption in the Union of Burma. *Thai-Yunnan Project Newsletter, 18*, 9–17.

Thelen, K., & Mahoney, J., Eds. (2010). *Explaining Institutional Change: Ambiguity, Agency, and Power*. New York: Cambridge University Press.

Thomas, M. (2001). Free France, the British government, and the Future of French Indo-china, 1940–1945. In P. Kratoska (Ed.), *South East Asia, Colonial History: Independence through Revolutionary War* (pp. 223–251). Oxford: Taylor & Francis.

Thomas, M. (2011). *The French Colonial Mind*. Lincoln: University of Nebraska Press.

Thomson, V. (1937). *French-Indochina*. New York: Macmillan & Co.

Thomson, J. (1996). *Mercenaries, Pirates, and Sovereigns: State-Building and Extraterritorial Violence in Early Modern Europe*. Princeton, NJ: Princeton University Press.

Tilley, H. (2011). *Africa as a Living Laboratory: Empire, Development, and the Problem of Scientific Knowledge, 1870–1950*. Chicago: University of Chicago Press.

Tilly, C. (1985). War Making and State Making as Organized Crime. In P. Evans, D. Rueschemeyer, & T. Skocpol (Eds.), *Bringing the State Back In* (pp. 169–187). Cambridge: Cambridge University Press.

Tilly, C. (1992). *Coercion, Capital, and European States, AD 990–1992*. Oxford: Blackwell.

Torpey, J. (1999). *The Invention of the Passport: Surveillance, Citizenship, and the State*. Cambridge: Cambridge University Press.

Tracol-Huynh, I. (2010). Between Stigmatisation and Regulation: Prostitution in Colonial Northern Vietnam. *Culture, Health & Sexuality, 12*, 73–87.

Tran, K. M. (2017). *Vice and Statecraft: The Case of Vietnam*. MA thesis, Georgetown University.

Trevelyan, G. M. (1942). *English Social History, A Survey of Six Centuries: Chaucer to Queen Victoria*. London: Longman, Greens and Company.

Trinquier, R. (1961). *La Guerre moderne*. Paris: Éditions de la Table ronde.

Trocki, C. (1990). *Opium and Empire: Chinese Society in Colonial Singapore, 1800–1910*. Ithaca, NY: Cornell University Press.

Trocki, C. (1993). The Collapse of Singapore's Great Syndicate. In H. Dick & J. Butcher (Eds.), *The Rise and Fall of Opium Farming* (pp. 166–181). London: St. Martin's Press.

Trocki, C. (1999). *Opium, Empire, and the Global Political Economy: A Study of the Asian Opium Trade.* London and New York: Routledge.

Trocki, C. (2002). Opium and the Beginnings of Chinese Capitalism in Southeast Asia. *Journal of Southeast Asian Studies, 33*(2), 297–314.

Trocki, C. (2004). Internationalization of Chinese Revenue Farming Networks. In N. Cooke & T. Li (Eds.), *Water Frontier: Commerce and the Chinese in the Lower Mekong Region, 1750–1880* (pp. 159–174). Lanham, MD: Rowman and Littlefield.

Trocki, C. (2005). A Drug on the Market: Opium and the Chinese in Southeast Asia, 1750–1880. *Journal of Chinese Overseas, 1*(2), 147–168.

Tuck, P. (1987). *French Catholic Missionaries and the Politics of Imperialism in Vietnam, 1857–1914.* Liverpool: Liverpool University Press.

Turbiaux, M. (2009). Un psychiatre-psychanalyste à l'ombre des épées. *Bulletin de psychologie, 6*(504), 553–568.

Turnbull, M. (1989). *A History of Singapore, 1819–1988,* 2nd ed. Oxford: Oxford University Press.

Turner, A. (2014). *Saving Buddhism: The Impermanence of Religion in Colonial Burma.* Honolulu: University of Hawai'i Press.

Tyrell, I. (2008). The regulation of alcohol and other drugs in a colonial context: United States policy towards the Philippines, c. 1898–1910. *Contemporary Drug Problems, 35,* 540–571.

Tyrell, I. (2010). *Reforming the World: The Creation of America's Moral Empire.* Princeton, NJ: Princeton University Press.

United States. (1905). *Report of the Committee Appointed by the Philippine Commission to Investigate the Use of Opium and the Traffic There in and the Rules, Ordinances, and Laws Regulating Such Use and Traffic in Japan, Formosa, Shanghai, Hong Kong, Saigon, Singapore, Burmah, Java, and the Philippine Islands.* Washington, DC: Government Printing Office.

Victoria, F. (2015). 'The Most Humane of Any that Could be Adopted': The Philippine Opium Committee Report and the Imagining of the Opium Consumer's World in the Colonial Philippines, 1903–1905 (pp. 88–156). In P. Reyes (Ed.), *Towards a Filipino History: A Festschrift for Zeus A. Salazar.* Quezon City: Bahay Saliksikan ng Kasaysayan (BAKAS).

Wah, Y. K. (1981). The Guillemard-Maxwell Power Struggle, 1921–1925. *Journal of the Malaysian Branch of the Royal Asiatic Society, 54*(1), 48–64.

Wahid, A. (2013). *From Revenue Farming to State Monopoly: The Political Economy of Taxation in Colonial Indonesia, Java c. 1816–1942,* PhD thesis, Universiteit Utrecht.

Wakabayashi, B. (2000). From Peril to Profit: Opium in the Late-Edo to Meiji Eyes, In T. Brook & B. Wakabayashi (Eds.), *Opium Regimes: China, Britain, and Japan, 1839–1952* (pp. 55–77). Berkeley: University of California Press.

Walker, K. (2012). Intimate Interactions: Eurasian family histories in colonial Penang. *Modern Asian Studies, 46*(2), 303–329.

Walker, W. (1991). *Opium and Foreign Policy: The Anglo-American Search for Order in Asia, 1912–1954.* Chapel Hill: University of North Carolina Press.

Warren, J. (1985). The Singapore Rickshaw Pullers: The Social Organization of a Coolie Occupation, 1880–1940. *Journal of Southeast Asian Studies, 16*(1), 1–15.

Warren, J. (1986) *Rickshaw Coolie: A People's History of Singapore, 1880–1940*. Singapore: Oxford University Press.

Warren, J. (1990). Prostitution and the Politics of Venereal Disease: Singapore, 1870–1898. *Journal of Southeast Asian Studies*, 21(2), 360–383.

Weber, M. (1979) [1923]. Bureaucracy. In *Max Weber: Essays in Sociology*, edited by Hans Heinrich Gerth & C. Wright Mills. New York: Oxford University Press.

Webster, A. (2000). Business and Empire: A Reassessment of the British Conquest of Burma in 1885. *The Historical Journal*, 43(4), 1003–1025.

Wedeen, L. (1999). *Ambiguities of Domination: Politics, Rhetoric, and Symbols in Contemporary Syria*. Chicago: University of Chicago Press.

Wen, L. (1907). The Anti-Opium Movement in Malaya. *Straits Chinese Magazine*, 11, 3–8.

Wertz, D. (2013). Idealism, Imperialism, and Internationalism: Opium Politics in the Colonial Philippines, 1898–1925. *Modern Asian Studies*, 47(2), 467–499.

White, O. (2007). Drunken States: Temperance and French Rule in Cote d'Ivoire, 1908–1916. *Journal of Social History*, 40(3), 663–684.

Wilder, G. (2005). *The French Imperial Nation-State: Negritude and Colonial Humanism between the Two World Wars*. Chicago: University of Chicago Press.

Willcox, W. (1929). *International Migrations*, vol. 1. Cambridge, MA: National Bureau of Economic Research.

Williams, L. (1961). The Ethical Program and the Chinese of Indonesia. *Journal of Southeast Asian History*, 2(2), 35–42.

Wilson, J. (2008). *The Domination of Strangers: Modern Governance in Eastern India, 1780–1835*. Basingstoke: Palgrave Macmillan.

Wilson, J. Q. (1989). *Bureaucracy: What Government Agencies Do and Why They Do It*. New York: Basic Books.

Wilson, N. (2011). From Reflection to Refraction: State Administration in British India, circa 1770–1850. *American Journal of Sociology*, 116(5), 1437–1477.

Windle, J. (2012). The Suppression of Illicit Opium Production in Viet Nam: An Introductory Narrative. *Crime, Law, and Social Change*, 57, 425–439.

Winther, P. (2003). *Anglo-European Science and the Rhetoric of Empire: Malaria, Opium, and British Rule in India, 1756–1895*. Lanham, MD: Lexington Books.

Wiselius, J. (1886). *De Opium in Nederlandsch en Britsch Indië, Oeconomisch, Critische, Historisch* [Opium in the Dutch and British Indies, Economical, Critical, and Historical]. The Hague: Martinus Nijhoff.

Wolf, E. (2010). *Europe and the People without History*. Berkeley: University of California Press.

Wong, J. (2002). *Deadly Dreams: Opium and the Arrow War (1856–1860) in China*. New York: Cambridge University Press.

Woodruff, P. (1954). *The Men Who Ruled India: The Founders of Modern India*. New York: St. Martin's Press.

World Peace Foundation (1925). *Pamphlets*, vol. 8. Somerville, MA: World Peace Foundation.

Wright, A. (1908). *Twentieth Century Impressions of British Malaya: Its History, People, Commerce, Industries, and Resources*. London: Lloyd's Greater Britain Publishing Company.

Wright, A. (2008). Opium in British Burma, 1826–1881. *Contemporary Drug Problems*, 35(4), 611–647.

Wright, A. (2014). *Opium and Empire in Southeast Asia: Regulating Consumption in British Burma.* Cambridge: Cambridge University Press.

Wright, Q. (1924). The Opium Question. *American Journal of International Law, 18,* 281–295.

Wyrtzen, J. (2017). Colonial Legitimization-Legibility Linkages and the Politics of Identity in Algeria and Morocco." *European Journal of Sociology, 58*(2), 205–235.

Yang, T. (2012). Selling an Imperial Dream: Japanese Pharmaceuticals, National Power, and the Science of Quinine Self-Sufficiency. *East Asian Science, Technology and Society, 6*(1), 101–125.

Yashar, D. (2018). *Homicidal Ecologies: Illicit Economies and Complicit States in Latin America.* New York: Cambridge University Press.

Yoshimura, M., & Akashi, Y., Eds. (2008). *New Perspectives of the Japanese Occupation of Malaya and Singapore, 1941–1945.* Chicago: University of Chicago Press.

Young, E. (2013). *Ecclesiastical Colony: China's Catholic Church and the French Religious Protectorate.* New York: Oxford University Press.

Yvorel, J.-J. (1992). *Les poisons de l'esprit: drogues et drogués au XIXe siècle.* Paris: Quai Voltaire.

Yvorel, J.-J. (2012). La loi du 12 Juillet 1916: première incrimination de la consommation de drogue. *Les Cahiers dynamiques, 56,* 128–133.

Zacka, B. (2017). *When the State Meets the Street: Public Service and Moral Agency.* Cambridge, MA: Harvard University Press.

Zheng, Y.W. (2005). *The Social Life of Opium in China.* Cambridge and New York: Cambridge University Press.

Zhou, Y. (1999). *Anti-drug Crusades in Twentieth-Century China: Nationalism, History, and State Building.* Lanham, MD: Rowman & Littlefield.

Zinoman, P. (2001). *The Colonial Bastille: A History of Imprisonment in Vietnam, 1862–1940.* Berkeley: University of California Press.

Zinoman, P. (2014). *Vietnamese Colonial Republican: The Political Vision of Vu Trong Phung.* Berkeley: University of California Press.

INDEX

A NOTE ON THE TYPE

THIS BOOK has been composed in Arno, an Old-style serif typeface in the classic Venetian tradition, designed by Robert Slimbach at Adobe.